MANAGING GLOBAL RISKS IN THE URBAN AGE

Rethinking Asia and International Relations

Series Editor: **Emilian Kavalski**,
Australian Catholic University (Sydney)

This series provides thoughtful consideration both of the growing prominence of Asian actors on the global stage and the changes in the study and practice of world affairs that they provoke. It offers a comprehensive parallel assessment of the full spectrum of Asian states, organisations, and regions and their impact on the dynamics of global politics.

The series encourages conversation on:

- what rules, norms, and strategic cultures are likely to dominate international life in the 'Asian Century';
- how will global problems be reframed and addressed by a 'rising Asia';
- which institutions, actors, and states are likely to provide leadership during such 'shifts to the East';
- whether there is something distinctly 'Asian' about the emerging patterns of global politics.

Such comprehensive engagement not only offers a critical assessment of the actual and prospective roles of Asian actors, but rethinks the concepts, practices, and frameworks of analysis of world politics.

Other titles in this series

China's New Governing Party Paradigm
Political Renewal and the Pursuit of National Rejuvenation
Timothy R. Heath

Risk State
Japan's Foreign Policy in an Age of Uncertainty
Edited by Sebastian Maslow, Ra Mason and Paul O'Shea

Contentious Integration
Post-Cold War Japan-China Relations in the Asia-Pacific
Chien-peng Chung

The Long Peace of East Asia
Timo Kivimäki

Harmonious Intervention
China's Quest for Relational Security
Chiung-Chiu Huang and Chih-yu Shih

Managing Global Risks in the Urban Age

Singapore and the Making of a Global City

YEE-KUANG HENG

National University of Singapore, Singapore

Routledge
Taylor & Francis Group
LONDON AND NEW YORK

First published 2015 by Ashgate Publishing

2 Park Square, Milton Park, Abingdon, Oxfordshire OX14 4RN
711 Third Avenue, New York, NY 10017

Routledge is an imprint of the Taylor & Francis Group, an informa business

First issued in paperback 2017

British Library Cataloguing in Publication Data
A catalogue record for this book is available from the British Library

The Library of Congress has cataloged the printed edition as follows:
Heng, Yee-Kuang.
Managing global risks in the urban age : Singapore and the making of a global city / by Yee-Kuang Heng.
pages cm. – (Rethinking Asia and international relations)
Includes bibliographical references and index.
ISBN 978-1-4724-4799-9 (hardback) 1. Singapore–Relations. 2. Singapore–Foreign economic relations. 3. Urbanization–Political aspects–Singapore. 4. Regionalism–Singapore. 5. Globalization. I. Title.

DS610.45.H46 2015
337.5957–dc23

2015004245

ISBN 978-1-4724-4799-9 (hbk)
ISBN 978-1-138-57197-6 (pbk)

Contents

Acknowledgements

Many people and organisations have helped me immensely in the rather long gestation period for this book.

I should first of all thank my institution, the National University of Singapore (NUS) for actively supporting research endeavours through targeted initiatives. I am a grateful recipient of a Humanities and Social Sciences (HSS) Fellowship, which generously granted me time off from teaching and administrative duties to concentrate on writing. Research for this book was funded by a NUS Start-Up Grant WBS R-603-000-041-133. Through the efforts of the Dean, Prof. Kishore Mahbubani, the Research Excellence Committee and a dedicated Research Support Unit, the Lee Kuan Yew School of Public Policy (LKYSPP) has never been more conducive to research.

Institutional frameworks are not complete without the human dimension that provides the inspiration and encouragement to undertake a book project like this. I am grateful to LKYSPP colleagues for listening to me and bouncing ideas around. Discussions at NUS with Prasenjit Duara about 'Risk Society' helped propel the early stages of this project. Meanwhile, from Oxford and LSE respectively, Yuen Foong Khong and Christopher Coker were as always reassuring. Emilian Kavalski in Sydney encouraged me to persevere all the way to publication. Meanwhile, Syed Aljunied Ad'ha worked tirelessly in the background, providing timely research support. This project also benefitted from presentations at the British International Studies Association/International Studies Association Joint conference in Edinburgh in 2012, as well as at Aoyama Gakuin University and the University of Tokyo.

I would like to particularly thank Aoi Chiyuki, Fujiwara Kiichi and Shiroyama Hideaki for driving me on with their interest in the idea of risk. Earlier versions of some arguments presented here were published as 'A global city in an age of global risks' in *Contemporary Southeast Asia*, Vol. 35 No. 3, December 2013.

Last, but certainly not least, it goes without saying that none of this would be possible without the unwavering support of my family.

This book is dedicated to Dad, Mum, Hiroko and Akiko.

Chapter 1
Urban Order, Global Risks

Global Cities in the Firing Line

This book is about what it terms the global city-global risk nexus. The analysis contained herein is motivated by a central security paradox of the global age: the hyper-connected global cities that facilitate globalisation's key processes – such as air travel and financial transactions – are also paradoxically most vulnerable to security risks (WMD proliferation/pandemics/economic meltdown etc.) associated with globalisation. Yet, this bourgeoning global risk-global city nexus and the implications for Security Studies have so far neither been theorised nor assessed in depth. How can academics begin to systematically conceptualise and map this global city-global risk nexus? What are the implications for civil society, industry, and policymakers at various levels, from municipal to national and global? Such previously overlooked questions are addressed here, as the vulnerability of global cities to global risks now appears to be a constantly recurring pattern. The Severe Acute Respiratory Syndrome (SARS) outbreak in 2003 transmitted through air travel demonstrated how global connectivity, previously seen as unequivocally positive for a global city like Toronto, also heralded 'certain dangers and vulnerabilities'.[1] In 2009, the worldwide spread of H5N1 swine flu was an unwelcome reminder that for global cities such as Dubai and Tokyo – which responded by targeting its aviation sector for screening passengers and planes – air travel was seen to provide the initial 'sparks' or 'seeding' events for such undesirables to enter the city.[2] Fears of such rapidly-moving pandemics are here to stay. Singapore, perhaps more than any other global city, had unfortunately close-up experience of several different types of global risks in succession in the Noughties. Reflecting on the accumulative impact of the September 11th terror attacks, the SARS outbreak; and financial turbulence which adversely affected Singapore between 2001 and 2010, its Deputy Prime Minister summarised that these 'crises reinforce the reality of Singapore's vulnerability to dangers, some

---

1 Neil Brenner and Roger Keil, 'Editors' Introduction', in Neil Brenner and Roger Keil (eds), *The Global Cities Reader*. London: Routledge (2006), 4.

2 Some argue that air travel provided the initial seeds globally but spread within a country was determined more by short-distance mechanisms such as school children. See Julia Gog et al., 'Spatial transmission of 2009 pandemic influenza in the US', *PLOS Computational Biology* 10:6 (2014).

unexpected, that can originate at any time and place in today's globalised world'.[3] Singapore as a global city is particularly suited to study the impact of global risks because, as its Prime Minister mused, 'we are an open, cosmopolitan city, highly connected to the world. In our globalised world, disorder or worse breakdown of political authority in one country threatens regional and international security'.[4]

Thriving on being the most connected in an inter-connected world, these global cities face up to a cruel paradox on a daily basis. They are also acutely exposed to what the June 2011 OECD report *Future Global Shocks* termed 'events – such as pandemics, financial crises – that begin locally and rapidly spread their impacts through contamination or contagion to societies and economies ... interconnectedness could make global shocks more likely'.[5] According to the World Economic Forum's (WEF) 2011 'Global Risks Report', the world faces 'ever-greater concerns regarding global risks, the prospect of rapid contagion through increasingly connected systems and the threat of disastrous impacts'.[6] The 2013 version of the 'Global Risks Report' noted that 'global risks do not respect national borders'.[7] Many of these concerns expressed have particularly resonance for global cities. Riding on the coat tails of globalisation might have made global cities as important as they are, but they can also become rather precarious places in the process.

A better understanding of this emerging global risk-global city nexus can help explain the changing nature of security challenges in Asia as the region becomes increasingly urbanised and globalised at the same time. Indeed, while Asia's security context has usually been characterised by maritime territorial disputes and geopolitical moves by the major regional powers, a far wider spectrum of security risks also exists, particularly for its global cities where most of the population lives. In 2012, China declared that more than half of its citizens were now city-dwellers. By 2050, three-quarters of humans are expected to be urbanites and within Asia, more than 55 per cent of the population will be urban by 2030. In 2008, the UN announced that more than half of the world's population was urban for the first time in human history.[8] Consequently, it is often claimed that 'the

3 Teo Chee Hean, 'Speech by Teo Chee Hean' (Singapore Global Dialogue, 21 September 2011) <http://www.mha.gov.sg/news_details.aspx?nid=MjA5Nw%3D%3D-bI%2B0CdXnsxM%3D> accessed 30 March 2012.

4 Lee Hsien Loong, 'Opening address at opening ceremony of UN-Interpol Ministerial meeting and 78th Interpol General Assembly' (speech, Singapore, 12 October 2009) <http://www.pmo.gov.sg/content/pmosite/mediacentre/speechesninterviews/primeminister/2009/October/opening_address_byprimeministerleehsienloongattheopeningceremony.html#.U7umQ7GHWxc> accessed 15 January 2013.

5 Organisation for Economic Co-operation and Development (OECD), 'Future Global Shocks', June 2011, 3 and 6.

6 World Economic Forum, 'Global Risks Report 2011: Executive Summary', January 2011, 8.

7 World Economic Forum, 'Global Risks Report 2013', Preface, 8.

8 United Nations Habitat Program, 'State of the World's Cities', Nairobi, Kenya: UNHP (2007), 4.

influence of cities – in politics, business, and culture – has never been greater'.[9] The implications can be important because by studying how these cities relate to one another above and beyond the traditionally formal focus on nation-states, 'we stand to learn a great deal more about the nature of the world-system itself' and how it is evolving.[10] In a 'Special Issue on Global Cities' in the journal *Foreign Policy*, it was predicted – defying conventional wisdom – that 'the age of nations is over. The new urban age has begun. The 21st century will not be dominated by America or China, Brazil or India, but by the city'.[11] As we mark the 'world's inaugural urban and metropolitan century',[12] at the same time it must be noted that this phenomenon is relatively recent, whereby it is only in the past 30 years that urban places and urban living have become commonplace.[13] Cities are now seen as humanity's real building blocks: they generate over two-thirds of the total world economic output, have high population densities, wield political influence, and possess an innovative edge.[14] While contemporary globalisation has reshaped the world immensely, making it far more interdependent than before, the globalisation phenomenon is most apparent in cities where mass congregations of people live and work. Some geographers see urbanisation as intrinsically related to the accelerating globalisation of recent decades;[15] at the pinnacle are the shining 'global cities' that epitomise the globalisation phenomenon, whether in terms of business activities; human migration; cultural interaction or information exchange. The 2008 Global Cities Index compiled by A.T. Kearney claimed that 'the world's biggest, most interconnected cities help set global agendas, weather transnational dangers, and serve as the hubs of global integration. They are the engines of growth for their countries and the gateways to the resources of their regions'.[16]

This book makes the case that Security Studies would enhance its explanatory and analytical abilities by expanding its focus beyond nation-states towards increasingly significant Asian cities and urban centres that now have global relevance not just in terms of economics, finance, but increasingly, security too. Asia hosted five of the world's top twelve global cities – Seoul, Beijing, Singapore, Hong Kong, Tokyo – according to A.T. Kearney's Global City Index in 2014. The analysis contained herewith centres on Singapore (ranked ninth in

---

9 Matt Mabe, 'The world's most global cities', Bloomberg Businessweek, 29 October 2008.

10 David A. Smith and Michael Timberlake, 'Cities in Global Matrices: Toward Mapping the World-System's City-System', in Paul L. Knox and Peter J. Taylor (eds), *World Cities in a World-System*. New York: Cambridge University Press (1995), 81.

11 Parag Khanna, 'Beyond City Limits', *Foreign Policy* (September/October 2010), 122.

12 Bruce Katz, 'Global cities: the drivers of economic growth', Brookings Institution, 20 October 2011 <http://www.brookings.edu/blogs/up-front/posts/2011/10/20-global-cities-katz> accessed 9 January 2013.

13 David Clark, *Urban World/Global City*. London: Routledge (2003), Preface, xvii.

14 Khanna, 'Beyond City Limits'.

15 Ibid.

16 Foreign Policy, 'The Globalisation Index 2008', 15 October 2008.

the aforementioned A.T. Kearney Index in 2014), rather than a more conventional focus on Western cities, either London or New York. As existing literature on global cities 'tends to exhibit an Anglo-American bias',[17] there is a need to incorporate other global cities, recognising the richness in varieties by shifting the focus towards Pacific Asia.[18] Furthermore, Singapore depends more than any other global city on connectivity for its survival, but this very fact has also brought with it exposure to global risks. Beyond a narrow interest in Singapore however, this Asian global city's first-hand experiences of managing global risks reflect the changing nature of security in a global risk society. There are broader implications that arise through a comparative analysis of the shared experiences of other global cities such as London, New York, Hong Kong, and Tokyo, showing where active learning of 'best practices' is underway.

Scholars working in sociology, migration, architecture, the arts, political economy, cultural studies, developmental studies or geography and urban planning, have already generated a copious amount of publications on the concept of 'global cities'. Urban planners, environmental scholars and geographers have even started pondering some security challenges global cities face and implications for their respective fields. Within Security Studies however, there does not appear to be similar research momentum developing; theoretical and conceptual tools remain under-developed for examining global cities as the primary unit of security analysis. Yet, the field has broadened recently through concepts such as 'non-traditional' and 'human security'. Global risks such as WMD proliferation, financial crises, and terrorism are now firmly on the agenda, but how might scholars systematically evaluate the implications for global cities and their vulnerabilities? Developing an analytical framework derived from hitherto disparate fields of literature, this book seeks to establish and develop connections between sociologist Ulrich Beck's *World Risk Society* which has inspired a range of literature on globalisation and risk, with writers such as Saskia Sassen and Manuel Castells on global cities, and Stephen Graham on urban dimensions of security. In 2012, Beck posited that 'the concept of "global risk society" raises several questions: how does the anticipation of a multiplicity of manmade futures and its risky consequences affect and transform the perceptions, living conditions and institutions of modern societies?'[19] For all his renown on globalisation and global risks, strangely enough there has not yet been any attempt by Security Studies scholars to systematically

17 Kris Olds and Henry Yeung, 'Pathways to global city formation: a view from the developmental city-state of Singapore', *Review of International Political Economy* 11:3 (2004), 494. A point also made by John Rennie Short and Yeong Hyun Kim, *Globalisation and the City*. London: Longman (1999), 8.

18 Henry Wai-Chung Yeung, 'Globalisation Singapore: One Global City, Global Production Networks and the Developmental State', in Tarn Tan How (eds), *Singapore Perspectives 2010*. Singapore: World Scientific (2010), 109.

19 Ulrich Beck, 'Global Risk Society', in George Ritzer (ed.), *The Wiley-Blackwell Encyclopedia of Globalization*. London: Wiley-Blackwell (2012).

examine Beck's claims and their implications for global cities, an omission all the more startling considering the growing prominence of cities worldwide and their associated exposure to global risks. On the other hand, given Sassen's emphasis on how certain places are uniquely suited to translate productive power into global control, some academics suggest that her writings have potentially unexplored implications for security thinking, since she 'has done the most to contribute to our thinking about how urban advantage translates into grand strategy'.[20] Exploring the global risk-global city nexus by utilising insights from leading thinkers of global risk and global cities respectively is a key aim here.

This book therefore develops firstly, a theoretical and analytical framework for:

1. Breaking down and categorising the various types of global risks (from deliberate to unintentional; penetrative; exploitative, to destructive) that global cities face;
2. Analysing the different domains in which they can manifest (maritime/financial/aviation);
3. Examining how they spread ironically through the different types of critical infrastructure (airports/financial centres/ports etc.) that confer coveted 'global city' status.

Secondly, in terms of empirical analysis and methodological approach, this book employs a case study method. Singapore is closely examined to illustrate how it is suited to the study of different varieties of global risks because these risks ironically circulate through, or target its critical infrastructure that fuelled its development as a global city, namely its maritime port; its aviation hub; and its financial centre. Potential policy implications are then drawn for other global cities such as London and New York that face similar global risk governance challenges. This chapter will set the conceptual and academic template for what follows in the rest of the book. Existing approaches posited by scholars such as Saskia Sassen, Manuel Castells, Kris Olds and Henry Yeung are first presented of what a global city is and the process through which cities such as Singapore developed. Drawing from such works, the chapter develops its definition of global cities based on several unique traits which in turn make them ideal candidates in general, and Singapore specifically, for study and analysis through ideas of global risk and security. The chapter then turns to assemble an analytical platform by engaging with intellectual developments and concepts drawn from urban studies, geography, and sociology. Two thematic categories structure the analytical framework developed. The first concerns the *mechanics* of how global cities with their critical infrastructure servicing the desirable 'good' flows of globalisation (financial investment; tourism; information etc.) also circulate or attract 'bad' flows such as financial contagion, terrorist financing, and pandemics: 'all of these phenomena form a part of the dark side of the globalised world: contamination, contagion, instability, interconnection,

20 Khanna, 'Beyond City Limits', 126.

turbulence, shared fragility, universal effects, and overexposure'.[21] The second category relates to the *policy* implications for managing complex global risks that range beyond any single entity's capacity to resolve. Globalisation not only provides the vector for spreading security risks but also complicates attempts at finding solutions. How have global cities who are the most vulnerable responded? As Benjamin Barber has argued in light of the nation-state's continued resilience, the foremost political challenge today is to forge new arrangements that can somehow address the global problems of interdependence without foregoing democracy and sovereignty of nation-states. Barber believes the solution lies in cities – 'the most networked and interconnected of our political associations … let mayors rule the world'.[22] They can govern through voluntary cooperation and shared consensus across borders.[23] Barber's call to 'change the subject: from states to cities, from top-down formal global governance to bottom-up informal global governance as an unfolding intercity reality'[24] is taken up in this book's focus on global cities as the referent object of security and global risk governance.

Defining the Global City

A global city 'acts as a – and preferably *the* – major nodal point between a region and other parts of the world, attracting disproportionate amounts of foreign trade, personnel, international services and expertise coming to the area'.[25] A concept closely associated with Saskia Sassen, who studied the impact of globalisation of capital and labour movements on urban centres, the fundamental driver is that as the world economy becomes ever more integrated and globalised, there is an ever-growing concentration of command and control functions in a relatively relatively small number of global cities. Sassen's counter-intuitive argument that very specific territorial spaces are still required even for highly globalised sectors such as finance, contradicts assumptions that the globalised economy is now 'placeless'.[26] A global city provides highly specialised services such as financial products.[27] Such cities

21 Javier Solana and Daniel Innerarity, 'The New Grammar of Power', Project Syndicate, 1 August 2011 <http://www.project-syndicate.org/commentary/solana10/English> accessed 1 August 2011.

22 Benjamin Barber, *If Mayors Ruled the World*. New Haven: Yale University Press (2013), 4.

23 Ibid., 5.

24 Ibid., 357.

25 Karl Hack and Jean-Louis Margolin, 'Singapore: Reinventing the Global City', in Karl Hack and Jean-Louis Margolin (eds), *Singapore from Temasek to the 21st Century: Reinventing the Global City*. Singapore: National University of Singapore Press (2010), 29.

26 Taken from web profile of 'Professor Saskia Sassen', LSE Sociology, 23 February 2011 <http://www.lse.ac.uk/sociology/whoswho/academic/Sassen.aspx> accessed 9 November 2014.

27 Saskia Sassen, *The Global City: London, New York, Tokyo*. New Jersey: Princeton University Press (2001), 5.

jostle for favourable positions at the centre of global trade, technology, tourism and services, banking on their deepening ties with the global economic system. This is due to a rather novel 'complex duality', that of the 'spatially dispersed, yet globally integrated organization of economic activity'.[28] Sassen contends global cities function in four ways: as highly concentrated command points in the organisation of the world economy; key locations for finance and specialised service firms as the leading economic sectors; as sites of production in these leading industries; and as markets for the products and innovations produced. Their capability for 'producing global control' is central in producing and reproducing the management of a global production system and global marketplace for finance.[29] Their power and influence comes from their position as command points and centres of planning, setting the framework for other cities to operate in the global economy.[30]

The notion that such leading cities are defined primarily by their core economic functions in the world economy is widespread.[31] The global city debate had predominantly strong political economy roots, typified by works on issues such as industrial restructuring in Hong Kong and Singapore.[32] These discussions about global cities have made little headway in security studies. Consider how Sassen's abiding purpose was to understand the place of global cities in the organisation of global specialised services and finance, as well as to problematise the practice of power, control and inequalities.[33] In her revised 2001 edition of *The Global City*, she presented seven hypotheses on the main features of global cities. These include rising levels of inequality, highly specialised and networked services sectors, the number of foreign headquarters, air travel links or stock market activities, and how these cities can become increasingly disconnected from their own broader national economies as they focus on cross-border transactions.[34] Examining issues such as foreign direct investment flows, employment and earnings, labour markets and location of producer services, central to Sassen's analysis is a need to 'emphasize that a whole new arrangement has emerged for accumulation around the centrality of finance in economic growth'.[35] As a result, the 'dominant focus on economic globalization (in the form of market forces, private firms and inter-firm networks) in the global cities of North America and Western Europe has led to a relatively

---

28 Ibid., 3.

29 Ibid., 6.

30 Arthur S. Alderson and Jason Beckfield, 'Power and position in the world city system' *American Journal of Sociology* 109:4 (2004), 812.

31 Fu-Chen Lo and Yue-man Yeung, 'Introduction', in Fu-Chen Lo and Yue-man Yeung (eds), *Globalization and the World of Large Cities*. Tokyo: United Nations University Press (1998), 1–2.

32 Stephen Wing-kai Chiu and Kong-Chong Ho, *City-States in the Global Economy: Industrial Restructuring in Hong Kong and Singapore*. Colorado: Westview Press (1998).

33 Sassen, *The Global City*, 351.

34 Ibid., xix–xxi.

35 Ibid., 344.

coherent global city discourse'.[36] Indeed, regardless of how global cities differ in their histories and cultural roots, some observers claim that 'the *economic* variable, however, is likely to be decisive for all attempts at explanation'.[37] They are above all, seen to 'serve as the organizing nodes of a global economic system'.[38]

Scholars have lamented this long-standing tendency towards economism and the corresponding neglect of social or cultural phenomena.[39] Indeed, this book would argue that security challenges for global cities also warrant more attention. From its political economy roots, the debate on global cities now tends to be varied and wide-ranging. While geographers have been pioneering the study of the urban world, no single discipline can monopolise the study of the city, since urban-related questions and problems in fact cut across many academic disciplines.[40] Questions about the global city have now covered topics as diverse as migration and migrant workers,[41] architecture, urban planning for terrorism resilience and cinema,[42] the arts and cultural studies,[43] development studies[44] or geography and urban planning.[45] Los Angeles and Singapore have even been re-imagined as 'sexy cyber cities'.[46] John Short concluded that four research topics capture the interest of researchers:[47]

36 Olds and Yeung, 'Pathways to global city formation', 497.

37 John Friedmann, 'Where We Stand: A Decade of World City Research', in Paul Knox and Peter J. Taylor (eds), *World Cities in a World-System*. New York: Cambridge University Press (1995), 69.

38 Ibid., 25.

39 Natalie Oswin and Brenda Yeoh, 'Introduction: mobile city Singapore', *Mobilities* 5:2 (2010), 168.

40 Clark, *Urban World/Global City*, 5.

41 Ligaya Lindio-McGovern, *Globalization, Labor Export and Resistance: A Study of Filipino Migrant Domestic Workers in Global Cities*. London: Routledge (2011); A.M. Findlay et al., 'Skilled international migration and the global city: a study of expatriates in Hong Kong', *Transactions of the Institute of British Geographers* 21:1 (1996).

42 For example, Linda Krause and Patrice Petro (eds), *Global Cities: Cinema, Architecture, and Urbanism in a Digital Age*. London: Rutgers University Press (2003); Jon Coaffee, *Terrorism, Risk and the Global City: Towards Urban Resilience*. Aldershot: Ashgate (2009); Robert Powell, *Singapore: Architecture of a Global City*. Singapore: Archipelago Press (2000).

43 See, for instance, Singapore Tourism Board, *Singapore: global city for the arts* (2000); Terence Chong, 'Singapore's cultural policy and its consequences', *Critical Asian Studies* 37:4 (2005), 553–68.

44 Olds and Yeung, 'Pathways to global city formation'.

45 For instance Ananya Roy and Aihwa Ong (eds), *Worlding Cities: Asian Experiments and the Art of Being Global*. Malden, MA: Wiley-Blackwell (2011); Brenda Yeoh, 'The global cultural city? Spatial imagineering and politics in the (multi-) cultural marketplaces of South-east Asia', *Urban Studies* 42:5/6 (2005), 945–58; Brenda Yeoh, 'Global/globalizing cities', *Progress in Human Geography* 23:4 (1999), 607–16.

46 Terrell Carver, 'Materializing the metaphors of global cities: Singapore and Silicon Valley', *Globalizations* 7:3 (2010), 383–93.

47 John Rennie Short, *Global Metropolitan*. London: Routledge (2004), 10.

1. The global city as a planning issue;
2. The global city as command centre;
3. The global network of cities;
4. The global city as polarised city.

In further developing the definition of a global city adopted in this book, several key features derived from Sassen and other leading writers on global cities and their development are identified below.

Feature 1: Global Cities and Global Flows

The notion of global flows is fundamental to understanding how global cities operate and the key functions they serve. For Sassen, a key purpose of the global city model is to 'conceive of economic globalization not just as capital flows, but as the work of coordinating, managing and servicing these flows'.[48] Manuel Castells, more latterly known for his work on Network Societies, had in the 1970s also studied the role of social movements in transforming cities. By the 1980s, while working on technologies and economic restructuring, Castells introduced the concept of 'spaces of flows' referring to the global networks needed for coordinating the global economy through long distances. Global cities for him are the 'most direct illustration' of these hubs and nodes of global flows.[49] This unique characteristic of global cities to serve as spaces of flows, according to Castells, is deemed 'critical for the distribution of wealth and power in the world'.[50] These flows can range from financial capital; maritime trade and cargo; air passengers; information and data to migrants and tourists and businessmen. The significance of flows drawn from Sassen and Castells' works forms a centrepiece of this book's analytical framework. Ali and Keil note also that irrespective of how one defines globalisation, it crucially involves the 'increased and intensified level of connectivity between diverse sites across the world … such connectivity is predicated upon flows that give material form to the interconnections between those sites'.[51] Through this idea of global flows, one can also better position recent attempts to conceptualise the global city as a 'mobile city' premised on 'the disciplined notion of movement (and subsequently disciplined mobilities)' in order to connect global cities literature with the so-called 'mobility turn' within

48 Sassen, *The Global City*, 347.

49 Manuel Castells, *The Rise of the Network Society*. Oxford: Wiley-Blackwell (2000), 377 and 415.

50 Ibid., 386.

51 S. Harris Ali and Roger Keil, 'Securitising networked flows: infectious diseases and airports', in Stephen Graham (ed.), *Disrupted Cities: When Infrastructure Fails*. London: Routledge (2010), 97.

the social sciences.[52] Of particular relevance to our purposes here is the fact that as Tim Creswell noted, 'mobility is more than just about getting from A to B. It is about mobilities rubbing up against each other and causing friction'.[53] Such friction that threatens to stymie a world of global inter-connections can stem from several sources, for instance cultural diversity and local resistance in the forests of Kalimantan to deforestation can derail the timber and paper industry feeding hungry Japanese companies, in Anna Tsing's ethnographical analysis.[54] This idea of interruptions or disruptions runs contrary to images of smooth, cool efficiency in global cities dedicated to coordinating and circulating the 'frictionless, speedy flow of metropolitan labour and capital'.[55] The dualism of both mobility and friction directs scholars to consider carefully the flows and movements in and through the global city that can also introduce downsides because 'mobility has become an evocative keyword for the twenty-first century ... Issues of movement, of too little movement or too much or of the wrong sort or at the wrong time, are central to many lives, organisations and governments'.[56] Flows of all varieties are crucial to sustaining the 'urban metabolism' of a city defined as 'the sum total of the technical and socio-economic processes that occur in cities, resulting in growth, production of energy, and elimination of waste'.[57] These flows are not all benign or beneficial. In a high-tech globally connected age, 'cities have to confront unstoppable flows, unpredictable mobility, and the risk of these enormously complex technological systems being perverted to disrupt, destroy and kill'.[58] Consequently, the circulations of flows traversing the city have become the main 'battlespace'.[59] Taken together, this growing focus by urban studies and geography scholars on global flows, friction, mobilities, and unwanted phenomena suggest a move away from a prior economics-centred research on global cities which 'is most often articulated as a way of speaking or connecting to the global economy ... (but) the mobile city approach understands the city as much more than a calculation of border-crossing labour and capital inputs and outputs'.[60] This book contributes to such debates by highlighting how these border-transcending flows and mobilities also carry distinctive types of security risks for global cities.

52 Oswin and Yeoh, 'Introduction', 169.

53 Tim Creswell, *On the Move: Mobility in the Modern Western World*. London: Routledge (2006), 265.

54 See Anna Tsing, *Friction: An Ethnography of Global Connection*. New Jersey: Princeton University Press (2005), 4.

55 Patrick Deer, 'The ends of war and the limits of war culture', *Social Text* 25:2 (2007), 2.

56 John Urry, *Mobilities*. Cambridge: Polity Press, 6.

57 C.A. Kennedy, J. Cuddihy, and J. Engel Yan, 'The changing metabolism of cities', *Journal of Industrial Ecology* (May 2007).

58 Ibid.

59 Stephen Graham, *Cities Under Siege*. London: Verso (2010), xv.

60 Oswin and Yeoh, 'Introduction', 170.

Feature 2: The 'Infrastructure' Approach and Circulating Global Flows

The aforementioned global flows and mobilities all rely on complex infrastructures and networks which invariably revolve around mega-cities as dominant nodes.[61] Globalisation is dependent on such key sites that tend to be co-located within leading urban centres, more commonly known as global cities.[62] Sassen has argued that, 'globalization can be deconstructed in terms of the strategic sites where global processes materialise and the linkages that bind them. Among these sites are export processing zones, off-shore banking centres, and, on a far more complex level, global cities. This produces a specific geography of globalization and underlines the extent to which it is not a planetary event encompassing all of the world'.[63]

The so-called 'infrastructure approach' to studying global cities thus recognises that 'well-connected cities are typified by the presence of vast enabled infrastructures'.[64] This realisation is additionally critical for constructing an analytical framework, for it prompts Security Studies scholars to also consider the various types of infrastructure that global cities employ in order to attract and circulate global flows, which may in turn expose them to global risks. In understanding the *mechanics* of new security challenges in a global age, the term 'circulation' describes the problems 'posed by interdependencies and flows rather than problems posed by demarcations between internal and external affairs'.[65] The security problematic today is characterised by how 'the basic transaction processes engendered by globalisation – instantaneous communication and transportation, exchanges of information and technology, flow of capital – catalyse certain dangerous phenomena or empower certain groups in ways unimagined previously'.[66] Recent works by Goldin and Mariathasan show how accelerating globalisation has the potential to destabilise whole societies. In an interconnected world, systemic risks, they argue, are now everywhere from supply

---

61 Stephen Graham, 'When Infrastructures Fail', in Stephen Graham (ed.), *Disrupted Cities: When Infrastructure Fails*. London: Routledge (2010), 2.

62 Fu-Chen Lo and Yue-man Yueng, 'World City Formation in Pacific Asia', in Fu-Chen Lo and Yue-man Yeung (eds), *Globalization and the World of Large Cities*. Tokyo: United Nations University Press (1998), 139.

63 Saskia Sassen, 'The global city: strategic site/new frontier', Globalization: A symposium on the challenges of closer global integration, July 2001 <http://www.india-seminar.com/2001/503/503%20saskia%20sassen.htm> accessed 8 June 2011.

64 Ben Derudder, et al., 'Airline data for global city network research: reviewing and refining existing approaches', *Geojournal* 71 (2008), 7.

65 Michael Dillon, 'Global security in the 21st century: Circulation, complexity and contingency', in *The Globalisation of Security*, Chatham House ISP/NSC Briefing Paper 05/02, December 2005.

66 Victor Cha, 'Globalisation and the study of international security', *Journal of Peace Research* 37:3 (2000), 394.

chains to pandemics and financial crises.[67] Rather than military threats or cross-border invasion, the primary analytical preoccupation should instead be with the processes of global/local 'circulation' and the critical infrastructure that facilitates such movement. For Dillon,

> circulation in this context means every conceivable kind of circulation or flow of peoples and things, of energy and of finance, of water and food, of capital and information, of images and discourses, of science and technology, of weapons and ideas, of drugs and of sex (AIDS to prostitution), of microbes and diseases. In a systemically interdependent world everything is connected or, in principle, is able to be connected, to everything else. The very smallest perturbations or anomalies in one system of circulation have the potential to cascade rapidly into large-scale crises affecting very many other local and global systems of circulation. A virus gets loose, a passenger jet crosses an ocean, a population is infected, a city is closed down – SARS and Toronto – and financial markets begin to react. Health, tourism, urban vitality and systems of global finance display connectivities hitherto unknown or unanticipated.[68]

Static territorial demarcations of 'inside' and 'outside' have been superseded by a globalised world in which the focus is 'geared towards trying to separate people and circulations deemed risky or malign from those deemed risk-free or worthy of protection'.[69] Sifting through flows tends to be naturally concentrated in global cities with the necessary infrastructure where such flows congregate. After all, 'the town exists only as a function of circulation and of circuits; it is a singular point on the circuits which create it and which it creates. It is defined by entries and exits: something must enter it and exit from it'.[70] Within these entry and exit points, 'the notion of connection is not enough. Something has to circulate too. If one place is to be globalised, it has to be linked to others'.[71] Indeed, Graham notes that everyday urban life is underpinned by a vast infrastructure that

> continually bring into being the mobilities and circulations of the city and the world … highway, airline, train and road complexes support the complex and multiscaled flows of commuters, migrants, tourists and refugees, as well as materials and commodities wichin and through the global urban system … electronics communications systems … (are) the lifeblood of digital capitalism based on assumptions of always being "on" … energy, water, sewerage,

67 Ian Goldin and Mike Mariathasan, *The Butterfly Defect: How Globalization Creates Systemic Risks*. New Jersey: Princeton University Press (2014).

68 Dillon, 'Global security in the 21st century', 2.

69 Graham, *Cities Under Siege*, 89.

70 Gilles Deleuze and Félix Guattari, 'City/State', *Zone 1/2* (1997).

71 Michael Callon and John Law, 'Guest editorial', *Environment and Planning D: Society and Space* 22 (2004), 4.

> transport, trade, finance and communication infrastructures allow modern urban life to exist … sustain the flows, connections and metabolisms that are intrinsic to contemporary cities.[72]

As the movement of these flows is facilitated by physical infrastructures such as airports and financial centres,[73] increasingly we are concerned with 'vital systems security' which refers to the need to protect 'networks and infrastructures that function by virtue of their connectivity, and this connectivity is typically supranational'.[74]

For Allen Feldman, US 'securocratic wars' against cyber-warfare, terrorism, crime, and biological threats are driven by the fear of urban infrastructure disruptions and that 'good' infrastructural mobilities sustaining tourism or financial globalisations are threatened by malign circulations and flows.[75] This is especially significant when one considers how transportation technologies constitute a central pillar facilitating the linkages between global cities which thrive on connecting dense patterns of interaction between people, goods, finance and information.[76] So-called 'security events' therefore arise from 'improper or transgressive circulations' when these alleged threats manifest through the disruption or misappropriation and exploitation of urban infrastructure for nefarious purposes.[77] These events are contrasted with the 'normal' flows of global logistics, tourism, labour and financial flows that are seen as 'safe circulation'. As such, 'the interruption of the moral economy of safe circulation is characterised as a dystopic 'risk-event'.[78] The various infrastructures, forms and modes of transport and communications that drive global cities thus deserve to play a central role in theories and models concerned with genesis, growth and change of global cities.[79] With the high premium placed on fluidity, mobilities and connectivity in the global city, these urban nodes which host critical infrastructure are prime candidates for analysing how they confront and manage undesirable risks circulating from the outside.[80]

---

72 Graham, 'When Infrastructures Fail', 1.

73 Ali and Keil, 'Securitising networked flows', 97.

74 Deborah Cowen, 'Containing insecurity: logistic space, U.S. port cities and the "war on terror"', in Stephen Graham (ed.), *Disrupted Cities*. London: Routledge (2010), 78.

75 Cited in Graham, 'When Infrastructures Fail', 16.

76 David Keeling, 'Transport and the world city paradigm', in Paul Knox and Peter Taylor (eds), *World Cities in a World-System*. Cambridge: Cambridge University Press (1995), 115.

77 Allen Feldman, 'Securocratic wars of public safety', *Interventions: International Journal of Postcolonial Studies* 6:3 (2004), 333.

78 Ibid.

79 Keeling, 'Transport and the world city paradigm', 129.

80 Brenda Yeoh and T.C. Chang, 'Globalising Singapore: debating transnational flows in the city', *Urban Studies* 38:7 (2001), 1026.

Feature 3: The Role of the Developmental State in Global City Formation

In light of preceding discussions about the centrality of critical infrastructure for global cities, one should also consider their long gestation periods: they do not simply appear overnight.[81] As Olds and Yeung argue, there is a need to focus attention on the '*processes creating global/world cities*, especially those associated with operation, relations, and networks of transnational corporations … as well as *governance* issues and implications, including the role of the state'.[82]

Consider how London's leading global city status is linked to its long history and imperial past as capital of the British Empire. Other urban geographers like Henry Yeung and Kris Olds argue that the role of developmental states in global city formation can also be crucial in other cases. This is particularly relevant for Singapore where a whole range of state-led agencies and projects exist whose sole aim is attracting global flows. This is a key factor why Singapore is particularly suited to study the impact of global risks on global cities: its excellent infrastructure in the form of its financial centre, air hub and maritime port provides not just the connectivity to circulate global flows of capital and goods but also potentially undesirable phenomena such as WMD proliferation and pandemics. Here, the developmental state and the infrastructure approach to growing a global city's infrastructural ability to attract global flows converge. This is also where perhaps most clearly, 'the political power and control of the developmental city-state of Singapore distinguishes it from municipal governments in most global cities because it is able to bypass national-state/provincial-city politics typical in many global cities'.[83] As Lo and Yeung point out, 'in the present era of large-sale and rapid exchange of goods, people, and ideas, the importance of ports, airports and teleports (indeed infrastructure as a whole) cannot be overemphasised'[84] Such high levels of connectivity for Singapore certainly did not come about by chance. Oswin and Yeoh argue that 'long before John Friedmann, Saskia Sassen and others began to articulate scholarly understandings of the 'global city', the ambitious postcolonial government of the Southeast Asian city-state of Singapore was self-consciously trying to create one'.[85] Former Prime Minister Goh Chok Tong echoed such claims that 'the term global city is not just a new buzzword for Singapore. This global city strategy in fact goes back some 35 years … We have been relentlessly pursuing the strategy of making Singapore a global city over the past

81 Hack and Margolin, 'Singapore: Reinventing the Global City', 28.

82 Olds and Yeung, 'Pathways to global city formation', 494.

83 Henry Wai-Chung Yeung, 'Global cities and developmental states: understanding Singapore's global reach', GaWC Annual Lecture 2000, 3 March 2000, <http://www.lboro.ac.uk/gawc/rb/al2.html> accessed 8 August 2014.

84 Lo and Yeung, 'Introduction', 10.

85 Oswin and Yeoh, 'Introduction: mobile city Singapore', 165–75.

few decades. We have excellent infrastructure and global connectivity'.[86] The case of Singapore consciously striving to *become* a global city therefore speaks to several critiques of how existing literature overlooks the rise of global cities, and neglects the role of developmental state policies in intentionally devising pathways to global city formation.[87] Indeed, Sassen argues that dominant narratives of economic globalisation privilege the capability for global control by major economic actors such as multi-national corporations, obscuring the deliberate development of infrastructure by authorities that make transmission of global control possible in the first place.[88] Attention should shift from simply ranking global urban hierarchies to the *process* of becoming a global city.[89]

The ways in which Singapore's planners have tried to translate their existing assets into an overarching blueprint for survival and connectivity demonstrates how the global city is not simply an accidental by-product of amorphous trans-national capital flows. Rather one should think of Singapore's global city status as an outcome of the developmental state instrumentally developing critical infrastructure in its maritime port, financial centre, and air hub for harnessing global flows.[90] To this point, cities have tended to be reified as if they were actors in and of themselves. This bypasses the crucial analytical challenge of interrogating issues of structure and agency in the understanding of 'the city'. It is an intrinsically political question about what agendas assume priority and how they are arrived at. As such, there is a need for dissembling the political regimes and alliances that inhabit and traverse the boundaries of global cities. Singapore has thrived as a global city because its success was underpinned by a carefully crafted policy package of selected interlinked niches such as the management of global maritime and financial trade flows that would keep its economy afloat and one step ahead of competitors.[91] The capacity for global control which determines global city status should thus not be taken for granted; 'it needs to be produced' and this leads us to a focus on multi-level actors involved in the practice of global control, the work of producing and reproducing the organisation and management of a global production system and a global market place for finance.[92] The importance of

86 Chok Tong Goh, 'Making Singapore a Global City' (speech, Singapore Institute of Architects 46th Annual Dinner, 4 May 2007 <http://www.nas.gov.sg/archivesonline/speeches/record-details/7e73fd0e-115d-11e3-83d5-0050568939ad>.

87 Olds and Yeung, 'Pathways to global city formation', 489–521.

88 Saskia Sassen, 'On concentration and centrality in the global city', in Paul Knox and Peter Taylor (eds), *World Cities in a World-System*. Cambridge: Cambridge University Press (1995), 64.

89 Short, *Global Metropolitan*, 21.

90 Daniel S.P. Goh, 'Capital and the transfiguring monumentality of Raffles Hotel', *Mobilities* 5:2 (2010), 175–95.

91 C.A. Airriess, 'Regional production, information-communication technology, and the developmental state: the rise of Singapore as a global container hub', *Geoforum* 32:2 (2001), 240.

92 Sassen, 'On concentration and centrality in the global city', 63.

building IT infrastructure for globally IT-connected Asian cities such as Singapore has been recently examined.[93] This book adds further emphasis on Singapore's other types of critical infrastructure, such as the financial, maritime, and aviation sectors.

Feature 4: Side-effects and Downsides

The prized critical infrastructure investments to attract global flows are meant to provide desirable benefits and gains to global cities. One often comes across positive descriptions of global city functions, such as the sought-after internal attributes and talents that allow creative cities to blossom.[94] However, there is rising interest in those marginalised and excluded by globalisation. Globalisation indices often rank countries according to winners and the bottom 10 losers.[95] The constant ranking of cities in terms of whether they are global or not leads to an exclusionary and exclusivist hierarchical ordering that unnecessarily pushes many urban centres 'off the map'.[96] Another indicator of negative side-effects is how global cities have also become associated with volatile economies, social polarisation, and inflated property markets that price out 'locals'. The plusses of cosmopolitanism, creativity, vibrancy and diversity through migration flows[97] go hand-in-hand with negatives such as sex industries of global cities.[98] Rapid influx of poor or migrant workers generated pressures on housing, education, health and welfare.[99] For Ross and Trachte, the most globally integrated US cities paradoxically contained difficult working conditions for many.[100] Globalisation has led to rapidly growing social and economic polarisation in leading cities.[101] For others, the implications of Sassen's arguments regarding immigration flows have received less attention than her claims about the industrial and financial

93 Alan Chong, '"Global City Foreign Policy": The Propaganda of Enlargement and Integration of an IT-Connected Asian City' in Alan Chong and Faizal bin Yahya (eds), *State, Society, and Information Technology in Asia.* Farnham: Ashgate (2014), 135–72.

94 Yeung, 'Globalisation Singapore', 110.

95 See, for instance, Foreign Policy, 'Measuring Globalisation', March/April 2004, 60 and 67.

96 J. Robinson, 'Global and world cities: a view from off the map', *International Journal of Urban and Regional Research* 26:3 (2002), 531–54.

97 Olds and Yeung, 'Pathways to global city formation', 495.

98 Ara Wilson, *The Intimate Economies of Bangkok: Tomboys, Tycoons and Avon Ladies in the Global City*. Berkeley: University of California Press (2004).

99 John Friedmann, 'The World City Hypothesis', *Development and Change* 17:1 (1986), 77.

100 Robert Ross and Kent Trachte, 'Global Cities and Global Classes: the peripheralisation of labour in New York city', in Neil Brenner and Roger Keil (eds) *The Global Cities Reader*. New York: Routledge (2006), 105.

101 Lo and Yeung, 'Introduction', 11.

foundations of global cities.[102] Within the literature, there is mounting concern with the unwanted social side-effects of *being* global cities, although Security Studies scholars have not quite paid sufficient attention to the *security* implications as well.

Global Cities as Candidates for Studying Global Risks

Through a combination of the four features outlined above, global cities then appear as ideal candidates for studying the transmission and impact of global risks. They are set up to process global flows of all kinds, using critical infrastructure that has been nurtured over the years by city and national authorities. This connectivity also brings exposure to security downsides and side-effects in the form of global risks. Take the example of critical infrastructure that global cities need such as airports to attract and circulate aviation flows. In 2003, Toronto became a 'city of pariahs' because of the (SARS) outbreak that had spread from thousands of miles away in Hong Kong.[103] Ironically, the 'same channels of transnational connectivity (in this case air routes) that are intended to facilitate business and financial transactions between Hong Kong and Toronto now became the basis for the transmission of a highly infectious disease'.[104] The fear here is that because trade and travel are increasing exponentially, 'a future pandemic may reach a globally connected city early and spread worldwide'.[105] The airports that global cities depend on so much for their prosperity have proved also to be its Achilles heel, for 'air travel is the major route of local to global propagation'.[106] The fact that severe SARS outbreaks also occurred in Hong Kong and Singapore not only highlights the question of how Toronto's linkages with other global cities shaped the global spread of the virus,[107] it also dramatically highlights the shared nature of global risks that global cities face because they all emphasise 'cosmopolitanism and movement, where transnationalism is as much the rule as locality'.[108] Since disruptions and failures in the finely-tuned myriad of flows can destabilise potentially whole cities, whether these are food supply chains or complex transport logistics systems, the

102 Michael Samers, 'Immigration and the Global City Hypothesis: Towards an Alternative Research Agenda', in Neil Brenner and Roger Keil (eds), *The Global Cities Reader*. London: Routledge (2006), 385.

103 *The National Post*, 'SARS kills two more in Toronto', 2 April 2003, A1.

104 Brenner and Keil, 'Editors' Introduction', 4.

105 Vernon J. Lee, et al., 'Influenza pandemics in Singapore, a tropical, globally connected city', *Historical Review* 13:7 (2007), 1052–7.

106 Harvey Rubin, *Future Global Shocks: Pandemics*. Paris: OECD (2011), 27.

107 S. Harris Ali and Roger Keil, 'Global Cities and the Spread of Infectious Disease: The Spread of Severe Acute Respiratory Syndrome (SARS) in Toronto, Canada', *Urban Studies* 43:3 (2006), 491

108 Andrew Gallery, 'City of Plagues? Toronto, SARS and the anxieties of globalisation', *Explorations in Anthropology* 9:1 (2009), 133–4.

crux here is to understand how cities seek to attract and influence these flows, while mediating their internal negative downsides for a city's residents.[109]

Besides disease pandemics transmitted through aviation flows, the convergence of economic activities in global cities' financial centres also means one should take note of disruptions in financial and economic flows. The 2008 financial meltdown, concluded the US Financial Crisis Inquiry Commission in 2011, originated partly from 'voracious' Wall Street banks in New York, the pre-eminent global city today. At its height, the Lehmann Shock rattled other global cities' financial cores. Across the Atlantic, on 6 October 2008, London's FTSE stock exchange recorded its steepest points fall ever in history. Tokyo's Nikkei index shed 5 per cent within the first 30 minutes of the opening bell. The yen soared as investors sought a safe-haven, in turn damaging Japan's trade-dependent economy. Indicative of how inter-connected different sectors of the global system are today, tourism flows to the world's most popular destination, Paris (itself another global city) were also hit, with visitor numbers dropping 11.4 per cent in the first quarter of 2009. Parisian consumer confidence plummeted to one of the lowest levels in 20 years. Even *haute couture* shows for the 2009 spring–summer season were curtailed. This was an excellent example of how disruption or destruction at a central node in the interconnected global system tends to send ripples ('the cascade effect') throughout the whole system, even in seemingly unrelated fields. Sassen linked the close infrastructural linkage between financial centres in global cities and the risks involved: 'Global cities are an integral infrastructure of the global financial systems. It is at their heart that these new and risky financial 'products' were designed. The urban embedding of global cities with global financial flows also makes them vulnerable. Indeed, London and New York City, for instance, are being dramatically affected'.[110] This was not the first time that undesirable financial flows had caused problems for global cities boasting important financial infrastructure. During the Asian financial crisis barely a decade earlier, the Thai baht's devaluation and the resulting contagion effects hurt Hong Kong's Hang Seng Index especially severely. It lost 23 per cent between 20 and 23 October 1997. The Dow Jones in New York plunged 554 points on 27 October 1997, with trading temporarily suspended.

Yet another crisis in New York, the September 11th terror attacks, also had a major effect globally. Indeed, highlighting the importance and vulnerability of critical infrastructure for global cities, what Graham terms 'infrastructural terrorism' on September 11th was carried out using everyday systems and infrastructure that we take for granted in the age of globalisation, such as trans-national instantaneous transfers of money flows, computers and aeroplanes, with

---

109 David Harvey, 'The City as Body Politic', in Ida Susser and Jane Schneider (eds), *Wounded Cities: Destruction and Reconstruction in a Globalised World*. Oxford: Berg (2003), 34–5.

110 Interview with *Le Monde Diplomatique*, 26 March 2009 <http://www.lemonde.fr/livres/article/2009/03/26/saskia-sassen-sociologue-globale_1172727_3260.html#ens_id=1176303> accessed 25 April 2012.

the aim to destroy such systems.[111] In the immediate aftermath of the attacks, global flows were severely disrupted. Air hubs of other global cities such as London and Paris faced massive knock-on effects with an unprecedented order from the US Federal Aviation Administration to 'clear the skies'. With tighter visa restrictions, student numbers also dropped. Equity markets in London, Paris and Tokyo by September 2002 remained at levels well below that of September 2001.[112] The global risk of terrorism took on an especially urban form and it was common after September 11th to come across discussions of 'cities under siege'.[113]

Global cities are often said to benefit disproportionately from globalisation, whether in terms of attracting talent, capital, tourism and investment flows or generating a cosmopolitan 'buzz' factor. However, there has been relatively less academic attention on how these very same global cities, by being so plugged into the global system, are also paradoxically most vulnerable to the increasingly noticeable downsides of globalisation. Worse, these global cities can be impacted severely both ways, whether globalisation is stuttering or intensifying. 'Accelerated' globalisation through increasing rates of air travel delivers waves of infectious diseases far faster than the rest of the country, as Toronto discovered. Indeed, such a downside of increasing globalisation is fingered as one of the biggest risks today.[114] Global cities are also most affected when economic meltdown accompanies 'de-globalisation' and decoupling in the international system in the form of protectionism, tariffs or restrictions on cross-border flows. Sassen points out how global cities like London or Tokyo tend to hold the largest populations as well as national employment within a country like Britain or Japan. London for instance held a share of 15.55 per cent of national employment in 1998 while Tokyo had almost 10 per cent of Japan's national employment.[115] These populations would be affected, by a disproportionately large extent than the hinterland, if financial capital flows or trade patterns were abruptly interrupted. The challenge of globalisation thus is an all-too-familiar two-pronged one, which global cities square up to more than others. They have to skilfully ride the waves of globalisation, while managing negative effects that will inevitably strike them first and hardest, compared to the rest of the country. But what does the current state of the art in Security Studies have to say about these trends?

---

111 Stephen Graham, 'Disruption by Design: Urban Infrastructure and Political Violence', in Stephen Graham (ed.), *Disrupted Cities: When Infrastructure Fails*. London: Routledge (2010), 113.

112 Dick K. Nanto '9/11 terrorism: global economic costs'. Congressional Research Service, 5 October 2004, <http://political-asylum.com/crs_country/CRSReport911TerrorismGlobalEconomicCosts(October5,2004)Updated.pdf>, DRS-4.

113 Bob Catterall. 'Cities under siege: September 11th and after', *City* 5:3 (2001), 383.

114 OECD, 'Globalisation ups risk of disease', *The Daily Telegraph* (Australia), 28 June 2011 <http://www.dailytelegraph.com.au/news/world/globalisation-ups-risk-of-disease-gfc/story-e6frev00-1226083296018> accessed 29 June 2013.

115 Sassen, 'The global city: strategic site/new frontier', 141–2.

Cities and Security Studies

As we have seen, global cities have borne the brunt of global risks recently but this has not translated into concerted analyses in the field of Security Studies. At the same time, it must be noted that, 'cities, especially global cities, have increasingly become accepted as objects of analysis'[116] although not so much as referent objects of security. Instead, some have called for innovation in theorising and case studies of how these sub-national actors play roles in global governance.[117] Others have shown how studying global cities allows a more nuanced account of world politics and appreciation of the strategic advantages such cities have in contemporary global governance.[118] Particularly popular have been attempts demonstrating the diplomatic advantages global cities bring to resolving specific global challenges like climate change. Despite this mini-avalanche of works on global cities, they have remained largely silent on the particular global city-global risk nexus examined in this book.

Take for example the existing 'Handbooks' or introductory textbooks, such as Cavelty and Mauer's 2012 collection surveying the rich landscape and subject matter that is Security Studies. There is no significant reference to the global cities either as referent objects of security or as actors in managing security. Other 'Introductory' textbooks, such as Paul Williams' effort in 2008, cover the grounds of key theories, concepts and institutions. The purpose of any attempt to analyse the global city-global risk nexus is not to dwell into the broader theoretical controversies between positivist/rationalist approaches and critical/reflexive approaches to security.[119] Instead, it speaks to the fact some of the global risks addressed in this book – such as terrorism, WMD proliferation, trans-national cime, and health issues – are usually classed as 'contemporary security challenges' in Cavelty and Mauer's or Williams' handbooks (and many others like them). Within the so-called 'traditionalists versus wideners-deepeners debate', our goal identifies more closely with the latter. The subject matter covered here engages with a more holistic understanding of security challenges and referent objects beyond the state. Security Studies has undergone significant change over the past

116 Mark Chou, 'The subject of analysis: global cities and International Relations', *Global Peace, Change, and Security* 24:2 (2012), 305.

117 Mark Amen et al. (eds), *Cities and Global Governance: New Sites for International Relations*. Farnham: Ashgate (2011).

118 Michele Acuto, *Global Cities, Governance and Diplomacy: The Urban Link*, London: Routledge (2013). For climate change, see Taedong Lee, 'Global cities and transnational climate change networks', *Global Environmental Politics* 13:1 (2013), 108–28; Harriet Bulkeley and Vanesa Castan Broto, 'Government by experiment? Global cities and the governing of climate change', *Transactions of the Institute of British Geographers* 38:3 (2013), 361–75.

119 The sub-field of Critical Security Studies has also generated its own handbook. See J. Peter Burgess (ed.), *The Routledge Handbook of New Security Studies*. Abingdon: Routledge (2013).

20 years, becoming one of the most dynamic areas of research such that 'wideners have succeeded enough for chapters on different sectors of security today to be necessary in any textbook introduction.[120] Yet, when textbooks discuss methods and actors confronting these challenges, it is often the EU or alliances or global governance or peace operations that are mentioned: global cities have not featured in any handbook or textbook. Meanwhile, Hughes and Lai's 2011 compilation of classic works provides overview of the 'past, current and developing trends in Security Studies' and 'state of the art' in security thinking.[121] Key theoretical paradigms such as realism, anarchy, and the security dilemma are introduced as a matter of course in discussing 'past' trends, but as for current and developing trends, there is no mention of how an increasingly urbanised world fits within these frameworks and the implications for questions of city-centred agency. Similar to the rubric of 'contemporary security challenges' contained in Cavelty and Mauer's Handbook, there is likewise an apparent sense of 'widening' security agendas reflected in Hughes and Lai's edition. Trans-national crime, migration, diseases and technology feature under the category of 'Security Dimensions and Issues', alongside more classic works on arms racing and deterrence. Besides the possible re-emergence of multi-polarity and security dilemmas, newer issues such as the impact of globalisation and the war on terrorism also merit discussion under the rubric 'Future of Security' which speculates on the implications of globalisation and the post-September 11th era.[122] Despite this growing recognition of globalisation's impact and the 'widening' of security agendas, there is nothing here on cities or the global city-global risk nexus. Crucially, when it comes to 'Security Frameworks and Actors' and the structures, organisations and actors and forms of power that maintain security, Hughes and Lai's collection unsurprisingly introduces concepts like bipolarity, regimes; security communities; alliance politics; multilateralism and even somewhat newer actors such as private military companies. The issue of agency here usually assumes the state remains central, even though private companies have made their presence felt. However, there is again no mention of the role that global cities can play in security governance.[123] Furthermore, the security responses of actors within global cities to issues such as pandemics and terrorist financing are more accurately classed as 'ordinary' and 'everyday' in nature, rather than 'exceptional' or 'dramatic' use of force often monopolised and wielded by nation-states.

Security Studies is multidisciplinary, driven by intellectual agendas outside the field and this is where opportunities lie in engaging across disciplines when

---

120 Myriam Dunn Cavelty and Victor Mauer, 'Introduction' in *The Routledge Handbook of Security Studies*. Abingdon: Routledge (2012), 2.

121 Christopher W. Hughes and Lai Yew Meng (eds), 'Preface', in *Security Studies: A Reader*. Abingdon: Routledge (2011), xiii–xiv.

122 Ibid.

123 Ibid.

examining new geographical concepts of boundaries, motion, space and time.[124] This open-minded mentality echoes some of the work of urban security thinkers such as Graham which we shall see below, but again does not relate specifically to global cities or global risks. Instead, Croft points to themes about culture, images and identity, as well as splits between more 'critical' versus 'realist/liberalist/constructivist' approaches.[125] Above all, Croft concludes that 'boundaries between security studies and other areas are always porous, thus allowing the construction of new forms of thinking about these issues, or at least in allowing that sense of 'newness to be shared by a number of like-minded researchers'.[126] This very porosity should allow, even encourage Security Studies researchers to draw from work in fields such as geography and urban studies in order to analyse the global city-global risk nexus.

Indeed, prominent academics working in geography or urban studies, rather than Security Studies per se, have done much of the early running in studying the urban dimensions of security. Stephen Graham for instance pointed out that war and the city have been deeply intertwined in the history of mankind; legendary urban centres such as Troy and Carthage etched in the annals of warfare.[127] Kabul, Nagasaki, Dresden, Sarajevo, Grozny, September 11th, and Baghdad serve as reminders that 'warfare like everything else is being urbanised'.[128] As modern life in the global economy becomes ever dependent on the critical infrastructures located in cities, Graham particularly noted how the destruction or disruption of mobilities, flows and circulations that cities depend on has become a potentially powerful political and military weapon.[129] Here, one can identify a link already being made between infrastructure and security implications for a city that forms the crux of our analytical framework, although with less direct linkage to notions of global risk and global cities. Appadurai has called this 'an implosion of global and national politics into the urban world'.[130] Political violence and the systematic targeting of cities has been extensively analysed by authors in Stephen Graham's excellent edited collection *Cities, War and Terrorism*. What concerns us here in particular is how unwanted mobilities and their attendant security implications increasingly shape agendas of global cities, from SARS and avian influena to

124 Stuart Croft, 'What future for security studies', in Paul Williams (ed.), *Security Studies: An Introduction*. Abingdon: Routledge (2008), 500, 505.

125 Croft, 503.

126 Croft, 510.

127 Stephen Graham, 'Introduction: Cities, Warfare and States of Emergency', in Stephen Graham (ed.), *Cities, War, and Terrorism*. London: Blackwell (2004), 1–2.

128 Ibid., 4.

129 Stephen Graham, 'Urban metabolism as target: Contemporary war as forced demodernisation', in Nik Heynen, Maria Kaika and Erik Swyngedouw (eds), *In the Nature of Cities: Urban Political Ecology and the Politics of Urban Metabolism*. London: Routledge (2006), 245.

130 Arjun Appadurai, *Modernity at Large: Cultural Dimensions of Globalization*. Minneapolis: University of Minnesota Press (1996), 152.

networked global terrorism.[131] Graham has forcefully highlighted the security downsides that mobilities bring to cities, albeit with less explicit reference to the global city-global risk nexus in particular: 'the technological mobilities that cross-cut cities – of machines, people, computer communications and potential biological pathogens – now threaten apparently unopposable carnage at any instant or any turn'.[132] Globalisation then means that 'in short, the new global security problematic is concerned with the circulation of everything'.[133] There are dangers that arise when the 'circuits sustaining the flows of energy, water, transportation or communications within or between cities break down, are deliberately attacked, or become infused with malign infiltration'.[134] In our new urban age, such mounting fears can have particularly adverse effects in an urban setting. Richard Norton's notion of 'feral cities' highlights how disorderly urban areas in the Global South pose threats to the industrialised North. Based on the notion of the city as a body politic capable of being collectively wounded, there has also been work done on how 'increasingly, urban wounds also result from globalisation processes, unfolding with few constraints since the 1980s'.[135] Security is no longer simply about military forces and the protection of borders, territory and sovereignty and here one can again identify implications for the wideners-traditionalist debate in Security Studies mentioned earlier. Instead, 'security is becoming more civic, urban, domestic and personal',[136] with important ramifications for global cities. Ali and Keil suggest, instead of concentrating as most do when studying global cities, on flows of capital, information, people or power, one should study the flows of microbes.[137] Municipal police forces in global cities such as New York and London facing heightened global terrorism threats have also drastically reorganised themselves with an expanded international reach.[138] Graham's work, amongst others, highlights how recently, 'the inclusion of cities in the realm of international security has the potential to create yet another challenge to the pre-eminence of the traditional state in international politics … cities are increasingly

131 Kevin Hannam, Mimi Sheller, and John Urry, 'Editorial: mobilities, immobilities and moorings', *Mobilities* 1:1 (2006), 1.

132 Stephen Graham, 'In a moment: on glocal mobilities and the terrorised city', *City* 5:3 (2001), 412.

133 Dillon, 'Global security in the 21st century', 2.

134 Graham, 'When Infrastructures Fail', 3.

135 Ida Susser and Jane Schneider, 'Wounded Cities: Destruction and Reconstruction in a Globalized World', in Ida Susser and Jane Schneider (eds), *Wounded Cities: Destruction and Reconstruction in a Globalized World.* Oxford: Berg (2003), 1.

136 Jon Coaffee and Murakami Wood, 'Security is coming home: rethinking scale and constructing resilience in the global urban response to terrorist risk', *International Relations* 20:4 (2006), 504.

137 Ali and Keil, 'Global Cities and the Spread of Infectious Disease', 493.

138 Brian Nussbaum, 'Protecting global cities: New York, London and the internationalisation of municipal policing for counter-terrorism', *Global Crime* 8:3 (2007), 228.

becoming relevant even in that most state-centric of realms: security'.[139] Yet, in spite of the impressive works done by geographers and urban planners, how should Security Studies scholars begin to engage intellectually with the global risk-global city nexus that remains substantially under-theorised?

The Vocabulary of Risk and Ulrich Beck's Global Risk Society

The aforementioned discussions of a global city – circulating global flows through critical infrastructure and the security implications for such connected cities dependent on uninterrupted flows – can now be brought to bear on the idea of global risks, the final missing piece in the analytical puzzle. For former UK Defence Secretary Liam Fox, globalisation brought plusses such as trade and prosperity, but also the 'unavoidable importation of strategic risk'.[140] The 1999 US *National Security Strategy* unequivocally declared that 'globalisation also brings risks',[141] in the form of ethnic conflicts, weapons of mass destruction and terrorism, diseases, and environmental degradation. Indeed the term 'proliferation' now describes any of the above trans-national dangers that spread across porous boundaries, apart from its original meaning relating to WMD.[142] The idea of spreading risks around the world through globalisation is particularly apt here, yet the implications remain unexplored for global cities that host the very infrastructure allowing these risks to circulate. Indeed, the insecurities and sense of dread invoked by late-modern systems such as air travel and global financial systems has become a prominent scholarly theme. For Zygmunt Bauman, the events of September 11th where hijackers from the Middle East were able to strike at the heart of New York using commercial airliners, highlighted dramatically what everyone had long known: 'it was the symbolic end to an era of space' where security was inherently linked to territorial boundaries.[143] Bauman's 'liquid modernity' refers to the increasingly under-defined and fluid structure of the global system that mandates re-evaluation of concepts of time-space and human individuality. The sense of change and flux particularly resonates with previous discussions of global cities as characterised by mobilities and fast-moving flows. This 'liquid modern' age has in turn generated what Bauman terms 'liquid fear' where people exhibit a state of constant anxiety

139 Ibid., 230.

140 Liam Fox, 'Oral evidence before the House of Commons Defence Committee on the SDSR and NSS' (speech, 9 March 2011) <https://www.gov.uk/government/news/dr-liam-fox-responds-to-defence-committee-report-on-sdsr> accessed 9 March 2013.

141 The White House, 'A National Security Strategy for a New Century'. Washington D.C: The White House (December 1999), Chapter I, 1.

142 David Mutimer, 'Reconstituting security? The practices of proliferation control', *European Journal of International Relations* 4:1 (1998), 99–129.

143 Zygmunt Bauman, 'Reconnaissance wars of the planetary frontierland', *Theory, Culture and Society* 19:4 (2002), 81.

about the dangers that could strike unannounced and at any moment.[144] Here, such a background of fear has not yet been linked to the preceding concerns raised by Graham about unrelenting mobilities and global flows that can appear unstoppable in wreaking massive disruption and destruction to hyper-connected cities. Further explaining this sense of an epochal transition and uncertainty, Martin Albrow noted that modernity and its sense of centrality of control and direction has lost its hold on the imagination. There is thus a need 'to bring our language into a closer fit with our experience of the present'. In place of modernity, Albrow touts the 'Global Age Hypothesis' to 'provide us with ample illustration of newly emergent social forms and forces which enable us to see ... modernity as ephemeral, and not permanent'.[145] The 'global' thus takes centre stage and yet, Albrow's analysis has overlooked global cities, the very places which reflect the new forces and forms that drive his new 'global age'. In this context of change, sociologist Anthony Giddens claimed that the new language lies in a generalised 'climate of risk' characteristic of late modernity. 'Thinking in terms of risk' becomes more or less inevitable and thus becomes unsettling for everyone: no one escapes.[146] Together with this sense of foreboding, Giddens posits the onset of 'runaway globalisation' where distant events such as globally-integrated financial markets, Internet-linked stock trading, airports, and new communications technologies now have the ability to impact and influence local events. This creates a process of 'dis-embedding' and sense of insecurity where individuals lose their place-based local orientations.[147] The infrastructure that underpins modern global cities also appears to have a part to play in generating risk. Timothy Luke noted that in order for critical infrastructure such as global finance and stock exchanges to operate optimally in late-modern capitalism, these technical systems must be open and receptive to a certain amount of flux and exchange which can never be totally controlled. This in turn fuels a sense of insecurity because 'defence against the insecurities of all those who now live amidst these linked assemblies in big market-driven systems is neither certain nor final'.[148] While these authors are different from each other in many significant ways, they allude to a similar sense of risk and foreboding arising from trepidation and unease; the loss of familiarity and control in the face of complex late-modern systems and technologies that comprise critical infrastructure today. They have also neglected the extent to which their concerns are relevant to highly connected

144 Zygmunt Bauman, *Liquid Fear*. Cambridge: Polity Press (2006).

145 Martin Albrow, *The Global Age: State and Society Beyond Modernity*. Cambridge: Polity Press (1996), 185.

146 Anthony Giddens, *Modernity and Self-Identity. Self and Society in the Late Modern Age*. Cambridge: Polity Press (1991), 123–6.

147 Anthony Giddens, *The Consequences of Modernity*. Stanford: Stanford University Press (1990), 21.

148 Timothy Luke, 'Everyday Technics as Extraordinary Threats: Urban Technostructures and Non-Places in Terrorist Actions', in S Graham (ed.), *Cities, War and Terrorism: Towards an Urban Geopolitics*. Malden, MA: Wiley-Blackwell (2004), 120–36.

global cities, which this book argues, serve as veritable repositories of modernised risk given their openness and critical infrastructure processing global flows. Indeed, 'greater interconnectedness of the world has changed the nature of risk and increased exposure', declared the UK Cabinet Office's Strategy Unit report on Risk in 2002. To better understand the nature of risks in an inter-connected world, the World Economic Forum's 'Global Risks Report 2011' helpfully supplies a 'risk inter-connectivity' map, whereby it attempts to map the inter-linkage between a staggering array of risks. It warns, 'we face ever-greater concerns regarding global risks, the prospect of rapid contagion through increasingly connected systems and the threat of disastrous impacts'.[149]

In such a perilously inter-connected world, it is perhaps unsurprising that researchers have been drawn not just to Giddens, Bauman and Albrow, but also to Ulrich Beck's notion of the world risk society.[150] Beck's early focus was on domestic issues, particularly how industrial societies previously predicated on the need to manufacture 'goods' had morphed into anxiety-ridden 'risk societies' preoccupied with managing side-effects and 'bads', such as pollution, nuclear disasters, and health hazards. Turning his attention towards international affairs, Beck's central claim is that the bipolar world of Cold War enemies has been replaced by a world of vague dangers and elusive globalised risks such as terrorism and ethnic conflict.[151] What Beck terms the 'triple axis' of World Risk Society is constituted by climate change, terrorism, and financial meltdown. There is an urgent need to recognise the global challenges we face because Beck argues 'the disregard for the globalizing risks aggravates the globalization of risk'.[152] Beck who has emerged as one of the foremost thinkers on globalisation and risks, declared that 'being at global risk is the human condition at the beginning of the twenty-first century … The experience of global risks represents a shock for the whole of humanity'.[153] Yet, he has not examined the experience of global cities at the frontlines facing global risks on a daily basis. For Beck, the shared *experience* of global risk is shaped by firstly de-localisation whereby causes and consequences are not limited to one geographical space, and secondly, incalculableness whereby consequences are in principle unknowable or calculable in advance.[154] The de-localisation of risks brings with it *spatial* challenges whereby there is no respect for borders and

149 World Economic Forum 2011 News Release, 'In East Asia, concerns about the world's response to global risks', 12 June 2011 <http://www.weforum.org/news/east-asia-concerns-about-world%E2%80%99s-response-global-risks> accessed 20 June 2011.

150 Eike Krahmann, 'Beck and beyond: selling security in the world risk society', *Review of International Studies* 37:1 (2011), 349.

151 Ulrich Beck, *World Risk Society*. Cambridge: Polity Press (1999), 3

152 Ulrich Beck, *World at Risk*. Cambridge: Polity Press (2009), 47.

153 Ulrich Beck, 'Living in the world risk society', *Economy and Society* 35:3 (2006), 329–45, 330.

154 Ulrich Beck, 'The terrorist threat: the world risk society revisited', *Theory, Culture and Society* 19:4 (1999), 50.

social implications whereby because of its complexity, assignment of causes and consequences is not possible with any reliability (e.g. global financial crises).[155] To Beck, ongoing debates over global risks have highlighted the 'cosmopolitan significance' of fear and the globalisation of emotions as humans in distant parts of the world share the same anxieties over common global risks. From Rio de Janeiro to Beijing, the same sense of shock accompanied the images of September 11th, a truly global event.[156] As Beck argues, 'the anticipation of catastrophe is changing the world'.[157] Hence, what is perhaps most important is not so much the catastrophe itself, but rather the efforts undertaken to avert a predicted negative result from actually materialising. 'Risk means the anticipation of catastrophe. Risks concern the possibility of future occurrences and developments'.[158]

Beck's focus on epochal change is not unique. Others such as Martin Albrow have written of the 'Global Age' where modernity has been supplanted by globality, triggering a fundamental change in the basis of action and social organisation for individuals and groups. Albrow points to five ways where this has occurred: global environmental consequences of human action; loss of security in the face of globally destructive weaponry; globality of communication systems; rise of a global economy; and the 'reflexivity of globalism' whereby people of all kinds refer to the globe as the frame for their beliefs'.[159] These five trends that Albrow highlights hold significance for global cities which remain unexplored. Albrow further notes how the 'global interconnectedness of human relations … makes it possible to conceptualise global risks' and cites Beck's work for demonstrating how the importance of risk is being seen as not merely a local matter of concern, but a global one with huge political implications.[160] Perhaps nowhere else can this sense of global interconnectedness and perception of global risk be seen than in global cities. Albrow continues that the influences and drivers of change in the personal milieu of an individual anywhere in the world may be linked to the operation of processes which are worldwide in their scope. The global reference is central and the 'recognition of their interconnection is the final step in the passage to the Global age'.[161]

Beck's world risk society accentuates the fact that no single country can properly manage global risks alone, for 'global risks are the expression of a new form of global interdependence, which cannot be adequately addressed by way of national politics or by the available forms of international co-operation'.[162] For Albrow, there are emerging 'configurations of the global age' whereby 'the world is

155 Beck, 'Living in the world risk society', 334.
156 Ulrich Beck, *Cosmopolitan Vision*. Cambridge: Polity Press (2006), 72.
157 Beck, *World at Risk*, 1.
158 Ibid., 9.
159 Albrow, *The Global Age*, 4.
160 Ibid., 85
161 Ibid., 106
162 Beck, *Cosmopolitan Vision*, 336, 342.

spanned by institutions with global concern even if there is no world government'.[163] This statement and possible *policy* implications is particularly pertinent to global cities that indeed have global concerns with global risks but face the conundrum of no overarching world authority to manage them. Yet, neither Beck nor Albrow have considered what global cities can do in the face of this global city-global risk nexus. For Albrow, the pressing task is conceptual and intellectual arising from a need to recognise that globality belongs to a new age with its own shape and characteristics that belie the previous framework of modernity.[164] In this new era, Beck declared that the only solution is intensified transnational cooperation.[165] This same theme was repeated in the 2011 OECD report *Future Global Shocks: improving risk governance* noting how,

> recent global shocks, such as the 2008 financial crisis, have driven policy makers and industry strategists to re-examine how to prepare for and respond to such events in the future, whether they arise in financial, natural, public health or even political systems ... Never before have global risks seemed so complex, the stakes so high, and the need for international co-operation to deal with them so apparent.[166]

Globalisation not only provides the vectors for circulating risks, but also complicates policy solutions. As Dillon observed,

> if circulation poses the generic problem of global security, complexity poses its epistemic challenges. How are we to understand how these complex systems of global circulation operate and how to manage them in ways that will avoid the potential for disaster stored up within them? This is as much a political as a technical challenge ... The more things circulate the more complex they become.[167]

The hope is that humankind's gradual realisation of this common set of challenges also stimulates more global cooperation.[168] Beck stresses the importance of 'staging' global risk, in the sense that only by imagining and staging global risk does the future catastrophe become present – often with the goal of averting it by influencing present decisions'.[169] The basic thesis of Beck's *World Risk Society* is that the new scale and types of global risks that have to be averted is reshaping the foundations of societies and global politics.[170] He suggests that three reactions

163 Albrow, *The Global Age*, 123.

164 Ibid., 119.

165 Beck, *World at Risk*, 41.

166 OECD, 'Future Global Shocks', 2.

167 Dillon, 'Global security in the 21st century', 2.

168 K.M. Venkat Narayan et al., 'Global non-communicable diseases: where worlds meet', *New England Journal of Medicine* 363 (2010), 1196–8.

169 Beck, *World at Risk*, 10.

170 Beck, *World at Risk*, 52.

to such global risks are possible: denial, apathy, and transformation.[171] It is the last, 'transformation' that concerns this book, for it raises the possibility of new cooperative actions and arrangements that arise across and within borders to tackle shared global risks.[172] This leads to a form of *co-operative trans-national states* that are better able to cope with the impact of globalisation: 'the great political challenge of our time'.[173] Beck's *prescriptions* for a *global cosmopolis* to manage global risks are based on principle of equality and cooperation between a wide range of actors to be realised through corresponding reform of international law and international organisations.[174] While Beck has stressed that crucial roles remain for reinvigorated trans-national states and international institutions to play, where global cities could fit into this jigsaw puzzle of myriad actors remains unexplored.

While he has hinted at how environmental change and rising seas would swamp global cities like London, New York, and Tokyo,[175] Beck has yet to examine in detail the implications of his global risks thesis for the world's global cities and how they would try to manage these globe-spanning risks. Neither did Beck scrutinise how risks are transmitted through global city infrastructures that circulate global flows. As for those who have utilised or criticised Beck's ideas, they have written on a range of topics: from governmentality and global governance; to war and strategy; the use of drones; AIDS; and the NATO alliance.[176] None have zeroed in on the global city-global risk nexus. Urban specialists Ali and Keil make a passing reference to Beck, noting 'the airports as a location where the risks of social and technological interactions of global capitalism manifest themselves in the so-called risk society',[177] but they did not undertake a more systematic in-depth analysis of the relationship between Beck's risk society thesis and global cities. While there is some existing literature of how cities respond to global terrorism risks,[178] the focus has tended to be on governance, urban design, and planning issues. For instance, Nussbaum notes that the theoretical approach employed in

171 Beck, 'Living in the world risk society', 331.

172 Ulrich Beck, 'The Cosmopolitan State: Towards a Realistic Utopia' <http://www.eurozine.com/articles/2001-12-05-beck-en.html> accessed 14 November 2007.

173 Ulrich Beck, 'In the new, anxious world, leaders must learn to think beyond borders', *Guardian*, 13 July 2007 <http://www.guardian.co.uk/commentisfree/story/0,2125317,00.html> accessed 12 November 2007.

174 Beck, *Cosmopolitan Vision*, 132.

175 Beck, *World at Risk*, 85.

176 See, for instance, Yee-Kuang Heng, *War as Risk Management*. London: Routledge (2006); Yee-Kuang Heng and Kenneth McDonagh, *Risk, Global Governance and Security*. London: Routledge (2009); Christopher Coker, *War in an Age of Risk*. Cambridge: Polity Press (2009); Claudia Aradau and Rens Van Munster, 'Governing terrorism through risk', *European Journal of International Relations* 13:1 (2007), 89–115; Michael J. Williams, *NATO, Security, and Risk Management*. London: Routledge (2009).

177 Ali and Keil, 'Securitising networked flows', 109.

178 For instance, Stephen Graham (ed.), *Cities, War, and Terrorism: An Urban Geopolitics*. London: Blackwell (2004); Coaffee, *Terrorism, Risk and the Global City*.

Coafee's important 2003 book *Terrorism, Risk and the Global City* 'is better suited to an analysis of Geography or Planning' rather than Security Studies.[179]

The flaws of Beck's thesis such as questions on risk definition, perception, neglect of power relationships and patterns of political engagement have already been addressed.[180] Beck's statements are generalised, sweeping, hardly nuanced and to a certain extent exaggerated. He stresses epochal breaks in historical continuities at the expense of logical consistencies, and more academic definitional and conceptual issues.[181] Notwithstanding the critiques of Beck, when it comes to the semantics of security, today it is 'the management of risks that characterises contemporary security practices'.[182] Other scholars working on global risk argued that alternative solutions are being found that run contrary to Beck's 'cosmopolitan' emphasis'.[183] The OECD recommends more emphasis on early warning systems and foresight capacities that can help 'produce a probability of the transmission of risks through complex and interdependent systems'.[184] Ortwin Renn et al. argue that since global risks are not confined to national borders; they therefore present global risk governance challenges.[185] Rather than Beck's sociologically-inspired understanding of risk derived from the processes of modernisation and industrialisation, Renn et al. apply frameworks developed by the independent organisation, International Risk Governance Council (IRGC). While the IRGC's approach is different from Beck's, they share common ground in a need for integrated solutions, involving not just governments, but civil society, industry and intergovernmental organisations. Yet, there is a real danger of global governance failures. One has to grapple with divergent interests of the Great Powers, the inequality of the international system and differentials in governance capabilities. The number-one risk today is 'de-globalization – the failure of the global system to cope with the complex issues we are confronted with'.[186] In such a connected world, global cities have the highest stakes because they are 'key nodes in the economic and technological networks that constitute the world community. They represent a sort of international critical infrastructure underpinning the global economy. They also face potentially higher threats because of the high profiles, high number of international travelers and

179 Nussbaum, 'Protecting global cities', 216. Also see Coaffee, *Terrorism, Risk and the Global City*, Preface, xii.

180 For instance Gabe Mythen, *Ulrich Beck: A Critical Introduction to the Risk Society*. Cambridge: Polity Press (2004).

181 See a critique of Beck's works in 'War and the Risk Society', in Hans Joas, *War and Modernity*. Cambridge: Polity Press (2003), 171–80.

182 Oliver Kessler and Christopher Daase, 'From insecurity to uncertainty: risk and the paradox of security politic', *Alternatives* 33:2 (2008), 211–32.

183 For instance, see Krahmann, 'Beck and beyond', 350.

184 OECD, 'Future Global Shocks', 3.

185 Ortwin Renn and Katherine D. Walker (eds), *Global Risk Governance*. Amsterdam: Springer (2008).

186 World Economic Forum 2011 News Release, 'In East Asia, concerns about the world's response to global risks'.

citizens, and target-rich environments'.[187] Some observers claim that the terrorist attacks on Mumbai in 2008 were precisely because of the city's iconic status as a global city. The chosen 'targets had a deep symbolic resonance: as hangouts for the legion of adventurous foreigners and the new Indian elite ... attracted by the project to re-make India's commercial capital as a global hub to rival Shanghai, New York or London ... it's precisely the elite infrastructure of the "global city" that the terrorists attacked ... it seems to be Mumbai's connection to globalisation that made it a target'.[188] With so much at stake for global cities in this new age of globalised risks, exactly what roles they can play in managing Beck's global risk society is therefore another crucial focus of this book.

Conclusion

It is often said that Hollywood has its hand on the pulse of the cultural *zeitgeist*, society's fears and concerns. During the Cold War, it delivered the classic *Dr. Strangelove or: How I Learned to Stop Worrying and Love the Bomb.* Consider a more recent offering from Tinseltown. The 2011 movie, *Contagion*, tracked the rapid spread of an airborne virus across the world's travel hubs. On the film's promotional poster, the word 'Contagion' is composed of letters derived from leading global cities such as Tokyo, London and Hong Kong. With a menacing subtitle of 'the world goes viral', the film epitomises the anxieties of an inter-connected world that pirouettes around on its global cities.

One can add other descriptive metaphors popular in contemporary discourse that characterise the global transmission of security challenges: 'ripple effects', 'circulation', 'inter-connectedness', 'inter-dependence', 'shockwaves', 'falling dominoes'. Pandemics that contaminate highly-globalised global cities are sadly not the only global risks that have caused urgent concern. This is especially true for global cities that, with their critical infrastructure, serve as gateways to the world.

Global cities have been discussed in the context of emerging infectious diseases, urbanisation, developmental studies, migration flows and of course, political economy and global capitalism. Others have looked at it through the lens of cinema, architectural icons and the promotion of arts within such cities. Despite recognition of the socio-political downsides of being a global city (high costs of living; traffic snarls, illegal immigration etc.), the far more sinister range of global flows such as trans-national terrorism, WMD proliferation, diseases and financial meltdown and policy responses of global cities remain under-conceptualised in the existing Security Studies literature. Instead, it has been geographers and urban planners that have taken the first stab at such problems. As Graham points out,

---

187 Nussbaum, 'Protecting global cities', 214.

188 Mukul Devichand, 'Where East meets West', *Guardian*, 27 Nov 2008 <http://www.guardian.co.uk/commentisfree/2008/nov/27/mumbai-terror-attacks-india6> accessed 18 April 2009.

'the politics of international, state, corporate or urban security are now especially preoccupied with the sense that the infrastructures sustaining urban life provide an urban Achilles heel to be attacked and exploited by all manner of state or non-state threats'.[189] This chapter has developed its definition of a global city based on four key features drawn from leading figures in the field, ranging from Sassen and Castells to Olds and Yeung. These include: 1) the ability to attract and circulate global flows; 2) the infrastructure approach stressing the centrality of critical infrastructure to global city functions; 3) the role of the developmental state; 4) increasing concern with side-effects and downsides. Security Studies researchers can more precisely identify two key aspects to zero in on: firstly, the *mechanics* of how highly-connected global cities as 'spaces of flows' and their different types of critical infrastructure help attract and facilitate unwanted global flows or mobilities; secondly, the policy *implications* for global cities and how to manage global risks. Heavily reliant on servicing and harnessing globalisation's flows to thrive, the crucial policy dilemma for global cities is 'how to differentiate good circulation from bad circulation, devising means of preventing bad circulation without collapsing circulation as such'.[190] Although several perspectives and modes of inquiry exist for global cities, none systematically engage with the roles of global cities in Beck's global risk society. Equipped with the analytical framework developed in this chapter, the following chapters can now begin to scrutinise perhaps the most vulnerable yet self-consciously 'global' global city today, Singapore.

189 Graham, 'When Infrastructures Fail', 16.
190 Dillon, 'Global security in the 21st century', 3.

Chapter 2
Mobilities, Flows and Infrastructures: The Making of Global City Singapore

Why Singapore?

Perhaps alone amongst other leading urban centres, being a global city has been a key plank of Singapore's foreign policy since its early post-independence years, as eloquently outlined by the country's first Foreign Minister S. Rajaratnam's famous 'Global City' speech in 1972. Acharya noted that Rajaratnam's vision was driven by a desire to 'achieve security through participation in the global economy'[1] and inviting foreign presence in the Singaporean economy so as to create stakes for external powers in its survival. Overcoming the constraints of its immediate geography, Singapore has preferred to define itself as a 'global city' with the whole world as its 'hinterland'.[2] What Desker terms the 'globalisation paradigm' has remained one of the key thrusts of foreign policy to this day.[3] By 1986, the island-nation of Singapore had acquired the distinction of a 'primary world city'.[4] Loughborough University's Globalization and World Cities Research Network also rated Singapore favourably as a leading 'Alpha World City'.[5] From a variety of databases and indices, Singapore's credentials as a globally significant urban node appear strong. Yet, as this chapter will show, such high standing does not come about by accident. Dissecting exactly how and where Singapore's global connectivity stems from allows us to engage with several critiques of existing global city research, particularly the neglect of how a global city comes into being. Keeping in mind the recurrent themes of the 'infrastructure' approach and a global city as a space of flows and the need to filter out 'good' from 'bad' circulations and mobilities highlighted previously, a close reading of Singapore's global city project vindicates the role of the developmental

1 Amitav Acharya, *Singapore's Foreign Policy: The Search for Regional Order*. Singapore: World Scientific (2008), 44.

2 Tan See Seng, 'Faced with the dragon: perils and prospects in Singapore's ambivalent relationship with China', *Chinese Journal of International Politics* 5:3 (2012), 245–65.

3 Barry Desker and Mohd Nawab Mohd Osman, 'S. Rajaratnam and the Making of Singapore Foreign Policy', in Kwa Chong Guan (ed.), *S. Rajaratnam on Singapore: From Ideas to Reality*. Singapore: World Scientific (2006), 7.

4 John Friedmann, 'The World City Hypothesis', *Development and Change* 17:1 (1986), 71.

5 Jon Beaverstock et al., 'A roster of world cities', *Cities* 16:6 (1999), 456.

state. Its leaders have consistently chosen to pour resources into carefully targeted sectors of critical infrastructure that enhance its ability to serve as a key intersection attracting and coordinating global flows. The high-level Economic Strategies Committee reiterated in 2010 a need to 'invest ahead in the fundamentals that will drive Singapore's success … the infrastructure and connectivity of a global city'.[6] It points to how in light of booming Asian trade and economic patterns, 'as a well-connected global city in the heart of Asia, we would be well-positioned to facilitate these flows'.[7] Yet, as we shall see, Singapore's impressive infrastructural ability to attract and circulate global flows (aviation; maritime; financial) also translates into a vulnerability to global risk.

Testament to Singapore's strengths in infrastructure, Price Waterhouse Cooper's survey in 2012 of 'Cities of Opportunity' placed Singapore in the top 10 in a new category 'City Gateway' which measures a city's global connectedness and attraction to others. Three types of infrastructure can be seen as pillars sustaining Singapore's global connectivity: its airport; its financial centre; and its global maritime port hub. Correspondingly, these critical gateways allow Singapore to service three types of global flows that will be individually scrutinised in subsequent chapters: financial flows; aviation flows; and maritime trade flows. For now, the point being made here is that these flows, either attracted to, or facilitated by Singapore's deliberate investment in world-class infrastructure, also deliver what Beck calls spatially-delimited global risks right into the heart of Asia's leading global city. Terrorism, which can involve home-grown radicalised groups with trans-national links to the Middle East, for instance poses a threat to disrupting mobilities and flows in the aviation, financial and maritime sector that pass through Singapore. This often triggers intense social reflexivity on how to manage global risks and perils of globalisation, in perhaps the most self-conscious of global cities.

A.T. Kearney's Global Cities Index of 2014 placed Singapore as number 9 within the top 10: 'Singapore is clearly in a league of its own among cities in Southeast Asia, with no close rivals in business activity, human capital, or information exchange'.[8] Academic studies comparing the period 2000 to 2008 consistently show Singapore moving up from number 6 to number 5 on the list of the connected cities in the world.[9] Sociologist Chua Beng Huat observed that there is the 'globalisation of everything' in Singapore.[10] At the same time,

---

6 Ministry of Finance, Singapore, 'Economic Strategies Committee Report', February 2010 <http://app.mof.gov.sg/data/cmsresource/ESC%20Report/ESC%20Full%20Report.pdf> accessed 15 April 2011, 10.

7 Ibid., 37.

8 A.T. Kearney, 'Global cities, present and future', <http://www.atkearney.com/research-studies/global-cities-index/full-report> accessed 9 May 2014.

9 Ben Derudder et al., 'Pathways of change: shifting connectivities in the world city network 2008–08', *Urban Studies* 47:9 (2010), 1861–77.

10 Cited in Asad Latif, 'Singapore: Surviving the Downsides of Globalisation', in Daljit Singh and Chin Kin Wah (eds), *Southeast Asian Affairs 2004*. Singapore: ISEAS (2004), 233.

data from the 2014 Revision of the UN's World Urbanisation Prospects report show that 100 per cent of Singapore's population is classified as urban, one of only three territories in the world with this figure. The tiny island epitomises the twin concurrent trends of urbanisation and globalisation. Assad Latif claims that Singapore's 'character derives from the fact that it is, exceptionally, a product of globalisation. Singapore saw itself as a global city long before it became fashionable to either lubricate or jam the wheels turning the world into a single factory'.[11] Described as a 'perennial powerhouse' when it comes to global connectivity, Singapore topped the list in the 2006 A.T Kearney/*Foreign Policy* Globalization Index.[12] It repeated the feat again in 2007, for the fourth time in seven years.[13] In 2010, Singapore came in eighth on the list of 'Most Global Cities 2010' by A.T. Kearney, and emerged third on Ernst & Young's Globalization Index.[14] In 2011, Price Waterhouse Coopers installed Singapore as Asia's leading global city.[15] Commercial estate firm CB Richard Ellis found that 67.5 per cent of international companies surveyed in July 2011 had a business presence in Singapore, making it the second most popular city for business in the world.[16] The Economist Intelligence Unit's inaugural Global City Competitiveness Index in March 2012 ranked Singapore third in the world, behind London and New York. As for its provision of services as global convention hub, the pocket dynamo has also been crowned Asia's 'Top Convention City' in 2014 for the 12th year running, by the International Congress and Convention Association. In December 2011, Harvard economist Edward Glaeser and Saskia Sassen listed Singapore as one of the 'Top 16 Global Cities to Watch' in the journal *Foreign Policy*. In October 2011, Singapore had the highest trade-to-GDP ratio in the world, standing at 404.9 per cent.[17] For the two-year period 2011 to 2013, the ratio was 366.2 per cent. These astounding figures highlight the level of openness and connectivity the city has with the wider global system.

Positivist taxonomies in existing global cities literature also obscure the fact that the 'global cities are best thought of as a historical construct, not a place or

11 Ibid., 225–6.

12 Paul Laudicina, 'The Globalisation Index', *Foreign Policy*, 19 October 2006.

13 Foreign Policy, 'The Globalisation Index 2007', November/December 2007.

14 Ernst & Young, 'Globalization Index 2010' <http://www.ey.com/SG/en/Newsroom/News-releases/News-release---Singapore-takes-third-spot-on-Globalization-Index-2010> accessed 1 July 2011.

15 Rachel Kelly, 'Singapore ranked as Asia's leading global city: report', Channel NewsAsia, 15 June 2011 <http://www.channelnewsasia.com/stories/singaporebusinessnews/view/1135350/1/.html> accessed 16 June 2011.

16 Channel NewsAsia, 'Hong Kong pips Singapore as most popular city for international business', Channel News Asia, 20 July 2011, <http://www.channelnewsasia.com/stories/singaporebusinessnews/view/1141966/1/.html> accessed 20 July 2011.

17 World Trade Organization, 'Trade profile: Singapore', October 2011 <http://stat.wto.org/CountryProfile/WSDBCountryPFView.aspx?Language=F&Country=SG> accessed 8 April 2012.

'object' consisting of essential properties that can be readily measured outside the process of meaning-making'.[18] This attests to the political importance and rhetoric in Singapore's political discourse about how being a global city is an existential issue. Such critical meaning is invested in the desirability of being a global city consistently placed into the public discourse by its senior leaders. In the previous chapter, scholars such as Olds and Yeung, and John Rennie Short argued that global cities literature tended to exhibit a predominantly Anglo-American bias towards London, New York, and occasionally Tokyo. There is a greater need now to broaden the existing knowledge of other global cities especially in the Asia-Pacific. Singapore as a global city has already been the subject of several studies, mainly from a political economy and developmental perspective; architecture; or its cultural policy.[19] Even more significant for our purposes are recent attempts by Oswin and Yeoh to conceive of Singapore as a 'mobile' city, essentially linking the global city literature with the mobilities turn emphasised in the first chapter.[20] This book continues this emerging scholarly focus on connectivity, mobility and attempting to harness flows, but provides a different twist by examining how Singapore the global city has also been exposed to a myriad of global risks because of its connectivity. A key dynamic that explains the significance of global cities like Singapore is how they have been able to develop the infrastructure that generates a high level of connectivity and capability for global control, coordination and management of global flows. This deliberate intention to become a global city is the subject of the next section.

S. Rajaratnam's 'Global City' Vision for Singapore

The tropical island of Singapore had for much of its known history been subsumed within a larger political entity (whether the British Empire or Malaya or the earlier Johor-Riau Sultanate). Upon gaining independence in 1965, the tiny island's traumatic experience of being booted out of post-colonial Malaysia convinced its leaders to pursue the global city pathway years before academics and planners

18 Michael Peter Smith, 'The Global Cities Discourse: A Return to the Master Narrative', in Neil Brenner and Roger Keil (eds), *The Global Cities Reader*. London: Routledge (2006), 378.

19 Kris Olds and Henry Yeung, 'Pathways to global city formation: a view from the developmental city-state of Singapore', *Review of International Political Economy* 11:3 (2004); Brenda Yeoh, 'The global cultural city? Spatial imagineering and politics in the (multi-) cultural marketplaces of South-east Asia', *Urban Studies* 42:5/6 (2005), 945–58; Terence Chong, 'Singapore's cultural policy and its consequences', *Critical Asian Studies* 37:4 (2005), 553–68; Robert Powell, *Singapore: Architecture of a Global City*. Singapore: Archipelago Press (2000).

20 Natalie Oswin and Brenda Yeoh, 'Introduction: mobile city Singapore', *Mobilities* 5:2 (2010), 167.

began speaking of the global city.[21] As the Globalisation Index 2007 observed, 'when you're a flyweight, globalising is a matter of necessity ... (Singapore) can't rely on their limited domestic markets the way the United States can. To be globally competitive, these countries have no choice but to open up and attract trade and foreign investment'.[22] Singapore's 'hinterland' de facto became other regions of South-East Asia and distant parts of the world. For a 100 per cent urbanised area with one of Asia's highest population densities that is only about the size of Chicago, the starting premise for Singapore planners is that they are irrelevant. So, the guiding vision has always been to do whatever necessary to become relevant and in such a way as to guarantee its survival. The challenge for Singapore is 'how to offset its vulnerability by increasing its national capacity and international presence'.[23] This is why former Deputy Prime Minister Wong Kan Seng consistently drummed up the importance of being a global city,

> becoming a global city is not merely an aspiration. It is a pre-requisite for our survival. Being open is the only viable option for us if we wish to be self-reliant and continue to prosper. Closing our doors will only turn us into an island of no consequence; we will become irrelevant to the world. Being open allows us to connect and trade with the rest of the world, and in doing so attract investments and the best talent to Singapore.[24]

Singapore initially considered several possible models for emulation, from post-colonial Cambodia to the siege mentality of Israel before eventually settling on Venice 'as a model of a global city it could learn from': Singapore was to 'become a hub of global trade, like Venice had been'.[25]

For some researchers, Singapore has been a global city at different times in its history, constantly reinventing itself to provide different niches. It has always been positioned as a 'hub' or 'nodal point' proving services ranging from entrepot trade

21 Henry Yeung Wai-Chung, 'Globalisation Singapore: One Global City, Global Production Networks and the Developmental State', in Tarn Tan How (eds), *Singapore Perspectives 2010*. Singapore: World Scientific (2010), 113.

22 Foreign Policy, 'The Globalisation Index 2007', 72.

23 Kwa Chong Guan, 'Relating to the World: Images, Metaphors, and Analogies', in Derek De Cunha (ed.), *Singapore in the New Millennium: Challenges Facing the City-State*. Singapore: ISEAS (2002), 108.

24 Keynote address by Wong Kan Seng, Deputy Prime Minister and Coordinating Minister for National Security, 'Singapore Perspectives 2011 Conference' (speech, Singapore, 17 January 2011) <http://www.nptd.gov.sg/content/NPTD/news/_jcr_content/par_content/download_18/file.res/Keynote%20address%20by%20DPM%20Wong%20Kan%20Seng%20at%20the%20Singapore%20Perspectives%202011%20Conference%20170111.pdf> accessed 18 January 2013.

25 Kwa Chong Guan, 'Relating to the World: Images, Metaphors, and Analogies', in Derek De Cunha (ed.), *Singapore in the New Millennium: Challenges Facing the City-State*. Singapore: ISEAS (2002), 117–18.

in the beginning, to financial services, education and more recently, hi-technology niches in bio-technology.[26] Over the years, it has 'attained and defended a centrality in the region, and for goods, services and people passing through the region' by 'nurturing existing comparative advantages while also developing new attributes'.[27] Whilst it has been suggested that the Singapore government belatedly decided to re-package the city-state as a cosmopolitan global city in the 1990s,[28] the truth of the matter is that the 'global city strategy' has long existed in the minds of Singaporean policy-makers way before the 1990s.

In a landmark 1972 speech, former Foreign Minister S. Rajaratnam articulated in the clearest terms what was perhaps the most significant and earliest explicit manifestation of Singapore's foreign policy vision as a global city. Framing his question in terms of survival, Rajaratnam self-consciously pondered why an independent Singapore had not collapsed and to the contrary, things were looking up. The island did not have odds stacked in its favour: a 'small city-state, without a natural hinterland, without a large domestic market and no raw materials to speak of, has a near-zero chance of survival politically, economically, or militarily'.[29] Salvation lay in being a global city, for Rajaratnam argued that 'once you see Singapore as a global city, the problem of hinterland becomes unimportant. For a Global City, the world is its hinterland … An independent Singapore survives and will survive because it has established a relationship of interdependence in the rapidly expanding global economic system'.[30] Thus, 'the whole world becomes the interior space of a global city' and the fate of Singapore 'will depend on its ability to establish a niche in the global economic system which is experiencing increasing expansion'.[31]

Rajaratnam could anticipate how global cities are increasingly linked intimately with one another via sea lanes, telecommunications and air routes: in other words, vital infrastructure. In this conception, Singapore was to be connected to other global cities 'like New York, London and Tokyo – moving freight from the regions where it abounds and is produced to where there is greater market demand'. Mirroring Sassen's later work on key urban centres in the global economy, Rajaratnam had already grasped the strategic importance of this 'chain of cities which shape and direct, in varying degrees of importance, a world-wide system

26 Karl Hack and Jean-Louis Margolin, 'Singapore: Reinventing the Global City', in Karl Hack and Jean-Louis Margolin (eds), *Singapore from Temasek to the 21st Century: Reinventing the Global City*. Singapore: National University of Singapore Press (2010), 3.

27 Ibid., 4.

28 Marystella Amaldas, 'The Management of Globalisation in Singapore: Twentieth Century Lessons for the Early Decades of the New Century', *Journal of Alternative Perspectives in the Social Sciences* 1:3 (2009), 984.

29 S. Rajaratnam, 'Singapore: global city' (speech to the Singapore Press Club, 6 February 1972) <http://newshub.nus.edu.sg/news/1202/PDF/GLOBAL-st-6feb-pA17.pdf> accessed 7 February 2012, 2.

30 Ibid., 8.

31 Ibid.

of economics'.[32] Pre-dating the 'infrastructure' approach to studying global cities, Rajaratnam ran through a list of assets that supplied connectivity for Singapore: 'our shipping statistics show clearly that the world is our hinterland. Our port is not merely a regional port, but a global port. Our port makes the world our hinterland. The sea gives us ready access to other global cities. Singapore is linked in other ways, through cable and satellite communications, by air, through the international financial network'.[33] Here, he presaged the contemporary importance placed on connectivity by presenting what amounted to a wish-list of critical infrastructure that global cities should depend on. Rajaratnam suggested that technological developments helped Singapore in 'transforming itself into a new kind of city – the Global City ... Ecumenopolis the world-embracing city. The Global City is the child of modern technology. It is the city that electronic communications, supersonic planes, giant tankers and modern economic and industrial organisation have made inevitable'.[34] Singapore had to capitalise on these developments to build its infrastructure and boost its global connectivity as a global city. Ahead of his time in foreshadowing the contemporary emphasis on 'connectivity' and being a 'hub', Rajaratnam stressed that Singapore needed to be 'plugged into' the international system because 'by linking up with international and multinational corporations, Singapore not only comes within the framework of a world economy but is offered a shortcut to catch up or at least keep pace with the most advanced industrial and technological societies. By plugging-in in this way, we can achieve in 20 to 30 years, what otherwise would have taken us a century or more to achieve'.[35]

Remarkably, Rajaratnam's somewhat prescient visions about the irresistible impetus of urbanisation were spot-on especially now that the world has entered its urban age: 'Whether cities are good or bad, the trend towards urbanisation is irreversible. However much we may denounce them, the cities have been the creators and sustainers of civilisation, culture, technology and wealth. Nothing short of a total collapse of world civilisation can halt the take-over of the world by the cities'.[36] With the benefit of hindsight, Rajaratnam's emphasis on infrastructural developments and boosting connectivity has been proven right on all fronts. As a maritime hub, Singapore's port is arguably the world's busiest trans-shipment hub, with 140,000 port calls annually connecting the island to over 600 other ports in more than 120 countries.[37] Changi International Airport has become an established aviation hub in 2014, with over 6,900 weekly scheduled flights to 280 cities in 60

32 Ibid., 3.

33 Ibid., 8.

34 Ibid., 3.

35 Ibid., 11.

36 Ibid., 5.

37 Maritime and Port Authority of Singapore, 'Premier Hub Port' <http://www.mpa.gov.sg/sites/maritime_singapore/what_is_maritime_singapore/premier_hub_port.page> accessed 9 April 2014.

countries and territories worldwide. It was named the 'World's best airport' in the 2014 Skytrax awards. On 22 December 2012 a daily record of 180,400 passengers passed through Changi within 24 hours. The airport handled a record 53.7 million passengers in 2013, processing 343,800 landings and take-offs. Singapore has also emerged as a major node in the international financial network, and in September 2013, overtook Tokyo to become Asia's largest foreign exchange centre for the first time and the third largest foreign exchange market in the world after London and New York. The city's average daily foreign-exchange volume increased 44 per cent to USD$383 billion as of April 2013 from USD$266 billion in the same month in 2010.[38] Assets under management rose fivefold to SGD$1.82 trillion in 2013 since 2001.

Striving to be a global city continues to be one of the guiding pillars for Singapore's leaders. In 1997, former Prime Minister Goh Chok Tong delivered perhaps the most significant and closely-watched speech in Singapore's political calendar, the National Day Rally, with the theme '*Global City, Best Home*'. Goh argued that to meet future competition, 'Singapore must become a cosmopolitan, global city, an open society where people from many lands can feel at home'.[39] The vision of being a global city is emblazoned all over official planning documents and reports. The 2000 'Renaissance City Report' published by the Ministry of Information and Arts states that its goal is: 'To establish Singapore as a global arts city. We want to position Singapore as a key city in the Asian renaissance and a cultural center in the globalized world. The idea is to be one of the top cities in the world to live, work, and play in, where there is an environment conducive to creative and knowledge-based industries'. The website of its highly-influential Economic Development Board (EDB) trumpets loudly the benefits of doing business in a 'dynamic global city'.[40] Even programs to wire up homes with broadband, the Intelligent Nation 2015 campaign, come with the slogan: 'A Global City, Powered by Infocomm'.[41] The Embassy in Washington presents its visions for Singapore as 'a global city with a world of opportunities … a cosmopolitan society and a dynamic, well-connected economy'.[42] In May

38 Kristine Aquino, 'Singapore overtakes Japan as Asia's top foreign exchange hub', Bloomberg, 6 September 2013 <http://www.bloomberg.com/news/2013-09-05/singapore-overtakes-japan-as-asia-s-biggest-foreign-exchange-hub.html> accessed 8 September 2013.

39 Lee Hsien Loong, 'National Day Rally Speech: Global City, Best Home' (Singapore, 24 August 1997) <http://www.pmo.gov.sg/content/pmosite/mediacentre/speechesninterviews/primeminister/2013/August/prime-minister-lee-hsien-loong-s-national-day-rally-2013--speech.html#.U4KpMnKSySo> accessed 25 August 2012.

40 Economic Development Board, 'A dynamic global city' <http://www.sedb.com/edb/sg/en_uk/index/why_singapore/dynamic_global_city.html> accessed 16 June 2011.

41 Koh Buck Song, *Brand Singapore: How nation branding built Asia's leading global city*. Singapore: Marshall Cavendish (2011), 36.

42 Singapore Embassy. 'Singapore 2006: Global city, world of opportunities', (an update from the Singapore Embassy, October/November 2005) <http://www.mfa.gov.sg/washington/Oct_Nov_05.pdf> accessed 16 June 2011.

2009, an Economic Strategies Committee (ESC) was tasked to develop strategies and opportunities based around the theme of 'Singapore: The Global City in Asia'. This ESC reported back on February 2010[43] and recommended developing strategies for Singapore to tap into three overlapping geographical areas that constitute its hinterland: ASEAN, Asia and the global economy. Singapore should be positioned as a 'Global-Asia' financial and business hub; a global node for commercialisation and innovation pioneer, to test-bed and export 'future-ready' green urban solutions, and a global base for complex manufacturing and manufacturing-related service.

By 2006, another significant event on the Singapore political calendar, the National Day Parade, was themed 'Our Global City, Our Home', almost 10 years after Goh had adopted this slogan portraying Singapore as a vibrant cosmopolitan city and an international hub of the global community. The notion of Singapore as a global city was meant to bring benefits for the country. Former Minister of Education Tharman Shanmugaratnam argued, 'An enduring Singapore brand is also based on 'our openness to people, enterprise and ideas from all over the world. We have to be relentless in this. It will give us value, and we can do this better than most other Asian cities'. Citing examples ranging from French hotel chain Accor to Bahrain investment bank, Arcapita setting up their HQs in Singapore, he contended that they are endorsements of Singapore's relevance to the world, and advancing along the value chain.[44] In 2011, Prime Minister Lee Hsien Loong reiterated the leitmotif driving the city-state's development strategies: 'Singapore's long-term vision is to become a global city in Asia'.[45]

Singapore's decades-long policy has been to globalise in such a way as to become a hub for as many things as possible, from international manufacturing, transport, communications to data and information and finance. Being a global hub increased its strategic relevance to the world, which in turn developed an economic stake in the city-state's continued survival and viability.[46] In August 2011, Prime Minister Lee Hsien Loong reiterated Singapore's reliance on its global city strategy because 'our fundamental constraints remain and we need to remain

---

43 Economic Strategy Committee, 'Making Singapore a Leading Global City', 4 February 2010 <http://www.news.gov.sg/public/sgpc/en/media_releases/agencies/mof/press_release/P-20100204-3/AttachmentPar/0/file/Subcommittee%20on%20Making%20Singapore%20a%20Leading%20Global%20City.pdf> accessed 7 June 2011.

44 Public Relations Academy, 'Opening address at the 6th Annual PR Academy Conference: Markets and Brands: Positioning for the 21st century' (Singapore, 23 May 2007) <http://www.ne.edu.sg/files/Minister%20Speech%206th%20Annual%20Conference%20Media.pdf> accessed 24 May 2013.

45 Lee Hsien Loong, 'Singapore: long term vision is to become a global city' (*Global: the international briefing*, magazine of the Commonwealth Secretariat, 2011) <http://www.global-briefing.org/2011/01/interview-with-prime-minister-lee-hsien-loong/#auth> accessed 1 January 2013.

46 Latif, 'Singapore: surviving the downsides of globalisation', 226.

connected to the world in order to survive'.[47] While globalisation went through a bad patch with the Euro debt crisis, Finance Minister Tharman Shanmugaratnam maintained that it remained the only long-term option, and Singapore just had to be patient and cope as well as it can.[48] Scholars have recently raised critical questions about the pivotal role of the Singapore state in the global city strategy. This presents a narrow view of the ways the city has sought such status and also crowds out alternative pathways in the future.[49] Oswin and Yeoh agree that 'global connections are narrowly cast as the key to progress'.[50]

A Global City's Roller-coaster Ride: Accelerating Globalisation and De-globalisation

Nevertheless, as its leaders maintain unwavering commitment to globalisation, what is of more concern to this book is how the global city of Singapore has also faced up to disturbances and downsides in the inter-connected global system that hit it hard and fast. This is why, as Prime Minister Lee Hsien Loong noted at the World Economic Forum in June 2011, 'you can see all the opportunities of globalisation, but something can go wrong'. Singapore has made a good living as a global city,

> but globalization has its downside and when it appears, it serves as a reminder that the city-state's fortunes are written globally whereas not only is its ability to control world affairs limited by its small size and population, but also the effects of a downside are multiplied by the degree of its openness to the world.[51]

The danger for Singapore from global financial contagion, as MIT professor Simon Johnson quipped, 'it's about de-globalisation'.[52] Words like 'freefall' were used to describe the stalling economy as its maritime hub port became a giant parking lot for idled super tankers and container ships. Singapore's global city status also made it more vulnerable, a point not lost on Prime Minister Lee's observations that 'we were also dragged down faster than others because we are more open and globalised'.[53] By August 2009, Lee felt confident enough to declare that 'the eye

47 Cited in *The Business Times*, 'Singapore stays the course on fundamentals: PM', *The Business Times Singapore*, 2 August 2011 <https://singaporepropertyhighlights.wordpress.com/2011/08/02/spore-stays-fundamentals-pm/> accessed 2 August 2013.

48 Cited in Anthony Faiola, 'Globalisation's demise sinking Singapore', *Washington Post*, 9 March 2012 <http://www.theage.com.au/business/globalisations-demise-sinking-singapore-20090308-8sfe.html> accessed 10 April 2012.

49 Hack and Margolin, 'Singapore: Reinventing the Global City', 7.

50 Oswin and Yeoh, 'Introduction', 167.

51 Latif, 'Singapore: Surviving the downsides of globalisation', 226.

52 Cited in Faiola, 'Globalisation's demise sinking Singapore'.

53 Lee Hsien Loong, 'Keynote Address', in Tarn Tan How (ed.), *Singapore Perspectives 2010*. Singapore: World Scientific (2010), 5.

of the storm had passed'.[54] Singapore then rebounded spectacularly to experience perhaps the highest economic growth rate in the world of 17.9 per cent in the first half of 2010: 'we have had a roller-coaster ride'[55] was how Lee described it. By June 2011, its economic growth had slowed to 0.5 per cent. This rapid turn-around amply demonstrates how fickle the forces of globalization can be.[56]

The year 2009 was particularly noteworthy in terms of Singapore's exposure to global risks. Prime Minister Lee noted that

> we have been hit by the most serious recession in half a century … to see our GDP go down -10%, was something unimaginable. Day to day we watch keenly the economic numbers – growth data, unemployment data, trade data, all the statistics. It is like monitoring the temperature chart of an H1N1 patient.[57]

Lee's reference to both the economic recession and H1N1 swine flu is significant, for it encapsulates the range of global risks (financial and pandemic) Singapore faced in 2009 at roughly the same time. These are the very same de-localised risks that Ulrich Beck warns of. The dilemma for global cities, Prime Minister Lee mused, is that 'whatever the difficulties of globalization, we have got to connect ourselves to the world and reach out to the distant horizon'.[58]

The Downsides of Globalisation

To be a global city is usually seen in the eyes of its leaders as bestowing positive blessings. As Prime Minister Lee argued, 'we seek to be a global city, attracting talent around the world, lively, vibrant, and fun to live and work in. We want Singapore to have the X-factor – that buzz you get in London, Paris or New York'.[59] However, there are increasingly visible signs that globalisation is not completely rosy. Rajaratnam's landmark global city speech had already hinted at some lurking dangers: 'There are admittedly grave political and economic dangers implicit in the entry of powerful foreign concerns into weak and underdeveloped countries.

54 Lee Hsien Loong, 'National Day Rally Speech' (Singapore, 16 August 2009) <http://www.pmo.gov.sg/content/pmosite/mediacentre/speechesninterviews/primeminister/2009/August/national_day_rallyspeech2009part4shapingsingaporetogether> accessed 17 August 2013.

55 Lee Hsien Loong, 'People's Action Party Youth Wing 25th Anniversary Rally' (speech, Singapore, 17 April 2011) <http://maintmp.pap.org.sg/uploads/ap/8170/documents/pmspchyp25thanniversaryrallyeng.pdf> accessed 18 March 2013.

56 Foreign Policy, 'The Globalisation Index 2007', 71.

57 Lee, 'National Day Rally Speech'.

58 Lee, 'Keynote Address', 11.

59 Lee Hsien Loong, 'Statement to Parliament on the Integrated resorts' (Singapore, 18 April 2005) <https://www.mti.gov.sg/MTIInsights/Documents/PM%20Lee%20Hsien%20Loong-Parliament-18Apr2005.pdf> accessed 18 April 2013.

But Singapore must be prepared to undertake these risks simply because the alternative to not moving into the global economic system is for a small Singapore, certain death'.[60] While dealing mainly with the economic pitfalls, Rajaratnam also acknowledged that 'the political, social and cultural implications of being a global city are no less important'. These, he felt, 'would be far more difficult to tackle' and may emerge to be the 'Achilles heel' of global cities.[61] The trade-off is simple: Singapore survived with its global city strategy only by accepting the risks and rewards that are par for the course in this highly-connected position.[62]

That being a global city is a dual-edged sword is gaining traction in political and academic discourse. Singapore's Deputy Prime Minister observed in 2010 that 'cities are often at the forefront of global challenges and change', facing two sides of the coin both positive and negative.[63] Veteran political observer Latiff uses a weather analogy: 'in a city-state like Singapore, to complain about globalisation is to criticise the sky for raining. Sunshine, too falls from above'.[64] It is of course the rain storms that arouse concern. The Centre for Liveable Cities in Singapore recognised the peculiar dangers that global cities face, organising a public lecture in 2009 on the topic 'Global Cities at a time of Crisis' delivered by Saskia Sassen. Founding Prime Minister Lee Kuan Yew noted in 2010 that Singapore since 1965 has plugged into and took maximum gains from globalisation, but its people must also be prepared to manage the drawbacks.[65] Concerns are especially mounting about the socio-economic implications, as Idris points out, 'there is a price that comes with being great cities … .One invariable side-effect of a successful global city is the high cost of living'.[66] In 2014, the Economist Intelligence Unit declared Singapore the priciest city in the world for expats. Deputy Prime Minister Tharman Shanmugaratnam accepted with no small measure of resignation that Singapore will also have a high Gini coefficient measure of income inequality, 'that's our fate in life. We are small, we can only survive and do well by staying open, but it brings inequality … it's a fact of life as a global city, somewhat higher

---

60 Rajaratnam, 'Singapore: global city', 11.

61 Ibid., 12.

62 Cited in Lui Tuck Yew, 'The Opening of Project 3/12: A Nation Remembers' (speech, City Hall Chambers, Singapore, 3 December 2009) <http://app.mica.gov.sg/default.apsx?tabid=79&ctl=details&mid=540&itemid=1092> accessed 4 December 2012.

63 Teo Chee Hean, 'Opening ceremony of Singapore International Water Week 2010' (speech, Singapore, 28 June 2010) <http://www.nas.gov.sg/archivesonline/speeches/record-details/80c63ef8-115d-11e3-83d5-0050568939ad> accessed 29 June 2012.

64 Latiff, 'Singapore: Surviving the Downsides of Globalisation', 235.

65 Lee Kuan Yew, 'The Fundamentals of Singapore's Foreign Policy: Then and Now', (speech, S. Rajaratnam Lecture, Singapore, 9 April 2009) <http://www.news.gov.sg/public/sgpc/en/media_releases/agencies/pmo/speech/S-20090409-1.html> accessed 10 April 2012.

66 Nizam Idris, 'The Future of Singapore as a Global City and its Socio-economic Implications', in Tarn Tan How (ed.), *Singapore Perspectives*. Singapore: World Scientific (2010), 97–8, 104.

degree of inequality'.[67] Prime Minister Lee warned of 'less benign possibilities' that might result from globalisation slowing or going into reverse but Singapore had little option but to survive by remaining open to servicing global flows.[68] Other social issues are also bubbling to the surface, in particular immigration has become a hot political potato.[69] From 2005 to 2009, 150,000 foreigners migrated to Singapore each year to top up its ageing population.[70] This range of concerns about openness and connectivity in a global city reflects not solely socio-cultural gripes. They have taken on more of a security tinge. Leading Singaporean businessmen appreciate that,

> while being one of the most "free trade" economies increases business opportunity, it also exposes Singapore to a multitude of global threats. One cannot expect to enjoy the benefits of global trade without having to contend with its associated risks. Such issues may come in the form of economic disruptions, natural disasters, civil unrest, epidemics or even terrorism.[71]

Its diplomats freely accept that 'the problem is that, the more connected you are to the world, the more vulnerable you are to the external environment'.[72]

While the dangers associated with being a global city are surfacing in the political and academic discourse, there exists sparse *academic* literature that systematically examines Singapore's experience of such global security risks. Prime Minister Lee Hsien Loong's speech at the inaugural 2012 Singapore Summit stressed that 'while we embrace globalisation, we must also strengthen ourselves to cope with the risks of globalisation'.[73] Academics have examined the main ways in which Singapore has been positioned as a global city over the

---

67 Tharman Shanmugaratnam, 'Singapore Perspectives 2012 conference' (speech, Singapore, 16 January 2012) <http://app.mof.gov.sg/newsroom_details.aspx?type=media&cmpar_year=2012&news_sid=20120121608784777037> accessed 17 January 2013.

68 Cited in *The Business Times*, 'Singapore stays the course on fundamentals'.

69 Lee, 'Keynote Address', 8.

70 Figures cited in Annie Koh, 'One Global City', in Tarn How Tan (ed), *Singapore Perspectives 2010*. World Scientific: (2010), 85.

71 Welcome Speech by Victor Tay, 'Acting CEO Singapore Business Federation at Business Continuity Management (BCM) Conference 2011' (speech, Singapore, 10 March 2011) <http://www.sbf.org.sg/public/newsroom/details/20110310sp.jsp> accessed 11 March 2013.

72 Speech by Singapore Ambassador to France, His Excellency Burhan Gafoor, 'MEDEF Université Debate at L'Ecole Polytechnique' (Paris, 28 August 2008) <http://app.mfa.gov.sg/data/paris/statements/REMARKS_FOR_MEDEF_28_Aug_08.html> accessed 28 August 2012.

73 Tharman Shanmugaratnam, 'Singapore Human Capital Summit' (speech, Singapore, 19 September 2012) <http://app.mof.gov.sg/newsroom_details.aspx?type=speech&cmpar_year=2012&news_sid=20120919503641796214> accessed 20 September 2013.

centuries, but less so the security dimensions. Indeed, existing academic tomes suggest that Singapore's experience can often be seen as positive, from which other aspiring global cities can learn.[74] The A.T. Kearney Globalisation Index usually places Singapore squarely 'within the winners' circle' when it comes to globalisation.[75] By comparison, far less attention has been placed on the global risks that come with Singapore being a global city, and the following sections will examine how to go about doing so.

Singapore as a Global City of Flows and Mobilities: Infrastructure

As discussed in the previous chapter, scholars such as Oswin and Yeoh have utilised the analytical lens of 'mobile city' to highlight how Singapore as a global city emerged.[76] Their work focuses predominantly on the 'instrumental incorporation of various sorts of flows into the pursuit of Singapore's particular global city project'.[77] Scholars assembled by Oswin and Yeoh are unravelling the impact of trans-national flows and how mobility is shaping Singapore, through examples such as migrant workers, weekend enclaves of foreign domestic workers and workplaces with large expatriate populations. These are important and significant contributions to understanding how certain types of global flows and mobilities are in fact central to contemporary Singapore polity and society.[78] Singapore thrives as a global city because it is 'a hub open to the flow of people, ideas, capital, goods and services', according to Khoo Teng Chye, executive director of Singapore's Centre for Liveable Cities.[79]

The 'mobilities' turn should also direct our attention to how these flows enter and exit the city in the first place. Scholars have to focus the analytical gaze on the critical infrastructure that allows a global city like Singapore to perform its core function of coordinating global flows. Combined with the 'infrastructure' approach to studying global cities, the main cause of concern is how 'a globalised world means that the vectors of prosperity can quickly become vectors of insecurity'.[80] In his writings on transport and telecommunications among world cities, Peter Rimmer focused on several types of global flows such as air freight and passenger travel, freight forwarders and maritime container movements by

74 Hack and Margolin, 'Singapore: Reinventing the Global City', 3.

75 Foreign Policy, 'The Globalisation Index 2007', 71.

76 Oswin and Yeoh, 'Introduction', 168.

77 Ibid., 170.

78 Ibid., 172.

79 Cited in Yingyue Han, 'Singapore as a global city', *The Diplomat*, 16 March 2012 <http://the-diplomat.com/asean-beat/2012/03/16/singapore-as-a-global-city/> accessed 17 March 2013.

80 John Hamre, 'Foreword', CSIS Commission on Smart Power (2007), 3.

sea and information networks.[81] It is often said that the 'dirty little secret' of global cities research relates to how 'the dominance of London, New York and Tokyo is more often asserted than demonstrated'.[82] Indices based on stock market capitalisation; headquarters of major banks and corporations have been tallied in attempts to empirically measure global cities. Sociologists have deployed several methods such as blockmodelling techniques to rigorously rank cities in the world system.[83] This book utilises data on the global flows that traverse Singapore in order to empirically assess connectivity of the global city. One of the crown jewels in Singapore's toolbox of connectivity is its global maritime hub port essential to ensuring smooth functioning of the global supply network. Such ports are 'critical nodes in complex economic inter-modal subsystems that facilitate the movement of goods and cargo around the world'.[84] Indeed, as Lee Kuan Yew notes, 'the presence and comprehensive suite of maritime ancillary services, and our extensive air connectivity, make Singapore a convenient base of operations for the Asia market. This is our value proposition to the maritime community'.[85] Maritime accessibility through its global port is thus only one of several crucial infrastructural factors that bolster Singapore's claim to global city status.[86] Fortunately for Singapore, it has two other trump cards: its booming aviation hub and its financial services industry which will be discussed in subsequent chapters. Singapore thus achieved and maintained its position in the world economy 'based on mastery of flows of production and purchasing power rather than on stock of goods'.[87]

Connectivity Also Brings Global Risks: The Spatial Aspects of De-localised Risks

The infrastructure capabilities outlined in the preceding section are all geared towards one thing: enhancing connectivity and ensuring frictionless movement of global flows as far as possible. This is why EDB promotes Singapore as a global transportation hub for air and sea cargo based on its 'unparalleled connectivity and infrastructure' which translates into 'better market access and trade flows for

---

81 Peter Rimmer, 'Transport and Telecommunications Among World Cities', in Fu-Chen Lo and Yue-man Yeung (eds), *Globalization and the World of Large Cities*. Tokyo: United Nations University Press (1998), 439.

82 Arthur S. Alderson and Jason Beckfield, 'Power and position in the world city system' *American Journal of Sociology* 109:4 (2004), 812.

83 Ibid., 814.

84 J.R. Harrald, et al., 'A framework for sustainable port security', *Journal of Homeland Security and Emergency Management* 1: 2 (2004), 1–13.

85 Cited in Paul Richardson, 'The Singapore maritime story', *Singapore Nautilis* (Q1 2008); Port Authority of Singapore (PSA), 'Sage Advice'. Singapore: Portview (Q2 2010), 12.

86 Rimmer, 'Transport and Telecommunications Among World Cities', 433–70.

87 Zielonka, 'Europe as a global actor: empire by example?', 473.

companies'.[88] Being 'connected' is one of Singapore's four core selling points (the others being 'trust, knowledge, and life') as a global city that give it a competitive advantage over others.[89] Short is undoubtedly correct in his claim that 'urban imagineering in the present era is dominated by selling the global connection'.[90] In terms of aviation flows, EDB highlights how 'Changi International Airport is linked to some 200 cities in 60 countries, with about 5,400 weekly flights, providing convenience and effective connectivity for passengers and cargo ... Companies here have the necessary land, air, sea, and telecommunications linkages necessary to move freight and services anywhere in the world, whenever they are needed'.[91] Another example of 'selling' Singapore based on its connectivity can be seen in the maritime domain. Singapore's Maritime Port Authority trumpets that 'global connectivity is the key to Singapore's success as a world-leading hub for container transhipment'.[92] Singapore's very status as a global city hinges on these notions of connectivity, which has also attracted environmental movements like Earth Hour to relocate from Sydney to Singapore instead. Co-founder Andy Ridley explained that 'As a global hub, Singapore offers us a level of connectivity and opportunity that the campaign needs and desires moving forward'.[93]

Singapore's ex-President S.R. Nathan explained in 2008 that 'connecting Singapore to the world' remained one of the country's 'fundamental principles' of foreign policy.[94] Variations of the need for Singapore to be 'connected' continue to appear. Former Head of Civil Service Peter Ho observed that 'Singapore's continued success as a hub depends both on its connections to the world ... and also in other domains – an R&D hub, an intellectual hub, and even a cultural and entertainment hub'.[95] In 2012 at a speech in Washington, Ho argued that Singapore should serve as a 'connector hub' linking America to other cities and parts of East and South-East Asia because

> in a globalised world, it is the hub that can provide leverage, extend reach and amplify impact within a larger network or system ... higher value-added activities are densely concentrated and clustered in hubs. The world's economic geography is dominated by hubs that are the focal points of opportunity, growth and innovation. We are a connector hub ... many cities and hubs around the world are linked to one another through Singapore ... Singapore-the-hub can be

88 Economic Development Board, 'Why Singapore: unparalleled connectivity and infrastructure'.

89 Economic Development Board, 'A Dynamic Global City'.

90 John Rennie Short, *Global Metropolitan*, 23.

91 Economic Development Board, 'Why Singapore: unparalleled connectivity and infrastructure'.

92 Maritime Port Authority of Singapore, 'Global Port Hub'.

93 Earth Hour, 'Singapore – home of Earth Hour'.

94 Nathan, 'Diplomatic Academy's Inaugural S. Rajaratnam Lecture'.

95 Ho, 'The future of a hub: can Singapore stay on top of the game?'.

> tapped by the US to take advantage of its connectivity to other hubs, both large and small, in the region and around the world.[96]

Tiny Singapore's development as a global city thus reinforces the point that population size alone is not a key indicator when identifying and determining the prospects and status of such leading cities. Instead, a more accurate indicator is the quality of its infrastructure, level of accessibility in transport and communications networks and on the degree of interactivity between them.[97] To sum up, being connected and possessing infrastructural capability to manage these types of flows is the raison d'etre for the global city that is Singapore today. Its policymakers have strategic intent to become a global 'hub of hubs'[98] to broaden its linkages in any way possible and relentlessly capitalise on its advantageous geographic location to capture global flows of people, goods, finance, capital, data and information.

The continuing focus on 'remaining connected to the world' however raises the spectre of the 'problems of circulation' that Dillion outlined in the previous chapter. Trans-national terrorism for instance poses a severe risk of disrupting the mobilities and flows that Singapore seeks to attract and process as a global city. In terms of the *spatial* questions Beck and other scholars have raised about how global risks are transmitted, Beck has indicated a rough typology of risks whereby '*unintentional* large-scale risks (such as climate change) are gaining prominence; on the other hand, the anticipation of the new kinds of threats emanating from *deliberate* terrorist attacks represents a persistent public concern'.[99] Derived from Beck's typology of intentionality, Singapore as a global city is exposed in two ways, and here Beck's typology can be further refined in terms of the types of flows these global risks represent. As the previous chapter points out, the dangers and global risks that accompany such flows can be classified in two forms. One, there are negative *penetrative* flows that, inadvertently or not, piggyback on the circulation of flows enabled by globalisation. Being so connected brings the strategic importation of global risks – the negative penetrative flows such as financial contagion and infectious diseases which are largely unintentional or lack a clear cause-effect mechanism. During the global financial crisis, Singapore as a key financial node also provided a 'window to the reversal of the forces that brought unprecedented global mobility'.[100] The dangers of WMD proliferation and terrorist financing on the other hand are clearly deliberate and intentional.

The second type of global risk that concerns us is negative *destructive*. When it is perceived as a leading global city coordinating and commanding the

96 Ho, 'Broadening partnerships for an Asian century'.

97 Rimmer, 'Transport and Telecommunications Among World Cities', 466.

98 ASEAN Focus Group, 'The strategic intent of a global hub of hubs', Asian Analysis, August 2005 <http://www.law.smu.edu.sg/research/documents/the_strategic_intent_global_hub.pdf> accessed 8 January 2012.

99 Ulrich Beck, *World at Risk*. Cambridge: Polity Press (2009), 15.

100 Faiola, 'Globalisation's demise sinking Singapore'.

various flows associated with globalisation, those who wish to disrupt the global economy (such as terrorists or cyber-hackers) can target key infrastructure such as Singapore's port or airport to generate the greatest magnitude ripple effects on the global economy. This is very much what a 'city-as-target'[101] model would suggest. When 'economic disruption is a stated terrorist goal,[102] such negative *destructive* flows attempt to disrupt, undermine or impair the crucial functions that global cities provide for the global economy.[103] As a leading global financial hub, Singapore, like its counterpart stock exchanges around the world faces 'systemic risks' from cyber-security that tend to be 'disruptive in nature'.[104] In July 2013, a World Federation of Exchanges report stated that 'a majority of exchanges (89 per cent) view cyber-crime in securities markets as a potential systemic risk, citing the possibility of massive financial and reputational impact; loss of confidence; effect on market availability and integrity; the interconnectedness and dependencies in securities markets; and related knock-on effects on market participants from an attack'.[105] With regards to terrorism, Singapore's 2004 *National Security Strategy* observed that 'globalization and our open borders present many more possibilities for the unexpected, which can inflict great damage and even alter our way of life'.[106] This reminds us of Graham's claim that 'circulations and spaces of the city are becoming the main battlespace both at home and abroad'.[107] As former Defence Minister Tony Tan warned in 2003, 'with a global economy built on integrated supply chains, any disruption to the safety and security of navigation in these waters would be a shock to the international system … sea lanes and sea-borne commerce are attractive terrorist targets. They are the lifelines of the international economy and symbols of the globalised international system that the terrorists want to repudiate'.[108] Singapore, with its global maritime port hub, is thus seen by its politicians, as an 'iconic target' for terrorists, in other words the 'city-as-target' model writ large.

---

101 Ryan Bishop, Gregory Clancey and John W. Phillips, *The City as Target*. London: Routledge (2012).

102 Jon D. Haveman, et al., 'The Container Security Initiative and Ocean Container Threats', *Journal of Homeland Security and Emergency Management* 4:1 (2007), 1547–7355.

103 I am grateful to Saw Shi Tat for introducing these terms to me in our discussions.

104 International Organisation of Securities Commissions and the World Federation of Exchanges, 'Cyber-crime, securities markets and systemic risks', 16 July 2013 <http://www.csrc.gov.cn/pub/csrc_en/affairs/AffairsIOSCO/201307/W020130719521960468495.pdf>, 3.

105 Ibid., 38.

106 National Security Coordination Centre Singapore, 'The Fight against Terror: Singapore's National Security Strategy'. Singapore: National Security Coordination Centre (2004), 40.

107 Stephen Graham, *Cities Under Siege*. London: Verso (2010), xv.

108 Tony Tan, 'Maritime security after September 11' (speech at the IISS Conference Plenary Session, Singapore, 1 June 2003) <http:// http://www.mindef.gov.sg/imindef/press_room/official_releases/nr/2003/jun/01jun03_nr2.html#.U4VY7HKSySo> accessed 2 June 2013.

Social Aspects of Global Risks: Reflexivity and Reinvention

Singapore is one of the most painfully self-aware 'global cities' that exist: 'Singapore as a global city has now become the dominant self-image of the city-state'.[109] The flip-side of this is that in an age of global risks, Beck would recognise how the city-state's planners and politicians have also become instinctively reflexive, constantly re-evaluating the foundations of its global city status, the precarious nature of that status and the need for rapidly reforming its policies and institutions. Given its openness and exposure to global flows, Singapore's planners have also fixated on the need to filter undesirable flows. This can be seen in a metaphor used by the Minister for Community Development, Youth and Sports when describing its U-turn on casinos to attract tourists and investment flows: 'that's part of the secret to our success: maintaining this semi-permeable membrane. Make it permeable to success, impermeable to the unsavoury elements'.[110] The membrane metaphor seems to be rather popular among its leaders. Former Foreign Minister George Yeo described how on one hand Singapore sought to become a global media hub but at the same time, its leaders remain deeply suspicious of outside influence because 'we need a kind of semi-permeable membrane to preserve our own bubble in Singapore'.[111] Former Deputy Prime Minister Wong Kan Seng referred to the fact that 'balancing policy trade-offs is particularly complex when global issues intersect with the local' especially in a global city like Singapore that needs to remain open.[112] Singapore has practiced what some call 'selective globalization', encouraging certain aspects of globalisation such as the economic and financial capital flows but it also keeps at bay what it feels are 'unwholesome global commodities' such as pornographic magazines.[113] This simply reflects the need to connect with the world for national interests but at the same time, retain certain notions of tradition and conservatism that protect specific dominant interests.[114] Such a dilemma now arguably extends to the security domain as well. The remainder of this book will show how the very flows that a global city manages and coordinates can also bring about unwanted security side-effects that Singapore's leaders are so wary of, precisely the types of 'malign circulations' that scholars of mobilities and urban geography warn of in the previous chapter.

---

109 Kwa, 'Relating to the World: Images, Metaphors, and Analogies', 121.

110 Cited in Wayne Arnold, 'The nanny state makes a bet', *The New York Times*, 23 May 2006, <http://www.nytimes.com/2006/05/23/business/worldbusiness/23casino.html?pagewanted=all&_r=0>.

111 Cited in Geoffrey Murray and Audrey Perera, *Singapore: The Global City-State*. Folkestone: China Library (1996), 168.

112 Wong Kan Seng, 'Administrative Service Singapore' (speech, Singapore, 28 March 2011) <http://app.psd.gov.sg/data/Admin%20Service%20Dinner%202011%20on%2028%20March%202011%20-%20Speech%20by%20DPM%20Wong%20Kan%20Seng.pdf> accessed 29 March 2013.

113 Amaldas, 'The Management of Globalisation in Singapore', 985.

114 Ibid., 986.

Tellingly, there is also increasing reflection on the complex nature of global risks Singapore has experienced as a global city over the past decade. Former Head of the Civil Service Peter Ho observed that,

> here in Singapore, we experienced in the last decade or so, a series of wild cards or black swans: the Asian Financial Crisis of 1997, December 7th, 2001 (the detention of members of a terrorist network, the Jemaah Islamiyah), the SARS crisis of 2003, and the sub-prime mortgage crisis of 2007, and financial meltdown of 2008, and the global economic crisis of 2009. These surprises were high-impact events that appeared out of the blue – not simple trends, but events that were characterised by their scope and speed. They suggested to me that we are operating not in a linear world where cause and effect are clear, but in a more complex environment where cause and effect are difficult to discern, if at all ... Today, we live in an interconnected and interdependent world. Events and actions in different parts interact with each other in complex ways, to produce effects that are often difficult to anticipate.[115]

Ho's observations about non-linear risks (also the very risks that Beck argues form the axis of his *World Risk Society*) in an inter-connected world appear at first glance to be strikingly reminiscent of Beck's claims about the social aspects of de-localised risks that are inherently difficult to attribute to a particular agent of responsibility. Indeed, there is certainly no lack of social contemplation amongst its policy-makers about the lurking dangers of globalisation and how they might spread,

> Singapore is aware of the downside of globalisation: influx of information through the Internet, of foreigners, and the liberalization of the financial and other services sectors such as telecoms and banking sectors. With globalisation, shocks and crises are transmitted around the world faster than ever.[116]

The notion of 'shocks' and 'transmission' being expressed here strongly echoes the metaphors and language deployed in the OECD *Future Global Shocks* report and the World Economic Forum's 'Global Risks Report' referred to in Chapter 1, as well as the spatial dimensions of de-localised security challenges in the works of Ulrich Beck and other urban scholars such as Graham. Yet, the broader debate on global risks in an inter-connected world has not been brought to bear in the case of Singapore's experiences as a global city. The subsequent chapters will set out to rectify this omission.

---

115 Peter Ho, 'The Interdisciplinary Conference: Adaptation, Order and Emergence – A Tribute to John Holland' (speech, Singapore, 12 February 2009) <http://www3.ntu.edu.sg/CorpComms2/Documents/2009/Feb/GOH%20Speech_090212_JohnHollandConf.pdf> accessed 12 March 2012.

116 Hawazi bin Daipi, 'Globalisation and its impact on social cohesion and rootedness' (speech, Singapore, 5 November 2002) <http://www.moe.gov.sg/media/speeches/2002/sp05112002.htm> accessed 5 November 2012.

Limits of a One-size-fits-all Approach to Global Cities

This chapter has outlined the reasons why Singapore deserves to be singled out for analysis as a global city exposed to global risks. However, as also noted in the previous chapter, there is no one-size-fits-all model to understanding the complexity of global cities, each with their own unique historical, cultural, political and economic contexts. Singapore for instance faces it own unique constraints and circumstances. As Prime Minister Lee Hsien Loong noted, 'we import all our food except for a few eggs. We import all our fuel and all our electricity is produced from imported either fuel oil or natural gas. When the world prices go up, how can we keep our rice prices, our petrol prices, our diesel prices, our electricity prices down? It can't be done'.[117] This set of constraints is not faced to the same degree by other global cities, as Lee explains that 'obviously, we cannot match London, New York or Tokyo in terms of size or depth of domestic markets. But that should not stop us from becoming a key global node in certain areas'.[118] According to economists, negative repercussions from the euro debt crisis, while difficult for global cities like London or New York, can be magnified several factors over, especially for small, open, global cities like Singapore that lack a domestic hinterland to cushion such shocks.[119]

Although lacking the strategic depth of London, Tokyo or New York, the good news for Singapore is that it is both a city *and* it also assumes the full sovereign powers, policy tools, resources, and diplomatic functions of full-fledged, legitimate, internationally recognised nation-states. For instance, 'by deploying its powers and capacities as a nation-state to transform society and space within the city, Singapore has successfully embedded itself within the evolving lattice of network relations that propel the global knowledge economy … State policies can be shaped to develop the city-state into a global city-state'.[120] It is also better placed to rapidly respond by developing new policy directions to mitigate the global risks that come with bring a global city. This can be best illustrated in how Singapore tackled the 2003 SARS crisis, which we will turn to in Chapter 4. We will also see how it has developed 'foresight' and horizon-scanning abilities in order to better decipher the complex non-linear nature of global risks. While sensitive to

117 Lee Hsien Loong. 'National Day Rally' (speech, Singapore, 17 August 2008) <http://www.pmo.gov.sg/content/pmosite/mediacentre/speechesninterviews/primeminister/2008/August/transcript_of_primeministerleehsienloongsnationaldayrally2008spe.html#.U4KqI3KSySo> accessed 18 October 2012.

118 Lee Hsien Loong, 'Building One Financial World' (keynote address, ACI World Congress, Singapore, 25 May 2001) <http://www.mas.gov.sg/news-and-publications/speeches-and-monetary-policy-statements/2001/building-one-financial-world--25-may-2001.aspx> accessed 25 May 2013.

119 Linette Lim, 'Singapore vulnerable in face of looming risks in global economy', *TODAYonline*, 23 May 2011 <http:// https://groups.yahoo.com/neo/groups/RealEdge/conversations/messages/18263> accessed 23 May 2012.

120 Yeung, 'Globalisation Singapore', 110, 111.

stark differences among global cities, the remaining chapters drawing on a close examination of Singapore's experience will highlight how peculiar vulnerabilities to global risks are broadly shared by all global cities because they thrive on one basic overarching premise: connectivity and the coordination of global flows.

Conclusion

While headlines screaming 'Europe sneezes, Asia catches a cold' are highly typical of the dangers of an interconnected world today, it does not sufficiently convey the uneven and differing impact that globalisation has. Hyper-connected global cities are intensely sensitive to fluctuations or perturbations in global flows. As one of these key urban 'nodal points', Singapore has become deeply enmeshed in the globalised world.[121] In 2012, it was reported that Singapore's ability to serve as a key hub commanding and controlling economic flows was being enhanced by major Japanese companies such as Panasonic and Mitsui chemicals moving key functions to the global city-state. Others such as Hoya Surgical Optics even moved its headquarters and CEO to Singapore. The reasons commonly cited pertain to Singapore's efficient infrastructure such as Internet connectivity, and having the world's busiest trans-shipment hub. In simple terms, it is the global city's critical infrastructure that enables its ability to attract, coordinate and manage global flows.

Singapore's long-standing drive towards achieving and cementing its prized global city status reiterates several points made by critics in the global cities literature that global cities do not magically materialise overnight. Building on a combination of existing works that analyse Singapore as a 'mobile city'; the importance placed on infrastructures and the role of developmental states; and conceptualising global cities as 'spaces of flows', this chapter has identified several infrastructural sectors (financial, maritime, aviation, information) that Singapore's planners have carefully nurtured and developed over the years. This allows researchers to pinpoint firstly the sources of connectivity and critical infrastructure which are the building blocks sustaining Singapore's global city status. Secondly, possessing such infrastructure in turn enables the attracting, command and control of global flows. These flows can in turn be categorised as:

1. maritime (materials, people, and trade traversing Singapore's maritime port hub);
2. aviation (cargo and passengers circulating through Singapore's Changi airport hub); and
3. financial (capital flows and investment services processed by Singapore's financial and banking sector).

---

121 Amaldas, 'The Management of Globalisation in Singapore', 982.

The global risks that accompany or are attracted to such flows can then be distinguished according to whether they are negative *penetrative* or negative *destructive*. Singapore's leaders in their use of the 'membrane' metaphor are acutely aware of the 'bad' vulnerabilities that accrue from globalisation and the need to make a living off the 'good' beneficial circulation of flows. Such sentiments have clear resonance with academic debates, particularly by urban studies professors such as Stephen Graham about cities becoming 'battlespaces' and the imperative to minimise 'malign circulations' of flows. Although Singapore has been at the sharp end of major global crises that were transmitted around the world in the past decade (the financial crises both Asian and Western; health pandemics; and trans-national terror networks), such fears expressed by Singaporean planners have not been expressly engaged through the analytical prism of global risks. Accordingly, two key aspects of global risks in Ulrich Beck's works as they pertain to Singapore's experiences will guide analysis in the chapters that follow. First, it will specify the spatial dimensions and mechanics of how de-localised global risks are attracted to, or transmitted through the types of global flows circulating through key infrastructure assets of global cities. Secondly, analysis centres around the reflexivity and policy responses that global risks trigger in Singapore where being a global city is a long-standing recipe for survival. Here, one needs to assess whether Beck's cosmopolitan significance of fear is triggering reconfigurations of multi-level relationships as a range of affected stakeholders within the global city cooperate to manage global risks. Whilst remaining cognisant of the limits of relevance to other global cities, the case of Singapore can generate theoretical and empirical insights into a global city's exposure to and subsequent response to managing global risks; risks that are functionally shared by other cities and countries which have, or aspire to, critical infrastructure such as financial centres, maritime ports, and air hubs.

Chapter 3
Financial Centres as Portals of Global Financial Risks

Global Financial Flows and Malign Circulations

According to the World Economic Forum's (WEF) 'Global Risks Report 2012', 'global risks are defined as having global geographic scope, cross-industry relevance, uncertainty as to how and when they might occur, and high levels of economic/social impact which require multi-stakeholder response'.[1] Global financial risks fall squarely into this category. The report lists 'major systemic financial failure' as one of the top five in terms of potential impact[2] particularly in an inter-connected global system where, as we have seen in previous chapters, the security problematic is now premised on managing the negative 'circulation' of undesirable flows. The 2008–2009 financial crisis highlighted the 'integrated nature of the global risk society, where anthropogenic manufactured risks are predominant'.[3] In particular, the self-inflicted 'manufactured risks' consistent with Beck's 'Risk Society' thesis arose from the pace of change and innovation in financial markets during the 'Golden Decade' from 1998 to 2008 that saw a proliferation of complex financial products and instruments such as credit default swaps, and collateralised debt obligations.[4] Beck justifies placing global financial risks at the heart of the World Risk Society because 'since all of the subsystems of modern society rely on the other subsystems, a failure of the financial system would be catastrophic. No other functional system plays such a prominent role in the modern world as the economy. Thus, the world economy is without doubt a central source of risk in the world risk society'.[5] Yet, Beck's statements remain undifferentiated and fail to sufficiently evaluate the specific transmission *mechanisms* through which de-spatialised global financial risks affect global cities; or even whether these are intentional or not. Secondly, Beck points out how 'the world can no longer control the dangers produced by modernity … The uncontrollable impacts of globalized financial flows for whole groups of

1 World Economic Forum, 'Global Risks Report 2012' <http://www.weforum.org/reports/global-risks-2012-seventh-edition> accessed 10 August 2014, 11.

2 Ibid.

3 Ian Goldin and Tiffany Vogel, 'Global governance and systemic risk in the 21st century: lessons from the financial crisis', *Global Policy* 1:1 (2010): 5.

4 Ibid., 6.

5 Ulrich Beck, *World at Risk*. Cambridge: Polity Press (2009), 203.

countries, as suddenly transpired during the Asian crisis, are also an expression of the radicalized capitalist market principle which has cast off the fetters of national and supranational controls'.[6] Yet, in spite of these concerns, Beck strangely does not pay enough attention to the diverse multi-level networks of actors that operate in and through a global city's financial hub, as they develop *policy responses* to better manage and regulate such risks.

In addressing these two issues, this chapter builds on the 'mobilities' turn outlined previously, for it has alerted scholars to the importance of studying flows and movements entering and exiting a global city. Foremost among these flows must be financial and capital movements, a raison d'être for a global city: 'International financial centres house the pivotal intermediaries who control and coordinate the exchange of capital, such as investments (infrastructure, stocks, and bonds), payments arising from trade in commodities and services, and currencies'.[7] This is why an 'infrastructure' approach to studying global cities would suggest that a financial centre is a form of critical infrastructure for a global city. Controlling and coordinating these massively profitable financial flows generates huge gilt-edged opportunities for global cities like Hong Kong and Singapore, for these 'longstanding financial centres in Asia ... exert a disproportionate and increasing dominance over the global exchange of capital'.[8] Often seen as poster boys for globalisation *because* of their deep involvement in economic and financial activities, Sharon Zukin notes that 'the global cities that have captured attention in recent years owe much to the intense competition in international financial services'.[9] These leading highly-connected urban nodes are the principal foci for global business travel and telecommunications networks.[10] The most valuable spaces in a global city are often those dedicated to serving global financial flows: 'the financial industry's vaults and computer networks, the corporate headquarters, and other network nodes where the flows of global capital and information are moored'.[11]

Indeed, 'open and fair financial markets' as well as 'free flow of capital' are one of the key building blocks for a world-class financial centre according to the Securities Industry Association, whether it is London, New York, or

6 Ibid., 8.

7 David Meyer, 'World cities as financial centres', in Fu-Chen Lo and Yue-man Yeung (eds), *Globalization and the World of Large Cities*. Tokyo: United Nations University Press (1998), 410.

8 Ibid., 414.

9 Sharon Zukin, 'The City as a Landscape of Power: London and New York as Global Financial Capitals', in Sam Whimster and Leslie Budd (eds), *Global Finance and Urban Living: A Study of Metropolitan Change*. London: Routledge (1992), 195.

10 David Clark, *Urban World/Global City*. London: Routledge (2003), 157.

11 S. Harris Ali and Roger Keil, 'Securitising networked flows: infectious diseases and airports', in Stephen Graham (ed.), *Disrupted Cities: When Infrastructure Fails*. London: Routledge (2010), 104.

Singapore.[12] Yet, the freedom of these flows can also bring with them negative repercussions. Sassen warns that 'the more we have focused, analysed, dissected the high-visibility components of globalisation, especially corporate, the more impenetrable the realities that operate on the dark side'.[13] While Finance Minister Tharman correctly stated that 'global connectivity must remain key strengths of Singapore's financial centre',[14] two types of negative *penetrative* risks categorised according to levels of intentionality are identified here:

1. Recurrent risks of financial contagion in 1998 and 2008 (inadvertent, rapid spread, and difficult to attribute responsibility), highlighting Beck's claims about de-localised spatial dimensions of global financial risks;
2. The risks of Singapore's financial sector being targeted and exploited by terrorist financiers and money launderers (intentional and deliberate) who attempt to surreptitiously circulate funds within the massive amounts of financial flows passing through a global financial centre.

Both risks can be classed as negative *penetrative* flows that share one thing in common: ironically, their ability to circulate is in fact dependent on Singapore's global financial infrastructure *not* being disrupted or destroyed. Sudden rapid movement of these flows – whether inflows or outflows – can create destabilising effects, not just for Singapore, but also the wider system.

This chapter scrutinises the relationship between a global city's financial connectivity and global financial risks by examining in detail two themes highlighted by Beck: the *mechanisms* by which these de-localised financial risks affect a global city's financial sector; and the restructuring of multi-level institutional arrangements and agents involved in 'a global city' as *policy response* in order to minimise malign circulations. If one approaches the problem through the analytical lens of the infrastructure approach; 'mobilities'; and circulation outlined previously, then it alerts us to first, how Singapore's financial architecture serves as the gateway for outflow and inflow of undesirable financial flows. Secondly, the desired response must be to ensure that at all levels from regulatory agency to industry to government and international institutions, all relevant stakeholders in Singapore's financial hub will cooperate to ensure its continued

12 Securities Industry Association, 'The Key Building Blocks of World Class Financial Centres' <http://www.ita.doc.gov/td/finance/publications/World_Class_Financial_Center.pdf> accessed 26 March 2010, 3.

13 Saskia Sassen, *The Global City: London, New York, Tokyo*. New Jersey: Princeton University Press (2001), xv.

14 Tharman Shanmugaratnam, '39th Association of Banks in Singapore Annual Dinner' (speech, Singapore, 28 June 2012) <http://app.mof.gov.sg/newsroom_details.aspx?type=speech&cmpar_year=2012&news_sid=20120629148451891878> accessed 29 June 2013.

ability to discharge its function of maintaining the smooth coordination of 'good' financial flows, while sieving out 'bad' infiltrations.

Being a Leading Global Financial Centre

Visionary Foreign Minister S. Rajaratnam had earmarked the financial and banking sectors as key industries that Singapore should not only cultivate as a matter of survival, it was also an indicator of global city status: 'Singapore's claim to being a global city does not rest on its communications network alone. We are also being connected to other Global Cities through the international financial network. Establishment in Singapore of a still growing number of foreign banks and merchant banks whose operations are world-wide is yet another indication of the fact that we are becoming a global city'.[15] From the late 1970s onwards, capital and financial accounts became highly open after restrictions were lifted. Competitive tax rates and regulations were passed to entice financial institutions to operate in Singapore. There is no capital gains tax in Singapore. IMF's Country Report on Singapore notes that 'the volume of international capital flows has been high, with gross flows averaging 40–50 per cent of GDP in 1980s and 1990s'.[16] As the Economic Review Committee stressed, 'the financial services industry is a significant component of Singapore's economy. Its share of nominal GDP has risen from an average of 6% in the 1970s to 13% in 2001. Among the services industries, the financial services sector contributes the highest value-added and is the largest source of tax revenue'.[17] The financial sector contributed about 12 per cent of GDP in 2013, double what it was four decades ago.

Various measures of the strong international financial role that Singapore plays in the global economy show why it was accorded 'Alpha' status as amongst the 'brightest shining global cities' by Beaverstock et al.[18] Foreign participation in the Singaporean financial sector by the mid-1990s was already 'probably one of the highest in the world'.[19] By August 2014, 125 commercial banks (including

15 S. Rajaratnam, 'Singapore: global city' (speech to the Singapore Press Club, 6 February 1972) <http://newshub.nus.edu.sg/news/1202/PDF/GLOBAL-st-6feb-pA17.pdf> accessed 7 February 2012, 11.

16 International Monetary Fund (IMF), 'Country Report No.01/177 for Singapore', October 2001 <http://www.imf.org/external/pubs/ft/scr/2001/cr01177.pdf> accessed 10 September 2010, 38.

17 Economic Review Committee, 'Positioning Singapore as the pre-eminent financial centre in Asia', September 2002 <http://www.mti.gov.sg/ResearchRoom/Documents/app.mti.gov.sg/data/pages/507/doc/12%20ERC_Services_Financial.pdf> accessed 7 March 2011.

18 Beaverstock, J.V. et al., 'World city network: a new metageography?', *Annals of the Association of American Geographers* 90:1 (2000), 123–34.

19 Chia Siow Yue, 'The Asian Financial Crisis: Singapore's experience and response', in H.W. Ardnt and Hal Hill, *Southeast Asia's Economic Crisis: Origins, Lessons and the Way Forward*. Singapore: ISEAS (1999), 52.

120 foreign banks), 39 merchant banks and 259 fund management firms were operating in Singapore. Assets under management have risen fivefold since 2001 to total approximately USD$2 trillion as of December 2013.[20] Singapore was ranked fourth in the 2014 Z/Yen Group's Global Financial Centres Index. Singapore is a major destination point for international equity and direct foreign investment, attracting a total of SGD$853.3 billion in foreign direct investment in 2013.[21] This explains Singapore coming in at No. 5 on the GaWC's ranking of financial network connectivity in 2008. Singapore has also become a major node in the international financial network, and in September 2013, overtook Tokyo to become Asia's largest foreign exchange centre for the first time and the third largest foreign exchange market in the world after London and New York. The city's average daily foreign-exchange volume increased 44 per cent to USD$383 billion in April 2013 from USD$266 billion in the same month in 2010.[22] This constituted roughly 5 per cent of global Forex trade. The Asia Dollar Market is considered the 'pillar of the Singapore financial sector'.[23] The Swiss central bank has set up a new Singapore office in 2013 to ease the round-the-clock management of its exchange rate cap, and manage its investments in Asia. Singapore's position as a regional bond-trading centre led to the choice of the city as the location of the first foreign branch in the Swiss National Bank's 106-year history, said President Thomas Jordan.[24]

Singapore is also a leading private banking centre for very High Net Worth Individuals (HNWI), second only to Switzerland. Singapore's Economic Committee recommended in 2002 that 'wealth management' is one key 'strategic thrust' and 'global niche' that Singapore should develop as a financial hub.[25] Among the various Asian financial hubs, Singapore occupies a special place for Citibank Global CEO for private banking Jane Fraser,

> We have our global chairman, our global head of investments, our global head of talent and human resources, and our global head of marketing based in

---

20 Monetary Authority of Singapore (MAS), 'Banking Sector' <http://www.mas.gov.sg/Singapore-Financial-Centre/Overview/Asian-Dollar-Market.aspx> accessed 9 July 2014.

21 Singapore Department of Statistics, 'Singapore's Foreign Direct Investment 2013', <http://www.singstat.gov.sg/docs/default-source/default-document-library/statistics/browse_by_theme/economy/findings/fei_infographic_findings2013.pdf> accessed 9 April 2015.

22 Kristine Aquino, 'Singapore overtakes Japan as Asia's top foreign exchange hub', Bloomberg, 6 September 2013 <http://www.bloomberg.com/news/2013–09–05/singapore-overtakes-japan-as-asia-s-biggest-foreign-exchange-hub.html> accessed 8 September 2013.

23 Ravi Menon, 'MAS Annual Report 2011/12' (opening remarks, Singapore, 25 July 2012) <http://www.mas.gov.sg/news-and-publications/speeches-and-monetary-policy-statements/2012/mas-annual-report-2011–2012.aspx> accessed 26 July 2013.

24 Aquino, 'Singapore overtakes Japan as Asia's top foreign exchange hub'.

25 Economic Review Committee, 'Positioning Singapore as the pre-eminent financial centre in Asia'.

> Singapore. These are four of our most critical roles and they have been in Singapore for several years. What we are seeing in Singapore, which I think is unique in Asia, is the amount of infrastructure to support vigorous wealth management. That comes from a talent base, a regulatory and legal framework that people have faith in, the city itself, and the infrastructure. I see clients the world over wanting to come to Singapore and have some of their wealth actually be held here. "One of the appeals of Singapore is the transparency here, and the regulatory standards give people confidence that if they invest their money here, they can get it out. And that's not the case everywhere in Asia".[26]

According to MAS figures, in July 2012, more than 70 per cent of assets under management came from abroad. As of 5 December 2011, there were 39 offshore banks in operation, all foreign-owned.[27] Large global players with private banking operations in Singapore include UBS, Merrill Lynch, Credit Suisse, Citigroup Private Bank and HSBC Private Bank. Societe Generale, a French lending company, set up a branch office in Singapore in 2007. Furthermore, many Chinese, Indian, Middle Eastern and European companies have listed their stocks on the Singapore Stock Exchange. Manchester United also considered very seriously listing in Singapore. Well-known established names in global insurance also have a presence, such as Lloyd's of London, providing services to the financial sector. The securities and bond market is also growing. According to Bloomberg data, 'trading volumes of Singapore government bonds increased 11-fold since 1988 with securities valued at SGD$3.05 billion changing hands daily in July 2012. A total of 56 businesses and organisations sold SGD$19.8 billion of Singapore dollar bonds, 19 per cent more than the amount offered in 2011 and a threefold gain from the past decade'.[28] In 2014, there were 1,742 bonds listed on the Singapore Exchange – up 19 per cent compared to a year ago.[29] Within these impressive figures however, risks lurk from the global financial flows continually entering and exiting a global city like Singapore.

---

26 Cited in Nicholas Fang, 'Drawn to a wealth magnet', *TODAYonline*, 4 September 2011, accessed 5 September 2013.

27 United States Department of State Bureau for International Narcotics and Law Enforcement Affairs, 'International Narcotics Control Strategy Report. Volume II: Money Laundering and Financial Crimes', March 2012 <http://www.state.gov/j/inl/rls/nrcrpt/2012/index.htm> accessed 30 March 2013, 158–60.

28 Bloomberg, 'Singapore bonds beat peers in shrinking AAA pool', Bloomberg, 17 August 2012 <http://www.bloomberg.com/news/2012-08-16/singapore-bonds-beat-peers-in-shrinking-aaa-pool-southeast-asia.html> accessed 20 August 2012.

29 'Subdued outlook for Singapore bond market', Channel NewsAsia, 8 July 2014 <http://www.channelnewsasia.com/news/business/singapore/subdued-outlook-for/1245730.html> accessed 9 August 2014.

Inadvertent Global Risks? The Spatial Aspects of De-localised Global Financial Contagion

Let us first begin with an inadvertent type of global financial risk that imperils global cities all too frequently. For Schinasi, financial crises are indicative of how 'the nature of systemic risk has changed as national, bank-based financial systems have given way to today's globally integrated, market-based financial system'.[30] The volatility of capital flows generates global repercussions because a closely-integrated global financial system also means all parts in the system are interlocking and interdependent.[31] This is often likened to a 'turbulent sea – massive, unpredictable and sometimes uncontrollable'.[32] A Bloomberg Businessweek commentary at the height of the Lehmann shock in October 2008 showed how the severest economic costs would fall particularly on those globalised cities most intimately dependent on global finance.[33] Scholars have made the relationship between globalisation and financial downsides plain and painfully clear. Alan Gilbert for instance contended that 'what the Mexican crisis shows is that economic and social volatility is part of the new form of globalisation ... The financial world is living constantly on a knife-edge'.[34]

What does this mean for a small, open global city like Singapore which prides itself on its world-class financial core? As the IMF reported in 2013, 'Singapore is exposed to a broad array of domestic and global risks, especially in light of its interconnectedness with other financial centers'.[35] Highly reliant on commercial trade, with merchandise exports representing over 220 per cent of gross domestic product (GDP), analyst Sanchita Das notes how this increases Singapore's vulnerability to global economic shocks.[36] In March 2014, the WTO reported that Singapore's trade-to-GDP ratio for the years 2010–2012 was a staggering 400.2

30 Garry J. Schinasi et al., 'Managing global finance and risk', *Finance and Development: a quarterly magazine of the IMF* 36:4 (1999) <http://www.imf.org/external/pubs/ft/fandd/1999/12/schinasi.htm> accessed 26 May 2014.

31 Sam Whimster and Leslie Budd, 'Introduction', in Sam Whimster and Leslie Budd (eds), *Global Finance and Urban Living: A Study of Metropolitan Change*. London: Routledge (1992), 12.

32 Ibid., 13.

33 Matt Mabe, 'The world's most global cities', Bloomberg Businessweek, 29 October 2008 <http://www.businessweek.com/globalbiz/content/oct2008/gb20081029_679467.htm> accessed 8 April 2011.

34 Alan Gilbert, 'World cities and the urban future: the view from Latin America', in Fu-Chen Lo and Yue-man Yeung (eds), *Globalization and the World of Large Cities*. Tokyo: United Nations University Press (1998), 187.

35 IMF, 'Singapore: Financial System Stability Assessment', 14 November 2013 <https://www.imf.org/external/pubs/cat/longres.aspx?sk=41051.0> accessed 30 April 2014.

36 Sanchita Basu Das, *Road to Recovery: Singapore's Journey Through the Global Crisis*. Singapore: ISEAS (2010), 44.

per cent.[37] It was even worse in 2006–2008 when Singapore's trade-to-GDP ratio was 443.2, according to the World Trade Organization. America's, in contrast, was only 28.7 while Hong Kong's was 406.5. In 2009, the average trade-to-GDP ratio for OECD countries was 41 per cent. Singapore also is a significant consumer of imports: it has an import to GDP ratio of more than 200 per cent, far more than the average 81 per cent of other Asian economies.[38] All these deep global financial and economic links meant that Singapore – 'the house globalization built' – also became the 'epicentre' of a rapidly de-globalising world in the wake of the sub-prime crisis in 2008.[39] First in East Asia to fall into a recession, Singapore experienced its worst economic reversal in its history as exports collapsed by a stunning 35 per cent in January 2009. The so-called peak-to-trough decline in GDP reached double digits of 16 per cent.[40] Das provides figures to highlight the battering Singapore received from global financial sector turmoil. GDP declined by an alarming rate of 15.2 per cent and 7.1 per cent quarter-on-quarter in Q4 2008 and Q1 2009.[41] By 2011, the world's attention shifted across the Atlantic to Europe so much so that the Monetary Authority of Singapore's managing director described the 'chief global risk' to Singapore's economic growth as the debt crisis in Europe, 'if there is contagion and banks in core Europe are affected, there could be a severe credit squeeze and pullback in economic activity'.[42] Identifying the transmission mechanisms in the case of Singapore shows the multiple ways through which global financial risks can affect global cities.

Unlike other financial crises in the 1990s which sprung from emerging economies in Asia or Latin America, the sub-prime mortgage crisis in late 2007 began in the US. There was, as 'Dr Doom' Noriel Roubini prophesised, 'real reason to worry that an American financial virus could mark the beginning of a global economic contagion'.[43] The negative effects were transmitted to Singapore in several ways, and again these can be analysed through Castells' notion of global

---

37 World Trade Organization, 'Trade profile: Singapore', October 2011 <http://stat.wto.org/CountryProfile/WSDBCountryPFView.aspx?Language=F&Country=SG> accessed 8 April 2012.

38 Ibid., 71.

39 Anthony Faiola, 'Globalisation's demise sinking Singapore', *Washington Post*, 9 March 2012 <http://www.theage.com.au/business/globalisations-demise-sinking-singapore-20090308–8sfe.html> accessed 10 April 2012.

40 Shelley Smith, 'Hong Kong and Singapore vulnerable to global slump, Nomura says', Bloomberg News, 25 May 2009 <http://www.bloomberg.com/apps/news?pid=newsarchive&sid=aUgbgKSCnM6I> accessed 8 April 2011.

41 Basu Das, *Road to Recovery*, 45.

42 Ravi Menon, 'MAS Annual Report 2010/2011 Press Conference' (opening remarks, Singapore, 21 July 2011) <http://www.mas.gov.sg/news_room/statements/2011/Opening_Remarks_at_MAS_AR_2010_11_Press_Conference.html> accessed 22 July 2013.

43 Nouriel Roubini, 'The coming financial pandemic', *Foreign Policy*, 2008 <http://www.foreignpolicy.com/articles/2009/02/19/the_coming_financial_pandemic> accessed 10 April 2013, 44.

cities as 'spaces of flows'. One can therefore look at how the global financial inflows and outflows processed by Singapore's financial hub experienced disruptions or volatility due to the crisis, rather than the smooth circulation one expects in 'normal' times. For instance, 'the financial sector was affected by the cessation of credit flows'.[44] Former Managing Director of the MAS Heng Swee Keat further noted how 'these shocks to the international financial system severely disrupted credit flows and led to dislocations in economic activity globally'.[45] The transmission mechanisms can be explained further as follows.

There is a psychological dimension fuelling the volatile financial flows that Singapore's financial centre experienced. The role of perceptions is stressed by Beck: 'the reflexive appropriation of information tends to increase the instability of financial markets – they can develop in unexpected directions, become chaotic, be used by free riders. For the financial wizard and multimillionaire George Soros, the financial markets must be classified among those momentous global risks which are influenced by information about and perceptions of these risks'.[46] Singapore Prime Minister Lee Hsien Loong referred to how jittery perceptions further exacerbate financial turmoil in the markets, which will take time to recover some stability.[47] Financial guru Roubini agreed that such 'market volatility culminates in a kind of panicky groupthink'[48] where investors dump assets en masse, sometimes based on unsubstantiated rumours and fears. Billions of dollars' worth of stocks and capital can be withdrawn in an instant. With the 2011 fears over Greek default, analysts pointed to how 'we have a wide-ranging contagion issue here – or at least the *perception* of one – and that is making people nervous'.[49] Furthermore, 24-hour news cycles and information flows that spread instantaneously across the globe have injected new uncertainties, creating abrupt sentiment shifts and loss of investor confidence.[50] 'The speed at which events unfolded and triggered a series of domino effects', in the words of MAS Director Heng, was 'exceptional'.[51]

---

44 Das, *Road to Recovery*, 44.

45 Heng, Swee Keat, 'MAS 2008/09 Annual Report Press Conference', (opening remarks, Singapore, 16 July 2009) <http://www.mas.gov.sg/news-and-publications/speeches-and-monetary-policy-statements/2009/opening-remarks-by-managing-director-heng-swee-keat-at-mas-annual-report-2008–09-press-conference.aspx> accessed 17 July 2012.

46 Beck, *World at Risk*, 120–21.

47 Cited in Angela Balakrishnan, 'Singapore slides into recession', *Guardian*, 10 October 2008 <http://www.guardian.co.uk/business/2008/oct/10/creditcrunch-marketturmoil1?INTCMP=SRCH> accessed 9 April 2012.

48 Roubini, 'The coming financial pandemic', 48.

49 Karl Schamotta, 'EU row over Greek aid sparks fears crisis could spread', *The Straits Times*, 12 July 2011, A4.

50 Heng, Swee Keat, 'The International Institute of Finance Asia Regional Economic Forum' (speech, Singapore, 4 March 2009) <http:// http://blog.finetik.com/2009/03/06/crisis-will-bring-new-opportunities-in-asia-monetary-authority-of-singapore/> accessed 5 March 2009.

51 Ibid.

The actual transmission mechanism can be seen in the sudden fluctuations and withdrawal of financial flows which were processed by the financial core in Singapore. Such extreme and rapid movements or 'waves' of international capital flows in the 1980s and 1990s have become more commonplace.[52] Here we are mostly concerned with 'contagion through financial linkages' which causes investors to stop investing abroad and bring their money home instead, usually from global financial centres where they had parked monies.[53] The US subprime meltdown led to a liquidity and credit crunch on Wall Street's banks, which soon spilled over to financial markets around the world.[54] Many toxic assets were also sold to investors around the world, and very quickly the Eurozone with deep financial ties with the US got embroiled.[55] In Singapore's case, while monetary and financial systems remained largely unscathed, the shocks were mostly felt through drying up of credit and capital flows due to heightened risk aversion.[56] Much of the impact on Singapore was felt in terms of financial flows that were either disrupted or excessive, demonstrating the merits of our analytical framework premised on cities as 'spaces' of global flows and mobilities. In the third quarter of 2008, which was around the peak of the global financial crisis, data from the private sector illustrated the large movements of capital flows out of Singapore. The Singapore Fund Flows Insight Report compiled by the Investment Management Association of Singapore and Lipper (a Reuters company), reported that 'the Singapore unit trust market registered net outflows of SGD$854.1 million, a significant turnaround from the positive net inflows of SGD$287.9 million recorded the quarter before'.[57] Meanwhile, in the public sector, MAS Director Ravi Menon explained the problem in terms of excessive abnormal capital flows, how 'financial market stresses will be felt most keenly in capital flows, currency markets, and interbank funding. There could be larger and more volatile capital flows. We must be prepared for both excessive inflows as well as outflows'.[58] External observers such as the IMF noted that 'Singapore is a net capital exporter, but during the 2008–2009 financial crisis it experienced extraordinarily large outflows from banks'.[59] Analyst Das also outlined how Singapore's heavy reliance on FDI inflows contributed to the sharp decline in its growth rate because inward FDI comprised

52 Kristin J. Forbes and Francis E. Warnock, 'Capital Flow Waves', Macroeconomic Review Special Feature B, Monetary Authority of Singapore Economic Policy Group, October 2011 <http://web.mit.edu/kjforbes/www/Papers/MAS%20Article-Macro%20Review-Oct%202011.pdf> accessed 16 April 2012, 77.

53 Ibid., 81.

54 Roubini, 'The coming financial pandemic', 47.

55 Heng, 'Speech at the International Institute of Finance Asia Regional Economic Forum'.

56 Basu Das, *Road to Recovery*, 70.

57 Investment Management Association of Singapore, 'Singapore Fund Flows Summary', 30 September 2008, 1.

58 Menon, 'MAS Annual Report 2011/12'.

59 International Monetary Fund (IMF), 'Country Report No.12/42', February 2012 <http://www.imf.org/external/pubs/ft/scr/2012/cr1242.pdf> accessed 26 August 2012, 24.

60 per cent of its gross fixed capital formation in 2007, compared with an average of 9.8 per cent among other Asian economies (excluding Hong Kong). FDI flows into Singapore literally dried up, collapsing from SGD$7.3 billion to a mere SGD$0.7 billion in the first three quarters of 2008.[60]

Roubini offers a tip that the best way to see how financial flu spreads is by watching global stock markets.[61] The Lehmann Shock in New York sent ripples around the world in a matter of seconds, rattling other global cities. On 6 October 2008, London's FTSE stock exchange recorded its steepest points fall ever in history. Tokyo's Nikkei index shed 5 per cent within 30 minutes of opening. 'The Singapore capital market mirrored the sell-offs in the global equity markets. The domestic equity market tumbled from 3500 points in December 2007 to 1700 points in the last quarter of 2008. As portfolio investment reduced, it became difficult to raise funds in Singapore's domestic capital market'.[62] For a global city that lived off servicing global financial flows, when these flows get disrupted or experience massive swings in volatility, the impact can be magnified. The hiring and retrenchment trends for Singapore's financial sector year-on-year reflect the topsy-turvy impact of the financial crisis. According to 2012 statistics for the financial and insurance industries from the Ministry of Manpower, 170 workers were made redundant in 2007, rising sharply to 1,440 employees losing their jobs in 2008, with another rise to 1,840 in 2009. The number improved to 610 by 2010 as some semblance of financial stability returned, but the numbers worsened again to 860 in 2011 with the onset of new fears about the Euro debt crisis.[63] The official Economic Survey of Singapore 2009 shows that the overall financial services sector experienced negative 1.4 per cent growth for the whole of 2009, with fund management activities especially plummeting 20.7 per cent.[64] Proprietary trading, wealth management and hedge fund activities based in Singapore were hit as investors withdrew funds to cover losses back in Europe or the US. One wealth manager estimated an outflow of 30 per cent of his funds under management.[65] According to Ministry of Trade and Industry figures for 2008, growth in the financial services sector dropped by 8.1 per cent as a result of significant declines in foreign exchange and stock brokerage, fund management and Asian Currency Units. This decline was attributed to the 'spill-over' from the global financial

60 Basu Das, *Road to Recovery*, 50.

61 Roubini, 'The coming financial pandemic', 47.

62 Basu Das, *Road to Recovery*, 54–5.

63 Ministry of Manpower, Singapore, 'Singapore Yearbook of Manpower Statistics, 2012' <http://www.mom.gov.sg/Documents/statistics-publications/yearbook12/mrsd_2012YearBook.pdf> accessed 14 April 2012, D10.

64 Ministry of Trade and Industry, Singapore, 'Economic Survey of Singapore, 2009', February 2010 <http://www.mti.gov.sg/ResearchRoom/Pages/Economic%20Survey%20of%20Singapore%202009.aspx>, accessed 29 March 2011, iii.

65 Megawati Wijaya, 'A dent in Singapore's financial hub dream', *Asia Times*, 6 November 2008 <http://www.atimes.com/atimes/Southeast_Asia/JK06Ae01.html> accessed 8 January 2009.

crisis.[66] In November 2008, Singapore bank DBS announced it was cutting 900 jobs as net profits slumped 38 per cent. Together with another leading financial centre Hong Kong, Singapore's financial sector experienced the greatest decline in cross-border loans as a percentage of GDP.[67] Several thousand investors also lost their money (estimated up to USD$360 million) when Lehman Brothers 'high note five' product (managed by Singapore bank DBS) collapsed. Paradoxically in 2012, with uncertainty over the Euro and US economies, Singapore became seen as a safe-haven with its Triple A credit rating, attracting funds and investors looking for somewhere safe to park their money.[68]

The situation of a global financial centre like Singapore experiencing disruptive capital outflows unfortunately had eerie precursors in the 1998 Asian financial crisis, where a classic currency crisis in Thailand spread through 'contagion effects' to its Southeast Asian neighbours.[69] As Ara Wilson notes, the term 'contagion' was first introduced in July 1997, when the currency crisis quickly spread throughout East Asia and then Russia and Brazil. This has 'become an exemplar of the risks of rapid global financial flows and bubble economies'.[70] A currency crisis emerges when a country with fixed exchange rate accumulates large current account deficits, only to find that for whatever reason, it can no longer cover such deficits when inflows of foreign capital dry up.[71] As the country depletes its reserves to prop up exchange rates, investors withdraw their funds to avoid what they believe will be inevitable currency devaluation. Like the 2008 crisis, the same psychology of fear and anxiety marked the 1998 Asian crisis: 'the immediate cause of the crisis was a classic case of investor panic that triggered a massive withdrawal of capital funds from the region, leading to a liquidity crunch that evolved into a broader financial and macroeconomic crisis'.[72] As in 2008, watching stock market prices

---

66 Ministry of Trade and Industry, Singapore, 'Economic Survey of Singapore, 2008' 26 February 2009 <http://www.mti.gov.sg/ResearchRoom/Pages/Economic%20 Survey%20of%20Singapore%202008.aspx> accessed 19 March 2014, 1.

67 Lee Yong Yong, 'The Singaporean economy and macrofinancial linkages', 9 February 2012 <http://www.fairobserver.com/article/singaporean-economy-and-macrofinancial-linkages> accessed 9 February 2013.

68 Senior Economist Alvin Liew at UOB Bank cited in Bloomberg, 'Singapore bonds beat peers in shrinking AAA pool', Bloomberg, 17 August 2012 <http://www.bloomberg.com/news/2012–08–16/singapore-bonds-beat-peers-in-shrinking-aaa-pool-southeast-asia.html> accessed 20 August 2012.

69 Linda Lim, 'Free Market Fancies: Hong Kong, Singapore, and the Asian Financial Crisis', in T.J. Pempel (ed.), *The Politics of the Asian Economic Crisis*. Ithaca: Cornell University Press (1999), 101.

70 Ara Wilson, 'Bangkok, the Bubble City', in Ida Susser and Jane Schneider (eds), *Wounded Cities: Destruction and Reconstruction in a Globalized World*. Oxford: Berg (2003), 203.

71 Ibid.

72 Khor Hoe Ee and Kit Wei Zhang, 'Ten years from the financial crisis: managing the challenges posed by capital flows', MAS Staff Paper No. 48, November 2007, 2.

index fuelled fears of contagion spreading in 1998. Hong Kong's Hang Seng Index lost 23 per cent between 20 and 23 October 1997. The Dow Jones plunged 554 points on 27 October 1997. The Singapore Straits Times Index which had risen by 145 per cent between 1990–96, declined by more than 60 per cent by third quarter of 1998. Leading bank DBS saw profits decline 50.2 per cent in first half of 1998. Again, here the impact on Singapore's financial centre is seen in terms of financial capital flows declining, withdrawn or disrupted. The IMF reports that for the year 1998, overall, Singapore posited a gloomy negative SGD$29,050 million of capital flows.[73] This was nearly double the figures of negative SGD$14,762 million for the previous year 1997. In 1998, in terms of its balance of payments, Singapore experienced a gross capital outflow of more than negative SGD$15 billion while this outflow almost tripled to nearly negative SGD$45 billion at the height of the 2008 crisis.[74] Figures from the Monetary Authority's annual report in 1998/99 show the extent of the setbacks inflicted on Singapore's financial hub,

> the commerce and financial services sectors experienced the sharpest deceleration in growth, with both sectors registering negative growth for three consecutive quarters in Q2-Q4 1998. The financial services sector contracted by 0.5% compared with 15.3% growth in 1997. It saw a sharp pullback in activity in the foreign exchange market and the Asian Dollar Market (ADM).[75]. Total assets in the Asian Dollar Market decreased by 9.6% in 1998 to US$503.6 billion, Average daily foreign exchange trading volume fell by 14.9% to US$142.0 billion. In the first quarter of 1999, the financial services sector contracted by 5.3% due to weak lending sentiment to nonbank customers in the domestic and offshore markets.[76]

The human cost was also substantial as the financial sector created just a net addition of 6,900 jobs in 1998 compared to 28,000 in 1997.[77] The Singapore dollar depreciated against US greenback by 13 per cent between second quarter 1997 and second quarter 1999.

Another transmission mechanism beyond volatile capital flows affecting Singapore's financial sector and investor panic is the knock-on effects on employment, productivity and other measures of the 'real' economy. Here we are concerned with 'contagion through trade flows'.[78] Interdependence is positive

---

73 IMF, 'Country Report No.01/177 for Singapore'.

74 Forbes and Warnock, 'Capital Flow Waves'.

75 Monetary Authority of Singapore (MAS), 'Annual Report 1998/1999' <http://www.mas.gov.sg/~/media/resource/about_us/annual_reports/annual19981999/MASAnnual9899.pdf> accessed 10 April 2014, 22–3.

76 Ibid.

77 Ministry of Trade and Industry, Singapore, 'Economic Survey of Singapore 1998', 22.

78 Forbes and Warnock, 'Capital Flow Waves', 81.

in good times but close trade and financial links also mean that an economic slowdown in one place can drag down others.[79] This is especially pertinent for a global city because 'Singapore cannot avoid being hit. We earn our living by trading with and servicing the world'.[80] Prime Minister Lee's concerns are not just about 'the transmission of shocks through financial institutions, but also 'the knock-on effects on the whole global system, on confidence, the financial system, or even the attitude towards globalisation and free trade'.[81] As consumer confidence in the West plummeted, Singapore experienced a fall in non-oil domestic exports (NODX). Unfortunately, Das highlighted how Singapore is not only trade-reliant but its vulnerability is compounded by how its export basket is concentrated in a few products like electronics, which accounts for nearly 40 per cent of NODX. The NODX crumbled 35 per cent in January 2009, the largest ever on record. In March 2009, about 70 per cent of all retrenchments came from the manufacturing sector, in fact outpacing losses in the financial sector.[82] In the second half of 2008 job creation slowed to 21,300 in Q4-2008, less than half the number of jobs created in Q3.[83]

Figures from the Ministry of Trade and Industry show that for the whole of 2008, 13,400 workers were retrenched, substantially higher than the 7,700 in 2007. Manufacturing formed the bulk of retrenchments (8,300), concentrated on the electronics segment (4,100).[84] Singapore also experienced global shocks through its communications (transportation, logistics), tourism, and other linkages to the rest of the world. Both sea port and airport experienced declines as maritime trade and aviation flows also stuttered. The 1998 Asian Financial crisis also delivered similar shocks to the 'real' economy. Singapore's exports to key partners Thailand, Indonesia and Malaysia collapsed. GDP growth rates fell from 8.9 per cent in 1997 to 0.3 per cent in 1998. The petrochemical industry was also hit, with oil exports sharply by 15.3 per cent in 1998.[85] For Ulrich Beck, this was an example of how 'the risks of transnational capital flows predictably affect labour that is culturally tied to the locality and threaten the foundations of society and the state – as millions of new poor and unemployed people well know in Indonesia and other South-East Asian

---

79 Roubini, 'The coming financial pandemic', 48.

80 Lee Hsien Loong, 'New Year Message' (statement, Singapore, 2009) <http://www.pmo.gov.sg/content/pmosite/mediacentre/speechesninterviews/primeminister/2008/December/prime_minister_leehsienloongsnewyearmessage2009.html#.U4KqRXKSySo> accessed 19 October 2013.

81 Cited in Greg Sheridan, 'Thoughtful wisdom from Lee Hsien Loong', *The Australian*, 29 September 2012 <http://www.theaustralian.com.au/national-affairs/thoughtful-wisdom-from-lee-hsien-loong-a-leader-with-proven-record/story-fn59niix-1226483762571> accessed 5 October 2012.

82 Basu Das, *Road to Recovery*, 48, 62.

83 Figures from Basu Das, *Road to Recovery*, 61.

84 Ministry of Trade and Industry, Singapore, 'Economic Survey of Singapore, 2008', 8.

85 Chia, 'The Asian Financial Crisis', 55.

countries'.[86] The painful lesson from the 1998 Asian financial crisis was that de-localised financial risks were becoming unattributable, compared to the past when foreign states were seen to pose economic risks.

> economic vulnerability to other governments no longer loomed large among security threats. Even the new transnational security threats that accompanied more open borders paled in significance when compared to the risks brought home by the crisis. Instead, a new vulnerability to international markets and an awareness of the economic and political volatility imported through those markets became central to a redefinition of economic security.[87]

Global financial crises are becoming the 'new normal' that global cities and their financial hubs, have to get accustomed to. Beck is right to say that 'this global market risk is also a new form of 'organized irresponsibility … the financial flows determined the winners and the losers'.[88] This is why global financial risks are seen to be largely inadvertent: the investors in Bangkok or US sub-prime mortgages were after personal gain, and had no inkling that their investments would eventually generate global ripple effects. Yet, these seemingly innocuous actions 'can destabilise the whole financial system in unforeseeable ways'.[89] How can global cities help to restore smooth circulation of financial flows within the global system? Having so discussed the transmission mechanisms of de-spatialised financial risk, we now move to address the second theme of Beck's thesis: the response.

'Attending' to the Global Financial Network

Leading global cities engage in both cooperation and competition. At the height of the 2008 crisis, the London Financial Services Board was set up to fend off challenges from other cities like Dubai dangling lower tax incentives. Beijing and Shanghai were seen to be benefiting from London's difficulties. Singapore Prime Minister Lee also warned that 'competition from emerging financial centres in the region is intensifying'.[90] While global cities are often seen as rivals, Beaverstock et al.

86 Ulrich Beck, *The Brave New World of Work*. Cambridge: Polity Press (2000), 73.

87 Miles Kahler, 'Economic security in an era of globalisation: definition and provision', *The Pacific Review* 17:4 (2004), 486.

88 Beck, *World at Risk*, 199.

89 Lee Hsien Loong, 'We will do more for middle-income PMETS' (speech, Singapore, 22 February 2009) <http://www.pmo.gov.sg/content/pmosite/mediacentre/speechesninterviews/primeminister/2009/February/we_will_do_more_formiddle-incomepmetspmlee.html> accessed 23 March 2013.

90 Lee Hsien Loong, '40th Anniversary Dinner of MAS' (speech, Singapore, 28 November 2011) <http://www.mas.gov.sg/news-and-publications/speeches-and-monetary-policy-statements/2011/speech-by-pm-lee-hsien-loong-at-the-mas-40th-anniversary-dinner.aspx> accessed 29 November 2013.

argue that these cities also cooperate in order to maintain, repair and transform the global network, as seen in the 1998 Asian financial Crisis: 'they work together to maintain flows through the network' because the disconnection of one or more cities from the network can have systemic consequences for the system as a whole. In a crisis, for these cities, in their own intertwined interests, there will be a need to cooperate to somehow normalise the resumption of normal flows.[91] Taylor insists on 'debunking the competitive presumption' because cooperation can arise also from network processes: 'cities need each other and all contribute to the wellbeing of the network.[92] Central here are the regulators and institutions that oversee individual firms within sectors. The state is another key player, together with international bodies like the Bank of International Settlements (BIS): all conceivably 'attend' to the global financial architecture by stabilising the system and policy regulation. The US lowering of interest rates in the late 1990s was seen as beneficial to maintaining finance flows through New York. Finally, the 'global city' itself should not be reified, but is seen to comprise networks of various multi-level actors from the City of London, individual banks, to trade associations, national governments and global financial bodies. These actors help in enabling the global city's financial core to discharge key command functions circulating global financial flows.

The notion that various actor networks within and between global cities can cooperate could provide an answer to the conundrum Beck posed in his *World Risk Society*, whereby 'the traditional methods of steering and control are proving to be inoperable and ineffectual in the face of global risks'.[93] One solution, as Benjamin Barber has argued, is that financial centres and cities should grasp the mantle in addressing global economic problems, and recommended Singapore and New York take the lead.[94] Yet, the Global Financial Stability Report of the IMF in 2010 did not mention the word 'financial centre' in its musings on how to maintain global financial system on an even keel. Wojcik goes further to argue that global financial centres must be included:

> Much of the discussion on the global financial reform assumes that the reform is a matter of decisions of state governments and inter-governmental organisations … In my view, for global finance to change, a significant degree of change must be generated internally within the financial sector, and given the concentration of

91 J. Beaverstock et al., 'Attending to the world: competition, cooperation and connectivity in the world city network', *Global Networks: A Journal of Transnational Affairs* 2:2 (2002), 115.

92 P.J. Taylor, 'Competition and cooperation between cities in globalization', GaWC Research Bulletin 351, Loughborough University, 2011 <http://www.lboro.ac.uk/gawc/rb/rb351.html> accessed 8 January 2012.

93 Ibid., 200.

94 Richard Florida, 'What if mayors ruled the world', 13 June 2012 <http://www.citylab.com/politics/2012/06/what-if-mayors-ruled-world/1505/> accessed 9 April 2015.

> key personnel, expertise, knowledge, transactions, and power of global finance in New York and London, the axis should also be considered in the ongoing debates.[95]

Wojcik however acknowledges that 'the issue of agency in relation to financial centres is complicated'. The main actors are usually seen to be international producer services firms and global banks, whereas cities themselves have apparently little agency. Wojcik however highlights for example the power of municipal-level actors such as the City of London Corporation or securities industry lobby groups, such as the London Investment Banking Association, SIFMA in the USA, and International Securities Dealers Association with offices in New York and London. Let us not forget of course what the Financial Stability Board (FSB) has termed 'G-SIBs': Globally Systemically Important Banks whose failure can have global repercussions. The need to restructure existing arrangements, to Beck, means to 'closely involve stakeholders in the co-production of new types of regulation'.[96] This is where a multi-stakeholder approach involving different actors in a global city could prove useful. Interconnected global risks are beyond the ability of any single country, industry or sector to confront or prevent on their own. As a result, 'global risks *empower* states and civic movements because they uncover new sources of legitimation and options for action for these groups of actors'.[97]

Once again, an analytical framework sensitive to the importance of 'frictionless' flows and circulations through a global city also allows researchers to understand the underlying drivers and goals of policy responses. In this case, how did the various constituencies that comprise Singapore as a global financial centre respond to financial crisis and work to restore normalcy to the inward and outward flows of capital? The IMF's Financial System Stability Assessment reported in 2013 that 'Singapore's current regulation and supervision are among the best globally'.[98] Logically speaking then, one should begin at the level of central bank and regulator, the Monetary Authority of Singapore (MAS). At the onset of the 2008 crisis, to maintain confidence and smooth functioning and circulation of financial flows in the market, the MAS ensured there was a high level of dollar liquidity in the banking system and set up a precautionary USD$30 billion swap arrangement with the US Fed in October 2008. Das explained that 'as the largest US dollar and FOREX centre in Asia outside of Japan, MAS needed to avoid any seizures experienced by other financial centres in the world'.[99] The idea of 'seizures' is central here, for it suggests disruptions to global financial flows.

95 Daruisz Wojcik, 'The dark side of NY-LON: financial centres and the global financial crisis'. Oxford Working Papers in Employment, Work and Finance 11–12, Oxford (2011), 11.

96 World Economic Forum, 'Global Risks Report 2012', 22.

97 Beck, *World at Risk*, 66.

98 IMF, 'Singapore: Financial System Stability Assessment'.

99 Basu Das, *Road to Recovery*, 73.

One desired policy goal was therefore to maintain and restore normalcy to the flows of capital into and out of the global city. As such, a priority was 'to prevent a potential outflow of bank deposits' by placing bank guarantees for all banks in Singapore, including foreign banks.[100] At the height of the 2008 crisis, MAS policy was 'aimed at protecting the economy and its financial sector against any erosion of confidence. It maintained a comfortable level of Singapore dollar and US dollar liquidity throughout the period of high uncertainty'.[101] Reflecting the cooperation with other regulators in global financial centres to maintain smooth circulation of financial flows, MAS also works with Hong Kong Securities and Futures Commission (HKSFC) and the UK Financial Services Authority (FSA) for enhanced sharing of supervisory information. It also participates in the Executives' Meeting of East Asia Pacific Central Banks (EMEAP) to support regional financial stability. As a member of the co-operative oversight arrangement of the Continuous Linked Settlement (CLS), led by the Federal Reserve Bank of New York, MAS is able to utilise the CLS for the safe and efficient settlement of foreign exchange trades involving 17 currencies, including the Singapore dollar. In July 2011, the China Banking Regulatory Commission (CBRC) and MAS agreed to cooperate on crisis management. As MAS observes, 'following the recent global financial crisis, there is recognition of the need for greater international cooperation to manage crises'.[102] Globally, MAS became a member of the Financial Stability Board (FSB) Steering Committee in January 2012. It chaired the FSB workgroup on Risk Governance, and participates in the workgroup on FSB Capacity, Resources and Governance. MAS co-chairs the Basel Committee on Banking Supervision Core Principles Group which is reviewing the Basel Core Principles for Effective Banking Supervision. In March 2011, MAS was admitted to the newly-formed Standing Committee on Risk and Research, which coordinates members' monitoring of systemic risks within securities markets, as well as to the newly-formed Assessment Committee, which will conduct assessments on the level of compliance with IOSCO Standards and Principles by its members. These webs of arrangements are all designed to forestall and manage any potential threats to the smooth circulation of global financial flows globally.

Besides financial regulators, the frightening scale and speed of the 2008 crisis prompted an unprecedented national response at the governmental level, also to maintain uninterrupted liquidity flows in the banking system. Prime Minister Lee said, 'As an open and exported oriented economy, Singapore felt the impact of the

100 Goh Chok Tong, '50th Anniversary of the Centre for Development Economics, Williams College, USA' (speech, United States of America, 14 October 2010) <http://www.news.gov.sg/public/sgpc/en/media_releases/agencies/micacsd/speech/S-20101015-1.html> accessed 14 October 2013.

101 Basu Das, *Road to Recovery*, 96.

102 Monetary Authority of Singapore (MAS), 'MAS Annual Report 2011/2012' <http://www.mas.gov.sg/annual_reports/annual20112012/partners01_08.html> accessed 14 September 2012.

global crisis more than most countries. We responded aggressively with emergency measures'.[103] Breaking precedent, the government drew SGD$4.9 billion from its financial reserves to fund a Jobs Credit Scheme and Special Risk-sharing Initiative under the SGD$20.5 billion 'Resilience Package – described as 'Singapore's most radical budget ever'.[104] These were designed to improve cash flows and maintain employment levels and stimulate bank lending as the Government absorbed 80 per cent of the default risk on loans up to SGD$5 million, and 75 per cent of the risk on trade financing. Indicative of the importance of a multi-stakeholder approach when responding to global financial risks, the Ministry of Finance added that 'Government assistance schemes can be complex and multi-faceted with numerous policy and implemenation considerations. This makes it difficult for any single government agency to design and implement such schemes on its own'.[105]

Engaging with regional or international bodies working to minimise disruptions in the global financial system, Singapore contributed to the Financial Stability Board's work on drafting principles for compensation, which were eventually adopted at the G20. FSB presently brings together finance ministries, central banks, regulators and supervisory authorities from major financial centres (G7 plus five); the IMF, World Bank, BIS, OECD, and European Central Bank; the international regulatory and supervisory standard setting bodies, and committees of central bank experts. Much as Beck postulated on the 'social explosiveness' of global risks that undermined pre-existing arrangements, Foreign Minister Shanmugam referred to how new arrangements and smaller regional groupings like the G20 and G8 may be more efficient and dynamic in decision-making.[106] In 2009, the G20 decided on concerted fiscal expansion of USD$5 trillion to combat the crisis as well as toughen financial regulations. Singapore has been invited several times to G20 summits as one of only five guests, because of its financial hub status. However, the G20 has also sparked negative reactions from the many smaller economies left out of the group.[107] Consequently, Singapore launched the Global Governance Group (3G) to articulate a coordinated position by smaller countries. Regionally, ASEAN plus 3 partners also worked to facilitate the smooth flow of capital through the financial system by expanding the Chiang Mai Initiative (set up after the 1998 crisis to ease credit crunches) from USD$90 billion to USD$240 billion

103 Lee Hsien Loong, 'APEC CEO Summit' (speech, Singapore, 13 November 2009) <http://www.news.gov.sg/public/sgpc/en/media_releases/agencies/micacsd/speech/S-20091113-2.html> accessed 13 November 2012.

104 Bernard Yeung, 'Foreword', in Sanchita Basu Das, *Road to Recovery: Singapore's Journey Through the Global Crisis*. Singapore: ISEAS (2010).

105 Ibid.

106 K. Shanmugam, 'Statement at the UN General Assembly General Debate' (27 September 2011) <http://gadebate.un.org/66/singapore> accessed 29 August 2014.

107 Menon, Vanu Gopala, 'Remarks at Wilton Park Conference on Reforming International Governance, Luxemborg, 15 June 2011' <http://www.mfa.gov.sg/content/mfa/overseasmission/newyork/nyemb_statements/global_governance_group/2011/201102/press_201106_2.html> accessed 12 March 2013.

in 2012. Singapore has committed USD$4 billion to the IMF to maintain stability of the overall global system.

Apart from financial regulators and national governments, banks are central in maintaining the stability of a global city's financial core, particularly those of systemic importance. Ex-Fed chief Ben Bernanke defined a 'too-big-to-fail' bank as 'one whose size, complexity, interconnectedness, and critical functions are such that, should the firm go unexpectedly into liquidation, the rest of the financial system and the economy would face severe adverse consequences'.[108] Singaporean policy makers have emphasised that 'contagion amongst banks is a fact of life. Financial systems can be severely stressed by their weakest points, even if it involves a single bank or a group of small banks. Confidence is therefore about banking systems, not just about individual banks'.[109] Hence, each and every bank has a stake in ensuring 'normal' financial flows are not disrupted. Clearly demonstrating Beaverstock's claims about cooperating in order to 'attend' to the financial system, Chairman of the Association of Banks in Singapore stated that 'although we are competitors, I believe all of us can have a shared collective agenda, which is to make Singapore an even more important financial hub ... we should work together ... to position Singapore at the forefront of international best practices'.[110] To prevent collapse of financial institutions destabilising the financial system and flow of funds, the ABS issued guidelines whereby lenders are encouraged to adopt a 'Rescue culture' and to be supportive to a company in financial difficulty.[111] Local Singaporean 'anchor' banks were holding an average 11.3 per cent of Tier-1 capital, nearly three times the BIS recommendation of 4 per cent and double the MAS guidelines of 6 per cent.[112] Besides prudent regulators, resilient banking systems in Singapore also require strong anchor banks that take a long-view and align their interests with the economy. These may find themselves compelled to acquire ailing financial institutions to minimise systemic disruption.[113] To keep funds flowing, Singapore banks responded to

108 Ben S. Bernanke, 'Testimony before the Financial Crisis Inquiry Commission, Washington D.C.', 2 September 2010.

109 Tharman Shanmugaratnam, '39th Association of Banks in Singapore Annual Dinner' (speech, Singapore, 28 June 2012) <http://app.mof.gov.sg/newsroom_details.aspx?type=speech&cmpar_year=2012&news_sid=20120629148451891878> accessed 29 June 2013.

110 Piyush Gupta, 'Incoming ABS Chairman 38th Annual Dinner' (speech, Singapore, 28 June 2011) <http://www.abs.org.sg/pdfs/Newsroom/Speeches/2011/Speech_280611_MrPiyush.pdf> accessed 29 June 2013.

111 The Association of Banks in Singapore, 'Principles and Guidelines for Restructuring of corporate debt: The Singapore Approach' <http://www.abs.org.sg/pdfs/Publications/spore_approach.pdf> accessed 14 September 2012.

112 Basu Das, *Road to Recovery*, 66.

113 Shanmugaratnam, '39th Association of Banks in Singapore (ABS) Annual Dinner'.

government calls to lend to SMEs, with some SGD$2.8 billion of loans approved for disbursement.[114]

A similar range of actors took on the 1998 financial crisis in Singapore, arguably providing lessons to cope with the later 2008 version. At the national level, a series of corporate and personal tax rebates was launched to reduce the costs of business and provide relief to individuals and businesses worth SGD$2 billion in 1998. At the regional level, the Chiang Mai Initiative bilateral swap network was established, with the core objectives of addressing balance of payment and short-term liquidity difficulties in the region. The state was once again a key player. With stronger macroeconomic fundamentals and a healthy domestic financial system that helped maintain investor confidence, the impact on Singapore was not as severe as in other less open regional economies.[115] The financial regulator, MAS also appeared crucial in 1998, as in 2008. Its managed-float exchange rate regime where the Sing dollar floated against a weighted basket of currencies such as the US dollar, Japanese yen and Malaysian ringgit, limited the loss of competitiveness suffered by Singapore's export sectors.[116] Leifer attributed this to 'underlying resilience based on a system of governance respected for its efficiency and probity'.[117] This same point was stressed by former Prime Minister Goh: 'One essential requirement of good governance is fiscal responsibility, Good governance is central to Singapore's competitiveness as a business hub'.[118]

Intentional Exploitation of Global Financial Architecture: Malign Circulations

Volatile fluctuations of global financial flows, *inadvertent* they may be, have severely affected Singapore as a global city, as outlined above. Unfortunately, there are more sinister and *deliberate* exploitations of a global financial hub's architecture in financial flows. This is particularly significant, bearing in mind how earlier discussions noted that security challenges today are 'geared towards trying to separate people and circulations deemed risky or malign from those deemed risk-free or worthy of protection'.[119] Singapore facilitates legitimate movements, investments and protection of funds in or through the global city, but here another

114 David Connor, 'Outgoing chairman of ABS' (annual dinner, 26 June 2009) <http://www.abs.org.sg/pdfs/Newsroom/Speeches/2009/Speech_260609_MrDavid.pdf> accessed 8 January 2010.

115 Chia, 'The Asian Financial Crisis: Singapore's experience and response', 51.

116 Ibid., 108–9.

117 Michael Leifer, *Singapore: Coping with Vulnerability*. Singapore: Routledge (2000), 157.

118 K. Shanmugam, 'Singapore Corporate Awards' (speech, Singapore, 23 April 2009) <http://www.mlaw.gov.sg/news/speeches/speech-by-law-minister-k-shanmugam-at-the-singapore-corporate-awards-2009.html> accessed 24 April 2012.

119 Stephen Graham, *Cities Under Siege*. London: Verso (2010), 89.

concern is how illicit terror or criminal networks can also transfer their monies through the same critical infrastructure. Such risks are different from financial shocks being transmitted from overseas. This can be seen a variant of the 'city-as-target' model whereby a global city is purposely targeted in order to take advantage of its connectivity, rather than destroy or disrupt it.

In 2004, Singapore, along with other major financial hubs Hong Kong and London, was blacklisted in a U.S. State Department report as a centre of 'primary concern' for money laundering. The danger, as London discovered with recent financial scandals from HSBC's involvement in money laundering, is that failing to weed out malign financial flows threatens its position as a leading financial hub. The Financial Action Task Force (FATF) has reported that 'Singapore is a major financial centre in the Asia Pacific region ... The size and growth of Singapore's private banking and assets management sector poses significant money laundering (ML) risk based on known typologies. There are also terrorist financing risks'.[120] According to Rohan Bedi, head of anti-money laundering services at PricewaterhouseCoopers in Singapore, private banks face the highest risks as they provide an unwitting link between Politically Exposed Persons from high-risk countries and terrorist financing.[121] Singapore was dropped from the Organisation of Economic Co-operation and Development's so-called 'grey' list only in 2009. Further compounding the risk is the nature of assets managed in Singapore, a large proportion of which belongs to overseas-based clients. According to FATF figures, half of these are non-institutional, including 43 per cent from the Asia-Pacific region (excluding North America) and from jurisdictions with relatively low levels of AML/CFT compliance. For instance, of the total assets held in this section, SGD$180 billion (USD$115 billion) was from non-institutional clients in the Asia-Pacific region (excluding North America).[122]

Mechanisms of Transmitting Terrorist Financing

As with previous sections, this part examines the mechanisms through which terrorist financing and/or money-laundering flows circulate through key financial nodes such as Singapore, given their systemic importance.[123] Once again, the analytical framework premised on flows and circulations provides a starting point

120 Financial Action Task Force, 'Third Mutual Evaluation Report on Anti-Money Laundering and Combating the Financing of Terrorism Singapore', 29 February 2008, 6.

121 Cited in Muralikmar Amamtharaman, 'Bank clients in spotlight in dirty money fight', Reuters, 25 August 2003 <https://www.world-check.com/media/d/content_pressarticle_reference/reference-182.pdf> accessed 9 April 2015.

122 Financial Action Task Force, 'Third Mutual Evaluation Report', 6.

123 Willam F. Wechsler, 'Follow the Money', *Foreign Affairs* 80:4 (2001) <http://www.foreignaffairs.com/articles/57052/william-f-wechsler/follow-the-money> accessed 12 May 2013.

to address the problem. Given how funds flowing throughout the global financial system are channelled through key nodes, eventually the dirty money trail will hit a financial hub at some point. Most of the funds for the September 11th hijackers for instance were wired from the Persian Gulf financial centre of Dubai. Relying on the anonymity provided by Dubai and the vast international monetary system, the amounts sent were inconspicuous, buried within the billions of dollars circulating daily. This was a good example of the spatial dimensions of de-localised risks that Beck referred to. Singapore as a clearing hub for US dollars and offering complex products such as securities and foreign exchange further makes it easier for potential terrorist financiers to disrupt the audit trail through 'layering'. Australia has reported fund flows associated with illegal activity utilising Singapore financial service providers as a transit point for funds ultimately destined for other parts of Asia.[124] With the high number of visitors that enter and exit Singapore (exceeding 10 million annually), the FATF also warns of vulnerabilities from cash couriers (money mules) seeking to physically move funds.

Again, utilising the notion of cities as spaces of flows allows researchers to identify the mechanisms through which terrorist financing might be illicitly transmitted within global financial flows that global cities process on a routine daily basis. The task for Singapore is to ensure there is 'enhanced vigilance against suspicious flows'.[125] Director of MAS Ravi Menon said that Singapore 'neither wants nor will tolerate these illicit inflows'.[126] Menon warned that: 'September 11 has highlighted a more threatening dimension of the problem – the use of the financial system to mobilise and direct funds for terrorist activities. As the conduit through which money flows, the financial sector has been the natural focal point for money laundering and terrorism financing … as an international financial centre, Singapore has a compelling interest in combating money laundering and terrorism financing'.[127] As Minister for Law, K. Shanmugam explained that the survival of terrorist groups turns on their ability to 'manipulate flows of money through financial systems'. Given how quickly and easily capital can now transfer across global financial markets, combined with new emerging techniques such as mobile payment systems, criminals and terrorists have ample means to exploit financial

124 Financial Action Task Force, 'Third Mutual Evaluation Report', 15.

125 Ng Sam Sin, 'Society for Trust and Estate Practitioners Asia conference' (speech, Singapore, 1 November 2011) <http://www.mas.gov.sg/News-and-Publications/Speeches-and-Monetary-Policy-Statements/2011/Keynote-Speech-By-Mr-Ng-Nam-Sin-AMD-MAS-STEP-Asia-Conference.aspx> accessed 2 November 2013.

126 Luzi Ann Javier, 'Singapore May Toughen Penalties for Money Laundering, Terrorism Financing', 27 October 2011 <http://www.bloomberg.com/news/2011-10-27/singapore-may-toughen-penalties-for-money-laundering-terrorism-financing.html> accessed 28 October 2011.

127 Ravi Menon, 'Asia Anti-money Laundering Conference' (speech, Singapore, 31 July 2003) <http://www.mas.gov.sg/news-and-publications/speeches-and-monetary-policy-statements/2003/combating-money-laundering-and-terrorism-financing.aspx> accessed 30 July 2013.

hubs.[128] The idea of undesirable flows passing through Singapore is repeated by MAS Director Menon, 'Like any international financial centre, Singapore is vulnerable to being used as a conduit for illicit funds. And given our growing prominence as a centre for wealth management, the vulnerability is greater. We need to guard against financial flows relating to corruption, terrorism, politically exposed persons, and weapons proliferation'.[129] Data from the FATF and US State Department suggest that Singapore has identified and frozen financial assets of individuals affiliated with the regional Jemaah Islamiyah terror network, although these are not publicly available. Singapore government reports to the FATF suggest that the amount of terrorist funds held in the city is 'small'. The FATF reports that up to 2008, Singapore had no terrorist financing prosecutions or convictions and investigations into frozen assets did not yield sufficient evidence to prosecute or confiscate.

Table 3.1 Statistics on Financing of Terrorism Investigations (data taken from FATF Mutual Evaluation Report of Singapore 2008)

	2004	2005	2006	2007
Total Number of Cases in which Assets are Seized	6	1	4	1
Number of Accounts in which freezing order is effected	6	5	11	2

Singapore's Suspicious Transactions Reporting Office (STRO) investigated 8, 11 and 18 cases of terrorist financing in the years 2005, 2006 and 2007.[130]

128 K. Shanmugam, '13th Annual Meeting of Asia-Pacific Group on Money Laundering' (speech, Singapore, 13 July 2010) <https://www.mha.gov.sg/news_details.aspx?nid=MTc2MA%3D%3D-g0QQBHqhZ%2FQ%3D> accessed 14 July 2013.

129 Ravi Menon, 'A Competent, Trusted and Clean Financial Centre' (speech, Singapore, 28 October 2011) <http://www.mas.gov.sg/news-and-publications/speeches-and-monetary-policy-statements/2011/a-competent-trusted-and-clean-financial-centre-welcome-address-by-mr-ravi-menon-md-mas-at-the-wmi-connection.aspx> accessed 29 October 2013.

130 Financial Action Task Force, 'Third Mutual Evaluation Report', 60.

Table 3.2 Funds Seized / Frozen relating to ML / TF pursuant to STR Information

Year 2004	SGD$5,824,396; USD$360,038; AUD$130,000
Year 2005	USD$1,500,303
Year 2006	SGD$7,938,155; USD$4,229,694
Year 2007	SGD$8,815,369; USD$70,000; MYR 7,000; EUR€46,538,535

Source: FATF Mutual Evaluation Report of Singapore 2008, 65.

In 2010, the use of financial intelligence helped investigators seize more than SGD$54 million of suspected criminal proceeds.[131]

Table 3.3 Financing of Terrorism Investigations

	2004	2005	2006	2007
STRs relating to Financing of Terrorism	34	49	73	313
FT related STRs concerning which STRO invoked Police Powers to gather more information	34	17	35	56
Other FT Investigations	43	33	42	39

Source: FATF Mutual Evaluation Report of Singapore 2008, 73.

Since 2005, Singapore's Suspicious Transactions Reporting Office (STRO) has also observed an emerging trend whereby account holders who have satisfied the Customer Due Diligence (CDD) requirements are recruited as transaction managers or 'money mules' to assist in the transfer of illegally obtained funds. As at 14 November 2007, STRO disseminated over 100 STRs relating to money mule. This led to nine money laundering investigations into 77 entities. In total, SGD$59,000 in proceeds of crime were identified and/or surrendered. Investigations further revealed that more than SGD$1.7 million has been transferred through money mules in Singapore.[132] In 2010, the number of suspicious transaction reports received was 11,934, reflecting a trend of suspicious flows of funds in the Singapore financial system. Between 2010 and 2013, STRO data suggests that there has been increasing requests for assistance from

131 Commercial Affairs Department Singapore, 'Annual Report 2011' <http://www.cad.gov.sg/NR/rdonlyres/4B459ADE-5B86-4034-8403-5E8E24A4DC08/28122/CAD_AR2011_web.pdf> accessed 8 July 2012, 33.

132 Figures taken from Financial Action Task Force, 'Third Mutual Evaluation Report', 15–16.

foreign intelligence units overseas, as well as proactive provision of suspicious transactions to foreign partners. The number of such spontaneous provision of information to foreign FIUs has increased from 34 to 75, while requests from overseas rose from 105 to 164.[133]

In 2012, the U.S. Department of State reported that in Singapore, 'terrorist financing in general remains a risk'. It continues that 'Singapore is a major international financial and investment center as well as a major offshore financial center. Secrecy protections, a lack of routine large currency reporting requirements, and the size and growth of Singapore's private banking and assets management sector' make the city a 'potentially attractive' destination for terrorist financiers.[134] The State Department also pointed out that there was no current requirement at that time to report large transactions, missing the chance to track significant financial flows. In July 2012, it was revealed in US Senate investigations into the HSBC money-laundering scandal that the Singapore branch of HSBC Bank USA (HBUS) was implicated in seeking to open an account for the Islami Bank – a bank thought to have links with Bangladeshi terrorist financiers – to supply it with physical US dollars and wire transfer facilities in US dollars.[135] While terrorist financing is different from money-laundering, available data suggests that there are also numerous small enterprises such as money changing and remittance businesses catering for the large migrant workforce in Singapore that a global city inevitably attracts. These approximately 870,000 foreign guest workers are the main users of alternative remittance systems that could also potentially be exploited to transmit funds.

The opening of two new large Singaporean casinos also brings possible terrorist financing risks, being as they are cash-intensive businesses with high volumes of daily transactions. According to the International Bar Association's Anti-Money Laundering forum, 'Casinos work with large and erratic inflows and outflows of cash and have the potential to be a channel for money laundering and/or terrorist financing'.[136] The U.S. Treasury's Financial Crimes Enforcement network reported in 2010 an increase in suspicious activities reporting by casinos worldwide. Singapore may not be immune to such risks.

---

133 Social Trade Organisation (STRO), 'Statistics on International Cooperation', 24 June 2014 <http://www.cad.gov.sg/content/cad/en/aml-cft/suspicious-transaction-reporting-office--stro-/statistics.html> accessed 30 July 2014.

134 United States Department of State Bureau for International Narcotics and Law Enforcement Affairs, 'International Narcotics Control Strategy Report', 158–60.

135 United States Senate, 'US vulnerabilities to money laundering, drugs, and terrorist financing: HSBC Case History', 17 July 2012 <http://www.hsgac.senate.gov/subcommittees/investigations/hearings/us-vulnerabilities-to-money-laundering-drugs-and-terrorist-financing-hsbc-case-history> access date 27 August 2014, 225–7.

136 IBA Anti-Money Laundering Forum, 'Entry on Singapore', 27 January 2012 <http://www.anti-moneylaundering.org/asiapacific/Singapore.aspx> accessed 13 April 2012.

'Attending' to the Global Financial Network

As seen previously, a 'global city' responds to financial crises through the multi-level network of actors that bring it into being and work to ensure its continued ability to process financial flows efficiently. Similar processes are emerging in the responses to risks of terrorist financing. These include regulators like the MAS; the Singapore government; and industry actors like banks and the financial sector. Characteristic of Beck's *World Risk Society*, terrorist financing, like global financial meltdowns, are now trans-boundary, requiring changes to how different actors in different countries cooperate. This challenge is not lost on Minister Shanmugam who stressed that 'A national-level response is not going to be enough to defeat a transnational enemy. Every member of the global community will need to have in place equally robust anti-money laundering and counter terrorist-financing – or AML/CFT – regimes'.[137] Singapore has emphasised collaborative efforts between the banking industry and the Government; tighter regulatory frameworks by the MAS; and cooperating with global and regional bodies such as the World Bank, the IMF, APG and FATF as well as other countries.

Starting with the government's engagement with regional and global bodies, Singapore has been a member of FATF since September 1991. There is a FATF-style regional grouping known as the Asia/Pacific Group on Money Laundering (APG). Singapore is a founding member of the APG and hosted the 13th annual meeting in 2010. STRO, as Singapore's Financial Intelligence Unit, was admitted in June 2002 into the Egmont Group, which was established in June 1995 to facilitate timely sharing of information and provision of assistance on financial-related crimes. In May 2003, Singapore issued a regulation pursuant to the MACMA and the Terrorism Act that enables the government to provide legal assistance to the United States and the United Kingdom in matters related to terrorist financing offences. Singapore has mutual legal assistance agreements also with Hong Kong India, and Laos. Singapore responded positively to a legal assistance request by the Financial Investigation Branch (FIB) for the US to extradite Balraj Naidu, a Singaporean. Naidu faced trial in the US in July 2009 for brokering the sale of weapons and terrorism financing in the US. The Singapore government has also acceded to requests by foreign governments to freeze funds during 2004 (SGD$13,549), 2005 (SGD$17,883), 2006 (SGD$21,859), and 2007 (as at 14 November) (SGD$4,467).[138] The Singapore state's engagement and cooperation with regional and global partners is motivated by self-interest to preserve the attractiveness of its financial sector to legitimate 'clean' financial flows, and to minimise the risk of malign infiltrations of terrorist funds or laundered money.

137 K. Shanmugam, '13th Annual Meeting of Asia-Pacific Group on Money Laundering'.

138 Financial Action Task Force, 'Third Mutual Evaluation Report', 52.

Being placed on the 'blacklist' for non-compliance could potentially lead to higher costs and penalties for financial institutions, resulting in the last thing a global city wants: the diversion of financial flows away. Singapore has adopted a risk-based approach such that customers deemed low risks are provided simplified CDD measures while high-risk ones undergo extra scrutiny. Before its two new casinos opened in 2010, Singapore passed the Casino Control (Prevention of Money Laundering and Terrorism Financing) Regulations 2009, specifically providing measures such as due diligence and suspicious activities reporting that casinos have to comply with. Singapore's Casino Regulatory Act of 2010 prohibits the conversion of money from one form to another without being used for gambling, including the receipt of cash for electronic transmittal on behalf of a patron or making cash payments to a patron from funds received through electronic wire transfers. The U.S. Department of State notes that 'The opening of Singapore's two casinos in 2010 increased concerns about the potential for illicit flows to pass through Singapore. Singapore has implemented legal and regulatory changes involving cash transactions at casinos to better align itself with the international standards for anti-money laundering/counterterrorist financing regimes'.[139] Further, MAS (Anti-Terrorism Measures) Regulations; and Terrorism (Suppression of Financing) Act – criminalises terrorist financing and requires report of 'suspicious transactions'. To tackle the dangers of cash couriers (money mules), from 1 November 2007, any person who moves into or out of Singapore cash exceeding SGD$30,000 (the prescribed amount) or its equivalent in a foreign currency, is required to give a report in respect of its movements. In late 2011, Singapore announced new measures to make laundering of proceeds from tax offenses a crime and tighten laws on tax evasion. All moneychangers and remittance agents must now be licensed and are subject to the Money-Changing and Remittance Businesses Act (MCRBA), which includes requirements for record keeping and filing of suspicious transaction reports.[140]

Mirroring the response to financial contagion, a similar multi-stakeholder approach has been adopted. Instituting new partnership arrangements within its government agencies designed to enhance inter-agency cooperation, a high-level Steering Committee comprising Permanent Secretaries from the Home and Finance ministries plus the Director of MAS was set up in 1999. In 2013, drawing reference from the FATF guidance on national risk assessment, a first ever 'risk assessment' report of money laundering and terrorist financing risks was completed by the Home and Finance Ministries with the MAS, in cooperation with both public and private sectors.

---

139 U.S. Department of State, 'Country Reports on Terrorism', Washington D.C., 2010 <http://www.state.gov/j/ct/rls/crt/> accessed 27 August 2014, 46.

140 Bureau of International Narcotics and Law Enforcement Affairs. '2009 INCSR: Country Reports – Moldova through Singapore', 2009 International Narcotics Control Strategy Report (INCSR) 27 February 2009 <http://www.state.gov/j/inl/rls/nrcrpt/2009/vol2/116545.htm> accessed 9 October 2011.

As with financial contagion, regulators like MAS Director Ravi Menon are also playing key roles of 'attendant' cooperating with other regulatory institutions to ensure that 'normal' global financial flows continue to flow smoothly through Singapore, rather than 'undesirable' terrorist financing: 'Given the cross-border nature of illicit financial activities, it is not enough that we have strong regulation and supervision in Singapore; we must be able to co-operate effectively with supervisory authorities and enforcement agencies abroad'.[141] Based on regulations issued in 2002, MAS has broad powers to direct financial institutions to comply with international obligations related to terrorist financing. Banks and financial institutions cannot provide resources and services that will benefit terrorists or terrorist financing. STRO has Memorandum of Understanding (MOUs) concerning the exchange of financial intelligence with its US counterpart, FinCEN, as well as with Australia, Belgium, Brazil, Canada, Greece, Hong Kong, Italy, Japan, Mexico and the United Kingdom. According to the US State Department, 'Singapore is an important participant in the regional effort to stop terrorist financing in Southeast Asia'.[142]

Other key 'attendants' such as banks and the financial sector are also engaged in keeping unwanted financial flows out. 'The fact is, money laundering, terrorist financing, drug financing is a real problem and because it goes through the banking channel, a bank is a good agent to try and stop that', said Piyush Gupta, CEO of DBS Bank.[143] Singapore adopts a so-called 'total' approach premised on proactive prevention and a rigorous regulatory regime. There is strong emphasis on outreach to relevant industry actors who are on the frontlines exposed to terrorist financing risks. The inter-agency Steering Committee notes that 'the business and professional sectors, including the financial sector, are key partners in combating money laundering, terrorist financing, and the financing of proliferation. Their views and feedback are important to effectively implement these regime enhancements. We will conduct industry consultations and work in partnership with the private sector to strengthen the overall resilience of our system against threats from cross-border crimes'.[144] STRO has intensified its

---

141 Ravi Menon, 'A Competent, Trusted and Clean Financial Centre' (speech, Singapore, 28 October 2011) <http://www.mas.gov.sg/news-and-publications/speeches-and-monetary-policy-statements/2011/a-competent-trusted-and-clean-financial-centre-welcome-address-by-mr-ravi-menon-md-mas-at-the-wmi-connection.aspx> accessed 29 October 2013.

142 Bureau of International Narcotics and Law Enforcement Affairs, '2009 INCSR: Country Reports – Moldova through Singapore'.

143 'Banking chiefs say regulation of the industry needs to strike right balance' Channel NewsAsia, 26 July 2014 <http://www.channelnewsasia.com/news/business/singapore/banking-chiefs-say/1283126.html> accessed 9 August 2014.

144 Ministry of Home Affairs, Singapore, 'FATF's Enhanced Measures to Combat Money Laundering, Terrorist Financing And The Financing of Proliferation', 16 February 2012 <http://www.mha.gov.sg/news_details.aspx?nid=MjM2NQ%3D%3D-AL0iTNxUJSI%3D> accessed 17 February 2013.

cooperation and outreach to the private sector, resulting in an increase in quality and quantity of STRs. The emphasis is on leveraging off industry knowledge and perspectives on the ground, to ensure that initiatives translate to meaningful regulations.[145] The Private Banking Industry Group, or 'PBIG' co-chaired by Chairman of Citi Private Banking and Assistant Managing Director of MAS, has also issued a code of conduct on good practice to guide members on due diligence and know your customer procedures when it comes to countering terrorism financing and money-laundering. The Association of Banks in Singapore (ABS) holds a conference twice every year to discuss emerging industry threat analyses and promote best practices. ABS Chairman David Connor announced in 2009 that 'The threat of terrorism continues to remain very real and banks must play their part to counter terrorism financing. In this regard, ABS signed a tripartite MOU with the S.Rajaratnam School of International Studies and the Ministry of Home Affairs to establish the Consortium for Countering the Financing of Terrorism'.[146] Reflecting the need to sieve out undesirable flows, this is seen as 'vital towards safeguarding Singapore's role and reputation as a financial hub'.[147] Financial sector representatives interviewed by the FATF assessment team in 2008 indicated that they know who to contact with terrorist financing-related information.

The relatively low number of investigations and convictions however has been a bugbear for international assessments of Singapore's counter-terrorist financing abilities. There were 14 prosecutions and 18 convictions for money laundering in 2010. Money-laundering convictions in Singapore climbed to an average of 21 per year from 2008 to 2010, compared with four between 2000 and 2007, according to the Financial Action Task Force. In 2010 and 2011, a total of 44 people were convicted of money laundering offences in Singapore, mostly related to fraud, and close to SGD$130 million was seized or frozen. By comparison, Hong Kong had 360 money-laundering convictions in 2010, compared with 179 in 2007. The FATF expressed its concern in 2008 that 'given the risk of money being laundered in Singapore (particularly the proceeds of foreign predicate offences), the amount of money being frozen and seized seems low'.[148]

Conclusion

The de-localised nature of global risks such as financial meltdown and terrorist financing/money-laundering that global cities face are not only key planks of Ulrich Beck's emergent *World Risk Society*, they also generated impetus on regulatory and

145 Menon, 'A Competent, Trusted and Clean Financial Centre'.

146 Connor, 'Outgoing Chairman of ABS'.

147 David Connor, 'ABS 35th Annual Dinner' (speech, Singapore, 27 June 2008) <http://www.abs.org.sg/pdfs/Newsroom/Speeches/2008/Speech_270608_MrDavid.pdf> accessed 27 June 2013.

148 Financial Action Task Force, 'Third Mutual Evaluation Report', 4.

political arrangements for actors and networks within the global city to respond through developing new multi-stakeholder arrangements to manage such risks. Taking Singapore's financial centre as a case study, this chapter incorporated the 'mobilities' turn in the debates on global cities and Castells' idea of cities as spaces of flows. By drawing attention to the exit and entry gateways for the circulation of financial flows (i.e the financial sector), an analytical framework focused on the notion of flows draws us to several conclusions. Financial centres can expose global cities like Singapore to global risks in several ways that Beck neglected previously to elaborate upon. First, there are *inadvertent* transmission mechanisms of financial shocks which manifest through panic selling; direct impact on financial sector growth through volatile swings in inflows and outflows; and wider effects on the real economy. Singapore's experiences demonstrate how global financial risks are an ultimate form of 'organised irresponsibility' in Beck's words, since one cannot precisely attribute responsibility for volatile capital flows or investor panic. Second, terrorist financiers or money launderers can organise a *deliberately* planned and targeted exploitation of Singapore's financial connectivity in order to secretly transfer malicious funds and monies around the world, hoping these transfers stay unnoticed among the billions of other 'normal' flows transacted daily in a financial hub. The challenge here is how to facilitate smooth circulation of 'legitimate' flows while filtering out 'illicit' ones.

For both these global risks however, there is a question of 'agency' to contend with when considering responses. Who exactly speaks for a 'global city'? As Beaverstock et al. have demonstrated, there are multi-level stakeholders from most affected industry sectors (like banks and lobby group associations), to regulatory agencies, to state governments, and regional/global bodies, all of whom work together to restore the normal routine workings of the global financial network or to minimise the risks of exploitation. New multi-stakeholder cooperative arrangements are arising between these actors who all have a stake in ensuring that Singapore's financial hub is able to perform its central role of processing 'normal' financial flows even in the face of such risks.

Being a leading financial centre has cemented Singapore's global city status. As an 'infrastructure' approach to studying global cities might suggest, the island has benefitted from having the necessary critical infrastructure for attracting, coordinating, servicing and facilitating global financial flows, from private wealth management, unit trusts, to foreign exchange. But its financial connectivity and ability to circulate these flows has also added vulnerability to global risks associated with these flows such as terrorist financing or financial contagion. The 1998 crisis was an early precursor of how Singapore's role as a regional financial hub brought downsides through greater exposure to financial stresses in neighbouring economies.[149] This point is reiterated by Prime Minister Lee who said, 'we will always be vulnerable to the vagaries of external events, as the Global Financial Crisis reminded us. More economic integration will generate

149 Basu Das, *Road to Recovery*, 130.

greater prosperity for many countries, but it also has its downsides. Shocks will be transmitted more quickly and widely, economic cycles will become shorter and more unpredictable, and the potential for worldwide contagion will be much greater'.[150] The crisis may well have highlighted what Das calls the 'flaws of an export-led growth strategy'[151] and while the Singapore government will consider alternative sources of growth such as increasing domestic consumption, education and healthcare, external demand will for the foreseeable future still constitute the main driver of the economy.

Yet Singapore's leaders have often tried to turn crises in the global city into an asset. Indeed, the ability to do so is seen as an added comparative advantage, for 'dealing with crises, and seeking advantage when they occur, is now a capability in itself and a competitive strategy for firms as well as economies'.[152] Indeed, given Singapore's reputation for tight regulations, the Economic Strategies Committee believes that it will actually 'benefit from the increased premium that global companies are placing on jurisdictions that provide safety and stability, post-crisis'.[153] Besides immediate crisis management, Singapore has also implemented strategies focusing on improving competitiveness in the long run. As Chia noted, times of economic duress can also be harnessed to undertake restructuring and reform, upgrading key infrastructure, education, all in order to enhance competitiveness in the long term.[154] Even in a time of turmoil, Prime Minister Lee stresses that the city-state must hunt continually for opportunities, 'in the midst of the storm, we must keep pursuing new growth chances, and look beyond the immediate problems to ensure that Singapore emerges stronger after the downturn'.[155] This has become an emerging feature of Singapore policymakers when dealing with financial crises. In 1998 at the height of the Asian financial crisis, Singapore's commitment to being a global city and financial centre did not wither: 'our fundamental approach towards economic development has not changed: to rely on market forces, allow free capital flows, encourage foreign

150 Lee Hsien Loong, 'Economic Society of Singapore Annual Dinner' (speech, Singapore, 23 June 2012) <http://www.pmo.gov.sg/content/pmosite/mediacentre/speechesninterviews/primeminister/2012/June/speech_by_prime_ministerleehsienloongateconomicsocietyofsingapor.html#.U4KsV3KSySo> accessed 24 June 2013.

151 Basu Das, *Road to Recovery*, 109.

152 Tharman Shanmugaratnam, 'Singapore Human Capital Summit' (speech, Singapore, 19 September 2012) <http://app.mof.gov.sg/newsroom_details.aspx?type=speech&cmpar_year=2012&news_sid=20120919503641796214> accessed 20 September 2013.

153 Ministry of Finance, 'Economic Strategies Committee Report', February 2010 <http://app.mof.gov.sg/data/cmsresource/ESC%20Report/ESC%20Full%20Report.pdf> accessed 15 April 2011.

154 Chia, 'The Asian Financial Crisis', 65.

155 Lee Hsien Loong. 'New Year Message'.

investments, and plug ourselves into the global economy'.[156] There was to be 'no retreat from the international economy' but instead to push further liberalisation where MAS shifts from 'regulation to supervision' to further develop Singapore as a global financial centre.[157] In the midst of the recent crisis in 2009, Singapore launched the Economic Strategies Committee to develop recommendations for restructuring the economy. While focusing on skills and innovation, the key goal remains to make Singapore a 'distinctive' and 'leading global city'.[158] There are even some potential upsides for Singapore's global city status, stemming from global financial turmoil. 'A fast growing, low tax and bank-friendly environment like Singapore stands as a perfect antidote to the comparatively high tax and anti-banker sentiment of London and New York", according to Mark Cameron, operations chief at Astbury Marsden'.[159]

Just as repeated bouts of financial shocks have pummelled Singapore's financial centre, the terrorist financing risk is seen to be open-ended and constantly evolving, with no end in sight. Counter-terrorist financing measures can only go so far: 'We are playing a cat-and-mouse game with the terrorists; they will be looking for loopholes to exploit, even as we take measures against them'.[160] All stakeholders in Singapore's financial sector recognise it is a risk to be managed, so that it does not fatally derail the larger global city strategy based on attracting and commanding legitimate financial flows. Regulators such as MAS Director Menon referred to this point when he said that 'we will ensure that financial crime does not pay in Singapore and those who jeopardize Singapore's hard-earned reputation as a financial center of integrity face severe consequence … one key imperative is to keep the financial sector clean'.[161] Despite repeated criticisms of regulatory loopholes and low rates of prosecution, Singapore has responded to recommendations issued by the 2008 FATF mutual evaluation report to plug weaknesses. On the strength of improvements made, in 2012, the city was removed

---

156 Monetary Authority of Singapore (MAS), 'Coping with the Asian Financial Crisis: The Singapore Experience' (speech at Nomura Securities 'Singapore Seminar', Tokyo, Japan, 30 September 1998) <http://www.mas.gov.sg/news_room/statements/1998/Coping_With_the_Asian_Financial_Crisis_The_Singapore_Experience__30_Sep_1998.html> accessed 9 April 2011.

157 Hal Hill, 'An Overview of the Issues', in H.W. Ardnt and Hal Hill, *Southeast Asia's Economic Crisis: Origins, Lessons and the Way Forward*. Singapore: ISEAS (1999), 12.

158 Ministry of Finance, 'Economic Strategies Committee Report'.

159 'UK investment bankers prefer Singapore', *Financial Times*, 26 August 2012 <http://www.ft.com/cms/s/0/887f67a6-ee04-11e1-b0e4-00144feab49a.html#axzz39su2Tdyw> accessed 24 April 2014.

160 Wong Kan Seng, 'The Second Reading of the Terrorism (Suppression of Financing) Bill' (speech, Singapore, 8 July 2002) <http://www.mha.gov.sg/news_details.aspx?nid=ODQ3-D78tel4qsXU%3D> accessed, 9 July 2013.

161 Ravi Menon, 'WMI Connection' (speech, Fullerton Hotel, Singapore, 27 October 2011) <http://www.news.gov.sg/public/sgpc/en/media_releases/agencies/mha%20-%20htuc/speech/S-20100713-1.html> accessed 28 October 2013.

from a requirement to report annually and can now submit reports on a less frequent biennial basis instead. Singapore has improved its conviction of money launderers by five-fold and third party convictions by seven times. From being placed on the FATF's 'grey' list in 2004, Singapore in 2012 was termed as a 'largely compliant' country in criminalising money launderers. The FATF notes that STRO has been successful at identifying domestic predicate offences but should focus more on identification of money laundering from foreign predicate offences.[162]

Other stakeholders such as Premier Formations, a Singapore firm specialising in international taxation, also emphasised it is in the collective interest to fulfil and implement the latest FATF recommendations, otherwise there is the potential 'to damage the reputation of Singapore and that of our organization in the same process'.[163] As Beaverstock might suggest, all these cooperative efforts by industry actors are aimed at maintaining the collective interest in the ability of Singapore's financial centre to process financial flows, without being infiltrated by 'dirty' money such as laundered funds or terrorist money. The Singapore Police Forces' Commercial Affairs Department, in its 'Handbook for Anti-money laundering and Terrorism Financing' issued to banks and other financial sector actors, argued that robust counter-measures ultimately 'help build and maintain Singapore's strong reputation as a well regulated major financial centre'.[164] Above all, Singapore's openness and position as financial hub in the age of globalisation has brought about added vulnerability from undesirable mobilities. Whether it is financial contagion or terrorist financing, in order to filter negative circulations, new cooperative arrangements are emerging involving multiple stakeholders from industry to regulators, state government and global bodies. This 'opening-out' of governance arrangements based on 'risk cosmopolitanism' fills in gaps within Beck's *Global Risk Society* framework on the role of global cities in managing shared global risks. These actors are not coming together simply for some vague idealised, altruistic goals or humanity: they are also working towards their collective shared interests in minimising risks. In spite of such risks, the underlying global city leitmotif survives unscathed in the mind of Prime Minister Lee: 'Our fundamental constraints remain and we need to remain connected to the world in order to survive. We will continue to make ourselves an international hub, open to global investments and talent'.[165]

162 Financial Action Task Force, 'Third Mutual Evaluation Report', 4.

163 Premier Formations (Singapore), 'AML/CFT policy' <http://www.premier-formations.com/aboutus/aml.php> accessed 8 April 2012.

164 Commercial Affairs Department of the Singapore Police Force, 'The Anti-Money Laundering and Counter-Terrorism Financing Handbook', 3rd edition, March 2010, 4.

165 Lee Hsien Loong. 'Economic Development Board 50th Anniversary Gala Dinner' (speech, Singapore, 1 August 2011) <http:// http://news.asiaone.com/News/AsiaOne+News/Singapore/Story/A1Story20110802-292220.html> accessed 1 October 2013.

Chapter 4
Connectivity Hurts: Premier Airports as Gateways of Global Risk

Introduction

It should be clear by now, from preceding chapters, that global cities are defined by their central positions coordinating and commanding various kinds of global flows. For Harris and Keil, 'what is central to such conceptualizations of both the relationship amongst global cities, and within global cities, are the notions of mobility, flow, and dynamism'.[1] Applying concepts of mobilities; flows; and the 'infrastructure approach' to analysing Singapore's attributes as a global city, we have already seen how its financial core attracted and circulated financial flows. Connectivity however does not derive solely from being a financial centre, no matter how world-leading it might be. Connectivity in the aviation domain is also highly-prized: 'A big international airport with numerous airlines and many destinations is a sure sign of global status'.[2] Airports, particularly those serving leading global cities like London and New York, have become indispensable critical infrastructure facilitating aviation flows: from tourists; cargo goods and materials; migrants to businessmen. Manuel Castells, whose idea of cities as 'spaces of flows' is central to our analytical framework, particularly sees 'the airport as a space where people and things flow: where mobility is most active'.[3] Ali and Keil agree that 'airports are where different global flows converge'.[4] Airports and airliners have become symbolic of the trans-boundary flows that define globalisation: 'cutting across national and international boundaries, as well as economic, political, and social divisions, civil aviation is a vital sector of contemporary global life'.[5] Airplanes and their associated aviation infrastructure

---

1 S. Harris Ali and Roger Keil, 'Introduction: Networked Disease', in S. Harris and Roger Keil, *Networked Disease: Emerging Infections in the Global City*. Malden, MA: Wiley-Blackwell (2008), 3–4.

2 John Rennie Short, *Global Metropolitan*. London: Routledge (2004), 68.

3 Peter Adey, 'Surveillance at the airport: surveilling mobility/mobilising surveillance' *Environment and Planning* 36: 8 (2004), 1366.

4 S. Harris Ali and Roger Keil, 'Securitising networked flows: infectious diseases and airports', in Stephen Graham (ed.), *Disrupted Cities: When Infrastructure Fails*. London: Routledge (2010), 110.

5 Mark B. Salter, 'Imagining numbers: risk, quantification, and aviation security', *Security Dialogue* 39:2 (2008), 254.

help to define the current global system. Without them, what we understand as globalisation would be entirely different altogether.[6]

This chapter retains the analytical framework demonstrated in previous chapters but extends it to the aviation domain. Conceptualising global cities as spaces of aviation flows and mobilities prods researchers to turn their gaze towards how this connectivity is produced and maintained through critical enabling infrastructure, in this case airports. As Mike Crang notes, 'mobility is produced through specific places', especially 'gateway spaces – thresholds for people coming and going'.[7] Air hubs therefore serve as gateways circulating flows of people and goods around the world. Yet, being a global city hooked up through dense air linkages also brings exposure to global risks. Here we can think of

> cities as particular nodes made from the "traffic" that moves through them, and this "traffic" is understood to be made from multiple and interconnected entities. The human/nonhuman, inorganic/incorporeal, phenomenal/epiphenomenal are constantly encountering each other in new and different ways, to produce unexpected and unpredictable effects.[8]

In an inter-connected world, aviation flows in the form of people, cargo, and microbes mix, evolve, and interact in complex, unanticipated ways.[9] This element of unpredictability also characterises Beck's *World Risk Society*: 'populations, economies, nature and culture at the beginning of the twenty-first century are interconnected at the global level in a co-evolution in which the repercussions in one or other domain influence each other in unknown ways that are difficult to predict'.[10] Arab terrorists planning their activities in far-away Afghanistan were able to severely disrupt global aviation networks on September 11th: 'the end of the World Trade Centre gave the Americans an idea of what it means to awaken suddenly in the strange new world risk society'.[11] Although 'the threat posed by terrorist networks' is a lynchpin of the World Risk Society,[12] Beck's omission to relate this to academic debates on global cities' flows and mobilities is particularly glaring. Many of these unpredictable side-effects are imported, targeted and

6 John Urry, *Mobilities.* Cambridge: Polity Press (2007), 136.

7 Mike Crang, 'Between places: producing hubs, flows, and networks', *Environment and Planning A* 34:4 (2002), 569–71.

8 E. Van Wagner, 'Toward a Dialectical Understanding of Networked Disease in the Global City: Vulnerability, Connectivity, Topologies', in S. Harris Ali and Roger Keil (eds), *Networked Disease: Emerging Infections in the Global City*. Malden, MA: Wiley Blackwell (2008), 25.

9 S. Harris Ali and Roger Keil, 'Global Cities and the Spread of Infectious Disease: The Spread of Severe Acute Respiratory Syndrome (SARS) in Toronto, Canada', *Urban Studies* 43:3 (2006), 505.

10 Ulrich Beck, *World at Risk.* Cambridge: Polity Press (2009), 177.

11 Ibid., 68.

12 Ibid., 199.

experienced precisely at aviation hubs of global cities like New York, London or Singapore. The September 11th hijackers hid themselves within otherwise innocuous aviation passenger flows passing through air hubs of global cities. This is why 'aviation security is a vital but under-studied component of contemporary security'.[13] The only answer to the shared global risks of terror which respects no boundaries or distance, Beck insists, is greater transnational cooperation.[14] But what roles can global cities and their aviation gateways play, as Beaverstock might say, in 'attending' to global aviation flows?

In terms of classifying global risks, if terrorist threats to aviation systems constitute what Beck calls an 'intentional' *destructive* catastrophe, then another global risk related to global aviation in the form of infectious diseases can be classed as more of a 'side-effect'[15] inadvertent catastrophe: it is *penetrative* and perpetuated as part of the day-to-day routine processes of globalisation. Beck writes that 'there can be no doubt that the swine-avian-human flu has long become a global domestic political phenomenon'.[16] An ostensibly global risk now has domestic implications given worldwide mobility and interconnectivity. Yet, Beck does not sufficiently relate 'globalised risk phenomena'[17] such as pandemics with literature on the aviation flows transiting global cities on a daily basis. Despite his claims that 'the anticipation of catastrophe is changing the world',[18] there has been scarce analysis of the reconfiguration of relationships as various stakeholders embedded within a global city's aviation sectors scramble to respond. Indeed, the oft-proposed solution to 'minimize the risks of globalization is through more global cooperation'.[19] Beck claims that a constant awareness of risks can trigger actions that can re-shape the world,[20] but how far is this apparent in the most exposed and vulnerable global cities with dense aviation links? In terms of the analytical framework premised on mobilities, flows, and global risks that this chapter develops, it is clear that 'the SARS virus represented another flow type that connected global cities'.[21] Diseases were also one of the mobilities cross-cutting cities that Stephen Graham warned of, threatening apparently unimaginable devastation. In a NATO study of the policy implications of Beck's works, diseases such as avian flu were pinpointed as an 'example of a nascent global risk that is already posing policy makers with a series of conundrums

13 Salter, 'Imagining Numbers', 254.

14 Beck, *World at Risk*, 41.

15 Ibid., 20.

16 Ulrich Beck, *Twenty Observations on a World in Turmoil*. Cambridge: Polity Press (2012), 49.

17 Ibid., 50.

18 Beck, *World at Risk*, 1.

19 Hung Hoo-Fung, 'The politics of SARS: containing the perils of globalization by more globalization' *Asian Perspective* 28:1 (2004), 19–44.

20 Beck, *World at Risk*, 10.

21 Ali and Keil, 'Introduction', 12.

exacerbated by the global movement of goods and people'.[22] Unfortunately, infectious diseases are the wrong 'bad' type of flow because they not only disrupt desirable 'good' trade and economic flows, but also generate massive social repercussions.[23] This is why SARS illustrates 'both the promise and the perils of globalisation'.[24] Both diseases and terrorism constitute risks from global aviation flows through global cities, but one should distinguish them carefully. The former is unintentional, *penetrative* and like terrorist financing, ironically depends on uninterrupted connectivity to circulate. The latter is *destructive*, predicated on targeting and disrupting aviation flows.

Aviation infrastructure presents thus yet another analytical lens to interrogate how global risks are transmitted and managed through global cities. Hence, the first section demonstrates how Beck's de-spatialised global risks of terrorism are both targeted at, and transmitted through the very aviation gateways that global cities bank their connectivity and prosperity on. The second part turns to how multiple stakeholders play crucial roles in ensuring there is minimal disruption to the circulation of global aviation flows through a global city. Just as a coalition of financial sector actors got together to minimise the risks of terrorist financing in the previous chapter, of utmost importance here are the airline industry, government regulatory and planning agencies, and airports that make up a global city's aviation sector. The challenge is that 'governments and authorities must continually reaffirm and re-establish their control over uncontrollable risks'.[25] Yet, new types of global risks, suggests Beck, have rendered conventional modes of regulation and management obsolete and ineffective.[26] Beck's claim that 'risk becomes the cause and medium of social transformation'[27] thus far remains overlooked, particularly how multi-level actors 'attend' to ensuring uninterrupted aviation flows through a global city's aviation hub. A global city's aviation connectivity does not automatically exist but, rather needs to be constantly enabled and reproduced by various actors on a daily basis.

Airports and Global Cities as Spaces of Aviation Flows

The basic starting premise for airline-based studies of global cities is something most laymen would recognise, that interactions and linkages between global cities

---

22 NATO Parliamentary Assembly Committee Report, 'Policy Implications of the Risk Society', 2005 <http://www.nato-pa.int/Default.asp?SHORTCUT=672> accessed 3 November 2012.

23 John Wyn Owen and Olivia Roberts, 'Globalisation, health and foreign policy: emerging linkages and interests', *Globalization and Health* 1:12 (2005), 3.

24 John T. Bowen and Christian Laroe, 'Airline networks and the international diffusion of severe acute respiratory syndrome (SARS)', *The Geographical Journal* 172:2 (2006), 142.

25 Beck, *World at Risk*, 117.

26 Ibid., 200.

27 Ibid., 16.

are being enhanced, enabled and shaped by transnational aviation flows.[28] Indeed, 'airports are developing into small-scale global cities in their own right, places to meet and do business, to sustain family life and friendship'.[29] Air passenger travel facilitates economic globalisation by bringing people and goods together, overcoming geographical constraints and national borders.[30] Airports are a form of global critical infrastructure because they provide 'global transit points' that process and circulate flows of masses of people, goods and information around the world. Airports are the key 'space of flows', especially hub airports located in major global cities'. Global airline flows, Keeling contends, offer the best illustration of transport's role in facilitating transnational inter-urban connectivity; air networks and their associated infrastructure are the most visible manifestation of inter-city interaction, and dense airline links underline a city's aspiration to global status.[31] Airports are of the key mechanisms for cities to enhance their positioning within the global urban hierarchy.[32] London, Hong Kong and Singapore compete to become key hubs for international air traffic flows. Particularly prized are non-stop air services to major global cities because this 'symbolises both the globalization of society and trade and the emergence of an information-based economy'.[33] Focusing on air linkages admittedly suffers from a range of data problems. For instance, only non-stop and scheduled direct flights between two cities are considered, elevating the importance of cities that are also air transit hubs without necessarily capturing the actual inter-city relations. Derudder et al. point out how data does not capture reasons *why* people visit a city: a city with high passenger flows from tourism and holidays does not necessarily mean it is a global city with global command functions.[34]

Nevertheless, relating to our analytical framework, airports as critical infrastructure have become central to the study of mobilities and flows. They are without a doubt, 'the space par-excellence of postmodern, post-national flows … mobilities from the body to the global pulse and circulate through and around the airport'.[35] Without international air travel, a whole range of mobilities that define and criss-cross the current globalised world, both good and bad, from

28 Ben Derudder, et al., 'Pathways of change: shifting connectivities in the world city network 2000–08', *Urban Studies* 47:9 (2010), 8.

29 Urry, *Mobilities*, 138.

30 Peter Rimmer, 'Transport and Telecommunications Among World Cities', in Fu-Chen Lo and Yue-man Yeung (eds), *Globalization and the World of Large Cities*. Tokyo: United Nations University Press (1998), 454.

31 David Keeling, 'Transport and the world city paradigm', in Paul Knox and Peter Taylor (eds), *World Cities in a World-System*. Cambridge: Cambridge University Press (1995), 118.

32 Urry, *Mobilities*, 142.

33 Keeling, 'Transport and the world city paradigm', 118.

34 Derudder et al., 'Pathways of change', 8.

35 Tim Creswell, *On the Move: Mobility in the Modern Western World*. London: Routledge (2006), 220.

holidaymaking, money laundering, business travel, drugs smuggling, diseases, arms trading, people smuggling and slave trading, would simply not exist.[36] To understand the points and nodes where these 'aero-mobilities'[37] are facilitated, 'of all the spaces of a globalised world, airports may be the most emblematic'.[38] Architect Hans Iberlings enthuses that the airport encapsulates the spirit of the age: mobility, accessibility, infrastructure and unlimited access to the world.[39]

Aerial Connectivity and Flows in Singapore's Global City Project

As with Singapore's financial core, an analytical framework premised on mobilities, flows, and infrastructure sensitises researchers to how global cities create critical infrastructure for attracting and circulating flows. Once again, the developmental state has played a central role in the careful development of Singapore's air hub. As its Minister for Transport explained, 'we have pursued a liberal air services policy aimed at facilitating greater people and trade flows. To date, Singapore has bilateral air services agreements with over 100 countries, of which over 40 are Open Skies agreements'.[40] 'Singapore could not have become the global city it is today without a good airport with superior air connectivity', insisted former Prime Minister Goh Chok Tong. 'Good air connectivity enhances our attractiveness as a global city, an international business centre and a manufacturing hub'.[41] Transport Minister Lui described aviation as a 'strategic pillar' and that 'strong air connectivity helps bring Singapore closer to the world and strengthens our position as a global city, a financial and business hub and a trading hub'.[42] Leading global aviation industry figures echo this view. Singapore is one of the Asian cities that 'get it' when it comes to 'using aviation as a critical part of their economic strategy', claimed International Air Transport Asssociation (IATA) CEO

36 Urry, *Mobilities*, 153.

37 Ibid., 155.

38 Crang, 'Between places', 571.

39 Hans Iberlings, *Supermodernism: Architecture in the Age of Globalization*. Rotterdam: NAi (1998), 78–9.

40 Lui Tuck Yew, 'Changi Airline Awards 2011' (speech, Shangri-la Hotel Singapore, 18 July 2011) <http://www.nas.gov.sg/archivesonline/speeches/record-details/813cd11f-115d-11e3-83d5-0050568939ad> accessed 19 July 2013.

41 Goh Chok Tong, 'Singapore Aviation Centennial Evening Dinner' (speech, Singapore, 16 March 2011) <http://www.pmo.gov.sg/content/pmosite/mediacentre/speechesninterviews/seniorminister/2011/March/Speech_by_Senior_Minister_Goh_Chok_Tong_at_the_Singapore_Aviation_Centennial_Evening_Dinner.html#.U4KneXKSySo> accessed 16 March 2013.

42 Lui Tuck Yew, 'Aviation Community Reception 2013' (speech at Avalon, Marina Bay Sands, 14 May 2013) <http://www.news.gov.sg/public/sgpc/en/media_releases/agencies/mot/speech/S-20130514–1> accessed 15 December 2013.

Tony Tyler.[43] Using a liberal bilateral and multilateral air services policy, airline policy and massive investments in airport infrastructure to grow its aviation links, this emphasis has in most part paid dividends for Singapore's global city credentials. In 1995, Keeling concluded that within East Asia, 'Singapore controls connectivity with 831 non-stop flights each week serving 39 cities, more than twice as many flights and cities served than Tokyo'.[44] In his 1998 analysis, Rimmer concluded that using 'top-25' city-pair rankings in international air passenger movements, Singapore was one of only nine cities worldwide deemed worthy of being called an aviation hub.[45] By 2000, Singapore was ranked by Matsumoto in the first tier in terms of international airport traffic, together with Tokyo, London and New York. Based on a gravity model (composed of GDP, population and distance between city-pairs) to examine the 'hubness' of a city, Singapore was found to be a key hub in terms of international air traffic flows, and furthermore, as a trans-shipment hub for the Asian region, there was also high density for air cargo, not just passengers.[46] All these goes to show that 'the more links a node has, the more accessible and interconnected it is'.[47] How air freight hubs, besides passenger terminals, also confer connectivity has been under-studied.[48] Singapore's focus on growing its cargo hub provides a useful example.

For Urry, airports are de rigueur for global cities seeking to position themselves within a global order characterised by global flows and mobilities.[49] Singapore's Changi airport is highly ranked in terms of passenger comfort as one of the world's top 10 most loved airports for being 'the place that re-invented what airports can be'.[50] It has won numerous accolades, including Skytrax World's Best Airport award in 2014 (for the fifth time) and 'Top Worldwide Airport' from Wanderlust (for the twelfth time), the 'Best International Airport Award' from Condé Nast Traveller, and 'Best Airport in the World' from Business Traveller UK magazine for 27 times

43 Cited in Civil Aviation Authority of Singapore (CAAS), 'Bridging Skies: toward sustainable growth', February 2012 <http://www.bridgingskies.com/wp-content/uploads/2012/09/Bridging%20Skies%20Print%20-%20Feb%202012.pdf> accessed 7 July 2012.

44 Keeling, 'Transport and the world city paradigm', 123.

45 Rimmer, 'Transport and Telecommunications Among World Cities', 462.

46 Hidenobu Matsumoto, 'International air network structures and air traffic density of world cities', *Transportation Research Part E* 43 (2007), 274, 280. Also see Hidenobu Matsumoto, 'International urban systems and air passenger and cargo flows: some calculations', *Journal of Air Transport Management* 10 (2004), 241–9.

47 Guilherme Lohmann, et al., 'From hub to tourist destination – an explorative study of Singapore and Dubai's aviation-based transformation', *Journal of Air Transport Management* 15 (2009), 205.

48 Rimmer, 'Transport and Telecommunications Among World Cities', 444.

49 Urry, *Mobilities*, 142.

50 Jordan Rane, '10 of the world's most loved airports', CNNGo, 17 November 2011 <http://www.cnngo.com/explorations/life/10-most-loved-airports-981939?page=0,1> accessed 8 April 2012.

between 1988 and 2014. Comfort aside, it is reliable air connectivity that underpins Singapore's global city status. This is why the International Federation of Airline Pilots Associations (IFALPA) voted Changi in 2014 as a 'Deficiency-Free Airport' for the thirty-third time. Changi Airport Group has an Executive Vice President of Air Hub Development tasked to enhance connectivity and viability of air linkages. This ambition is shared by the Civil Aviation authority of Singapore whose avowed vision is to be '*A leader in civil aviation; a city connecting the world*'.[51]

Recent numbers show that this ambition is within reach. Just 10 years ago, Changi was linked to 139 cities in 50 countries. As at 25 November 2014, 106 airlines operate at Changi Airport, connecting Singapore to more than 300 cities in around 70 countries and territories around the world.[52] In 2011, passenger traffic at Changi airport grew 11 per cent to reach a new high of 46.5 million, and the aerospace sector had a record 7.9 billion worth of output in repair, maintenance and overhaul of aircraft parts.[53] For Singaporean leaders, Changi's air connectivity is intrinsic to global city status: 'For Singapore to maintain its position as a vibrant global city, Changi must work hard to stay ahead'.[54] In March 2012, Changi recorded the largest number of passengers travelling in March for 31 years. Taken together, these dense air linkages reflect 'the connectivity of Singapore with major cities and markets around the world'.[55] With more than 6,400 weekly scheduled flights, an aircraft takes off or lands at Changi roughly once every 100 seconds. For the first half of 2012, Changi Airport handled 25.0 million passengers, an increase of 11.6 per cent compared to the corresponding period in 2011. In first half of 2014, it handled 26.608 million passenger movements, 1.4 per cent more than a year before.[56] There were 26,700 landings and take-offs at Changi during June 2012, a growth of 6.4 per cent year-on-year. In December 2012, Changi marked a new milestone by welcoming 50 million passengers in a calendar year. This was all the more remarkable, given that this new record was achieved less than two years after the 40 million-passengers hurdle was cleared in 2010. The figures climbed to a new record 53.7 million travellers for 2013. Monthly and

---

51 Civil Aviation Authority Singapore (CAAS), 'Empowering Growth in Singapore Aviation', Annual Report 2010/2011, 1.

52 Changi Airport Singapore, 'Air Traffic Statistics', 25 Nov 2014 <http://www.changiairportgroup.com/cag/html/the-group/air_traffic_statistics.html> accessed 1 Jan 2015.

53 Karamjit Kaur, '5m fund to help aviation firms expand reach overseas', *The Straits Times*, 29 May 2012, B2.

54 Josephine Teo, 'Ministry of Finance Committee of Supply' (speech, Singapore, 7 March 2014) <http://app.mof.gov.sg/newsroom_details.aspx?type=speech&cmpar_year=2014&news_sid=20140307334420702206> accessed 7 April 2014.

55 Oxford Economics, 'Economic Benefits from Air Transport in Singapore', 2011 <http://www.benefitsofaviation.aero/Documents/Benefits-of-Aviation-Singapore-2011.pdf> accessed 23 April 2012, 8.

56 Changi Airport Group, 'Monthly breakdown of passenger movements', 23 July 2014 <http://www.changiairportgroup.com/cag/html/the-group/passenger_movement.html> accessed 13 August 2014.

daily records are tumbling. In December 2013, the airport handled 5.12 million customers, the first time it had processed more than 5 million travellers within a month. The daily record was also shattered on Saturday 21 December 2013, with 191,800 passengers and 1,100 flights facilitated during the 24 hours. At peak times, an aircraft lands or departs every minute. This is why former Head of Civil Service Peter Ho claimed that 'Singapore is one of the three most important centres of global air travel today'.[57] Indeed, an IATA-sponsored study in 2009 found that further liberalisation policies could increase passenger traffic by 5.5 million people, an increase of 21 per cent from 2007 levels.[58] This does not include connecting passengers transiting via Singapore.

Like Amsterdam's Schiphol airport which is 'an extremely successful node in a global network',[59] the local population in Singapore could never sustain such a large and well-connected airport. Changi is more likely to serve as a hub or connecting transit point between Asia and the rest of the world.[60] Aviation networks consist of a set of links (e.g. air routes) and nodes or hubs (terminals and interchanges) which are connected. Hubs and gateway airports capitalise on their key position and connectedness in the network because the large numbers of transiting air traffic flows passing through a hub are a lucrative market. Singapore has managed to attract large numbers of passengers who are on transit, whilst travelling on long-haul routes between Europe, Asia and the Pacific.[61] Announcing plans in September 2013 for a fifth terminal at Changi, Senior Minister of State for Transport Josephine Teo stressed 'super-connectivity' because 'the more cities that we are linked to, the more frequent the flights, and the more efficient the transfers, the greater the convenience that we can offer the passengers and the better we are as an air hub'.[62]

Singapore has become a global city and aviation hub, as predicted by S. Rajaratnam who noted in 1972: 'We are also linked to other global cities by

57 Peter Ho, 'Strategic Perspectives Conference' (speech, Singapore, 4 September 2006) <http://www.mfa.gov.sg/content/mfa/overseasmission/washington/newsroom/press_statements/2006/200609/press_200609_01.html> accessed 5 October 2012.

58 InterVistas-EU Consulting on behalf of IATA, 'Impact of international air service liberalisation on Singapore', July 2009 <http://www.iata.org/SiteCollectionDocuments/Documents/SingaporeReport.pdf> accessed 14 March 2011.

59 Creswell, *On the Move*, 234.

60 John Rennie Short and Kim Yeong Hyun, *Globalisation and the City*. London: Longman (1999), 44.

61 Guilherme Lohmann, et al., 'From hub to tourist destination – an explorative study of Singapore and Dubai's aviation-based transformation', 205–6.

62 Cited in Ministry of Transport, Singapore, 'Changi developments to open path to new opportunities', 31 August 2013 <http://app.mot.gov.sg/News_Centre/Latest_News/NewsID/1921B0000710A733/Changi_Developments_To_Open_Path_To_New_Opportunities.aspx> accessed 30 November 2013, and *TODAY*, 'New Changi Airport can handle 135m passengers', *TODAYonline*, 31 August 2013 <http://www.todayonline.com/singapore/new-changi-airport-can-handle-135m-passengers> accessed 7 September 2013.

air. In 1970 there were over 17,000 landings at our airport- almost treble what it was in 1960'.[63] The desire to expand Singapore's air connectivity is relentless. Changi currently operates on a two-runway system, just like London's Heathrow airport – touted to be the world's busiest dual-runway airport. A 2012 study by the UK's National Air traffic system, commissioned by the Civil Aviation Authority of Singapore concluded that Changi has the potential to handle up to 430,000 aircraft movements annually, about 90 per cent of Heathrow's capacity. In 2013, it was announced that Changi will have access to a third runway in 2020, currently used by the military, in order for it cope with increasing passenger flows.

With Changi already a leading commercial airline hub, the Changi Airport Group (CAG) together with the Civil Aviation Authority of Singapore (CAAS) and the Singapore Government have focused on enhancing business aviation, air cargo and aerospace industries. The aerospace industry has expanded by an average rate of 10 per cent in the last two decades. In 2012, the aerospace industry achieved a record output of SGD$8.7 billion. The number of people employed in the aerospace industry Singapore stood at over 19,900 in 2012. Ninety per cent of the jobs in the industry are skilled jobs. As former Prime Minister Goh emphasised, 'Aviation is now an integral part of our economy, contributing over 3% to Singapore's GDP in direct value-add. As an enabler of people and business connections, aviation has a far reaching impact on the economy and society. Through aviation, Singapore is connected to the international networks of enterprise, talent and ideas'.[64] A study by Oxford Economics in 2011 found that the aviation sector contributed SGD$14.2 billion, or 5.2 per cent of Singaporean GDP for the calendar year 2009.[65] Rolls Royce's SGD$700million investment in facilities in Singapore demonstrated the interest of global players. Prime Minister Lee, who opened the facility, reiterated that 'we depend on global connectivity to thrive, and aviation helps to connect Singapore to the wide world. It enhances our position as a global city, as an international business centre, and as a trading hub … we must improve the connectivity of our aviation hub as this is a self-reinforcing advantage'.[66] The Singapore Air Show is now a significant aerospace event in Asia, and close to the likes of Farnborough and Paris. Airbus' communications director for Asia said this

63 S. Rajaratnam, 'Singapore: global city' (speech to the Singapore Press Club, 6 February 1972) <http://newshub.nus.edu.sg/news/1202/PDF/GLOBAL-st-6feb-pA17.pdf> accessed 7 February 2012.

64 Goh Chok Tong, 'Singapore Aviation Centennial Evening Dinner' (speech, Singapore, 16 March 2011) <http://www.pmo.gov.sg/content/pmosite/mediacentre/speechesninterviews/seniorminister/2011/March/Speech_by_Senior_Minister_Goh_Chok_Tong_at_the_Singapore_Aviation_Centennial_Evening_Dinner.html#.U4KneXKSySo> accessed 16 March 2013.

65 Oxford Economics, 'Economic Benefits from Air Transport in Singapore', 3.

66 Lee Hsien Loong, 'Opening of Rolls-Royce Seletar Campus' (speech, Singapore, 13 February 2012) <http://www.pmo.gov.sg/content/pmosite/mediacentre/speechesninterviews/primeminister/2012/February/speech_by_prime_ministerleehsienloongattheopeningoftherolls-royc.html#.U4KsAXKSySo> accessed 14 February 2013.

had become 'the most important event on the air show calendar in the Asia-Pacific region'.[67] 'Singapore is a global aviation hub in the Asia Pacific region, widely considered to be the most promising market for the aerospace industry worldwide', stated US Department of Commerce Assistant Secretary Nicole Lamb.[68] Mega deals were completed at the 2012 air show: Indonesia's Lion Air agreed to buy 230 new 737-model aircraft from Boeing, totalling USD$21.7 billion, the largest commercial deal in company history. Boeing's president of South-east Asia operations, Ralph Boyce stated that 'Singapore as an aviation hub is positioned to tap into the opportunities that increased air travel present'.[69] The Singapore pavilion, comprising 30 home-grown companies in the 2014 air show carried the tagline: 'Singapore: Heart of Aviation'. The brand was developed by the Civil Aviation Authority of Singapore (CAAS) because it 'reflects the aspirations of the Singapore aviation community and their continuing determination to reinforce Singapore as a premier aviation hub'.[70] The 2014 air show attracted more than 1,000 companies from 50 countries.

The Working Group on Logistics of the Ministry of Trade and Industry visualised how Singapore should become a 'regional aviation hub with high connectivity and capacity, and state-of-the-art logistics and support capacities'.[71] The goal is to achieve a 'multimodal hub' built on extensive maritime and air connectivity. Here, we can see very clearly how the relevance of an analytical framework premised on the developmental state; mobilities, flows and connectivity applies closely to the case of Singapore's global city ambitions. The report goes on to state that 'to attract multimodal transport and logistics operators and maximize the potential of our air and sea links to entice more goods to flow through Singapore, we should enhance our multimodal connectivity, even as we continue to improve our air and sea connectivity'.[72]

---

67 Cited in *The Sunday Times*, 'Soaring to new heights', *The Sunday Times*, 9 February 2014, special on 'Singapore Airshow 2014' <http://business.asiaone.com/news/soaring-new-heights> accessed 18 April 2014, 16.

68 Guest blog on the U.S. Department of Commerce Website, 'Leading the way for US aerospace companies at the Singapore Air Show', 17 February 2012 <http://www.commerce.gov/blog/2012/02/17/leading-way-us-aerospace-companies-singapore-air-show> accessed 15 January 2013.

69 Cited in *The Sunday Times*, 'Key aviation hub', *The Sunday Times,* 11 February 2014, Special on 'Singapore Airshow 2014' <http://business.asiaone.com/news/key-aviation-hub> accessed 19 April 2014, 22.

70 Cited in *The Sunday Times*, 'Connected to the world', *The Sunday Times*, 9 February 2014, Special on 'Singapore Airshow 2014', accessed 20 April 2014, 22.

71 Ministry of Trade and Industry Singapore, 'Report of the Working Group on Logistics, Developing Singapore into a Global Integrated Logistics Hub', September 2002 <http://www.mti.gov.sg/ResearchRoom/Documents/app.mti.gov.sg/data/pages/507/doc/ERC_SVSLOG_MainReport.pdf> accessed 5 October 2012.

72 Ibid., 16.

Inadvertent Negative Penetrative Flows: Infectious Diseases

Aviation connectivity however exposes global cities to global risks that swirl around Beck's *World Risk Society.* The notion that infectious diseases represent a global risk is hardly new.[73] What is novel is the pace and aviation infrastructure through which it spreads. As the World Economic Forum's *Global Risk Report 2014* observed, 'perhaps the oldest form of systemic risk is that arising from viruses and pandemics, a threat that has entered a dangerous new phase as people and goods move at increasing speeds and over greater distances, with many passing through a small number of airports and other hubs'.[74] Such global risks can be categorised as un-attributable, inadvertent and negative penetrative flows that spread ironically because of the efficiency of critical aviation hubs processing aviation flows. High levels of aviation connectivity explain why Singapore ranked Number 1 on the list of places at 'Extreme Risk' on the Influenza Pandemic Risk Index compiled by the consultancy Maplecroft in 2012. Such hyper-connected cities are also 'where an outbreak would probably hit, where the international airports are'.[75] Such fears materialised in 2003, when a viral respiratory illness associated with a newly discovered virus (Severe Acute Respiratory Syndrome-CoV), produced symptoms such as high fever and flu-like illness. The SARS pandemic took 813 lives and infected 8,427 people worldwide. Spread through large droplets, infection occurs from close contact with infected persons. The index case for outbreaks in Hong Kong, Vietnam, Canada, and Singapore all traced back to a Chinese doctor from Guangdong Province who travelled to Hong Kong with a fever after treating patients suffering from serious atypical pneumonia.[76] Described as the 'first epidemic of the Internet Age' unfolding over cyber space in real time as millions around the globe watched in trepidation,[77] SARS also epitomised the age of 'globalised insecurity'[78] as events unfolding in distant parts threw the world into collective panic. This particularly illustrates Beck's claim that 'damage loses its spatio-temporal limits and becomes global and lasting'.[79]

---

73 See, for instance, Stefan Elbe, 'Microbes take to the sky: pandemic threats and national security' in Stefan Elbe, *Security and Global Health: Toward the Medicalization of Insecurity*. Cambridge: Polity Press (2000), 30–65.

74 World Economic Forum, 'Global Risks Report 2014 'Risks in Focus', <http://reports.weforum.org/global-risks-2014/part-2-risks-in-focus/2-1-introduction-understanding-global-systemic-risk/> accessed 24 June 2014.

75 World Health Organization Official, cited in S. Harris Ali and Roger Keil, 'Securitising networked flows', 97.

76 David P. Fidler, *SARS: Governance and the Globalization of Disease*. New York: Palgrave Macmillan (2004), 82.

77 Asad Latif, 'Singapore: Surviving the Downside of Globalisation', in Daljit Singh and Chin Kin Wah (eds), *Southeast Asian Affairs 2004*. Singapore: ISEAS (2004), 226.

78 Michael Fitzpatrick, 'Apocalypse from Now On', Spiked Online, 25 April 2003 <http://www.spiked-online.com/articles/00000006DD71.htm> accessed 8 April 2011.

79 Ulrich Beck, *World Risk Society*. Cambridge: Polity Press, 36.

Airports may be highly prized for global cities but for Harris and Keil, they are also 'where the risks of social and technological interactions of global capitalism manifest themselves in the so-called risk society ... In the global city system, airports play a specifically important role in the 'mobility stream' of disease'.[80] Ominously, the WHO considered every city with an international airport at risk.[81] Exponentially increasing levels of travel and trade connections means a globally connected city will in all likelihood be hit first.[82] Seen as bestowing global city status, 'airports are where different global flows converge'.[83] The problem is they also facilitate import of unwanted microbes on the back of 'normal' aviation flows.

The SARS episode illustrated how global risks imperil global cities because of their connectivity. Toronto's global connectivity was once viewed positively for those seeking transnational capital investments but the SARS case was a reminder of how connectivity also entailed vulnerabilities.[84] The qualities of greater interconnectivity, diversity and population congregation in a 'global city' are also the very same conditions that render it most vulnerable to imported pandemics: 'As no two airports in the world are more than 36 hours apart, airports become "interchanges" in disease transmission and spread'.[85] This perfectly typifies the misgivings scholars such as Graham have raised about mobilities and circulations: the need to ensure desirable flows continue to transit a global city while filtering out undesirable flows such as infectious diseases.

Transmitting De-spatialised Global Risks: Airlines and Global Cities' Air Hubs

While acknowledging the de-spatialised aspects of pandemics, Beck did not concern himself particularly with transmission mechanisms, or the wider literature on global cities and their command of flows and mobilities. Yet, global risks are having a disproportionately large impact on global cities – a connection Beck does not make explicitly. The fact that severe SARS outbreaks occurred in other global cities such as Singapore not only raised questions about how linkages with other global cities shaped transmission,[86] it also dramatically highlights the shared nature of global risks that global cities face. What was known as a 'super-

80 Ali and Keil, 'Securitising networked flows', 109.

81 Cited in Lawrence O. Gostin, et al., 'Ethical and legal challenges posed by SARS: implications for the control of severe infectious disease threats', *Journal of the American Medical Association* 290 (2003), 3229–37.

82 Vernon J. Lee et al., 'Influenza pandemics in Singapore, a tropical, globally connected city', *Historical Review* 13:7 (2007), 1052–7.

83 Ali and Keil, 'Securitising networked flows', 110.

84 Brenner and Keil, 'Editors' Introduction', in Neil Brenner and Roger Keil (eds), *The Global Cities Reader*. London: Routledge (2006), 4.

85 Wagner, 'Toward a Dialectical Understanding of Networked Disease in the Global City', 15.

86 Ali and Keil, 'Global Cities and the Spread of Infectious Disease', 491.

spreading' event highlighted the dangers of connectivity through aviation flows. At the Hotel Metropole in Hong Kong, a guest spread the disease to other guests from all over the world. These guests took the disease home with them on their airline flights.[87] This is why Singapore's Ministry of Home Affairs warned that 'in today's highly interconnected world, the spread of infectious diseases has emerged as a significant challenge to global security. If a pandemic occurs, millions of people could fall ill or die'.[88]

Indeed, for Harris and Keil point out, SARS illustrated the close uncomfortable link between global cities and spread of diseases in the age of globalisation.[89] The SARS epidemic had close symbiotic relationships with global aviation as airports and airlines were instrumental in spreading the disease.[90] Given how rapid and large flows of people around the world are creating new global vectors of disease spread, global cities can now serve as key transmission nodes for contagion.[91] The outbreak did not occur in cities of the underdeveloped (or more crucially, under-connected) Global South, rather it surfaced in the most connected global cities such as Beijing, Hong Kong, Toronto and Singapore.[92] The air hubs that global cities depend on so much for their prosperity proved to be an Achilles heel.[93]

The abilities of global cities' airports to circulate global aviation flows here is paramount to understanding disease transmission: 'Cities, now more than ever, play an important role in the distribution of disease, because under the conditions of globalization, they serve as ever-dynamic hubs in the intensified flow of people'.[94] The fact that transport networks facilitate disease is not new but the pace and speed is much faster today, particularly in the jet age. As Elbe notes, the accelerating rates of air travel globally drive this 'renewed microbial anxiety'.[95] Improvements in mobility as a result of improving transport technology have important implications for the spread of disease.[96] Shortening travel times can mean sick patients arrive at their destinations more infectious than they would be if their travel had taken longer. This is called epidemiological isolation of distance.[97] Or they might be infectious but not yet manifesting symptoms. Given

87 Bowen and Laroe, 'Airline networks and the international diffusion of severe acute respiratory syndrome (SARS)', 132.

88 Ministry of Home Affairs, 'Preparing for a Human Influenza Pandemic in Singapore', 2009 <http://app.crisis.gov.sg/Data/Documents/H1N1/NSFP.pdf> accessed 8 January 2010, 1.

89 Ali and Keil, 'Introduction: Networked Disease', 1.

90 Ibid., 99.

91 Short, *Global Metropolitan*, 127.

92 Ali and Keil, 'Securitising networked flows', 99.

93 Harvey Rubin, *Future Global Shocks: Pandemics*. Paris: OECD (2011), 27.

94 Ali and Keil, 'Introduction: Networked Disease', 3.

95 Elbe, 'Microbes take to the sky', 31.

96 J.D. Mayer, 'The surveillance and control of emerging infectious diseases', *Applied Geographical Studies* 2:4 (1998), 261–78.

97 A.D. Cliff et al., *Island Epidemics*. New York: Oxford University Press (1998).

their air hubs and dense air linkages and how the aviation system is currently structured, these disease carriers at some point will usually arrive at global cities first. Globalisation and the jet age means that microbes are no longer restricted to remote forests or rare reservoir species.[98] As Bowen and Laroe observe, SARS ironically spread much faster overseas than into the interior of China.[99] SARS spread globally through global cities, thanks to jet airliners.

One eye-catching dimension then of the SARS epidemic was how airline networks facilitated disease spread.[100] Airline network *accessibility* affected the spatial-temporal spread of the disease. Accessibility from those cities that were infected by SARS, and its connectivity by air links to other cities was mapped using IATA airline schedules. This measure was regarded as 'determinants of the speed with which SARS arrived in infected countries as well as its failure to arrive in most countries'.[101] For Bowen and Laroe, the central relationship of being connected by air and air transport network accessibility is measured by the IATA's publication, the global transport connectivity monitor.[102] This methodology comprises the number of scheduled flights among cities and via connections and intermediate hubs. Bowen and Laroe conclude that 'scheduled airline services can be conceptualized as possible pathways for disease diffusion, with greater frequency and directness of services among some cities facilitating the ease of movement for an infectious disease'.[103]

Preceding discussions about airline links transmitting global pandemic risks have deep resonance for Singapore: a global city that faced SARS in 2003 and H1N1 swine flu in 2009. Health Minister Khaw touched on the repeated challenges of global disease risks because 'after fighting against SARS in 2003, many of us in this room hoped that we would not have to fight another war against a novel virus. But H1N1 came along'.[104] Lee et al. argue that this unpleasant fact is down to connectivity and openness: 'Globally connected cities will be especially vulnerable to a future pandemic, and preparedness plans must be developed to include the megacities of the tropical world. The 20th-century pandemics swept through Singapore within 4 weeks'.[105] SARS killed 33 people

98 L. Garrett, *The Coming Plague: Newly Emerging Diseases in a World out of Balance*. New York: Farrar, Straus and Giroux (1994), 571.

99 Bowen and Laroe, 'Airline networks and the international diffusion of severe acute respiratory syndrome (SARS)', 140.

100 Ibid., 130.

101 Ibid.

102 International Air Transport Association (IATA), 'One Stop Security' <http://www.iata.org/whatwedo/safety_security/security/Pages/one-stop.aspx> accessed 9 December 2012.

103 Bowen and Laroe, 'Airline networks and the international diffusion of severe acute respiratory syndrome (SARS)', 133.

104 Khaw Boon Wan, 'A Tale of Two Wars' (speech, The National Medical Excellence Awards Ceremony, 22 July 2009).

105 Lee et al., 'Influenza Pandemics in Singapore', 1057.

out of 238 people who were infected in Singapore.[106] In June 2009, the WHO declared the H1N1 outbreak as a global 'pandemic'. Global city Singapore thus encapsulates the spread and impact of a global risk in Beck's *World Risk Society* because 'for urban centres with high population density and global connectivity' there is greater transmission potential in terms of speed and rate of infection.[107] Singapore fit these two criteria to a T: one of the most densely populated cities in the world with deep global connectivity.

When the first case of SARS was introduced into Singapore by a traveller returning from Hong Kong in 2003, SARS caused a huge demand shock. The service sector suffered as a result of decreasing numbers of travellers and consumer spending.[108] The economy grew only 1.1 per cent in 2003, compared to its neighbours' average rate of 4.5 per cent. Again, the notion of flows and mobilities being disrupted explains how Singapore as a global city was affected: 'SARS dramatized Singapore's vulnerability to sudden fluctuations in the global movement of goods and people'.[109] The aviation sector was hard-hit. Changi Airport Group (CAG) haemorrhaged about SGD$5–SGD$6 million dollars per day and a total of SGD$312 million losses during the first quarter of 2003 at the height of SARS. Over the period, Singapore Airlines (SIA) recovered its first quarter losses through several measures ranging from retrenchment to aggressive marketing.[110] Between April and May 2003, the company lost USD$3m a day as air passenger numbers plunged.[111] The crisis was described by SIA's chief executive as its 'worst-ever'.[112] Ten airlines suspended operations into Changi Airport. From first quarter growth in 2003 of 1.7 per cent, Singapore's economy suffered a -4.2 per cent reverse in the second quarter. The services sector which accounts for 65.7 per cent of Singapore's Gross Domestic Product (GDP) dropped by 3.9 per cent in

106 K.U. Menon and K.T. Goh, 'Transparency and trust: risk communications and the Singapore experience in managing SARS', *Journal of Communication Management* 9:4 (2005), 33.

107 Sadasivan, Balaji. 'Opening Ceremony of the Global Outbreak Alert and Response Network Steering Committee Meeting' (speech, Singapore, 7 December 2005) <http://www.moh.gov.sg/content/moh_web/home/pressRoom/speeches_d/2005/opening_ceremony_of_the_global_outbreak_alert_and_response_network_steering_committee_meeting.html> accessed 8 December 2013.

108 Grace O.M. Lee and Malcolm Warner, 'Singapore: a case study', in Grace Lee and Malcolm Warner (eds), *The Political Economy of the SARS Epidemic: The Impact on Human Resources in East Asia*. London: Routledge (2008), 131.

109 Latif, 'Singapore: Surviving the Downside of Globalisation', 228.

110 Singapore International Airlines (SIA), 'Annual Report' (2003/2004) <http://www.singaporeair.com/pdf/Investor-Relations/Annual-Report/annualreport0304.pdf> accessed 10 August 2014, 41.

111 BBC News, 'Singapore Airlines staff accept pay cut', 3 July 2003 <http://news.bbc.co.uk/2/hi/business/3042310.stm> accessed 23 November 2012.

112 BBC News, 'Singapore Air in worst-ever crisis', 21 May 2003 <http://news.bbc.co.uk/2/hi/business/3047203.stm> accessed 23 November 2012.

the second quarter of the year 2003.[113] A quarantine was imposed on air travellers who left Singapore and re-entered the global city from a SARS inflicted country. This interruption to 'normal' desirable passenger traffic and connectivity was a complete catastrophe for an airport that craved ever-increasing aviation flows.[114] Between 22 and 28 April 2003, visitor arrivals plummeted by 74 per cent on the same period the previous year.[115]

Equating SARS with another global risk of terrorism, former Defence Minister Tony Tan called SARS 'Singapore's September 11th'.[116] SARS became 'the defining metaphor of a people under global siege'.[117] A global city was face to face with a global risk in the *World Risk Society*. Prime Minister Lee recognises that Singapore's connectivity brings greater exposure to risks: 'we are vulnerable to trans-national diseases, because we are so highly connected to the rest of the world'.[118] In March 2013, speaking at the 10th anniversary of the SARS outbreak, Health Minister Gan reiterated the vulnerabilities for Singapore as a global city thriving on connectivity: 'in our highly globalised world, where cities are well connected by air travel, the transmission of infectious diseases has become much harder to control. There is a real risk of epidemics or outbreak of a new infectious disease spreading to Singapore, given our global connectivity'.[119]

Once a global city becomes central to global flows and mobilities, this also translates into vulnerability to global risks and potential disruption to those flows. Again, an analytical framework attuned to the notion of flows and circulations reveals how Singapore was affected. The permanent secretary at the Ministry of Health explained vulnerability as a factor of its ability to circulate flows, 'Singapore is a trading and talent hub, a crossroads in the middle of Asia, where people and goods flow in and out of the country constantly. We are also right in the midst of a region which is largely expected to be ground zero for the next pandemic'.[120] Diseases also

113 Lee and Warner, 'Singapore: a case study', 91.

114 Ibid., 94.

115 BBC News, 'SARS deters Singapore visitors', 5 May 2003 <http://news.bbc.co.uk/2/hi/business/3001717.stm> accessed 14 October 2012.

116 Cited in *Guardian*, 'SARS: global death toll tops 630', 19 May 2003 <http://www.guardian.co.uk/world/2003/may/19/china.sars> accessed 8 April 2010.

117 Latif, 'Singapore: surviving the downsides of globalisation', 226.

118 Lee Hsien Loong, 'Singapore Medical Association's 50th Anniversary Dinner on Saturday' (speech, Singapore, 16 May 2009) <http://www.pmo.gov.sg/ ... /speechesninterviews/primeminister/ ... /speech_by_mrleehsienloongprimeministeratsingaporemedicalassocia.html> accessed 17 May 2012.

119 Gan Kim Yong, 'Remembering SARS: 10 years on' (speech, Singapore, 20 March 2013) <http://www.moh.gov.sg/content/moh_web/home/pressRoom/speeches_d/2013/speech-by-minister-for-health-gan-kim-yong--at-tan-tock-seng-hos.html> accessed 21 March 2014.

120 Yong Ying-I., 'Developing a Regional Infectious Disease Hub' (speech by Ministry of Health Permanent Secretary, Singapore, 21 March 2009) <https://www.moh.gov.sg/content/moh_web/home/pressRoom/speeches_d/2009/developing_a_regional_infectious_disease_hub.html> accessed 10 August 2014.

have knock-on effects on other flows, generating likely disruption to the global flows that are coordinated and commanded by a global city: 'Due to its global nature, a pandemic will likely impact the flow of goods in and out of Singapore'.[121] This is because 'disease affects the operations of businesses locally and internationally, supply chains, flow of goods worldwide and provision of services'.[122] Air hubs which once served as gateways to the world for global cities like Singapore, now turned into portals for the importation of global risks. The SARS disease disrupted passenger and business flows emanating to and from Singapore. Singapore is a key source of investment and managerial expertise for China but the number of passengers leaving Singapore for China was down nearly 90 per cent in May 2003, compared to a year earlier.[123] The total human cost was almost a thousand deaths and the financial cost was estimated at nearly USD$40 billion for the Asia-Pacific region.[124]

The SARS crisis demonstrated that the networked relationships of global cities in contemporary globalisation are not just about global capital flows and human mobility – they are also about rapid and undetected viral transmission.[125] The rate, pace and scale of travel between Singapore to other cities worldwide explains the pace in which infectious diseases can be transmitted from one locality to another without being noticed since the incubation period of infectious diseases is between two to ten days duration.[126] This is what happened whereby three infected Singaporeans returned home without any clear indication of infection, only to trigger concerns from local authorities two weeks after the first case was defined as SARS. The connection between the local and regional, local and global demonstrates how a disease that starts 'elsewhere' in the world has severe implications on Singapore the global city.

Deliberate Negative Destructive Flows: Global Terrorism and Aviation Security

If *penetrative* infectious diseases are especially hard to attribute in terms of human causality and responsibility, another global risk that air gateways of global cities face is more *destructive*, intentional and deliberate: global terrorism. The events of September 11th, argued Beck, revealed not only 'the vulnerability of

121 Ministry of Home Affairs, Singapore, 'Preparing for a Human Influenza Pandemic in Singapore', 37.

122 Ibid., 15.

123 Civil Aviation Authority of Singapore (CAAS), 'Air Transport Statistic', May 2002 and May 2003.

124 Michael T. Osterholm, 'Preparing for the next pandemic', *Foreign Affairs*, July/August 2004 <http://www.foreignaffairs.com/articles/60818/michael-t-osterholm/preparing-for-the-next-pandemic> accessed 10 August 2014, 24–37.

125 Wagner, 'Toward a Dialectical Understanding of Networked Disease in the Global City', 14.

126 Ali and Keil, 'Global Cities and the Spread of Infectious Disease', 498–9.

western civilisation' but also 'the kind of conflicts that economic globalization can lead to'.[127] A global city like New York, for Kurt Campbell, also served as a prime symbol of globalisation, with its cosmopolitan population and 24-hours operations reaching every part of the world. Its air hubs also reflected many of the vulnerabilities in the global aviation network, such as just-in-time delivery of air packages and curbside-check in; freer immigration policies that arise from the very efficiencies demanded by globalisation's impetus for productivity and circulating global flows.[128] Hijackers from distant parts of the world – Saudi Arabia, Egypt, UAE – exploited air connectivity to reach the US for flight training. On September 11th, without disguising their names or identities, they slipped through the massive passenger flows going through New York's air hub on any given day. Air connectivity, as we have seen with SARS, also doubles as the transmission mechanism for de-spatialised global terrorism risks in Beck's *World Risk Society*. One crucial difference however, is that these terrorists *deliberately* seek to wreak havoc and massive disruption to aviation flows.

Using our analytical framework based on infrastructure, mobilities, and flows, September 11th's impact can be seen in terms of the disruption caused: 'terrorism has literally thrown a spanner into global trade flows and added considerable friction to the wheels of the global economy'.[129] Whereas pandemics are more inadvertently spread, terrorists purposefully target critical infrastructure in the aviation network to inflict economic destruction and chaos because 'civil aviation is an important economic enabler, facilitating trade, tourism, business and travel'.[130] This is one reason why 'the airline and air industry continues to be a prime target for terrorists … airlines are a special target' according to the Head of Interpol Roland Noble.[131] For a global city like Singapore that survives off greasing the wheels of global trade, any friction or disruption creates negative impact, as we shall see. Air hubs are targeted for their symbolic value and also because a successful attack could severely snarl aviation flows. Researchers at RAND Corporation have shown how terrorists understand that cascading effects and crippling disruptions to complex interdependent networks (such as financial centres, tourism and airline industries) can result from attacks on critical infrastructure such as airports. Civil aviation was grounded for 24 hours after September 11th and took almost two weeks to recover

127 Ulrich Beck, 'The silence of words: on terror and war', *Security Dialogue* 34:3 (2009), 262 .

128 Kurt Campbell, 'Globalization's first war', *The Washington Quarterly* 25:1 (2002), 7–14.

129 Khaw Boon Wan, 'Opening of Aviation Security Conference' (speech, Singapore, 24 April 2002) <http://www.nas.gov.sg/archivesonline/speeches/record-details/76144877–115d-11e3–83d5–0050568939ad> accessed 25 March 2012.

130 Civil Aviation Authority Singapore (CAAS), 'Asia-Pacific Aviation Security Action Plan jointly presented by Singapore and Japan'. 47th Conference of Directors General of Civil Aviation Asia Pacific Regions, China Macao, 25–29 October 2010.

131 IATA, 'One Stop Security'.

a semblance of normalcy.[132] There are also an increasing number of plots targeting airports themselves rather than aircraft.[133] The potential for disruption is all the greater at air hubs in global cities such as New York, London, and Singapore, that if successfully attacked, can generate massive knock-on effects globally because of their central roles as hubs and transfer airports coordinating aviation flows. This global risk from aviation-related terrorism can be classed as negative *destructive*. While Beck has called such risks 'intentional', they can be better understood for their destructive ability to unhinge, interrupt and destabilise global connectivity and smooth circulation of flows facilitated by hub airports in global cities.

This is why the Transport Ministers' Statement on Counter-Terrorism at the International Transport Forum in 2002 vowed to 'ensure the safe, secure and reliable and seamless flow of air and sea transportation from any terrorist action'.[134] Security measures are now implemented not just at the geographical borders of a country, but increasingly at the air gateways into global cities that global aviation flows enter and exit. In several ways, 'the war against terror is obsessed with aeroplanes and airports' as the 'economic functions of airports to distribute wealth is blended with the need to defend against terror',[135] highlighting the intrinsic relationships between global risks, mobilities and aviation flows. Those with bad intentions can now take advantage of the accessibility of aviation flows to get closer to their targets, whether in the developed or developing world.

Although it was skyscrapers such as the World Trade Centre that were targeted and collapsed, the aftermath of September 11th has instead seen security measures predominantly focused on the airport, deemed to be the portal for circulating global risks such as terrorism. As the U.S. Deputy Secretary for Homeland Security admitted, the pre-September 11th security system was 'focused chiefly on efficiency'.[136] The overarching goal was to facilitate and circulate global aviation flows as quickly and smoothly as possible. New security procedures attempt to filter out undesirable passenger flows such as would-be hijackers and terrorists. The Computer Assisted Passenger Prescreening System (CAPPS II) was designed to 'greatly enhance TSA's ability to prevent terrorists from boarding commercial

132 Martin Libicki, Peter Chalk and Melanie Sisson, *Exploring Terrorist Targeting Preferences*. Santa Monica, CA: RAND Corporation (2007), 59.

133 Ben Brandt, 'Terrorist threats to commercial aviation: a contemporary assessment', November 2011, Combating Terrorism Centre, West Point Military Academy <http://www.ctc.usma.edu/posts/terrorist-threats-to-commercial-aviation-a-contemporary-assessment> accessed 8 April 2012.

134 'Transport Ministers Statement on Terrorism' (Tokyo, Japan, 15 January 2002) <http://www.internationaltransportforum.org/IntOrg/ecmt/crime/pdf/Tokyo2002.pdf> accessed 16 January 2014.

135 Mika Aaltola, 'The international airport: the hub-and-spoke pedagogy of the American Empire', *Global Networks* 5:3 (2005), 262.

136 James M. Loy, 'National Commission on Terrorist Attacks Upon The United States' (statement, United States of America, 27 January 2004) <http://www.9–11commission.gov/hearings/hearing7/witness_loy.htm> accessed 28 January 2012.

airlines while preserving the efficient flow of passengers'.[137] The notion of a filter and sieve with regards to circulating good and bad global flows, seen previously with financial centres, is mirrored in the aviation sector of a global city as well.

Airports facilitate not just passenger flows but global cargo flows as well. According to statistics from the International Air Transport Association (IATA), cargo carried on aircraft accounts for 35 per cent of all international trade by value, and the sector supports some 32 million jobs and generates USD$3.5 trillion of economic activity globally. By 2030, IATA expects air cargo traffic to triple to an estimated 150 million tonnes. Demand for air cargo traffic is expected to continue to rise with growing demand for high-value and time-sensitive goods.[138] In the US alone, around 120 million pounds of cargo is carried on cargo and passenger planes daily, according to the International Air Cargo Association.[139] The multibillion-dollar air cargo industry, much of it facilitated through air hubs of global cities worldwide has been described as 'an essential lubricant of the global economy'.[140] These air cargo linkages have also been targeted and exploited by terrorists. In 2010, improvised explosive devices (IEDs) hidden in printer toner cartridges were sent from Yemen via commercial air cargo UPS and FedEx flights through the air hub of a global city Dubai, destined for synagogues in the United States, while one was designed to detonate in mid-air. Experts argue that the greatest risks come from 'one-off' random parcels like those from Dubai that escape detection amidst the millions of other 'regular' parcels. Given the central position of air cargo in the world economy, 'you cannot stop the flow of time-sensitive air freight', said Yossi Sheffi, the director of the Center for Transportation and Logistics at the Massachusetts Institute of Technology. 'It is simply not realistic'.[141] Indeed, 'the air cargo supply chain is, by definition, a high velocity supply chain. For shippers that move their products by air, lead times are critical and speed is of the essence; they are willing to pay significant premiums for it over other modes of transportation'.[142]

---

137 Ibid.

138 Pang Kin Keong, 'Joint Conference on Enhancing Air Cargo Security and Facilitation' (speech, Orchard Hotel, Singapore 5–6 July 2012) <http://www.customs.gov.sg/NR/rdonlyres/6185D945-DC37-4EA6-B5B7-3EC35CC8C60E/24064/PS_T_OpeningSpeechattheICAOWCOJointConference_Fina.pdf> accessed 7 July 2013.

139 Barry Meier and Eric Lipton, 'In air cargo business, it's speed versus screening, creating weak link in security', *The New York Times*, 1 November 2010 <http://www.nytimes.com/2010/11/02/business/02cargo.html?pagewanted=all&_r=0> accessed 10 January 2012.

140 Ibid.

141 Cited in Meier and Lipton, 'In air cargo business, it's speed versus screening, creating weak link in security'.

142 John Muckstadt, Sean Conlin and Walter Beadling, 'Securing the air cargo supply chain, expediting the flow of commerce', October 2009 <https://www.securecargo.org/content/securing-the-air-cargo-supply-chain-expediting-the-flow-of-commerce-a-collaborative-approach> accessed 7 March 2011.

The air hubs of global cities have to service this need for speedy and efficient processing of air cargo flows, while paying heed to securing these flows.

Recent plots such as the unsuccessful 'underpants' plot highlight the vulnerabilities of the air transport system as the presumptive attacker transited through several air hubs in the Middle East and took advantage of global connectivity epitomised by his connecting US-bound flight through Amsterdam Schiphol (one of Europe's busiest hub airports). This was an excellent example of how Beck's de-spatialised global terrorism risk moved swiftly unimpeded through global aviation hubs. Other plots such as the 'shoe bomber' Richard Reid in 2002 highlight the extent to which a terror group will seek to attack the aviation network. The attack on Moscow's Domodedovo Airport in 2011 was another indication of terrorist groups targeting aviation infrastructure, especially less secure land-side parts compared to screening of departing passengers conducted air-side. Despite increased security, terrorists remain undeterred because attacking airports generates symbolic value, creates ripple effects through disruption, and guarantees international news coverage.[143]

The preceding discussion on transmission of undesirable global aviation flows and targeting of airports has relevance to the global city of Singapore which has experienced its fair share of aviation-related security risks. 'We are so much more connected to the world compared to twenty or thirty years ago', the Head of Planning at Changi Airport Emergency Services observed, 'any incident that happens could have a ripple effect on us'.[144] When aviation flows originate from airports where security might be perceived as lax, this is crucial for air hubs such as London or Singapore since they process numerous passengers from other airports who then connect to another flight. On 26 March 1991 Singapore Airlines shuttle service SQ117 from Kuala Lumpur (KL) to Singapore was hijacked by four passengers, claiming to be members of the Pakistan People's Party. This was the first hijacking of an SIA plane and the first such incident at Changi. Aerial connectivity in this sense provided access to Singapore for terrorists from Pakistan who transited through KL, where questions were raised about security. There have also been several plots physically targeting Singapore's air hub itself. Southeast Asian terror group Jemaah Islamiyah conspired to hijack and crash airliners onto the runway at Changi Airport in 2002. Singaporean analyst Bilveer Singh writes that 'there is almost a kind of an "amazing race" to bomb the nation'.[145] In

143 Brian Michael Jenkins, 'Terrorists can think strategically' (testimony presented before the Senate Homeland Security and Governmental Affairs Committee, Washington D.C., 28 January 2009) <http://www.rand.org/pubs/testimonies/CT316.html> accessed 19 August 2012.

144 Edwin Lim, 'Standing ready in the face of crisis', *Bridging Skies* 15 (2012) <http://www.bridgingskies.com/> accessed 10 January 2013.

145 Bilveer Singh, 'Why Singapore is an iconic target', *TODAYonline*, 22 July 2011 <http://www.themalaysianinsider.com/sideviews/article/why-spore-is-an-iconic-target-for-terrorists-bilveer-singh> accessed 10 April 2012.

2009, it emerged that there was yet another plot to attack Changi Airport by Indonesian terrorists.[146]

Many of these plots often are intended to influence a larger audience rather than Singapore itself (for instance the Pakistani government in the 1991 hijack). But, as Singapore becomes an attractive high-profile global city, worries are mounting about a successful terrorist strike that generates global publicity. Former Senior Minister and Coordinating Minister for Security S. Jayakumar mused that previously 'we just happened to get caught as a transit point ... (but) today, Singapore is an "iconic" target for terrorists'.[147] Terrorists target Singapore for several reasons, not just because of its perceived pro-Western stance, but also because of the high volumes of passenger flows through its air gateway. As Bernard Lim, Director of International Relations and Security Division, Ministry of Transport, put it, 'Owing to the high profile of the civil aviation industry and the potential high volume of casualties, civil aviation is one of the targets where terrorists hope to exploit as a means to achieve their demands'.[148] Because the air hubs of global cities process thousands of passengers a day (that is their abiding purpose to facilitate flows), terrorists get a lot of victims at once. 'There is a lot of bang for the buck ... The system works, but it is struggling to cope with the volumes of today'.[149] Besides passenger flows, September 11 elevated the value of secure airports which adopt international best practices to secure aviation trade flows. These need to become, in the words of former Senior Minister of State Khaw Boon Wan, 'trusted nodes' in the global trade network where customers are confident of their ability to process aviation flows securely. Changi takes its responsibility of being a trusted node seriously'.[150] As a key node in the global manufacturing system with integrated transport and logistics, it has to ensure that smooth flow of trade and air cargo is not disrupted. The toner cartridge plot of 2010 therefore has potentially significant ramifications for a nascent air cargo hub like Singapore. 'Cargo connectivity' is touted by Changi Airport Group[151] as one of its key strengths whereby 15 airlines operate more than 300 weekly scheduled pure freighter flights linking Singapore to about 17 cities in 7 countries. Changi

146 Jakarta Globe, 'Terror plot at Singapore's Changi Airport foiled by arrests', 28 July 2009 <http://www.thejakartaglobe.com/home/singapore-airport-terror-plot-foiled-say-solo-police/320409> accessed 27 August 2012.

147 Cited in Francis Chan, 'Twenty years after SQ117, terror threat looms larger'. *The Straits Times*, 29 March 2011<http://soufangroup.com/20-years-after-sq117-terror-threat-looms-larger/> accessed 9 December 2012.

148 Civil Aviation Authority of Singapore (CAAS), 'Keeping security threats at bay', *Bridging Skies*, July 2010, 8.

149 Tony Tyler, 'Singapore Air Show' (speech, Singapore, 16 February 2012) <http://www.iata.org/pressroom/speeches/pages/2012-02-13-01.aspx> accessed 17 February 2013.

150 Khaw Boon Wan, 'Opening of Aviation Security Conference'.

151 Changi Airport Group, 'Cargo connectivity', 1 December 2011 <http://www.changiairportgroup.com/cag/html/business-partners/air-cargo/cargo-connectivity.html> accessed 15 March 2012.

handled 1.87 million tonnes of cargo in 2011. Singapore hosts 3,000 logistics and supply chain management firms such as DHL and UPS. The Singapore Airline Terminal Services *Coolport* scheme is Asia's first perishables handling facility at an airport, while a new Air Cargo Express Hub is aimed at enabling air express companies to use Singapore more efficiently as a gateway into Asia. In October 2012, global cargo giant FedEx opened its new consolidated operations centre in Singapore as the anchor tenant at the new Air Cargo hub. Reflecting the two-faced nature of global connectivity that this book stresses, enhanced cargo connectivity could also provide additional transmission mechanisms for terrorists to infiltrate Singapore's air cargo supply chain, as we have seen with the Dubai plot.

Attending to the Global Aviation Network: Speed Versus Security

Global cities do not just exist. As the previous chapter on financial flows demonstrated, they need to come into being, with an array of actors working to sustain its connectivity. These actors have the largest stake 'attending' to this connectivity, making sure it is not disrupted or if the worst happens, to restore normal circulation of flows as quickly as possible. Like financial centres discussed in Chapter 3, airports thus also need various actors to enable these aviation links. Prime spaces where mobility of bodies and identities is most associated with a globalising world, airports are also sites for monitoring, sifting and differentiation of these movements into undesirable or desirable flows through surveillance and biometric systems: 'The border zones through which people must move are, then, the likely candidates for the focus of new and intensified forms of surveillance and control. This is nowhere truer than at the airport'.[152] Maintaining 'good' flows while preventing 'bad' ones is the overriding challenge, as we have seen for Singapore's financial sector. Based on a similar premise, the Privium program at Amsterdam's Schiphol airport fast-tracks 'pre-approved' travellers through immigration using iris scans because they are deemed to be low-risk and frequent passengers. Likewise, the TSA Registered Traveler Program in the United States operates on the same basis: 'Lowering the cost of travel in terms of reduced screening time, less physical strain, and more certainty will be the benefit that travelers who register in the RT program receive'.[153] As Salter points out, developing these passenger profiles does not seek to eliminate the risk, but to manage the circulation of the risk through targeting resources where they are most needed.[154] These programs illustrate Beck's claims about the unfortunate side-effects of global risk which exclude and stigmatise: those classified as 'risk persons' or 'risk groups' count as

152 Peter Adey, 'Surveillance at the airport', 1365.

153 Charles A. Stone and Anne Zissu, 'Registered traveler program: the financial value of registering the good guys', *Review of Policy Research* 24:5 (2007), 452.

154 Salter, 'Imagining Numbers', 254.

nonpersons whose rights are threatened.[155] What these programs effectively do is separate 'desirable' from 'undesirable' circulations; legitimate aviation passenger flows from those more 'risky' requiring additional checks. Airports serving global cities are expected to facilitate seamless flows of 'desirable' goods and passengers: 'the flows of right people, businessmen and tourists should also be efficient and the facilities the latest and most sophisticated'.[156] To ensure it continues to serve this crucial purpose, airports have become the 'loci of reassurance and security ... against disruptions in the vital flows'.[157] The IATA suggests that up to one quarter of passengers at hub airports are in transit to connect to another flight. Quick and efficient connections are imperative and central to the aviation system.[158] New tools and practices of security should allow passengers and goods to flow as quickly as possible but reduce the risk of further terrorist attacks sufficiently for confidence to remain in the aviation system.[159] Key here is how to maintain a balance between security and facilitation of smooth flows of aviation traffic. Before September 11th, the average throughput of an airport security checkpoint was 355 passengers per hour. Today, that average is 149 passengers per hour.[160] The volumes of passenger flows in aviation are quite astounding. It is estimated that US airports alone will have to screen one billion passengers by 2024 or even sooner.[161] When designing and implementing aviation security policies to thwart would-be terrorists, 'it would be critical to balance the needs of airport facilitation, operations and cost effectiveness to allow the civil aviation industry to continue functioning efficiently'.[162] The Joint Statement of the ICAO's Regional Conference on Aviation security in Kuala Lumpur in 2012 declared that 'We underscored the importance of maintaining a balance between the effectiveness of aviation security measures and their operational and economic impact in order to achieve the highest degree of facilitation'.[163]

---

155 Beck, *World at Risk*, 16.

156 Aaltola, 'The international airport', 269.

157 Ibid., 275.

158 IATA, 'One Stop Security'.

159 Heng Yee-Kuang and Kenneth McDonaugh, *Global Governance and Security: The other war on terror*. London: Routledge (2009), 116.

160 See Tony Tyler, 'We can make airport security faster and more secure', *The Business Times*, Singapore, 22 October 2012 <http://www.iata.org/pressroom/Documents/OpEd-Airport-Security-Faster-moreSecure-October2012.pdf> accessed 23 October 2013.

161 Bart Elias, 'Airport Passenger Screening: background and issues for Congress'. Congressional Research Service, Washington D.C, R4053 (2009), 2.

162 CAAS, 'Asia-Pacific Aviation Security Action Plan jointly presented by Singapore and Japan'.

163 International Civil Aviation Organization (ICAO), 'Joint Statement of the Regional Conference on Aviation Security' (Kuala Lumpur, 12 January 2012) <http://www.icao.int/Security/Documents/Malaysia%20Regional%20Conference%20Statement%20FINAL.pdf> accessed 6 February 2013.

While filtering out undesirable flows, at the same time air hubs must also discharge their primary functions of commanding, coordinating and circulating global aviation flows of cargo and passengers. At various levels of engagement from its domestic aviation industry to government agencies and global bodies, Singapore has worked to minimise the possibilities of disruptions to global aviation flows whether these are from terrorist threats or disease pathogens. The difficulties of doing so relate closely to Changi air hub. The Singapore Customs newsletter *Insync* highlights how 'the challenge lies in making sure the goods flow smoothly and efficiently without impeding global trade, all the while ensuring high security for air cargo'.[164] The Civil Aviation Authority of Singapore (CAAS) stresses that 'while facilitating seamless passenger and cargo movements, CAAS is committed to aviation security not being compromised'.[165] This brings our attention to those who actually 'attend' to the aviation system to ensure continued circulation of aviation flows. Roberto Kobeh, President of the ICAO Council paid tribute to 'the monumental collective efforts of the individuals' who make the global aviation system 'function so seamlessly and safely each day'.[166] One of Beck's central claims is how global risks are triggering a reconfiguration in relationships at all levels as actors come together to manage shared risks. While arguing that 'neoliberalism loses its force in the face of global risks',[167] Beck has remained adamant that the state take charge, with the input of multiple stakeholders.[168]

The developmental state has indeed taken the lead in a global city like Singapore. CAAS formed the National Air Transport Facilitation Committee (NATFC), complying with the standards in ICAO Annex 9, with a task force set up to facilitate the movement of aircraft, crew, passengers and air cargo. At the regulatory level, Singapore established an Aviation Security Task Force to undertake a comprehensive review of airport and airline security measures and to recommend improvements. The National Civil Aviation Security Committee coordinates aviation security policy. The Singapore Government has brought together various agencies to raise awareness and vigilance against terrorism.[169] The inaugural Joint Aviation Security and Facilitation Seminar, hosted by the Civil Aviation Authority of Singapore (CAAS) and the Airport Police Division

164 Singapore Customs, 'Forging global partnerships to strengthen air cargo security'. *Insync: Singapore Customs E-Newsletter* 19 (July/August 2012).

165 CAAS, 'Empowering Growth in Singapore Aviation', 20.

166 Cited in CAAS, 'Bridging Skies'.

167 Ulrich Beck, 'The terrorist threat: the world risk society revisited', *Theory, Culture and Society* 19:4 (1999), 39–55.

168 Beck, 'The silence of words: on terror and war', 262.

169 Wong Kan Seng, '8th National Security Seminar' (speech, Singapore, 9 November 2010) <http://www.singaporeunited.sg/cep/index.php/Our-News/DPM-Coordinating-Minister-for-National-Security-Mr-Wong-Kan-Seng-8th-National-Security-Seminar> accessed 10 November 2012.

(APD) in 2012, also aimed to attain greater collaboration among the authorities and the airport community to ensure secure and smooth facilitation of passengers and cargo. More than 200 representatives from various government agencies and aviation industry practitioners participated. In early 2011, the CAAS Safety Series was launched as a platform to regularly share safety information with the industry. All interested parties with stakes in maintaining the smooth aviation flows through Changi have crucial roles to play. Despite all precautions, when the worst does happen in an aviation-related crisis, a crisis management framework is in place to allow air operations to resume as quickly as possible. The CAAS works with several agencies such as the Civil Defence Force; Police; Immigration and Customs; and the Ministries of Defence, Health, and Foreign Affairs. These agencies work together to assess impact and provide strategic guidance to those on the ground.[170]

At the level of the airport and its operators, several 'hard' security measures were introduced to minimise the risks of disruptions to aviation flows. In early 2004, an automated 100 per cent Hold Baggage System was introduced in Changi, employing the latest explosive detection technology. In 2007, in line with international regulations, restrictions on aerosols and gels on hand-luggage were implemented. There have also been joint armed patrols by the army and police force in the passenger terminals. In 2012, Changi introduced a new Fence Intrusion Detection System (FIDS) based on fibre sensor technology for quicker and more accurate detection of breaches. The notion of air hubs circulating aviation flows enables researchers to instantly understand the rationale behind several initiatives and their relevance to Changi. In 2011, the International Air Transport Association (IATA) demonstrated a model of their 'Checkpoint of the Future' system whose ultimate goal is to enhance security but ensure minimal hassle to passenger flows. Changi does not seem to face congestion problems to the same degree with centralised screening that airports in the UK and US face. As a spokesman explained, 'we conduct decentralised screening at the gates. With dedicated security screening resources at each gate, we do not often face bottlenecks. We can also sieve out persons of interests at the gate for enhanced screening if needed'.[171] Premised similarly on filtering out undesirable flows, Changi's Threat-Oriented Passenger Screening Integrated System (TOPSIS) even ropes in and trains non-security staff such as check-in staff, taxi handlers, and cleaners to identify anyone or anything amiss. Since they interact daily with 'normal' passenger flows, the assumption is that they can easily detect anything out of the ordinary. Singapore's Homefront Security Division senior director John Lim explained, 'they (airport staff) have an understanding of what's normal,

170 CAAS, 'Bridging Skies'.

171 Cited in Hedy Khoo, 'Airport checkpoint of the future?', *The New Paper*, 4 January 2011 <hhttp://www.pvtr.org/pdf/ICPVTRinNews/AirportCheckpointOfTheFuture.pdf> accessed 9 April 2012.

which also means they have a higher chance of identifying what's not normal'.[172] The basic idea is to pick out anything that is untoward within the massive flows thronging Changi, for instance 'an individual going against the crowd flow'.[173] Such programmes reflect what Graham described as the central security challenge of filtering and sieving 'bad' from 'good' normal global flows.

Just as financial centres in London and Singapore shared information to combat terrorist financing flows, air hubs are also training air hubs in other cities on how to maintain security for smooth circulation of aviation flows. Of course, Changi Airport Group (CAG) profits from providing such consultancy services but it also benefits if aviation flows remain uninterrupted. Changi Airports International (CAI), a CAG subsidiary, is transplanting its expertise to more than 40 airports in over 20 countries across four continents. CAI jointly established a premier aviation training academy with other air hubs such as Xiamen International Airport Group Co. Ltd to train Chinese personnel on ground operations as well as security procedures. The United Arab Emirates (UAE) Abu Dhabi Airports Company also contracted CAI from 2006 to 2008 to design procedures to balance smooth passenger flows with rigorous security screening.

Civil aviation threats such as terrorism are global problems that require global solutions. However, it is often said that 'the 1st Law of Supply Chain Physics is '*Local Optimization = Global Disharmony*'.[174] In an interconnected world, Singapore recognises that the global supply chain is only as secure as its weakest link. Security enhancements therefore should cover the entire chain ideally through a globally coordinated effort by ICAO Contracting States to 'ring-fence the global aviation security system'.[175] The ICAO's Annex 17 and the World Customs Organisation's SAFE Framework to Secure and Facilitate Global Trade contain the standard measures for aviation supply chain security. 'The issue is you don't have a seamless set of standards that apply globally from end to end in the global network with the same level of sensitivity', said Robert W. Mann Jr., an aviation industry expert in Port Washington, N.Y.[176] Not all airports and cities have necessary capacities or resources to properly implement these guidelines. To help plug gaps in the system, the Singapore Cooperation Programme has provided training to ICAO

172 Channel NewsAsia, 'Border security system sees results', Channel NewsAsia, 12 October 2011 <http://www.channelnewsasia.com/stories/singaporelocalnews/view/1158831/1/.html> accessed 8 December 2012.

173 David Millward, 'Spy system for airlines to tackle terrorism', *The Daily Telegraph*, 27 June 2010 <http://www.telegraph.co.uk/finance/newsbysector/transport/7857880/Spy-system-for-airlines-to-tackle-terrorism.html> accessed 20 January 2011.

174 Muckstadt, Conlin and Beadling, 'Securing the air cargo supply chain, expediting the flow of commerce'.

175 Ministry of Transport, 'Aviation security' <http://app.mot.gov.sg/page_air.aspx?p=/Air_Transport/Contributions_to_International_Civil_Aviation/Aviation_Security.aspx&AspxAutoDetectCookieSupport=1> accessed 22 December 2012.

176 Meier and Lipton, 'In air cargo business, it's speed versus screening, creating weak link in security'.

member states and developing countries. Singapore has supported global efforts through its participation as vice-chair of the ICAO Aviation Security (AVSEC) Panel and contributes to the ICAO Comprehensive Aviation Security Strategy. Regionally, Singapore stresses 'the need for ASEAN aviation security agencies to work together to restore public confidence' through operational efficiencies and minimising inconvenience to passenger flows.[177] The Singapore Aviation Academy has conducted workshops for ASEAN security agencies on aviation security, intelligence analysis, post blast investigation, as well as bomb and explosives identification.

From cooperation between airports, to its national government engaging at the regional to global level, Singapore has sought to engage those with a stake in keeping the global aviation infrastructure ticking along without interruption in the face of terrorism threats. The International Civil Aviation Organization (ICAO) and the Civil Aviation Authority of Singapore (CAAS) signed a Memorandum of Understanding (MOU) in 2010 to establish the ICAO-Singapore Aviation Security Leadership and Management Seminar (LAMS). Targeted at senior management of governmental aviation agencies, airlines and airport authorities, the seminar is intended to disseminate best-practices and harmonise global standards. This is the only advanced level AVSEC programme available for Director-General level officials and was attended by 9 DGs from the Asia and Pacific Region and from Africa.

Security applies not only to passenger flows but goods and other cargo carried on airplanes. The 2010 toner cartridge plot highlighted the serious risks that air cargo hubs face from being exploited by terrorist groups. With effect from July 2011, the enhanced ICAO standards concerning air cargo security include a requirement for its 191 member States to establish a supply chain security process. Singapore works at three levels of collaboration on aviation cargo security – regulators, States, and industry.[178] This multi-stakeholder approach could be what Beck had in mind, with different actors configuring new relationships to tackle shared global risks. It also demonstrates Beaverstock's notion of networks cooperating to 'attend' to global flows between global cities. The first level involves regulatory authorities and the private sector. As we have seen with a multi-stakeholder approach to terrorist financing and financial contagion, the same is applied to aviation security. Singapore's policymakers realise that 'airport authorities alone cannot ensure that Singapore continues its success as a global air hub … the air cargo industry too has a role to play in strengthening the security of their own cargo'.[179] With the Advance Export Declaration (AED) framework operational in April 2013, declarations for all exports are made before leaving Singapore,

177 Ho Peng Kee, 'Counter Terrorism Workshop: Managing Civil Aviation Security In Turbulent Times' (speech, Singapore, 21 July 2003) <http://www.mha.gov.sg/news_details.aspx?nid=OTYx-Rll2t6J02oA%3D> accessed 22 July 2013.

178 Pang, 'Joint Conference on Enhancing Air Cargo Security and Facilitation'.

179 Ho Peng Kee, 'Launch of the Regulated Air Cargo Agent Regime' (speech, Singapore, 8 September 2008) <http://www.spf.gov.sg/rcar/forms/sms_writeup.pdf> accessed 9 September 2012.

to strengthen supply chain security. Customs Director-General Fong Yong Kian stated that 'Singapore is a key node in the international supply chain ... Singapore Customs needs to have timely information on all goods being exported, to position Singapore as a trusted and secure global trade hub and be more effective in trade facilitation'.[180] This initiative has attracted industry support from the Singapore Air Cargo Agents Association whose members have taken up certification because they see benefits. Being security-conscious can also help capture more business through the Changi air hub, 'for providing additional protection to the aviation industry from the aviation perspective ... will promote more cargo flows through Singapore as a regional hub'.[181] Since 2008, the Regulated Air Cargo Agent Regime (RCAR) means that cargo shipments on commercial passenger aircraft at Changi have to undergo security screening and clearance before they are loaded. Cleared cargo has to be protected from unlawful interference or contamination until they are loaded. The Singapore Air Cargo Agents Association has provided strong support. As of 15 August 2014, 263 companies were certified as Regulated Air Cargo Agents and 50 companies certified under the Secure Trade Partnership programme. Similar to the US Certified Cargo Screening Program, the rationale is easily understood when applying our analytical framework focused on processing flows and mobilities: the aim is 'to maintain supply chain velocity and the overall flow of commerce without loss from theft, terrorism or other threats'.[182]

The second layer of collaboration is co-operation between States. In April 2012, Singapore and the United States signed a Joint Statement to enhance collaboration to strengthen supply chain security bilaterally and with other partners. Another layer of collaboration is at the multilateral level. As the Joint Communique of the ICAO, World Customs Organisation, Singapore Customs and Singapore Ministry of Transport in July 2012 noted, 'the authorities responsible for customs and aviation security; airport and airline operators, shippers, freight forwarders and cargo agents and other stakeholders must coordinate their efforts to ensure the secure, safe and efficient movement of goods'.[183] This was first ever conference to bring together Singapore government agencies with the international civil aviation and customs communities, and their leaderships, to discuss security and facilitation issues related to air cargo.

---

180 Singapore Customs, 'All exports to be declared in advance come 2013' (media release, 12 January 2012) <http://www.customs.gov.sg/NR/rdonlyres/6185D945-DC37-4EA6-B5B7-3EC35CC8C60E/23735/PressReleaseonAEDImplementation_FinalWeb.pdf> accessed 14 January 2013.

181 Ibid.

182 Muckstadt, Conlin and Beadling, 'Securing the air cargo supply chain, expediting the flow of commerce'.

183 Singapore Customs, 'Joint communique on enhancing air cargo security and facilitiation: synergy through cooperation, Singapore', 6 July 2012 <http://www.customs.gov.sg/NR/rdonlyres/806059B3-FEBE-4D85-9717-C4270BE42857/24081/JointCommuniqueMOTSCICAO.pdf> accessed 10 November 2012.

'Attending' to Aviation Infrastructure in the Face of Disease Flows

Disease, as we have seen, is another type of negative mobility that penetrates highly-connected global cities through their air hubs. Airports again emerged as major points for managing global pandemic risks in global cities. The stakes are high because the issue of global health exemplifies 'the challenge of making globalization work … a challenge to our ability to act together at all levels that affect and are affected by these issues: the places we live; political communities and nations; across different countries; and in institutions of global governance'.[184] To tackle disease outbreaks, global cities have to 'break the chain on transmission'; in other words to do what is counter-intuitive to global cities whose existence is to facilitate circulation of global flows: they have to disrupt these flows in order to stem an outbreak. At the same time, however, global cities have to ensure the flow of 'healthy' individuals and goods is maintained to enable normal activities of the global economy. As in the case of terrorist financing and aviation security, regulators have to strike a balance between 'halting one type of flow while permitting another type of flow'.[185] This is why an analytical framework sensitive to notions of mobilities, infrastructure and flows, positions researchers to appreciate both the nature of global disease flows and the policy response emerging in global cities' air hubs. As airline networks and aviation infrastructure became the transmission modes for SARS, 'the world's international airports naturally become the setting for interdicting and screening passengers who might be infected'.[186] Airports became crucial interfaces between the global and the local, and with temperature screening stations and other restrictions, the symbolic meaning of airports changed from one of 'global mobility to one of local restriction'.[187] For instance, a policy drafted by Greater Toronto Airport Authority described the importance of 'sterilising passenger flow'.[188] For Wagner, paramount was the need to maintain smooth flows of people and goods without disruption and restore faith in air travel.[189] Harris Ali and Roger Keil demonstrate how the SARS crisis exemplified how 'a pivotal circuit of "normal" transnational mobility was infiltrated by malign pathogens … global airport and mobility flows were reorganized during the crisis in attempts to maintain global connectivity whilst attempting to interrupt the flows of the SARS pathogen'.[190]

184 Owen and Roberts, 'Globalisation, health and foreign policy', 1–125.

185 Pang, 'Joint Conference on Enhancing Air Cargo Security and Facilitation', 98.

186 Bowen and Laroe, 'Airline networks and the international diffusion of severe acute respiratory syndrome (SARS)', 132.

187 Ali and Keil, 'Securitising networked flows', 105.

188 Ibid.

189 Wagner, 'Toward a Dialectical Understanding of Networked Disease in the Global City', 20.

190 Stephen Graham, 'When Infrastructures Fail', in Stephen Graham (ed.), *Disrupted Cities: When Infrastructure Fails*. London: Routledge (2010), 26.

It was hardly surprising that 'many of the measures focussed on the airport'.[191] We have seen how financial centres in global cities cooperate against terrorist financing flows. Airports too face the same challenges in keeping aviation flows circulating in the face of disease risks. Any weak node within the dense aviation network generates vulnerabilities for others. Ensuring uniformity and consistency in robust disease screening protocols across airports is therefore essential. Based on the German air hub, the 'Frankfurt Model' for instance was proposed by Gaber et al. as a guideline for screening of infectious diseases at all international airports. The air hub of global city Singapore, with large concentrations of SARS, emerged as one of five disease hot-zones or 'epicentres from which the disease most likely spread to other countries, making them important areas in which to review the measures undertaken to contain the spread of the disease via air travel'.[192] Changi Airport, according to Menon and Goh, became a visible site of surveillance as well as detection of entry and exit of disease flows. There were two objectives: fulfilling the international community's desire to monitor and combat SARS by restricting suspected carriers; and imposing control over residents of the global city.[193] Changi was the first airport certified to be in full compliance with ICAO Anti-Sars Protective measures. The process of compiling these guidelines highlights the role that Singapore played in trying to facilitate continued aviation flows in the face of disease risks. The guidelines were formulated at a meeting at Changi Airport hosted by the Civil Aviation Authority of Singapore (CAAS) with participants from the World Health Organization (WHO), the International Air Transport Association (IATA) and senior public health officials from Singapore. Airports are meant to adhere to these standardised procedures to enhance surveillance of disease flows, while maintaining the balance with processing 'desirable' normal passenger flows. Hong Kong Airport followed suit with similar ICAO certification soon afterwards. Changi also pioneered the deployment of thermal scanners and indicative of how airports faced the same risks, these were soon quickly used by other air hubs in Hong Kong, China, Phillippines, Thailand and Taiwan.[194] This made managing passenger flows easier and less disruptive but questions remain over the efficacy of such scanners.[195] Changi Airport offered a 30 per cent discount on landing fees for airlines to encourage resumption of aviation flows; and airlines were given grants equivalent to USD$12 per incremental passenger over a base

191 Adam Warren, Morag Bell and Lucy Budd, 'Airports, localities and disease: representations of global travel during the H1N1 pandemic', *Health & Place* 16 (2010), 731.

192 Bowen and Laroe, 'Airline networks and the international diffusion of severe acute respiratory syndrome (SARS)', 138.

193 Menon and Goh, 'Transparency and trust', 378.

194 Bowen and Laroe, 'Airline networks and the international diffusion of severe acute respiratory syndrome (SARS)', 141.

195 Meng Kin Lim, 'Global response to pandemic flu: more research needed on a critical front', *Health Research Policy and Systems* 4:8 (2006).

load in May 2003. Airports desired such passenger flows. Airline chiefs like Geoff Dixon of Qantas were brought to Changi to endorse its anti-SARS measures. But Changi also wanted to keep out undesirables like SARS. On 30 march 2003, it was announced that there would be 'additional measures at Changi Airport to minimize the import of SARS',[196] including nurses to check on passengers who appear unwell. Airlines flying to Singapore were required to ask a set of health-related questions to passengers before embarking. In 2006, Changi again hosted meetings to develop guidelines for preventing spread of avian influenza, with assistance from WHO, ACI, IATA and CDC experts. The resulting ICAO Cooperative Agreement for Preventing the Spread of Communicable Diseases through Air Travel (CAPSCA) focused on cooperation in implementing guidelines between major airports such as Changi and Bangkok. A table-top exercise as part of the CAPSCA project was launched at the Singapore Aviation Academy involving representatives from ICAO, ACI and IATA amongst others.

Given that shared global health challenges provide stimulus for global cooperation,[197] one can discern relevant stakeholders coming together, a la Beaverstock, to 'attend' to the global city's aviation flows. Beck points to the 'assemblage' of institutions, governments, experts spanning great geographical distances that have arisen in response to a global risk such as SARS.[198] Using terminology familiar to scholars of mobilities, Beck even writes that the 'mobility streams of the SARS risk'[199] generated new transnational connections focused on risk management between hospitals and doctors in affected cities like Hong Kong linking up with the Centre for Disease Control in Atlanta. Singaporean clinicians and hospitals also participate in a WHO collaborative network of clinicians for diagnosis and SARS treatment with colleagues from Canada and Hong Kong. We have already seen how air hubs like Changi work with counterparts in Hong Kong or Bangkok. Other stakeholders seeking to revive aviation flows such as the regional trade association, Association of Asia Pacific Airlines (AAPA), comprising members such as Singapore Airlines, cooperated in ensuring health declaration forms are filled in properly and conducting pre-boarding screening. Airlines also agreed to increase air circulation in cabins and disseminated WHO information posters at check-in. Airline associations and other lobby groups also actively worked to clear misconceptions about the spread of SARS in flight. In order to maintain passenger flows, the AAPA issued a statement that air travel

---

196 Ministry of Health, Singapore, 'SARS: New measures at airport to curb importation of new cases', 30 March 2003 <http://www.moh.gov.sg/content/moh_web/home/pressRoom/pressRoomItemRelease/2003/SARSnew_measures_at_airport_to_curb_importation_of_new_cases_more_patients_recovering_and_discharged.html> accessed 14 January 2010.

197 K.M. Venkat Narayan, et al., 'Global non-communicable diseases: where worlds meet', *New England Journal of Medicine* 363 (2010), 1196–8.

198 Beck, *World at Risk*, 175.

199 Ibid.

is safe and the risk of infection in an aircraft is very low. The Airports Council International (ACI), which represents the interests of airports in industry and international talks, also played key roles disseminating information to its members. ACI convened a Regional Board Meeting on 3 June 2003 to discuss the situation with representatives from ICAO and IATA regional offices, AAPA and the Centre for Disease Control (CDC).

Similarly casting a wide net in responding to SARS, at the national level, when the Singapore government decided on contact tracing, it mobilised the human and technological resources of the police, army, People's Association, etc.[200] This is where the developmental state and its resources comes into play in a global city like Singapore. An inter-ministry coordinating committee led by the Health and Home Affairs Ministers, designated the Tan Tock Seng Hospital as the command and control centre.[201] Initially, there was lack of consensus and coordination between the Ministry of Health (MOH) and Ministry of Education (MOE) on whether to close schools.[202] Ooi and Phua point to how MOH had to be supported by the Armed Forces and Ministry of Defence to set up software for contact tracing as MOH was ill equipped for that task. Other responses included quarantine orders, tagging of quarantine breakers with movement sensors, sealing of hospitals, temporary closure of schools and thermal scanning at public and private offices. A wholesale vegetable market was closed when one hawker was infected, with hundreds quarantined. With all these restrictions in place, health officials continually stressed the need to balance security with free flows of goods: 'border controls must continue to facilitate the flow of essential goods and personnel into Singapore'.[203]

The biggest problem that SARS presented was the unknown. For example, when the virus emerged, it was just called 'atypical pneumonia'. It created a deep sense of fear as authorities did not know what to do. The SARS crisis was a classic example of a complex risk that cuts across different agencies from health, finance, to transport. Managing such global risks in a global city requires the embracing of multiple actors at various levels, just as Beck recommended. Singapore's Health Minister described 'a shared responsibility, requiring collective defence against transnational threats and public health risks. The WHO and Governments can no

200 Tommy Koh, 'The new global threat: SARS and its impacts' <http://www.spp.nus.edu.sg/ips/docs/pub/pa_tk_editorial_the%20new%20global%20threat.pdf> accessed 10 April 2012.

201 See Chua Beng Huat, 'SARS Epidemic and the Disclosure of Singapore Nation', *Cultural Politics* 2:1 (2006), 77–86; and Chris Hudson, 'Singapore at war: SARS and its metaphors', in John H. Powers and Xiaosui Xiao (eds), *The Social Construction of SARS: Studies of a health communication crisis*. Amsterdam: John Benjamins Publishing Company (2008), 163–77.

202 Ooi, Giok Ling and Phua, Kai Hong. 'SARS in Singapore – challenges of a global health threat to local institutions', *Natural Hazards* 48 (2009), 317–27.

203 Ministry of Home Affairs, Singapore, 'Preparing for a Human Influenza Pandemic in Singapore', 26.

longer be the sole stewards for public health. We need to rope in the private sector and the people sector more systematically in this endeavour ... none of us now can be absolved from our collective responsibility to uphold international health security'.[204] Thinking in terms of global cities processing global flows, the risk of pandemics also overlaps with other aspects of Singapore's critical infrastructure such as its financial centre and financial flows. This means that a broad range of stakeholders, both private and public, have common interests in ensuring these flows are not disrupted. Singapore's emergency preparations 'are deliberately kept adaptable so that they can be applied in other scenarios, for example, an outbreak of other infectious diseases or a terrorist attack'.[205] Exercise Raffles III for instance was held in September 2011 in Singapore's financial hub, the only financial centre to conduct a large-scale flu pandemic response exercise. Aiming to integrate the financial sector's business continuity and crisis response plans with those of Singapore's government agencies, the Exercise involved 137 financial institutions, including the Association of Banks in Singapore; banks, finance companies, insurance companies, securities and broking houses, the Singapore Exchange, the MAS as well as infrastructure providers such as NETS, Clearing and Payment Services and the Singapore Automated Clearing House.[206] The role of the community and industry is important, for Home Affairs Minister Wong Kan Seng said that 'the Government will do its utmost to mitigate the impact, it needs the cooperation of the private sector and the community for the success of any measure'.[207] Health Minister Gan stressed that 'We need to rope in the private sector and the people sector more systematically in this endeavour'.[208] The authorities have been working with privately-run essential services to ensure they have robust preparedness and continuity plans. Various exercises such as Sparrowhawk II in 2006 tested readiness and response plans at clinics and hospitals but also key entry checkpoints including Changi Airport. Learning lessons from SARS, when H5N1 came around in 2009, the Ministry of Home Affairs recommended that 'We will continue engaging and working with the private sector and the public to raise the level of preparedness at the individual, community and national levels. It is only through this Whole-of-Singapore approach that we can build a robust,

---

204 Gan Kim Yong, 'WHO Conference on multi-sectoral collaboration to manage public health risks' (opening remarks, Singapore, 13 October 2011) <http://moh.gov.sg> accessed 13 October 2013.

205 Ministry of Home Affairs, Singapore, 'Preparing for a Human Influenza Pandemic in Singapore', 48.

206 David Connor, 'ABS 35th Annual Dinner' (speech, Singapore, 27 June 2008) <http://www.abs.org.sg/pdfs/Newsroom/Speeches/2008/Speech_270608_MrDavid.pdf> accessed 27 June 2013.

207 Cited in Ministry of Home Affairs, Singapore, 'Preparing for a Human Influenza Pandemic in Singapore', 2.

208 Gan, 'WHO Conference on multi-sectoral collaboration to manage public health risks'.

multi-layered defence against pandemic influenza'.[209] Other key stakeholders such as doctors have also been involved. As Professor K. Satku, former Director of Medical Services noted, the Infectious Disease (ID) community, comprising Infectious Disease Physicians, Microbiologists and Public Health Specialists, has a significant role to play in safeguarding global health security, from surveillance to diagnosis and horizon-scanning.[210]

At the global level, Fidler points to how 'germs are epidemiological phenomenon. Passports are political phenomena' and SARS did not recognise borders.[211] Much of ICAO's efforts to implement a harmonised global response plan during the (SARS) outbreak in 2003 focused on air hubs. Changi hosted ICAO Working Group meetings to develop precautionary anti-SARS measures for airports and later for avian flu. Singapore also seconded an expert to ICAO to lead the first-ever CAPSCA project mentioned previously in 2006. Working with neighbouring countries and other international actors to develop mutually beneficial mechanisms, improving medical surveillance and reporting is essential for advance warnings. Global bodies such as the World Health Organization (WHO) therefore have a crucial role to play. The antidote is more globalisation, not less, to tackle global risks, 'the long term strategy to contain these diseases and to prepare for the "big one" was to construct effective and resourceful networks of global cooperation and, more importantly, to revitalize local public health systems'.[212] At the regional level, the Singapore Government also initiated the Special ASEAN Leaders' Meeting on SARS on 29 April 2003 which launched initiatives to screen passengers' health and an ASEAN SARS Containment Information Network.[213] Since a public health threat crossed national borders through air hubs, states have to cooperate and act in a collective and mutually beneficial manner to safeguard their populations.[214] Singapore pushed first for an ASEAN centred agreement on surveillance of SARS through the airline sector, while leaving APEC to generate a common land border management strategy.[215] There is, as Beck might recognise, growing recognition that global pandemic risks now mandated shared vulnerability, particularly in highly-exposed global cities like Singapore. WHO Director-General Margaret Chan said that 'an influenza pandemic is an extreme expression of the need for solidarity before a shared threat.

209 Ministry of Home Affairs, Singapore, 'Preparing for a Human Influenza Pandemic in Singapore', 48.

210 K. Satku, Speech at the 12th Western Pacific Congress on Chemotherapy and Infectious Diseases, 2 Dec 2010 <https://www.moh.gov.sg/content/moh_web/home/pressRoom/speeches_d/2010.html> accessed 23 April 2013.

211 Fidler, *SARS*, 15.

212 Hung, 'The politics of SARS', 27.

213 Melissa Curley and Nicholas Thomas, 'Human security and public health in Southeast Asia: the SARS outbreak', *Australian Journal of International Affairs* 58:1 (2010), 26.

214 Ibid., 29.

215 Ibid., 28.

The radically increased interdependence of countries amplifies the potential for economic disruption'.[216] Yet, health care scholars argued that there was, relatively speaking, insufficient institutional changes in the health care sector to take account of intensified globalisation.[217] In particular, there was concern over the lack of an information network among health care and public health institutions in globalising cities that are increasingly integrated through international travel and other business connections.[218]

Singapore received international acclaim from WHO for its SARS measures.[219] For Bowen and Laroe, this success 'reflects the unusual capability of Singapore's bureaucracy as well as the advantages of the city-state's small size'.[220] Chua however argues that the Singapore Government used the SARS epidemic episode to bolster its legitimacy as the sole organisation capable of mobilising Singapore's population against a deadly disease.[221] The ruling elite mobilised residents of the global city in battle against SARS for the sake of nation as well as state building agendas.[222] Parliament has given the Health Minister sweeping powers to commandeer the use of private hospitals and manpower in a health crisis. Hudson argues that society became both medicalised and militarised.[223] Using both the war in Iraq and SARS as military and biological wars in the discursive space of political communication, the war against SARS was evoked in terms of military strength; unity in diversity, and defence of national borders against the threat of pestilence.[224]

Conclusion

All leading global cities today without exception boast a significant air hub to capture global aviation flows of cargo and people. Travel writer Pico Iyer sees airports as 'the new epicenters and paradigms for our dawning post-national age'.[225]

---

216 Margaret Chan, 'Concern over flu pandemic justified' (speech, 62nd World Health Assembly Geneva, Switzerland, 18 May 2009) <http://www.who.int/dg/speeches/2009/62nd_assembly_address_20090518/en/> accessed 19 May 2009.

217 Ooi and Phua, 'SARS in Singapore – challenges of a global health threat to local institutions', 318.

218 Ibid., 320.

219 World Health Organization, 'Situation updates', SARS update #53, 12 May 2003 <http://www.who.int/csr/sars/archive/en/> accessed 13 June 2013.

220 Bowen and Laroe, 'Airline networks and the international diffusion of severe acute respiratory syndrome (SARS)', 140.

221 Chua, 'SARS Epidemic and the Disclosure of Singapore Nation', 77–86.

222 Ibid.

223 Chris Hudson, 'Singapore at war: SARS and its metaphors', 163–77.

224 Hudson, 'Singapore at war', 177.

225 Pico Iyer, 'Where worlds collide', *Harpers Magazine*, August 1995 <http://harpers.org/archive/1995/08/where-worlds-collide/> accessed 9 January 2012, 51.

International airport terminals have become what some call 'points of entry into a world of apparent hyper mobility, time-space compression and distanciation'.[226] They are 'indispensable gateways to the global city'.[227] A key contributor to the widely discussed time-space compression of globalisation, airports 'seamlessly' hook up major global cities.[228]

From its early years, the developmental state of Singapore has poured resources into developing the connectivity of Changi international airport, making the global city an important node in the global aviation infrastructure. A Changi Airport group brochure touts the connectivity of Singapore's ability to deliver through its air, IT and sea infrastructure 'the seamless flow of goods and services to markets around the world'.[229] Yet, as this book has argued, the ability to circulate global aviation flows also exposes global cities to a range of global risks. Castells singled out an existential alienation that exists at airports where people suddenly realise that they 'are alone, in the middle of flows, they may lose their connection, they are suspended in the emptiness of transition'.[230] Even worse, airports also serve as the portals for importation of global risks into global cities. This chapter has elaborated on how de-spatialised global risks discussed in Ulrich Beck's *World Risk Society* spread through airline networks and air hubs of global cities. With regards to the role that global cities can play in trans-national risk management, it also mapped out, to a far greater degree than Beck, the shifting reconfigurations of relationships between multi-level actors from airline associations and airports to cargo agents who have stakes in maintaining uninterrupted aviation flows through a global city's airport. This chapter has also sought to differentiate global risks such as pathogens from other global risks such as terrorism: 'An influenza pandemic is different from other crises such as a terrorist attack or an earthquake. It does not affect physical infrastructure such as buildings and computer networks, but it threatens human resources by removing employees for long periods of time. This impact is broad-based and will hit all industries including critical sectors'.[231] Two key categories of aviation-related risks were identified, depending in their level of intentionality and nature of circulation: inadvertent negative *penetrative* flows (such as infectious diseases that ironically depend on global aviation connectivity to spread) and intentional negative *destructive* flows (such as terrorists that target and seek to disrupt/undermine global aviation hubs and networks). Singapore as a global city has unfortunately had experience managing both types of global risks.

226 Ali and Keil, 'Securitising networked flows', 97.

227 Ibid., 104.

228 John Urry, *Sociology Beyond Societies*. London: Routledge (2000).

229 Changi Airport Singapore, 'Air Cargo: Set Your Sights Further'. Singapore: Changi Airport Group Brochure (2011), 3.

230 Manuel Castells, *The Rise of Network Society*. Oxford: Wiley-Blackwell (2000), 421.

231 Ministry of Home Affairs, Singapore, 'Preparing for a Human Influenza Pandemic in Singapore', 32.

SARS was the first severe infectious disease to imperil the highly globalised world of the twenty-first century.[232] These diseases particularly challenge global cities that are open to high volumes of flows with other cities, particularly through aviation links. The study of global infectious disease has been receptive to the deployment of multi-disciplinary perspectives from various analytical angles. As Warren, Bell and Ludd observe, 'When we merge the literatures on biosecurity and spread of disease, questions arise about "containment" and the traveller's journey. These include the complexities of managing risk at various scales – international, national and regional – and the role of the airport as a site for controlling the threat of disease spread'.[233] Likewise, this chapter has sought to merge literatures on global cities as 'spaces of flows' and mobilities with Beck's *World Risk Society*, by focusing on the aviation links that key urban nodes depend on. Singapore functions like a hub at the centre of movement of people, goods, services and ideas, linked to other alpha cities in the likes of London and New York. Facilitating flows of people, ideas, services and goods brought with it the risk of infectious diseases such as (SARS) and H1N1, as well as global terrorism. In 2014, the Ebola outbreak in West Africa once again revived fears of an infectious disease reaching a global city like Singapore. However, despite its dense web of aviation connections around the world, perhaps fortunately, its Ministry of Health deemed public health risks to be low because 'travel connectivity between Singapore and Africa is low'.[234] This was a reminder that connectivity is a key variable when assessing exposure of global cities to global risks. Other health-related risks arising could be seen in 2008 when Singapore banned the sale and import of milk products from China as a result of the melamine-tainted milk scandal.

One of the key challenges managing global risks in the aviation sector of global cities is striking a balance between facilitating global flows (the very reason for a global city's existence) and ensuring security. Whether it is disease or terrorists, the same principle applies: global cities need to filter undesirable flows (terrorists and pathogens), while maintaining its ability to circulate the right, normal type of flows (goods, people, and cargo). While global cities might face the same global risks, the differences between how Singapore and Hong Kong coped with SARS are striking.[235] In Singapore, Curley and Thomas argue that 'the rapid creation of a ministerial-level committee to provide oversight for all SARS-related government activities, on a daily basis, ensured that top-down management of the crisis across all political, economic and social sectors were efficiently implemented'.[236]

232 Fidler, *SARS*, 6.

233 Warren, Bell and Budd, 'Airports, localities and disease', 728.

234 Ministry of Health, 'Ebola virus disease: Health Advisory', 22 November 2014 <https://www.moh.gov.sg/content/moh_web/home/pressRoom/Current_Issues/2014/ebola-virus-disease-.html> accessed 29 December 2014.

235 Chua, 'SARS Epidemic and the Disclosure of Singapore Nation', 91.

236 Curley and Thomas, 'Human security and public health in Southeast Asia', 25.

Our analytical framework based on flows, infrastructure and mobilities in global cities facilitates the analysis of a highly inter-connected urban world, where flux and the movement of money, individuals and microbes intermingle in seemingly unanticipated ways across global city networks. This became most apparent in how 'SARS spread rapidly via a global airline network that, a century on from the Wright Brothers' first flight, afforded unprecedented mobility'.[237] Whether from diseases or the trans-national nature of terrorist plots, in an inter-connected air travel system, loopholes or weaknesses anywhere ultimately have repercussions. This is why when attending to the global aviation network and making sure that aviation flows through Changi are not disrupted by pathogens or terrorists, a multi-level approach that is as comprehensive as possible is desirable. From key industry players at the frontline (airlines, cargo agents and airports) to government agencies (Home Affairs, Police, Customs) to international organisations (ICAO, IATA, ACI, WHO), all these actors have a self-interested stake in managing the global aviation risks that stalk a global city like Singapore. The problem with ICAO is that it is a 'political' and official UN agency. Thus 'ICAO rules – the standards – are always the minimum acceptable'.[238] Wallis suggests that recognising the inability of ICAO to ensure global implementation of its supposedly global benchmark SARPs, the private sector in the form of the airlines most affected then developed their own response. This was far from an altruistic desire, but rather recognition that global coordination was the best way to manage their collective risks in aviation security.

Finally, there are constantly evolving global risks in aviation flows: 'one thing we should be careful about is the danger of being narrowly focused or overly preoccupied with the last sensational topical incident. Today, it is parcel bombs on aircraft. Last Christmas, it was bombs concealed in the perpetrator's underwear. Further back, it was Mumbai-style attacks'.[239] Likewise with regard to diseases, first there was SARS, and then swine flu came along and in 2014, concerns arose over Ebola and MERS. As long as Singapore continues to cement its global city status through increasing air connectivity, its ability to command and coordinate global aviation flows and aero-mobilities will expose it to fast-spreading global aviation risks in Beck's *World Risk Society*. Global cities and their command/control functions do not automatically materialise out of nowhere, nor should they be reified. Various actors at multiple levels that help bring about Changi's aviation connectivity have to come together to 'attend' to the networks and protect them from disruption and destruction in the face of aviation terrorism or pandemic risks.

237 Bowen and Laroe, 'Airline networks and the international diffusion of severe acute respiratory syndrome (SARS)', 142.

238 Rodney Wallis, *How Safe Are Our Skies?* Santa Barbara: Greenwood Publishing, 69.

239 Wong, '8th National Security Seminar'.

Chapter 5
Major Port Hubs and the Circulation of Global Maritime Risks

Introduction

The previous chapters dealt with dimensions of Singapore's connectivity as a global city processing global flows through its financial centre and aviation hub. Global risks in the form of negative *penetrative* flows were highlighted that ironically depended on a global city's critical infrastructure to circulate: global financial crises and pandemics which were largely un-attributable, and the more deliberate exploitation of the financial system by terrorist financiers. As for negative *destructive* flows, this was seen in aviation-related terrorism that deliberately sought to first exploit, then disable or massively disrupt an air hub like New York or Singapore. This chapter shifts the spotlight towards a third cornerstone of Singapore's connectivity as a global city: its ability to coordinate and service maritime trade flows and the associated global risks. What are the risks that concern us here? The World Economic Forum's 'Global Risks Report 2012' classified WMD proliferation and terrorism as 'global risks of humanity's own making'.[1] WMD diffusion is ranked as one of the highest in terms of impact. Terrorism on the other hand was seen to have a lower impact but higher likelihood. Both these risks manifest a maritime dimension and have been pinpointed in Ulrich Beck's works but he has hardly commented on the implications for global cities. Indeed, Beck does not sufficiently distinguish between these two types of global risks which are categorised here as negative *penetrative* (WMD proliferation that ironically depends on smooth uninterrupted circulation of maritime flows) and negative *destructive* (maritime terrorism explicitly designed to target, destroy or impede maritime movements). Nor does he outline in detail how these de-localised risks spread to adversely affect global cities through the maritime domain. The various ways in which multi-level actors involved in ensuring a global city's maritime connectivity respond to such risks has also been neglected. Once again, a 'global city' and its maritime links should not be reified or automatically assumed. These are issues that this chapter will address in detail.

Using our analytical framework based on mobilities, circulations, critical infrastructure and the global city as a space of flows allows us to approach this question in a systematic analytical fashion. In order to become a space of flows,

1 World Economic Forum, 'Global Risks Report 2012' <http://www.weforum.org/reports/global-risks-2012-seventh-edition> accessed 1 June 2014, 40.

a global city usually amasses and accumulates a concentration of capabilities and functions within its strategic core that are crucial to the smooth operation of the global economy, what Stephen Graham terms the 'concentrating logics of global city development'.[2] The developmental state has played a critical role in 'growing' Singapore's maritime infrastructure as a global city. However, this very concentration of key functions in a global city often proves to be the soft underbelly of the highly-connected international system. The attacks on New York on September 11th not only caused massive loss of life, but also highlighted the possibility of disrupting and destroying multiple mobility systems from financial flows to air travel as well as the hitherto taken-for-granted 'global discourse on unfettered mobility as a way of life'.[3] This can be seen in how 'the flows on which New York depends were seriously interrupted, if not closed down (like the airports, tunnels and bridges, Stock Exchange) … What Bin laden's strike did so brilliantly was to undermine confidence by hitting hard at the symbolic centre of the system and exposing its vulnerability'.[4] Al-Qaeda did not only target the United States as a country, but also specifically New York City as a 'global city' of transnational mobility of capital, information, and people'.[5] The World Trade Centre 'epitomized the spaces of global flows of capital'.[6]

If New York exemplified the control and coordination of global financial flows, Singapore arguably serves as its maritime counterpart, given its particularly high levels of connectivity and global links through the sea. Even in the global age of jet travel and aviation links, in 2013, figures from UNCTAD show that more than 80 per cent of international trade in goods is carried by sea. UNTAD's Review of Maritime Transport 2014 revealed that world container port throughput rose 5.6 per cent to 651.1 million TEUs in 2013, of which Asian ports such as Singapore dominated the league table for port throughput and terminal efficiency.[7] 2013 figures from UNCTAD estimates global seaborne trade to have increased by 4.3 per cent, with the total reaching over 9 billion tons in 2012 for the first time ever.[8]

A significant portion of these maritime flows is coordinated and serviced by Singapore's mega-port hub. Maritime trade flows passing through Singapore have

2 Stephen Graham, 'In a moment: on glocal mobilities and the terrorized city', *City* 5:3 (2001), 414.

3 Kevin Hannam, Mimi Sheller, and John Urry, 'Editorial: Mobilities, immobilities and moorings', *Mobilities* 1:1 (2006), 7.

4 David Harvey, 'The City as Body Politic', in Ida Susser and Jane Schneider (eds), *Wounded Cities: Destruction and Reconstruction in a Globalised World*. Oxford: Berg (2003), 40.

5 Hannam, Sheller and Urry, 'Editorial', 7.

6 Mike Douglass, 'From global intercity competition to cooperation for livable cities and economic resilience', *Environment and Urbanisation* 14:1 (2002), 54.

7 UNCTAD, Review of Maritime Transport. Geneva: United Nations Conference on Trade and Development (2014), Chapter 4.

8 UNCTAD, Review of Maritime Transport. Geneva: United Nations Conference on Trade and Development (2013), xiv.

generated immense economic benefits through the so-called maritime cluster. More than 5,000 shipping companies and others provide services including insurance, legal services, maintenance and engineering expertise to support the circulation of maritime flows through Singapore. Together, this cluster employed more than 170,000 people and contributed around 7 per cent to Singapore's Gross Domestic Product in 2013.[9] The Port of Singapore Authority has itself become a trans-national corporation operating 27 other container terminals globally. A tiny city-state without a natural hinterland, Singapore 'has succeeded in making a hinterland of the global economy with conspicuous success'.[10] This success however hinged a great deal on 'just-in-time' production features and a finely-tuned level of coordination and facilitation of maritime flows.

Singapore as Global Maritime Port Hub: Connectivity and Capturing of Maritime Flows

The WTO singles out the extreme reliance of Singapore on exports and global trade, for 'without a sizeable domestic market, Singapore is by necessity outward-oriented. In 2007, the trade to GDP ratio was 348%, the highest in the world'.[11] WTO figures for Singapore's trade-to-GDP ratio reached a mind-boggling 415.8 per cent from 2010–2012. Much of this trade is sea-borne. Connectivity through the ocean has from the start been indispensable to Singapore's development and survival. Already in 1972, the central role that maritime trade flows play in Singapore's global city strategy was flagged by S. Rajaratnam who noted that 'For a Global City, the world is its hinterland ... Our shipping statistics show clearly that the world is our hinterland ... Our port is not merely a regional port, but a global port. Our port makes the world our hinterland'. Rajaratnam continued that 'Global cities are linked intimately with one another. They form a chain of cities which shape and direct, in varying degrees of importance, a world-wide system of economics. The sea gives us ready access to other global cities'.[12] Founding Prime Minister Lee Kuan Yew was unequivocal that 'Singapore's raison d'être was its Port. Singapore must strive to remain a major hub port'.[13] Lee later reflected that

9 Maritime and Port Authority of Singapore, 'Singapore's 2013 maritime performance', 7 January 2014 <http://www.mpa.gov.sg/sites/global_navigation/news_center/mpa_news/mpa_news_detail.page?filename=nr140107a.xml> accessed 2 January 2015.

10 Michael Leifer, *Singapore: Coping with Vulnerability*. Singapore: Routledge (2000), 157.

11 World Trade Organization (WTO), 'Trade Policy Review, Report by Singapore'. Trade Policy Review Body, WT/TPR/G/202, Geneva: World Trade Organization (2008), 1–10.

12 S. Rajaratnam, 'Singapore: global city' (speech to the Singapore Press Club, 6 February 1972) <http://newshub.nus.edu.sg/news/1202/PDF/GLOBAL-st-6feb-pA17.pdf> accessed 7 February 2012.

13 Cited in Paul Richardson, 'The Singapore maritime story', *Singapore Nautilis* (Q1 2008); Port Authority of Singapore (PSA), 'Sage Advice'. Singapore: Portview (Q2 2010), 11.

on gaining independence, 'We were suddenly confronted with the challenge of making a living for two million people on a barren island at the southernmost tip of Asia, which gives us the advantage of servicing all the ships that cross the Atlantic and the Pacific'.[14] The 'advantage' Lee refers to is the favourable geographical location Singapore occupies that allows it to facilitate sea-borne flows of trade, materials and goods. Singapore sits astride the Straits of Malacca, one of the world's busiest shipping lines carrying one-third of the world's traded goods.

In a global economic system characterised by just-in-time production chains that depend on parts built and assembled all around the world, 'outsourcing and global logistics chains now reflect the declining significance of geography in determining production and trade process'.[15] Centrally positioned port hubs like Singapore are today indispensable in the smooth facilitation, coordination and servicing of these globally-dispersed maritime production and supply flows. Singapore is a self-styled 'global port' and the world's busiest container trans-shipment hub handling about 'one-seventh of the world's total container transhipment throughput, and 5% of global container throughput'.[16] PSA Singapore Terminals operates four container terminals and two multi-purpose terminals, connecting all kinds of vessels – from container ships, bulk carriers, to cargo freighters – to a network of 200 shipping lines with sailings to 600 ports in 123 countries. The Maritime Port Authority sells this impressive 'global connectivity' as 'hallmark of the Singapore port'.[17] In September 2014, the Singapore Registry of Ships ranked among the top 10 largest in the world, with more than 4,000 registered vessels totalling 80 over million gross tonnes. Key to Singapore's port hub status is transhipments, the transfer of containers from one vessel to another bound for a final destination, while in transit. Because of its connectivity and frequent sailings as a trans-shipment hub, it may often be faster and more economical to tranship through Singapore than send goods to their destination points directly. This is why PSA's official website claims 'unrivalled connectivity' in 'our core business- trans-shipment' with around 85 per cent of all containers arriving in Singapore trans-shipped to another port.[18] There are two to three ships arriving or leaving every minute and about 1,000 vessels in the port at any one time. On any given day, 100,000 containers occupy space in

14 Cited in Dylah Loh, 'Singapore is what it is today because of globalization: Lee Kuan Yew', *TODAYonline*, 21 September 2012 <http://www.channelnewsasia.com/stories/singaporelocalnews/view/1227352/1/.html> accessed 22 September 2013.

15 Ian Goldin and Tiffany Vogel, 'Global governance and systemic risk in the 21st century: lessons from the financial crisis', *Global Policy* 1:1 (2010), 5.

16 Port of Singapore Authority, 'About Us' <http://www.singaporepsa.com/aboutus.php> accessed 8 November 2012.

17 Maritime and Port Authority of Singapore, 'Global Port Hub' <http://www.mpa.gov.sg/sites/maritime_singapore/what_maritime_singapore_offer/global_connectivity/global_hub_port.page> accessed 9 January 2013.

18 Port of Singapore Authority, 'Our Core Business' <http://www.singaporepsa.com/transhipment.php> accessed 8 November 2012.

the container yards. It is no exaggeration when Ron Widdows Group CEO and President of major shipping firm Neptune Orient Lines declared that 'Singapore's the centre of the universe for us'.[19]

Just consider the impressive data for three consecutive years, even in the midst of a global economic downturn. World Port Source suggests that 'in 2010, the Port of Singapore handled a total of over 503 million tons of cargo including 289.7 million tons of containerized cargo in 28.4 million TEUs, 177.1 million tons of oil, 24 million tons of conventional cargo, and 12.6 million tons of nonoil bulk cargo. More than 182 thousand vessels called in the Port of Singapore'.[20] In 2011, PSA Singapore Terminals handled 29.37 million TEUs of containers and 530 million tons of cargo. Annual vessel arrival by gross tonnage surpassed the 2 billion gross ton mark to reach 2.12 billion for the first time. Singapore was the world's busiest port by vessel arrival tonnage in 2011, handling more than 127,000 vessels totalling 2.12 billion gross tons. For the whole year of 2012, PSA handled a historic high of 31.26 million TEUs: the first time it had surpassed the 30 million mark and a 6.4 per cent increase from 2011.[21] In 2012, Singapore also maintained its position as world's busiest port by vessel arrival tonnage with 2.25 billion gross tons (GT) for 2012, an increase of 6.1 per cent from 2011.[22] Singapore in 2012 also handled the most cargo by weight in its history. Total cargo tonnage rose 1.2 per cent from 2011 to 537.6 million tones.[23] In 2013, Singapore's port handled 32.578 million Twenty-Foot Equivalent Unit (TEUs) containers and 139,417 vessel arrivals and 2.33 billion tons of vessel tonnage. With its position and expertise, Singapore has held various leadership posts at the International Maritime Organisation (IMO), and currently serves as the vice-chairman of the IMO's Maritime Safety Committee which develops global standards for seafarers; codes for rescue and collision avoidance; as well as facilitation of maritime traffic. In November 2013, it was re-elected to the IMO Council, and has served on the council since being first elected in 1993.

Amongst many other accolades, Singapore in 2014 won 'The Best Seaport in Asia' for the 26th time by the Asian Freight and Supply Chain Awards, and 'Port Operator Award' for the 12th time by Lloyd's List Asia Awards. In achieving and maintaining its prized port hub status, Singapore has consistently kept its

19 Cited in Port of Singapore Authority, 'Sage Advice', 7.

20 World Port Source, 'Port of Singapore' <http://www.worldportsource.com/ports/commerce/SGP_Port_of_Singapore_244.php> accessed 9 November 2012.

21 Figures given in Jonathan Kwok, 'PSA International posts 10.7% rise in profit for 2012', *The Straits Times*, 29 March 2013, accessed 8 March 2014, C8.

22 Figures given in speech by Lui Tuck Yew, 'Singapore Maritime Foundation New Year Cocktail Reception 2013' (speech, Singapore, 10 January 2013) <http://www.news.gov.sg/public/sgpc/en/media_releases/agencies/mot/speech/S-20130110-11> accessed 11 January 2014.

23 Maritime and Port Authority of Singapore, 'Singapore's 2012 maritime performance', 10 January 2013 <http://www.news.gov.sg/public/sgpc/en/media_releases/agencies/mpa/press_release/P-20130110-1> accessed 12 January 2013.

eye on how to enhance competitiveness in rapidly changing environments, and crucially, much of this is designed to capture the largest percentage of maritime trade flows. This is where Castells' notion of global cities as 'spaces of flows' is most apparent. In an age of trans-national production and consumption strategies, globally dispersed production and consumption flows require a maritime hub to efficiently manage these flows swiftly to the right places without disturbance. In response, Singapore 'aggressively adopts ICT to more efficiently manage flow of products between different regions associated with trans-national corporation production strategies ... The most competitive global port-cities have become ICT-based transactional and logistics management junctions capturing a greater slice of the value chain of the global production system'.[24] Because shipping lines must balance the economies of size achieved while at sea with inefficiencies and diseconomies of size while anchored at port, IT has become for Singapore a 'critical ingredient to control ever increasing amounts of trade and transport-related information ... to capture greater amounts of container-based maritime traffic'.[25] The emergence of the global economy therefore required the parallel development of 'enabling' information and transport technologies so that goods might be spatially articulated across space and time'.[26] This required the rise of new inter-modal gateways that function as hubs for a larger network that 'facilitate connectivity between interacting places'.[27] These are often referred to as 'value-added transactional hubs'.[28] Computerised systems like Computer Integrated Terminal Operations System (CITOS) direct container handling operations in real-time to ensure best loading and unloading sequences by reducing cost and turn-around times for vessels. Such IT capabilities help Singapore 'by capturing regional and global flows'[29] because it is able to coordinate complex systems of container flows at the regional and global scale. In 2011, the next generation Vessel Traffic Information System (VTIS) was deployed at the Port Operations Control Centre – Vista. The upgraded VTIS has the ability to handle up to 10,000 vessel tracks at any one time, double the previous capacity. This is why Singapore is able to promote itself as a 'global maritime information hub'. Customs clearance of boxes in Singapore took several hours in 1997 while it took days in Malaysia. The Integrated Reefer Monitoring System (iRMS) also now allows real time and online tracking of refrigerated containers at each stage of operations. Customers can monitor the status of their reefer boxes anywhere in the world via Internet.

---

24 C.A. Airiess, 'Regional production, information-communication technology, and the developmental state: the rise of Singapore as a global container hub', *Geoforum* 32:2 (2001), 235.

25 Ibid.

26 Ibid., 237.

27 Ibid.

28 K.E. Haynes, Y.M. Hsing and R.R. Stough, 'Regional port dynamics in a global economy: the case of Kaohsiung', *Maritime Policy and Management* 21:4 (1997), 95.

29 Ibid., 243.

In 2008, the Maritime Port Authority of Singapore launched the Wireless-broadband-access for SEaPort, or WISEPORT, project where ships can access wireless mobile broadband connectivity, up to 15km from Singapore's southern coastline. It further reduces paperwork because procedures done in hard copy previously onshore, such as regulatory filings, can instead be completed online before even entering the port. Therefore, 'the economic logic of a transhipment hub such as Singapore allows for the maximum connectivity of transport routes serving the global production strategies of TNCs'.[30] This intense level of maritime connectivity that Singapore as a global city depends on for its success however also carries risks of several types.

The Exploitation or Destruction of Global Maritime Flows

Singapore's position as a key node coordinating far-flung maritime supply and trade chains from around the world means the types of global risks here can be classified in two ways: 'penetrative' (illicit hidden materials that *deliberately* exploit the massive amounts of circulating daily maritime trade flows) and 'destructive' (*intentional* targeting of key maritime port nodes to destroy and cause havoc in the global trading system). The first type of risk relates to trans-national dangers that spread across porous boundaries, especially relating to Weapons of Mass Destruction (WMD) proliferation.[31] Terrorists could exploit international maritime supply routes to move weapons or terrorists themselves, using key ports as a conduit. Describing the problem using the terminology of risk, Prime Minister Lee warned that 'This is not just a low probability, worst case scenario, but a disaster which can realistically happen, sooner or later, unless all countries do their part to secure nuclear material and combat illicit trafficking'.[32] The second type of risk is mentioned in the WEF 'Global Risks Report 2010', which cautioned that 'a major terrorist attack that closed a port ... for weeks would have severe economic consequences on world trade because it would inflict major disruptions in complex just-in-time supply chains that comprise the global economy'. In this scenario, terrorists attack a global port hub like Singapore or sink ships in the narrow strategic waterways such as the Straits of Malacca, halting much of the inter-connected global maritime supply chain and creating extensive disruptions to maritime flows. The range of concerns thus arises from smuggling of illicit goods in the cargo; or commandeering the vessel as a weapon of attack. The ubiquitous containers found on large shipping vessels can be used for either of these threats. Most of the world's maritime cargo is transported in containers – steel boxes that

30 Ibid., 247.

31 David Mutimer, 'Reconstituting security? The practices of proliferation control', *European Journal of International Relations* 4:1 (1998), 99–129.

32 Cited in Chua Chin Hon, 'Nuclear terrorism: it's real', *The Straits Times*, 14 April 2010.

are commonly referred to as 'twenty-foot equivalent units' (TEUs). 'An ever greater proportion of container shipping trade is being concentrated in giant ports with the modern facilities to handle the boxes',[33] and Singapore is clearly one such mega-port. Furthermore, terrorists often seek to

> devastate and interrupt the circulations of cities. Infrastructures and technologies of circulation are preeminent among the myriad of 'soft' targets that constitute contemporary cities in the eyes of such movements. They symbolize ... the transnational reach and power of 'global' cities'. They provide opportunities to engineer massive media events ... and they help generate incalculable economic costs as 'normal' circulations and flows sustaining globalised capitalism are interrupted by cascading disruptions unleashed unpredictably in space and time.[34]

As Phil Agre has put it, 'if you want to destroy someone nowadays, you go after their infrastructure'.[35] This is where once again, our analytical framework based on mobilities, flows and infrastructure enables researchers to focus on global cities and their maritime port hubs because 'it is the particular ways in which big systems of infrastructure intersect with global cities that seem to dominate the targeting strategies of contemporary terrorists'.[36] John Robb points out that the greatest political and economic leverage in an interconnected world comes from the manipulation, destruction, disruption of the tightly coupled infrastructure networks that sustain modern global urban capitalism.[37] Singapore has had past experience of deliberate attempts to create disruption to global supplies because of its hub status. In 1974, the Japanese Red Army and the Popular Front for the Liberation of Palestine attempted to storm the Shell oil refinery on Pulau Bukom – now known as the Laju Incident. Their goal was to disrupt the supply of oil from Singapore to war-torn South Vietnam. This was an early example of Singapore being targeted as a key node in the global economy's maritime supply flows of oil.

Transmission of Global Risks: WMD Proliferation and Maritime Flows

If the Laju Incident was an attempt to disrupt maritime flows through Singapore, would-be WMD proliferators to the contrary depend on the smooth uninterrupted

33 Michael Richardson, *A Time Bomb for Global Trade: Maritime-related Terrorism in an Age of Weapons of Mass Destruction*. Singapore: ISEAS (2004), 3.

34 Stephen Graham, 'When Infrastructures Fail', in Stephen Graham (ed.), *Disrupted Cities: When Infrastructure Fails*. London: Routledge (2010), 24.

35 Phil Agre, 'Imagining the next war: infrastructural warfare and the conditions of democracy', *Radical Urban Theory*, 14 September 2001 <http://www.rut.com/911/Phil-agre.html> accessed 19 April 2005.

36 Stephen Graham, *Cities Under Siege*. London: Verso (2010), 267.

37 Ibid., 270.

circulation of maritime cargo through Singapore's port for their illicit materials to reach their intended destinations. The U.S. President Barack Obama warned that 'black-market trade in nuclear secrets and nuclear materials abound, the technology to build a bomb has spread. Terrorists are determined to buy, build, or steal ... This is the most immediate and extreme threat to global security'.[38] Obama specifically invited Singapore Prime Minister Lee Hsien Loong to the global nuclear security summit in March 2010 because 'Singapore serves as a critical trading hub in the region', said U.S. National Security Council spokesman Michael Hammer.[39] Prime Minister Lee described nuclear terrorism and proliferation as an 'existential threat' to the densely-populated urbanised global city that is Singapore, particularly one with a global maritime port. Complex and highly integrated maritime supply chains now underpin the global economy but they also provide conduits for the spread of WMD risks. Al-Qaeda allegedly planned to smuggle high-grade radioactive material into the US, hiding them in packets of sesame seeds in shipping containers.[40] In 2001, officials stumbled across a stow-away in a container, complete with suspicious airport security passes and mechanic's certificate, in the southern Italian port of Gioia Tauro, a key trans-shipment node for the Mediterranean. This danger of undesirable circulations and mobilities within maritime trade flows has become 'doubly vital for places like Singapore, Hong Kong and Rotterdam that are not only very large seaports with global connections, but also giant container trans-shipment hubs'.[41] In the maritime domain, the porosity and massive expanse of sea borders to be patrolled mean that illegal activities often go undetected.[42] If September 11th exposed weaknesses in the global aviation infrastructure and airports, attention also turned to vulnerabilities in the maritime sector's container shipping system, particularly the covert shipment of contraband goods.[43] Writing from the perspective of mobilities, John Urry has argued that 'materials too are on the move, often carried by those moving bodies, whether openly, clandestinely, or inadvertently. Also multinational sourcing of different components of manufactured products involves just-in-time

38 Barack Obama, 'Remarks in Hradčany Square, Prague, Czech Republic', 5 April 2009 <http://www.whitehouse.gov/the_press_office/Remarks-By-President-Barack-Obama-In-Prague-As-Delivered> accessed 30 April 2012.

39 Michael Hammer, 'White House National Security Council' (statement, United States of America, 15 November 2009) <http://www.atimes.com/atimes/China/KI26Ad01.html> accessed 15 November 2013.

40 Richardson, *A Time Bomb for Global Trade*, 9.

41 Ibid., 2.

42 Nicholas Lim, 'The Information Fusion Centre: A Case for Information Sharing to Enhance Security in the Maritime Domain', *The Information Fusion Centre: Challenges and Perspectives*. Singapore: SAF Pointers Supplement (2011), 3.

43 Paul H. Barnes and Richard Oloruntoba, 'Assurance of security in maritime supply chains: conceptual issues of vulnerability and crisis management', *Journal of International Management* 11:4, 519–40.

delivery from around the word'.[44] It is not just people, machines and money, but dangers such as WMD too are 'on the move'.[45]

These concerns perturbed Singapore's Deputy Prime Minister (DPM) Teo who depicts the transmission mechanism for WMD proliferation risks interestingly in terms of the very flows and circulations that Singapore's mega-port processes: 'As a result of the high volume of trade and information *flows* circulating the globe, proliferators today have greater flexibility and options as they use these legitimate channels to mask their illicit trade and make detection and prevention more difficult'.[46] By virtue of geographical location at the juncture of key sea lines and its dependence on maritime connectivity, Singapore has 'an important role to play in the common fight against WMD proliferation'.[47] For those on the frontlines, such as the former Director General of Singapore Customs, the risks and obligations were equally clear: 'Singapore is in a unique position in Asia. We are heavily dependent on trade and shipping for our livelihood ... it is also our responsibility to ensure that Singapore is not used as a conduit for illicit trade in WMD'.[48]

Singapore's position as a major trans-shipment hub means that such illicit circulations are a real danger. External observers such as the International Institute for Strategic Studies note that despite having efficient controls in place, 'because of the sheer volume of trade, however, and the inadequate controls of many of its trading partners, Singapore's export-control system is not leak-proof. As one of the most important business and transhipment hubs in the world, Singapore has been targeted by arms dealers and proliferators'.[49] Prime Minister Lee agreed that there are proliferation risks arising from the massive maritime trade flows circulating through Singapore's global port hub, 'we hope that we will be able to play our part to keep the global trading system safe because all you need is one warhead to slip through and that will not only cause a big disaster but cause a complete loss of confidence in the whole trading system and may break down and it will be a disaster for the world'.[50] Several cases already illustrate the range of WMD risks that exist from negative penetrative maritime flows. US citizen

44 John Urry, *Mobilities.* Cambridge: Polity Press (2007), 5.

45 Ibid., 6.

46 Teo Chee Hean, 'Exercise Deep Sabre II' (opening address, Singapore, 27 October 2009) <http://www.mindef.gov.sg/imindef/press_room/official_releases/nr/2009/oct/27oct09_nr/27oct09_speech.html#.U4KxWXKSySo> accessed 28 October 2013.

47 Ibid.

48 Teo Eng Cheong, 'Global Trade Controls – Asia Conference' (speech, Singapore, 25 May 2006) <http://www.customs.gov.sg/NR/rdonlyres/29789BF9–39F4–4E7C-BADD-5E0DC1561422/22486/GTCAddress.pdf> accessed 26 May 2012.

49 International Institute for Strategic Studies (IISS) Strategic Dossier, 'Preventing Nuclear Dangers in South-east Asia and Australasia' (2009), 134.

50 Interview with Charlie Rose on *Chicago Tonight*, 14 April 2010 <http://160.96.2.142/content/pmosite/mediacentre/speechesninterviews/primeminister/2010/April/transcript_of_primeministerleehsienloongsinterviewwithustelevisi.html#.U4KeenKSySo/> accessed 15 March 2012.

Laura Wang-Woodford, director of an import-export Singaporean firm Monarch Aviation Pte Ltd, was arrested by US authorities in December 2007 on suspicion of illegally exporting components for *Chinook* military helicopters from the US via Singapore port and transhipped to Iran. In another incident, the A.Q Khan network allegedly transferred Malaysian-built centrifuge parts by Scomi Precision Engineering (SCOPE), via Singapore, to Libya's nuclear weapons programme. 'The Khan network, like so many legitimate commercial concerns, appears to have taken advantage of Singapore's superb trade facilities, sending SCOPE-built centrifuge parts to Dubai via Singapore'.[51] Singapore firm Bikar Metal Asia unwittingly sold aluminium tubing to SCOPE. Mitutoyo Corporation in Japan also sent equipment to SCOPE through Singapore for onward shipment to Libya. In April 2007, Sokkia Singapore Pte Ltd which makes advanced 3-D measurement machines was sanctioned by the US for 'actions that potentially make a material contribution to the development of Weapons of Mass Destruction in Iran and Syria'.[52] In 2008, Singapore permitted the transhipment of a computer numerically controlled (CNC) five-axis machining centre (Model MC 1020, Sr No ME 10261 with Siemens 840D controller) from Istanbul and bound for Karachi. The U.S. Embassy protested because Pakistan as the end-user is a state of concern and the machinery could enhance WMD programmes. In 2011, as part of its broader sanctions regime against Iran's WMD program, the U.S. Treasury designated Singapore-based Sinose Maritime, the agent of The Islamic Republic of Iran Shipping Lines (IRISL) in Singapore, effectively barring its access to US financial and commercial systems. Prime Minister Lee has recognised that a global risk exists and that 'It is important because unless you do something about it, one day you are going to have a disaster but it may not happen tomorrow and there are so many other priorities to worry about immediately'.[53]

Disabling Connectivity: the Intentional Disruption of Global Port Hubs

If negative *penetrative* risks such as WMD proliferation transmitted through Singapore's port are predicated on the uninterrupted circulation of global maritime trade flows, another far more sinister *destructive* global risk exists for global port hubs. A maritime terrorist strike would seek to create maximum disruption to maritime trade flows.

Much of the existing focus on global cities targeted by terrorists revolves around their critical financial or aviation infrastructures. Coaffee observed that global cities with important financial centres were attractive targets because a successful attack extends beyond physical destruction; immense psychological

51 International Institute for Strategic Studies (IISS) Strategic Dossier, 'Nuclear Black Markets: A.Q. Khan and the rise of proliferation networks' (2007), 154.

52 IISS Strategic Dossier, 'Preventing Nuclear Dangers', 133–5.

53 Interview with Charlie Rose on *Chicago Tonight*.

damage is also incurred through taking down a high-profile icon, disrupting social fabric, commercial activities and confidence. The IRA targeted the City of London 'due to its symbolic value as the traditional heart of British imperialism and its economic importance at the centre of the British and global financial system'.[54] The Provisional IRA also sought not just structural damage and rising insurance costs, but London's prestige as a world financial centre also tumbles.[55] Senior officers with the City of London Police note that terrorists are drawn to prestigious targets like financial centres because they can cause many casualties but also severely disrupt trade and economic transactions worldwide. The guarantee of 24-hour media coverage is irresistible for groups craving publicity.[56] In 2003, it was reported that the British Chancellor of the Exchequer was considering the power to 'freeze payment and settlement systems and run the Bank of England in the aftermath of an attack'. The reasoning was simple: a successful terrorist strike could mean that the 'millions of financial transactions which normally take place each day would stop … this would inflict serious damage on the UK's reputation as a world player in the financial markets'.[57] Likewise, Harrigan and Martin argue that the actual cost of September 11th for New York accrued beyond immediate deaths and destruction, but extended to the knock-on effects on slower transportation linkages due to security checks as well as increased insurance premiums.[58] The disruption caused to the connectivity of global flows hat global cities depend on is therefore crucial to understanding motivation of terrorists. The Commissioner of the City of London Police is right that 'if you want to hurt the Government, hurt people and you want to cause maximum disruption, where better to hit than at the financial centre?'[59] Nussbaum argues global cities represent 'a sort of international critical infrastructure underpinning the global economy. They face potentially higher threats because of the high profiles, high number of international travelers and citizens, and target rich environments'.[60]

---

54 Jon Coaffee, *Terrorism, Risk and the Global City: Towards Urban Resilience*. Aldershot: Ashgate (2009), 7.

55 *An Phoblacht*/Republican News, 29 April 1993, cited in Coaffee, *Terrorism, Risks and the Global City*, 106.

56 Coaffee, *Terrorism, Risk and the Global City*, 79.

57 M. Curphey, 'The Chancellor's emergency measures', *Guardian*, 26 February 2003 <http:// http://www.theguardian.com/politics/2003/feb/26/economy.uk> accessed 27 February 2012, 20.

58 J. Harrigan and P. Martin, 'Terrorism and the resilience of cities', *FRBNY Economic Policy Review* 8:2, 97–116.

59 Cited in *Edinburgh Evening News*, 'Terror attack on finance hub is inevitable', 10 August 2005 <http://www.edinburgnews.scotsman.com/uk.cfm?id=1759222005> accessed 11 September 2013.

60 Brian Nussbaum, 'Protecting global cities: New York, London and the internationalisation of municipal policing for counter-terrorism', *Global Crime* 8:3 (2007), 213–32.

A financial centre is not the only type of critical infrastructure that enables global cities to discharge their command and control functions in the world economy. There is a close maritime cousin, for according to the OECD, world trade depends on a system of maritime transport that is rendered 'as frictionless as possible' such that 'any important breakdown in the maritime transport system would fundamentally cripple the world economy'.[61] Attacks or disruptions at core maritime gateways such as Singapore with their port hubs would derail the global maritime transport infrastructure through far-reaching ripple and cascade effects. As a result, fears about potential disruption or destruction of trade flows are driving the reorganising of global port security systems.[62] Maintaining the 'orderliness' of everyday life[63] may also mean making sure global cities' port hubs remain functional, in order to coordinate, manage and service global maritime flows.

Several incidents suggest that terrorist groups such as Al-Qaeda and affiliated organisations, the Jemaah Islamiah in Southeast Asia, have targeted major chokepoints in global seaborne trade.[64] The attack on the oil tanker M.V. *Limburgh* in 2002 off the Yemen coast, close to the Bab el-Mandab Strait, occurred in a busy shipping lane. An Al-Qaeda statement claimed that it was not an 'incidental attack at a passing tanker but on the international oil-carrying line in the full sense of the word … one can assume the scope of risks facing the Western economic lifeline, oil'.[65] In 2014, it was reported that Al-Qaeda's English magazine carried an article titled 'On Targeting the Achilles Heel of Western Economies', which advocated attacks on shipping in maritime chokepoints.[66] In March 2010, the Singapore Shipping Association issued a warning received from the Singapore Navy Information Fusion Centre of a potential terrorist attack on oil tankers in the Malacca Strait. In past cases of successful terrorist attacks on tankers, smaller vessels such as dinghies and speedboats were used. Such attacks would pale in comparison to a successful nuclear or radiological bomb strike on a mega port like Singapore.[67] Britain's First Sea Lord Sir Alan West had warned in 2004 of grave 'knock-on effects' that maritime terrorism would have on developed economies

61 Organisation for Economic Co-operation and Development (OECD), 'Security in maritime transport', Maritime Transport Committee, July 2003.

62 Graham, 'When Infrastructures Fail', 3.

63 Richard Johnson, 'Defending ways of life: the (anti) terrorist rhetorics of Bush and Blair', *Theory, Culture and Society* 19:4 (2002), 212.

64 Richardson, *A Time Bomb for Global Trade*, 36.

65 Al-Qaeda Statement in Martin Libicki, Peter Chalk, Melanie Cission, *Exploring Terrorist Targeting Preferences*. Santa Monica, CA: RAND Corporation (2007), 40–41.

66 *Jane's Intelligence Review*, ' Al Qaeda indicates increased intent to target shipping transiting chokepoints', 9 November 2014 <http://www.janes.com/article/45596/al-qaeda-indicates-increased-intent-to-target-shipping-transiting-chokepoints-but-sustained-attacks-are-unlikely> accessed 9 January 2015.

67 Richardson, *A Time Bomb for Global Trade*, 39.

and global trade in an inter-connected world.[68] In this regard, Castells' notion of global cities as space of flows exhibits a security dimension which has hitherto remained unexplored: 'national security, at least in the ports, is conceptualized as almost interchangeable with the security of international trade flows'.[69] When applying a logistics-driven approach to security of global flows, this means thinking about how to ensure 'the security of supply chains rather than the people who live in and work in the city', because 'logistics is ostensibly about efficient movement and undisrupted flow'.[70] For a global city with a port hub working to achieve frictionless maritime flows, any potential interruption becomes a 'system vulnerability, and forces that interfere with flow are managed as security threats'.[71] This intense focus on global maritime logistical movements means that national security in now thought of in terms of 'preventing the disruption of commodity flows and protecting transportation infrastructure'.[72]

Interestingly, as the notion of flows was used to describe the dangers of WMD proliferation by Singaporean policymakers, once again the same idea is expressed in the case of maritime terrorism. Transport Minister Lui noted, 'As a premier hub port along important trade routes, Singapore places a strong emphasis on the safety of navigation to sustain the flow of maritime trade'.[73] Singaporean leaders are keenly aware of how a disruption in one node can easily affect others, and have illustrated this risk using the example of the US labour dispute that shut down all West Coast ports for almost two weeks in October 2003. This was not even a deliberately destructive terrorist strike but the resulting delays and backlog for more than 200 ships carrying 300,000 containers took more than a month to resolve. Former Minister Khaw Boon Wan explained the lessons learnt in terms of the mechanics of flows: 'a minor disruption in trade flow nowadays can have big impact on factories half a world away, and takes weeks for the flows to be set right again … It is now a finely tuned system, so even a small hiccup can bring it to a halt. That was what the US ports' shutdown has done'.[74] Consequently, terrorists could create massive disruption in a tightly integrated globalised world by targeting key nodes in the close-knit economic system. This is why 'military

68 *Lloyd's List Daily News Bulletin*, 'First Sea Lord warns of al-Qaeda plot to target merchant ships', 5 August 2004 <http://www.lloydslist.com/ll/sector/piracy-and-security/article123388.ece> accessed 29 Octobeer 2014.

69 Deborah Cowen, 'Containing insecurity: logistic space, US port cities and the war on terror', in Stephen Graham (ed.), *Disrupted Cities*. London: Routledge (2010), 136.

70 Ibid., 69.

71 Ibid., 71.

72 Ibid.

73 Lui Tuck Yew, 'Official Commissioning of the Port Operations Control' (speech at Changi Naval Base, 25 July 2011) <http://www.mpa.gov.sg/sites/global_navigation/news_center/speeches/speeches_detail.page?filename=sp110725.xml> accessed 10 August 2012.

74 Khaw Boon Wan, 'Speech at 17th gala dinner of Singapore Shipping Association', 25 October 2002 <http://www.moulmein.org.sg/speech/20021028_singapore_as_london_plus.htm> accessed 9 January 2012.

doctrine and strategy (would become) more and more closely geared to the tactical and strategic protection of the political and economy key sites, zones and spaces of the global capitalist systems'.[75]

When you depend on vast maritime flows, then the risk is these might be somehow disrupted. Recounting an alleged conversation with Osama Bin Laden, British terror suspect Saajid Badat emphasised the economic disruption in a globalised world, 'So he (Osama) said the American economy is like a chain … If you break one link of the chain, the whole economy will be brought down'.[76] There is growing anxiety that the infrastructures that urban life depends upon also constitute an 'urban Achilles heel' that could be attacked and exploited by state or non-state actors.[77] Global maritime trading networks are another type of 'everyday' infrastructure that, as Singapore's Transport Minister noted, 'is an important cog in the machinery of world trade. An attack on a port or shipping lane would seriously disrupt trade … Southeast Asia, Singapore included, cannot escape from such threats'.[78] Defence Minister Tony Tan also explained the dangers in terms of shocks and disruption to global maritime supply chains because 'sea lanes and sea-borne commerce are attractive terrorist targets. They are the lifelines of the international economy and symbols of the globalised international system that the terrorists want to repudiate'.[79] As frictionless, uninterrupted maritime trade flows fuels the just-in-time interlinked globalised trading and manufacturing systems, the scenario presented by former Foreign Minister George Yeo of a hijacked LPG tanker crashing into Singapore port would 'disrupt operations at the world's second busiest port and a super-hub crucial to the smooth operation of today's globalised trading and manufacturing system'.[80] This 'tight coupling' of infrastructure has resulted from the imperatives of economic globalisation as complex inter-linked research, production, and consumption processes are spread out around the world yet they need to be closely coordinated to carry out their functions properly.[81]

---

75 Graham, 'In a moment', 415.

76 Larry Neumeister and Tom Hays, 'Two NY cooperators give firsthand look at Al Qaida', Associated Press, 7 May 2012 <http://news.yahoo.com/2-ny-cooperators-firsthand-look-al-qaida-211626418.html> accessed 7 May 2012.

77 Graham, 'When Infrastructures Fail', 16.

78 Yeo Cheow Tong, 'Maritime Security Should Be Beefed Up at the Multilateral, National and Individual Levels' (speech, International Maritime and Port Security Conference, 21 January 2003) <http://www.mpa.gov.sg/sites/global_navigation/news_center/mpa_news/mpa_news_detail.page?filename=030121.xml> accessed 10 December 2013.

79 Tony Tan, 'Maritime security after September 11' (speech at the IISS Conference Plenary Session, Singapore, 1 June 2003) <http:// http://www.mindef.gov.sg/imindef/press_room/official_releases/nr/2003/jun/01jun03_nr2.html#.U4VY7HKSySo> accessed 2 June 2013.

80 Andrew Tan, 'Singapore's cooperation with the Trilateral Security Dialogue Partners in the War Against Global Terrorism', *Defence Studies* 7:2 (2007), 193–4.

81 Stephen Graham, 'Disruption by Design: Urban Infrastructure and Political Violence', in Stephen Graham (ed.), *Disrupted Cities: When Infrastructure Fails*. London: Routledge (2010), 111.

As a global maritime hub, Singapore is inevitably affected by how the 'complexity of interaction between ports, maritime operations and supply chains create vulnerabilities'.[82] Type 1 vulnerability stems from operational complexity within a port. Type 2 vulnerability relates to maritime movements on the high-seas. By their very nature, ports are vulnerable since they are designed to be accessible by sea and land: that is their purpose to promote connectivity. The need for accessibility also makes it difficult to apply the security measures one sees at airports for instance. Therefore, it is worrying that 'global supply chains and the intermodal transportation system that supports them remains a very vulnerable critical infrastructure to mass disruption'.[83]

Singapore's leaders believe that their central position in the global maritime system makes it an attractive 'iconic' target like New York was on September 11th, but also because any attack would generate outsized disruption throughout the system. Former Defence Minister Tony Tan warned that 'if terrorists were to seize a tanker, a large ship, and sink it into a narrow part of the Straits it will cripple world trade. It would have the iconic large impact which terrorists seek'.[84] Although analysts such as Catherine Raymond are skeptical about how plausible this scenario actually is,[85] Singapore has emerged as 'icing on the cake' for several reasons, argued analyst Bilveer Singh. As a global city and a global hub for trade, finance and telecommunications, this makes it a 'critical infrastructure' for the smooth functioning of the world economy and successful attacks would greatly derail the smooth coordination and management of global flows of trade, information and supplies.[86] This was the reasoning behind Prime Minister Lee Hsien Loong's warning that 'a spectacular terrorist attack on a tanker or an LNG carrier in the Straits of Malacca would be a major setback for the whole region ... Asia's transformation is based fundamentally on globalisation, free markets, and the free flow of goods and services worldwide'.[87] Minister of Defence Teo reiterated that 'the sea is our lifeline. The disruption of sea-borne commerce

82 Barnes and Oloruntoba, 'Assurance of security in maritime supply chains', 519.

83 Stephen Flynn, 'Written testimony on "Neutralizing the nuclear and radiological threat: securing the global supply chain" before a hearing of the Permanent Subcommittee of Investigations', Committee on Homeland Security, U.S. Senate, Washington D.C., 28 March 2006.

84 Yudhoyono Susilo Bambang (speech at the IISS Asian Security Conference, Singapore, 6 June 2012) <http:// http://www.thejakartapost.com/news/2012/06/01/keynote-speech-11th-iiss-asia-security-summit-shangri-la-dialogue.html> accessed 7 June 2013.

85 Catherine Zara Raymond, 'Maritime terrorism in South-east Asia: potential scenarios', *Terrorism Monitor* 4:7 (2006).

86 Bilveer Singh, 'Why Singapore is an iconic target', *TODAYonline*, 22 July 2011 <http://www.themalaysianinsider.com/sideviews/article/why-spore-is-an-iconic-target-for-terrorists-bilveer-singh> accessed 10 April 2012.

87 Lee Hsien Loong, 'Lloyd's City Dinner' (speech, London, 7 September 2006) <http://www.nas.gov.sg/archivesonline/speeches/record-details/7e6c2509-115d-11e3-83d5-0050568939ad> accessed 8 September 2012.

would have a serious impact on the international economy, with not just economic but also strategic repercussions for the whole world'.[88] The 2006 decision by Lloyd's Joint War Committee to place the Malacca Straits on its list of areas at risk from terrorism attacks further created consternation from the Singapore Shipping Association because the decision raised the costs of maritime insurance, threatening to create obstacles for maritime traffic flows through Singapore.

Certainly, there are several reasons why terrorists would want to strike Singapore. Its perceived closeness to the US, Israel, and Europe, for example. But there is another reason related to it being a global city circulating global maritime flows. High-volume, mainline trade has increasingly become concentrated on just a few mega-ports like Singapore that become critical nodes of global seaborne trade, so much so that 'it has been estimated that global economic impact from closure of hub port like Singapore alone could easily exceed $200 billion per year from disruptions to inventory and production cycles'.[89] As Young and Valencia put it, 'The nightmare for the US is that a supertanker will be hijacked and driven into Singapore, or some other large port, or sunk in the Malacca Strait, thus seriously disrupting or detouring the flow of oil to East Asia'.[90] Speaking after September 11th, former Deputy Prime Minister Lee Hsien Loong pointed out, 'Singapore is also vulnerable. We are a financial centre, we are an economic hub … It happened in the US. We can take precautions but we can never say it will not happen in Singapore'.[91] Singapore is a major trans-shipment hub and overlooks the main east-west route within the global hub and spoke container network.[92] The threat of loss of a substantial port like Singapore thus is a major critical infrastructure protection issue.[93]

To sum up, to be 'just-in-time' and just enough' are characteristics of a twenty-first century global trading system driven by free-flowing international trade developed to be 'as open and frictionless as possible' through reduced barriers and tariffs.[94] As Al-Qaeda has stated that 'we are hoping to enter the next phase, a war

---

88 Teo Chee Hean, 'Emerging Security Trends: Challenges for Singapore and South-east Asia' (speech, Institute of Defence and Strategic Analysis, New Delhi, India, 2004) <http://www.mfa.gov.sg/content/mfa/overseasmission/new_delhi/press_statements_speeches/2004/200401/press_200401_01.html> accessed 10 April 2013.

89 Joshua Ho, 'The security of sea lanes in Southeast Asia', *Asian Survey* 46:4 (2006), 563.

90 Adam J. Young and Mark J. Valencia, 'Conflation of piracy and terrorism in Southeast Asia: rectitude and utility', *Contemporary Southeast Asia* 25: 2 (2003), 276–7.

91 Agence France Press, 'Osama bin Laden footprints surround "vulnerable" Singapore', 1 October 2001 <http://www.mindef.gov.sg/imindef/publications/pointer/supplements/IFC/_jcr_content/imindefPars/0006/file.res/MINDEF_Pointer%20IFC%20Supplement%20FINAL.pdf> accessed 16 August 2013.

92 Ho, 'The security of sea lanes in Southeast Asia', 561.

93 Barnes and Oloruntoba, 'Assurance of security in maritime supply chains'.

94 Catharine Zara Raymond, 'Maritime terrorism in Southeast Asia: a risk assessment', *Terrorism and Political Violence* 18:2 (2006), 239.

against business, which will hit the enemy where he does not expect us to', then 'targeting of maritime infrastructure is now a real possibility'.[95] The key shipping routes which Singapore's port serves are key arteries of the global economy and uninterrupted flow of shipping is critical to world economic growth.[96] The disruption of crucial sea lines by terrorists can have severe economic repercussions since the sea is the major transportation medium for trade and raw energy and materials.[97] This especially relates to narrow key waterways such as the Malacca Straits which is 600 miles long but at its narrowest point is only 1.5 miles wide. A tanker carrying 600 tonnes of LPG would cause a fireball 1200m wide.[98]

Attending to Global Maritime Trade Flows: A Needle in a Haystack and WMD Proliferation

As we have seen in previous chapters, the intricate layers and web of global trade connections that global cities service do not arise spontaneously out of nowhere. Whether these are aviation, financial or maritime flows, they depend on multiple actors, from the global business sector to governments and international organisations that help enable this web of connections to come into existence and function smoothly. It is also in this multi-level domain that one can identify what Beaverstock called 'attendants' to the global system: these attendants seek to protect and ensure the smooth and secure circulation of maritime trade flows through the port hub of Singapore. Let us first begin with WMD proliferation. As a global city, Singapore is on one hand committed to safeguard global maritime trade flows that it depends on but also keen to maintain its image as an efficient and convenient port circulating these flows without undue impediment. As former CEO of the PSA observed, 'PSA strives to integrate security requirements with our operational processes to minimise disruption and make cargo flow as seamless as possible'.[99] Singapore ports have to strike a delicate balance between implementing beefed-up port and maritime security measures that do not unduly delay or impede swift servicing of maritime trade. Given the millions of containers carried daily around the world on thousands of ships, checking all legitimate cargo for WMD-related materials is akin to looking for 'the proverbial needle in the haystack'.[100] Mirroring what we have already seen with terrorist financing and aviation security, the goal here is to make sure that the right 'desirable' maritime flows are properly processed

95 Ibid., 241, 245.

96 Ibid., 242.

97 Ho, 'The security of sea lanes in Southeast Asia', 559.

98 Ibid.

99 Grace Fu, 'Singapore gears up to meet security deadline', 11 February 2004 <http://www.mpa.gov.sg/sites/global_navigation/news_center/mpa_news/mpa_news_detail.page?filename=040211.xml> accessed 27 March 2010.

100 Richardson, *A Time Bomb for Global Trade*, 84.

by Singapore's port hub and sent on their way, while filtering out the undesirable ones such as illicit WMD materials. According to Mr Fong Yong Kian, Director-General of Singapore Customs[101] the challenge here is to maintain connectivity and ability to command and coordinate global maritime flows: 'Singapore Customs is committed to safeguarding trade security, so that trade can continue to flow smoothly'. The Immigration and Checkpoints Authority's Commissioner also stated that 'Being an international maritime hub, Singapore views the enhancement of homeland and (shipping) container security as an important response to the threats posed by terrorism'.[102] The key point to bear in mind here is that supply chain security is multi-dimensional. 'It requires government-to-government cooperation, business-to-business collaboration as well as government-to-business partnership in the development of security and trade initiatives'.[103] Maintaining nuclear security and safety in a complex, inter-connected world is simply beyond the capabilities of any single country.[104] For Minister of Defence Teo, 'We all share a common interest in preventing the proliferation of WMDs. In this era of increasing interconnectivity and interdependence, it is vital that we work together to safeguard our countries and people'.[105]

At the global level, as previously seen with aviation security; pandemics and terrorist financing, the inter-connected global maritime system is only as strong as its weakest links. To help plug gaps and weaknesses, Singapore has signed various international counter proliferation treaties such as the Nuclear Non-Proliferation Treaty, the Chemical Weapons Convention, the Biological Weapons Convention, and the Comprehensive Test Ban Treaty. Specifically with regard to Singapore's maritime port hub, the World Customs Organization or WCO has developed the Framework of Standards to Secure and Facilitate Global Trade. The WCO Framework contains a common set of standards to secure cargo movement in and out of the country, rather similar to the FATF Recommendations to ensure financial flows are not exploited by terrorist financiers discussed previously. WCO is designed to minimise abuse of the global maritime trading system by WMD

101 Singapore Customs, 'Singapore Customs rattles sabre against WMD proliferation', *Insync: Singapore Customs E-Newsletter* 7 (2010).

102 Immigration & Checkpoints Authority of Singapore (ICA), 'United States and Singapore governments launch effort to detect terrorist shipments of nuclear material', 10 March 2005 <http://app4.ica.gov.sg/news_details.aspx?nid=3086> accessed 24 April 2011.

103 Teo, 'Global Trade Controls – Asia Conference'.

104 Lee Hsien Loong, '2nd Nuclear Security Summit: Plenary Sessions on "National Measures and International Cooperation to Enhance Nuclear Security, Including Future Commitments"' (speech, Seoul, Republic of Korea, 27 March 2012) <http://160.96.2.142/content/pmosite/mediacentre/speechesninterviews/primeminister/2012/March/interventions_byprimeministerleehsienloongat2ndnuclearsecuritysu.html#.U4KsO3KSySo> accessed 28 March 2013.

105 Teo Chee Hean, 'Asia Pacific Security Conference' (opening address, Singapore, 22 February 2004) <http://www.mindef.gov.sg/imindef/press_room/official_releases/sp/2004/22feb04_speech.html#.U4KxLHKSySo> accessed 23 February 2012.

proliferators while facilitating the flow of legitimate trade. Singapore adopted the WCO Framework in 2005. Singapore Customs was praised for its efficiency in terms of facilitating trade by the World Customs Organization (WCO) Secretary General, Mr Kunio Mikuriya, who said that Singapore's maritime hub is one of the real examples that demonstrate coordination, collaboration and cooperation. Mikuriya believed that World Customs Organization (WCO) and other global customs operators can learn from Singapore's best practices.[106] Singapore is seeking also to facilitate involvement of extra-regional powers such as Australia, Japan and USA.[107] Singapore also hosted the ASEAN Regional Forum Seminar on Non-Proliferation of Weapons of Mass Destruction (WMD) with China and the US in March 2006. In 2007, it hosted a pilot IAEA Sub-Regional Workshop on Illicit Nuclear Trafficking Information Management and Coordination.

At the bilateral level of cooperation, as a global port hub with deep economic links to the US markets, any US initiatives to improve port/container/maritime security inevitably will have an effect on Singapore.[108] For instance, the US-led Container Security Initiative (CSI) specifically focuses on major ports such as Singapore, Hong Kong or Yokohoma in Japan. Singapore was one of the 18 original ports to join the US Container Security Initiative (CSI) after the September 11th attacks. Like temperature screening to filter out desirable healthy travellers from undesirable sick passenger flows in aviation security, CSI is designed to identify high-risk shipments (or undesirable negative penetrative flows) from the circulations of maritime trade that traverse mega-ports every single day. CSI thus 'focuses on the series of maritime enclaves which orchestrate global divisions of labour and resulting trade flows … covers major seaports and the flows that link them'.[109] These ports pre-screen and target high-risk cargo containers travelling towards the US. Cargo manifests are to be emailed to US 24 hours before loading. US personnel are also posted to CSI ports to inspect high-risk cargo together with officials from the host nation. Gamma and neutron sensitivity scanning equipment are also deployed. In 2009, 58 foreign ports were participating in CSI, accounting for 85 per cent of container traffic bound for the United States.

Singapore is also part of the Megaports Initiative that is designed to deter, detect and interdict illegal shipments of nuclear weapons materials. The initiative has set up radiation detectors at over 230 locations at 30 major ports around the world. Former Commissioner of the ICA Lock Wai Han said, when signing the agreement with U.S. Ambassador Frank Lavin, 'Singapore's participation in the initiative demonstrates our commitment in safeguarding maritime security and the

106 'WCO Secretary-General Commends Singapore Customs' Contribution to Global Customs Community', *InSync: Singapore Customs E-Newsletter* 19, (2012), 7.

107 Tan, 'Singapore's cooperation with the Trilateral Security Dialogue Partners in the war against global terrorism', 194.

108 Mark Hong, 'Singapore's Security Concerns Post-9/11', *RUSI Journal* 148:1 (2003), 52.

109 Graham, *Cities under siege*, 135.

global trading system'.[110] Radiation detection equipment and infrastructure were set up at Brani terminal. The initiative is especially focused on trans-shipment cargo flows that go through Singapore's port. Another initiative Singapore has joined is the US-led Proliferation Security Initiative, an 'informal arrangement' among countries best viewed as 'an activity, not an organization'. According to the U.S. State Department, PSI partners cooperate at developing and maintaining effective measures for interdicting the illicit transfer of WMDs, delivery systems, and related materials to and from States and non-state actors of proliferation concern. PSI training exercises, which Singapore has hosted twice, are focused mostly on intercepting deliveries of suspect ships on the high-seas.

As we have seen when a global city like Singapore deals with global risks from SARS and terrorist financing, there is also an emphasis on coordinating across all relevant agencies to address the risk of WMD proliferation. Former Defence Minister Teo argued that 'to ensure effective enforcement, we adopt a "whole of government" approach to coordinate action across all relevant government agencies at both policy and operational levels'.[111] Singapore has implemented a Strategic Goods (Control) Act in 2003 to strengthen export controls. This Act, which is administered by Singapore Customs, regulates the transfer of strategic goods and related technologies. There is an Inter-Ministry Committee on proliferation, chaired by the Foreign Ministry, with representatives from other ministries such as Trade & Industry, Home Affairs, Defence, Customs, Transport and the Attorney General's Chambers. Other Agencies involved include: Monetary Authority of Singapore; Defense Trade Advisory Office; and National Security Coordination Secretariat. Singapore Customs for instance led the Port Search Phase of the PSI Deep Sabre Exercise hosted by Singapore in 2005 and 2009. Working together with the Singapore Armed Forces' Chemical, Biological, Radiological and Explosive (SAF CBRE) team and the Singapore Civil Defence Force, participants were taught how to go about identifying, unloading and inspecting containers suspected of containing radioactive materials. Other agencies participating included the Immigration & Checkpoints Authority, Maritime & Port Authority of Singapore.

Besides engaging with global organisations like WCO and coordinating between enforcement agencies like Singapore Customs, other key 'attendants' of the global maritime network such as the private shipping industry and global shipping lines need to be on board to ensure that smooth circulation of maritime flows is not exploited by presumptive WMD proliferators. As the Director General of Singapore Customs put it, 'Our export control system will not be effective without the understanding and co-operation from the industry'.[112] Industry-government collaboration is key in combating proliferation, to raise awareness and compliance of export controls through seminars and courses. Singapore Customs has been reaching out to the

110 ICA, 'United States and Singapore governments launch effort to detect terrorist shipments of nuclear material'.

111 Teo, 'Exercise Deep Sabre II'.

112 Teo, 'Global Trade Controls – Asia Conference'.

industry and organised an outreach session, titled 'Doing Our Part to Curb the Spread of Weapons of Mass Destruction', at the Revenue House on 28 October 2009. The session attracted more than 100 participants from the industry, including shipping lines, freight forwarders, and logistics providers. Customs also runs The Strategic Goods Control Programme, a one-day programme that consists of two modules, SC 201 Basics of Strategic Goods Control Seminar and SC 202 Essentials of Internal (Export Control) Compliance Programme Seminar. In 2007, Singapore Customs launched the Secure Trade Partnership (STP), a voluntary certification programme that encourages companies to adopt robust security measures in their trading operations, in order to 'prevent disruptions to the smooth flow of goods', once again highlighting the central role that notions of global flows play when conceptualising global risks.[113] Interested companies can ask for tailored '1-to-1 Company Consultation' from Customs officials when implementing this program. The STP programme is open to all supply chain stakeholders (importers, exporters, warehouse operators, transporters, and terminal operators, etc.) and is consistent with the World Customs Organisation (WCO) SAFE Framework of Standards to secure and facilitate global trade mentioned earlier. The STP is a good example of how global level guidelines can be translated into practice for industry stakeholders operating at the frontlines on a daily basis looking out for suspicious WMD flows.

The overarching goal here is to raise awareness among key industry players, and to improve enforcement of WMD counter-proliferation measures. Mutual cooperation in tackling WMD proliferation by both the government and the industry means getting all 'attendants' involved in minimising the possibility of WMD proliferation through the global maritime trade network. US assistance has been forthcoming in helping industry identify items of WMD concern. Japan's METI, in cooperation with Singapore Customs, also conducts outreach activities such as holding seminars and other programs for capacity-building for export control in Asian countries and regions. METI also offered to dispatch experts on Commodity Identification Technology in order to strengthen the enforcement of export controls by Singapore Customs. Recognising the need to enhance interoperability and cooperation across not just partner nations but also relevant industry sectors as well, the Deep Sabre II PSI exercise Singapore hosted in 2009 brought together 'a wide range of multi-national participants from not only the military forces, but also legal, law enforcement and intelligence agencies, port and civil aviation authorities and industry'.[114] Industry actors such as Neptune Orient Lines Ltd (NOL) and PSA Corporation Ltd (PSA) also participated in the port search phase of Deep Sabre in 2005. Under the auspices of APEC, Singapore hosted a symposium on Total Supply Chain Security in 2006. The symposium brought together experts from the public and private sector to share their views and best practices on the security of the global supply chain.

113 Singapore Customs, 'Secure Trade Partnership' <http://www.customs.gov.sg/leftNav/trad/Supply+Chain+Security.htm> accessed 18 April 2010.

114 Teo, 'Exercise Deep Sabre II'.

Despite Singapore's efforts and commitment to combat WMD proliferation, it suffers from several problems. The first is knowledge about commodity identification: it possesses limited technical expertise in identifying specific nuclear or missile parts even if these were seen in cargo holds of ships. It also has to consider how to balance increased licensing procedures without hampering trade and increased costs. This is a key challenge clearly understood by senior officials such as the Director-General of Singapore Customs.[115] For items on the control list, the Government would have to convince industry that controlling these items was important and could be done with minimal interruption to commerce and maritime trade. This reflect a fundamental dilemma of an open highly connected global city: how to facilitate smooth maritime flows without jeopardising security and its hub port status open for trade.

Security in an inter-connected world is only as strong as its weakest link, as we have seen with terrorist financing. In terms of global maritime trade flows, about 50 per cent of world shipping (by tonnage) is still processed through ports that are not part of the PSI. CSI also screens only a fraction of US imports from risky countries: all it takes is one container to get through. Between 140,000 to 1 million containers from risky countries could be arriving at US ports without CSI screening.[116] This highlights the stark inter-dependence and close linkage between ports around the world in terms of maritime trade flows. As Prime Minister Lee highlighted at the 2010 Nuclear Security summit, second-tier ports also need to put in place effective safeguards as well, 'Otherwise, instead of preventing the illicit movement of nuclear materials, we would simply divert them to less stringent jurisdictions … Our experience suggests that vessels with suspicious cargoes are already bypassing ports like Singapore with stricter controls'.[117]

Reducing the Risk of Maritime Terrorism Disrupting Trade Flows

The preceding discussion addressed the challenges of interdicting undesirable mobiliities such as WMD hidden within global maritime flows. The risk is penetrative in nature, as WMD proliferators depend on connectivity of the system to achieve their goals. However, the more destructive risk of a terrorist attack that intentionally seeks to unhinge the global maritime infrastructure also mandates a multi-level response from all stakeholders involved in 'attending' to the network of global maritime flows. When it comes to maritime terrorism, Singapore has stressed a similar coordinated holistic approach in its domestic national regulatory and enforcement framework: 'The cornerstone of Singapore's strategy

115 Teo, 'Global Trade Controls – Asia Conference'.

116 Jon D. Haveman et al., 'The Container Security Initiative and Ocean Container Threats', *Journal of Homeland Security and Emergency Management* 4:1 (2007), 1547–7355.

117 Cited in Chua, 'Nuclear terrorism: it's real'.

is a stronger and more robust inter-agency network'.[118] Only though 'a whole-of-government and whole-of-society approach, and through adept diplomacy to leverage on international cooperation, Singapore has to ensure a zero success rate for terrorists'.[119] A New National Security Secretariat was set up initially within the Ministry of Defence, and later moved to the PM's Office, in order to strengthen coordination between all security agencies. The approach is based on the principle of 'setting up a network to fight the terrorist network'.[120] A Homeland Security framework was also drafted for closer inter-agency coordination. A Home Front Security Centre surpervises security operations and joint exercises. Republic of Singapore Navy (RSN), the Police Coast Guard (PCG), and the Maritime and Port Authority (MPA) cooperate closely to protect Singapore against seaborne threats. Navy warships escort selected high-value merchant vessels in the Singapore Straits while coast guard boats have intensified patrols of sensitive vessels. Exercise Apex for instance is a maritime drill involving Coast Guard and Navy aimed at boosting the ability to tackle maritime terrorism in Singapore and Malacca Straits. 'To Singapore, it's very important because we thrive on shipping and that's one of our major sources of revenue. We must be ready at all times'.[121] A Maritime Security Task Force has been set up to consider further ways of enhancing maritime security. It comprises the Inter-Agency Coordination Group including representatives from the Police Coast Guard (PCG), the Maritime and Port Authority of Singapore (MPA), the Immigration & Checkpoints Authority (ICA), and the Singapore Customs (Customs). The Operations Group comprises operations planners from the Army, Navy and Air Force, while the Comprehensive Maritime Awareness (CMA) Group builds information-sharing networks. It works closely with national agencies, international partners and the shipping community (such as ship owners, ships charterers, agents and port operators) to share maritime information. Singapore Port has also gone beyond the provisions laid down by the International Maritime Organization to also equip smaller craft with transponder systems.[122] The Harbour Craft Transponder System (HARTS) is a world-first that automatically tracks and monitors small boats in Singapore ports. In 2011, Singapore's Exercise Northstar series of counter-terrorism drills involved 18 different agencies, including the Singapore Armed Forces (SAF), the Singapore

118 National Security Coordination Centre Singapore, 'The Fight against Terror: Singapore's National Security Strategy'. Singapore: National Security Coordination Centre (2004), 39.

119 Singh, 'Why Singapore is an iconic target'.

120 Hong, 'Singapore's security concerns post-9/11', 54–5.

121 Philip Alvar, Head of Operations for Coastal Command, 'Singapore holds maritime drill to combat terrorism, piracy', Bloomberg, 29 August 2006 <http://www.bloomberg.com/apps/news?pid=newsarchive&sid=ajg9HuWQn9aM> accessed 1 April 2010.

122 National Security Coordination Centre Singapore, 'The Fight Against Terror', 50–51.

Civil Defence Force (SCDF), the Singapore Police Force (SPF), the Immigration and Checkpoints Authority, the Maritime and Port Authority and Singapore Customs. A maritime Information Fusion Centre (IFC) has been established next to its Changi naval base, designed to be a regional maritime information hub to enhance maritime situation awareness and information sharing. Ten countries have sent International Liaison officers to the IFC.

Again, the various 'attendants' of the global maritime system are called into action here. Defence Minister Teo has stated that 'individual state action is obviously not enough in this as in other areas of the fight against terrorism. In this sector in particular, states do not have all the answers. Cooperation among the multiple stakeholders is key. This means not only governments and their agencies, but also our commercial partners. There has been an encouraging array of maritime security initiatives from multilateral forums such as the International Maritime Organisation (IMO), APEC, ASEAN and the ASEAN Regional Forum'.[123] Maritime Information-Sharing Exercise (MARISX) 2011 simulated a series of terrorist plots for maritime strikes from the sea. This involved 27 countries as well as intergovernmental arrangements such as the International Maritime Bureau (IMB) and Regional Cooperation Agreement on Combating Piracy and Armed Robbery Against Ships (ReCAAP).

Working with partners at the global level, Singapore has implemented special amendments to the International Convention for the Safety of Life at Sea (SOLAS) and the International Ship and Port Facility Security Code (ISPS Code). The Code provides standard global guidelines allowing both states and ship operators to evaluate the risk of terrorist attacks as well as develop contingency plans for responding. PSA port terminals that have implemented the IPSPS code incorporate the guidelines in their security designs from access control to transit security measures during navigation. Singapore shipping company Neptune Orient Lines in 2004 was the first to achieve certification of its entire fleet's compliance with the code. On the back of its maritime global port hub status, Singapore chaired the Asia-Pacific Economic Cooperation Trade Recovery Programme in 2009 on how to recover from a maritime terrorist strike. It was then asked by the World Customs Organisation to chair its Trade Recovery Subgroup in order to develop guidelines to secure global trade. This resulted in key principles such as 'Respond' (actions to be taken in immediate aftermath of an incident), 'Repair' (actions to identify and rectify capability and security gaps); 'Reconstitute' (actions to bring trade back to normal state).[124] The WCO then adjusted these guidelines and formally incorporated it into WCO's SAFE Framework of Standards, which seek to establish global standards for supply chain security and facilitation to promote predictability. According to Mikuriya, 'We made the Singaporean product into a

123 Teo, 'Emerging Security Trends'.

124 World Customs Organization, 'WCO Trade Recovery Guidelines', 2010 <http://www.wcoomd.org/en/topics/facilitation/instrument-and-tools/tools/~/media/558C64ADD8634558A123D75357E188EE.ashx> accessed 20 September 2014.

global one'.[125] This was a concrete example of how multi-level cooperation from local to global actors came about in order to reduce the potential of disruption from a maritime terrorist strike.

Besides setting global guidelines, the idea of partnership with those industry actors on the frontline in circulating maritime trade flows through Singapore port is fundamental here to understanding the response to maritime terrorism risks. The cooperation of these 'attendants' is indispensable to ensure security of port hubs and uninterrupted maritime flows. To that end, the Navy's Information Fusion Centre also works closely with the Singapore Shipping Association and many shipping companies through a two-monthly Shipping Shared Awareness meeting.[126] Singapore's Chief of Navy noted that 'the maritime security challenges faced are complex and trans-boundary in nature. There is a need for various stakeholders to come together and collaborate. Cooperation between navies, coast guards, other maritime agencies and the shipping community will be the key'.[127] In May 2004, the Maritime and Port Authority of Singapore (MPA), PSA Singapore Terminals (PSA) and major shipping firm Neptune Orient Lines (NOL) conducted a joint maritime security exercise for the first time. The exercise tested the operational effectiveness of port and ship security plans put in place as a result of the ISPS compliance. Other government agencies such as the Auxillary Police – AETOS, Singapore Police Force (Special Operations Command and Police Coast Guard), Immigration and Checkpoints Authority and the Republic of Singapore Navy also deployed their resources. Then-NOL group president David Lim said 'It is harder for terrorists to succeed if there is a close and effective working relationship between the authorities and the shipping community. Exercises such as this both practice security procedures and help build those relationships'.[128] Ms Grace Fu, CEO of PSA Terminals noted 'we look forward to working with our partners along the logistic chain to achieve our common objective of ensuring safe and efficient movement of goods'.[129] Once again, the stress here is on how multiple stakeholders can work together to maintain the uninterrupted maritime trade flows through Singapore as a global city. The NOL Group's container shipping business APL also conducted similar drills with other major ports like Seattle, Los Angeles and Yokohama.

---

125 'WCO Secretary-General Commends Singapore Customs' Contribution to Global Customs Community', *InSync: Singapore Customs E-Newsletter* 19 (2012), 7.

126 Lim, 'The Information Fusion Centre', 7.

127 Chew Men Leong, 'Foreword', The Information Fusion Centre: Challenges and Perspectives, 30 March 2011, Ministry of Defence Singapore <http://www.mindef.gov.sg/imindef/publications/pointer/supplements/IFC.print.html?Status=1> accessed 9 April 2014.

128 Cited in Maritime and Port Authority of Singapore, PSA Singapore Terminals and Neptune Orient Lines, 'First Joint Maritime Security Exercise', MPA Statement, 25 May 2004 <http://www.mpa.gov.sg/sites/global_navigation/news_center/mpa_news/mpa_news_detail.page?filename=nr040525.xml> accessed 26 June 2012.

129 Ibid.

As it has done with building networked partnerships with industry actors and outreach to combat WMD proliferation, the Maritime Port Authority of Singapore organised a conference on maritime security in 2003 bringing together representatives from international organisations like the International Maritime Organisation, other port operators like the Port of Los Angeles, to Singapore shipping companies such as Neptune Orient Lines (NOL). Then-acting chief executive officer of NOL Mr Ron Widdows highlighted the implications of maritime terrorism for 'stakeholders in international trade', of which NOL is clearly one.[130] Indeed, a key 'corporate responsibility' goal of NOL as stated on its website is to 'build better, more secure supply chains'[131] working with other shippers, carriers and government agencies like the Singapore Customs and U.S. Customs and Border Protection as well as trade bodies such as the World Shipping Council's Security Advisory Committee. Taken together, from the global level right down to the shipping industry (the likes of Neptune Orient Line) and port operators like Maritime Port Authority of Singapore, these actions demonstrate how new multi-level relationships are emerging in response to the global risks of a maritime terror strike. What motivates these actors is a shared collective desire to ensure minimal disruption to the circulation of maritime trade flows through the global city of Singapore. Indeed, these actors demonstrate that a global city and its command and control functions clearly do not automatically come about. It requires collective action on the part of multiple stakeholders for such connectivity to be achieved and maintained in the face of global risks to the maritime infrastructure.

Conclusion

Perhaps even more so than the financial or aviation sectors, maritime connectivity has long been a distinguished and defining characteristic of Singapore's global city status. Singapore first depended on its port to connect to the world, way before it started developing its financial centre or airport. Its world-leading global port hub is not only its raison d'etre; it is also a crucial node coordinating and servicing the complex maritime trade flows of goods and materials that constitute the 'just-in-time' integrated global supply chain today. Ensuring that these trade flows are not disrupted or exploited for nefarious purposes has emerged as a key challenge for all those multiple actors involved in enabling Singapore's maritime connectivity as a global city. As in earlier discussions on financial and aviation flows, this chapter set out to bridge on one hand the academic literature on mobilities and global cities as spaces of maritime flows, and on the other hand the global risks that Ulrich Beck

130 Maritime Port Authority of Singapore, 'Conference Program' <http://www.mpa.gov.sg/sites/pdf/030113-b.pdf> accessed 24 March 2011.

131 Neptune Orient Lines, 'About Us' <http://www.nol.com.sg/wps/portal/nol/aboutus/corporateresponsibility/security> accessed 9 April 2012.

emphasised but glossed over in terms of their impact on global cities. Two types of global risks were identified here that arise from Singapore's central position coordinating maritime trade flows – the negative penetrative (WMD proliferation) and the negative destructive (maritime terrorism). These de-localised risks have trans-national repercussions on global cities such as Singapore in an interdependent world. Both share similarities in that they are *intentional*, exploiting Singapore's maritime infrastructure either as a means of onward transmission, or targeting that very same maritime system to create world-wide disruption to trade flows. Singapore's leaders clearly recognised these global risks were related to the global city's intense maritime connectivity. This chapter then showed how the various multi-level actors (from international organisations to governments to the shipping industry sectors) that enable a global port hub to discharge its critical functions work together in response to managing these global maritime risks. Singapore's signature 'whole-of-government' inter-agency approach was not only a constant recurrent feature (as with managing global financial and aviation risks), it also emphasised outreach to relevant maritime industry players and multilateral frameworks. The key maritime services that global cities provide do not automatically come about, they have to be provided and continuously maintained. There are several similarities here with regard to how global cities seek to ensure their continued ability to function and stay connected in the face of global risks. Like Singapore's emphasis on outreach with private actors such as Neptune Orient Lines and the Singapore Shipping Association, London too has its Project Griffin launched jointly by the Metropolitan Police and the City of London Police. It brings together police and other emergency services, local authorities and private security sector to coordinate efforts in counter-terrorism. What Beaverstock called the 'attendants' of the global trade network are also very much in evidence in the highly integrated maritime trade domain where disruptions in any one node can easily send ripple effect throughout the whole system. These actors all have an interest in ensuring that disruptions to, or exploitation of the smooth flows of maritime trade through Singapore do not happen as far as possible. Scholars such as Dillon and Graham working on the notion of circulation in regard to global security will recognise the renewed emphasis in Singapore's ports that only the 'right' and desirable type of maritime flows are processed and sent on their way, filtering out the 'undesirable' circulation of WMD-related materials. The maritime shipping industry and logistics sectors are on the front-line when dealing with these risks.

Several implications arise from this securitisation of Singapore's maritime environment. Scholars have pointed out how 'the potential threat of urban terrorism in certain cities has necessitated attempts to "design out terrorism" through addition of advanced security design features'.[132] As Graham observes, 'military and geopolitical security penetrate utterly into practices surrounding

132 Coaffee, *Terrorism, Risk and the Global City*, 6.

governance, design and planning of cities and regions'.[133] This 'obsession with urban security in certain global cities has in recent years led architects and planners to design buildings and spaces that are infused with notions of security and defence in residential, leisure and commercial areas'.[134] This is also becoming evident in the ways in which the Singapore port is being designed to enhance its security features. What initially began as an emphasis on crime prevention through urban design has now evolved towards design solutions for reducing the potential of terrorist attack. These include physical barriers to restrict access, CCTV cameras, blast protection for individual buildings, armed checkpoints, and parking restrictions. Such measures are also now deployed commonly through the port of Singapore, whose security systems include armed checkpoints, intruder alarm systems, access control systems, CCTV systems, central alarm monitoring system, X-Ray machines, and door-entry systems.

One should not forget however that being seen to be secure also confers competitive benefits for a global city. For instance, the so-called 'ring of steel' that emerged around the City of London helped to 'create a secure platform upon which it could continue to develop and adapt to its role as the financial heart of a world city'.[135] Similarly, the London Resilience Forum was set up explicitly for this reason to demonstrate that businesses are ready to 'bounce-back' from any terror attack. Being security-conscious enhances the ability to attract and capture trade flows if a global city is perceived to be better prepared and more resilient than its competitors when managing global risks. It is paramount to be seen to be able to swiftly restore normal maritime trade flows as quickly as possible, with minimal fuss. Singapore Customs' Secure Trade Partnership is explicitly designed to 'profile Singapore as a secure trading hub'. Coaffee argues that 'there has been a paradigm shift from counter-terrorism towards resilience, which is becoming a key discourse in shaping how global cities and their business environments are structured'.[136] To demonstrate resilience, Singapore's Maritime Port Authority has developed comprehensive contingency plans reinforced by regular operational drills in order to ensure efficiency. Examples of multi-agency exercises include the Joint Oil Spill Exercise codenamed 'JOSE 2012' in October which simulated the collision between an oil tanker and a cargo vessel. Again, this involved a wide range of government agencies and industry partners such as ExxonMobil and Sinanju Tankers Private Limited. Vessel traffic management operations are conducted at the upgraded Port Operations Control Centre (POCC) – Vista and the newly commissioned POCC – Changi. The two POCCs are manned 24 hours and fully integrated to provide a mutual back-up system with multiple layers of built-

133 Stephen Graham, 'Special collection: reflections on cities, September 11th and the war on terrorism one year on', *International Journal of Urban and Regional Research* 26:3 (2002), 589.

134 Coaffee, *Terrorism, Risks and the Global City*, 215.

135 Ibid., 197.

136 Ibid., 298.

in redundancy. If one control centre is rendered out of action in an emergency, the other can quickly take full operational control in its place.

Singapore's leaders repeatedly point to how its global port hub is now an 'iconic' target because of its position as a key maritime trade node, but unfortunately the prominence of global cities in targeting is not unique. During the Cold War, the writer E.B. White wrote that 'all city dwellers must live with the stubborn fact of annihilation; in New York the fact is somewhat more concentrated because of the concentration of the city itself, and because of all targets, New York has a certain clear priority'.[137] The events of September 11th concentrated the world's attention on how to protect globally significant cities such as New York and London with their global financial centres. Even before September 11th, Martin Pawley noted in 1997 that 'fear of the dislocation of urban services on a massive scale is now endemic in the populations of all great cities'.[138] NYPD Commissioner Ray Kelly mused that 'as a matter of fact, we probably look more like London than we do like any other US city. (A terrorist attack in New York) has a ripple effect throughout the whole world'.[139] Therefore, 'terrorist targeting against the UK is still focused upon London, particularly the financial zones where maximum economic damage can be done'.[140] For all this entirely understandable fixation on protecting financial cores of global cities, one must not forget that servicing global financial flows is but one dimension of the multiple types of flows and connectivity that global cities depend on. This is why the analytical framework deployed throughout this book based on notions of circulation; mobilities; infrastructure and flows allows researchers to more closely appraise the security conundrum stated at the onset of this book: how and why do hyper-connected global cities also face global risks as a result. As this chapter has demonstrated, global cities with critical infrastructure that circulate and command maritime trade flows also confront a range of maritime risks that need to be properly managed. For Singapore, this is especially pronounced because it was and is a global port hub, way before it became a significant financial centre or aviation node.

137 Cited in Graham, 'In a moment', 411.

138 Martin Pawley, *Terminal Architecture*. London: Reaktion (1998), 162.

139 Speaking on 8 August 2006 cited in Nussbaum, 'Protecting global cities', 217.

140 Coaffee, *Terrorism, Risk and the Global City*, 277.

Chapter 6
Global Cities: Premium Sites and Paragons of Global Risk Management?

Introduction

It should come as no surprise to readers that globalisation is increasingly viewed as a double-edged sword, as Tony Blair warned,

> We are bound together as never before. And this coming together provides us with unprecedented opportunity but also makes us uniquely vulnerable.[1]

'September 11th was the dark side of this new age of global interdependence', echoed Bill Clinton. In humankind's inaugural urban and metropolitan century, this book has argued that a significant urban dimension to the downside risks of globalisation exists, with the negative effects disproportionately felt in highly connected global cities. For some geographers at least, humanity's historic crossing of the urban threshold went 'largely unrecognised and unreported, and its profound symbolic importance was overlooked'.[2] This book hopes to have redressed some of this oversight, by highlighting the hitherto unexplored nexus between global cities and global risks for IR and Security Studies. The conceptual innovation behind this project has been premised on bringing together several significant themes concurrently developing in academia. Mounting concerns about rapidly spreading global risks are reflected in academic works such as Ulrich Beck on a 'world at risk' and Ian Goldin on how globalisation creates systemic risks that can destabilise whole societies. There has also been a plethora of policy reports on global risks and shocks issued by global bodies such as the WEF and the OECD, as well as the publication of 'National Risk Registers' in Britain and the Netherlands. Despite increasing alarm about this so-called 'dark side of globalisation'[3] and the fanfare about humankind's new urban era, this has not translated into greater

---

1 Tony Blair, 'Joint Session of Congress' (speech, Washington D.C., 17 July 2003), <http://www.cnn.com/2003/US/07/17/blair.transcript/>.

2 David Clark, *Urban World/Global City*. London: Routledge (2003), 1.

3 Jorg Heine and Ramesh Thakur, *The Dark Side of Globalization*. Tokyo: United Nations University Press (2011).

academic attempts by Security Studies scholars to assess security implications for the global cities that are both highly globalised *and* urbanised at the same time.

On the other hand, geographers and urban studies scholars writing about highly-connected global cities – whether conceptualised in terms of their command and control functions; their infrastructure; or as 'spaces of flows' and mobilities – have developed largely autonomously of works about globalisation and risks such as Ulrich Beck's *World Risk Society*. This neglects the intriguing global city-global risk conundrum that this book posed at the beginning: hyper-connected global cities are also most vulnerable to global risks. Two critical dimensions of this question were drawn out for more detailed analysis in the preceding chapters. The first involves transmission mechanisms of de-spatialised global risks and the relationship with global cities, which Beck overlooked. To address this issue, the analytical framework developed in this book incorporated ideas from geography and urban studies scholars working on global cities as 'spaces of flows' and circulation, the 'infrastructure approach'; and the 'mobilities turn'. From London to New York and Singapore, it has been argued that global cities' critical infrastructure in the form of airports, maritime port hubs, and financial cores, served either as inadvertent transmission mechanisms (e.g. financial contagion and pandemics) or are more deliberately exploited and targeted (e.g. aviation and maritime terrorism) to generate maximum disruption to global flows. These gateways to the world thrive precisely because they are so open and connected. However, this ability to process global flows entails exposure to global risks in several forms that this book has highlighted: *inadvertent* negative *penetrative* flows (financial contagion, pandemics); *deliberately* negative *destructive* that seek to disrupt flows (aviation and maritime terrorism) and *intentional* negative *penetrative* flows (terrorist financing, WMD proliferation). While there clearly is concern in officialdom on how globalisation might affect Singapore's traditional understanding of vulnerability, this book has sought to overcome the dearth of academic works that engage in sustained and in-depth analysis on its changing vulnerability as a global city.

The second dimension of our question relates to how the 'cosmopolitan vision' Beck had articulated affects global cities in their attempts to manage global risks. How might his claim that 'global threats create global society'[4] be relevant to global cities that share the same global risks? It should be stressed from the onset that Beck's notion of 'cosmos' is far more limited and minimalistic than a conventional Kantian understanding. He simply refers to a world view or horizon wider than that of a nation-state.[5] Far from being a pessimist, it is the possibilities of 'transformation' in the face of shared global risks, rather than 'denial' or 'apathy' that animates Beck's thesis. Traditional nation-states need not face obsolescence but can instead enhance their capabilities for global risk management by cooperating

4 Ulrich Beck, *What is Globalisation?* Cambridge: Polity Press (2000), 38.

5 Bruno Latour, 'Whose cosmos, which cosmopolitics', *Common Knowledge* 10:3 (2004), 454.

with other states and non-state actors. If these various actors at multiple levels are now compelled to work together to overcome shared global risks, how does this affect relationships within and between global cities? This was a question Beck left unanswered. The Toronto Forum for Global Cities seeks to address major challenges faced by all global cities, such as energy, infrastructure, finance, and innovation. They confront similarly enormous public policy challenges: traffic congestion, environmental degradation, rapidly appreciating housing prices, growing social disparities and most pronounced income inequities'.[6] Low-lying global cities such as Singapore, New York, Tokyo and London are also vulnerable to climate hazards and global warming.[7] Global cities as a whole appear to share a rather distinctive set of problems and challenges. The role that global cities potentially have to play in global risk management remains under-examined. Global risks, according to Beck, connect various actors across borders who otherwise have nothing to do with each other. It is a kind of 'enforced integration'.[8] Beck's idea of 'risk-cosmopolitanism' therefore arises from the sense of participating in shared collective attempts to counter global risks.[9] As a result, new rules and norms are renegotiated not only between the national and international, but also between global businesses, transnational NGOs, and supranational organisations.[10] Critics of Beck argue that while he accepts the tensions between conflict, cooperation and power inequality in his notion of risk-cosmopolitanism, but 'this does not recognise the agency of actors in making cosmopolitanism and who can also reverse it'.[11] To this point, cities have tended to be largely reified as if they were actors in and of themselves. This bypasses the crucial analytical challenge of interrogating issues of structure and agency in the understanding of 'the global city', and more precisely who exactly are the actors that enable a global city to discharge its critical command and control functions servicing and circulating global flows. Building on Beck's claims of 'risk-cosmopolitanism' together with the work of Beaverstock et al. on 'attending' to the global city network, this book has examined how an array of multi-level actors in the global city of Singapore has worked to manage shared collective global risks to the global maritime; aviation and financial infrastructures.

---

6 Bruce Katz of the Brookings Institution, 'The enormous challenges of global cities', Spiegel Online, undated <http://www.spiegel.de/international/world/0,1518,589556,00.html> accessed 8 July 2011.

7 Alex de Sherbinin, Andrew Schiller and Alex Pulsiper, 'The vulnerability of global cities to climate hazards', *Environment & Urbanisation* 19:1 (2007), 39–64.

8 Ulrich Beck, *Cosmopolitan Vision*. Cambridge: Polity Press (2006), 5–6.

9 Ibid., 21.

10 Yee-Kuang Heng and Kenneth McDonagh, *Risk, Global Governance and Security: The Other War on Terror*. London: Routledge (2009), 33.

11 Luke Martell, 'Beck's cosmopolitan politics', *Contemporary Politics* 14:2 (2008), 129–43.

Furthermore, sceptics point to the lack of empirical evidence of a global risk consciousness as powerful states put their own economic or national interests ahead of collective risks. This can be seen in the case of climate change for instance.[12] Beck has remained decidedly vague on how his 'cosmopolitan outlook' might operate in practice, only pointing to the International Criminal Court (ICC) and NGO-led anti-globalisation movements as possible examples.[13] Of great interest to this book is the notable silence (with the exception of climate change issues) on what possible roles global cities can play in this ongoing global reconfiguration to manage global risks, especially if as urban scholars would have us believe, global cities are now increasingly influential in global politics, security, and economics. If anything, the previous chapters have shown how overlapping multi-level arrangements aimed at managing global risks are emerging, centred around the very global cities that are most exposed to them. Whilst such developments have been researched in terms of how global cities are engaged in combating climate change, much less has been done to evaluate the multi-level responses to other global risks such as WMD proliferation and terrorist financing. Risk is not only staged in order to gain attention, as Beck argues. It is also seldom objective, created by those seeking to regulate it, a point that Hulsse goes to great lengths to stress in the case of anti-terrorist financing regulations.[14] This is one reason why seeking a uniform global consensus on shared risks is elusive. One might also need to enquire into the nature of power relationships that underpin nascent relationships emerging to regulate global risks. Do more influential powerful actors set the rules and coerce weaker partners to comply? In what way can these ostensibly 'cosmopolitan relationships' be distinguished from interest politics?

In the light of this inability for global consensus at grand international forums, it might well be more productive to examine narrower and more specific issue-driven initiatives built around global cities that have a compelling collective self-interest in transnational risk management. Yet they do not have 'sovereign' international authority to negotiate 'formal' global norms on risk management. And how far can experiences of the uniquely global city-state of Singapore which *does* exercise sovereignty, be relevant for other global cities like Tokyo, London or New York? Presented on two levels of analysis, in what follows, the first section takes stock of Singapore's experience as a global city buffeted by global risks, positioning it within the context of wider global policy and academic discussions on circulation and *transmission* of undesirable phenomena and flows. Secondly, in reviewing the specific case of Singapore, it draws out broader policy implications for trans-national risk management by placing the analysis in the context of how other global cities faced with similar risks have responded and learnt from each other's best practices. The purpose here is to highlight the ways in which actors

12 Ibid., 136.

13 Heng and McDonagh, *Risk, Global Governance and Security*, 34.

14 Rainer Hulsse, 'Creating demand for global governance: the making of a global money-laundering problem', *Global Society* 21:2 (2007), 155–78.

at multiple levels are working to *'attend'* to global city networks, as Beaverstock et al. might suggest, in order to protect key urban nodes and infrastructure that enable smooth and uninterrupted circulation of global flows. While cognisant of the differences between various types of global cities, this section reflects on the emerging roles that actors operating within and beyond global cities have to play in regulating global risks in *World Risk Society.*

The Dark Side of Globalisation: Mobilities, Flows and Transmission of Global Risks

Global cities are rather curious spaces marked out by contradictions and paradoxes:

> It excites starkly contrasting emotional responses, sometimes all within the same individual. The global city is where "It" is Happening. It has all the restaurants, the nightclubs, the high budget musical theatre productions, the biggest concerts, the tallest buildings, the broadest wireless internet coverage, the most international of the international airports. It has the darkest alleys, the smoggiest summers, the most desperate poverty, the loosest morals, the least caring citizens.[15]

Notwithstanding these serious social downsides, at the core of this book's analysis is a fundamental security paradox: these highly-connected global cities are also most exposed to the vagaries of global risks. As Beck notes, 'the globality of risk does not, of course, mean a global equality of risk'.[16] Global cities as hubs of connectivity usually service the positive flows of globalisation (financial, investment; tourism; information; business) but are also thrust into the frontline when threatened by negative flows or attempts to destroy/disrupt those flows. There is an urgent need to recognise the global challenges we face because 'the disregard for globalizing risks aggravates the globalization of risk'. Failing to acknowledge the global spread of avian flu was accelerating the global risk of infection.[17] 'Spread' is a critical concept in the age of global cities. In identifying *transmission* mechanisms for global risks, this book, as an 'infrastructure' approach to the study of global cities suggests, has pinpointed global cities' critical infrastructure as either key gateways for circulating undesirable global flows, or as targets for disruption because of the magnitude of ripple effects that would arise from a key node being taken offline.

As Thomas Friedman observed, the relentless forces of globalisation had lowered all sorts of barriers to the flow of goods, services, people and ideas in

15 Andrew Gallery, 'City of Plagues? Toronto, SARS and the anxieties of globalisation', *Explorations in Anthropology* 9:1 (2009), 139.

16 Ulrich Beck, *World Risk Society*. Cambridge: Polity Press (1999), 5–6.

17 Ulrich Beck, *World at Risk*. Cambridge: Polity Press (2009), 47.

an increasingly connected world: 'nations are more tightly integrated than ever before. We're driving bumper to bumper with every other major economy today, so any misbehaviour or mistakes anywhere can cause a global pileup'.[18] In such a highly-strung world, a perturbation anywhere in the system generates ripples at all other parts of the system, as we have seen for instance, in our discussion of Singapore's role in coordinating far-flung global maritime supply chains in Chapter 5.

The global city of Singapore has long been acutely sensitive to globalisation's pitfalls and opportunities. Harnessing the benefits of globalisation, according to Michael Leifer, also brought additional security gains. The aim was to encourage external powers to develop a stake in Singapore's continued survival.[19] Indeed, Leifer suggested that Rajaratnam's Global City speech, whereby he set out Singapore's desire to survive by serving as a key node in the international economy and making itself useful to multiple major external powers, reflected a far more sophisticated update of crude balance of power practices of eighteenth-century Europe.[20] Here, the global city concept had clearly a security dimension too. Singaporean leaders accept that 'becoming a global city is not merely an aspiration. It is a prerequisite for our survival. Closing our doors would only turn us into an island of no consequence, unable to provide for our people. We will become irrelevant to the world'.[21]

Ensuring its relevance means making sure that its critical infrastructure continues to attract and service various types of global flows. This is where our analytical framework – drawn from works within urban studies and geography that stress the centrality of flows; mobilities; circulation; and infrastructure in the study of global cities – can be usefully deployed. Bearing such key concepts in mind, it becomes quickly apparent that there has been a consistent emphasis placed by policymakers on developing various kinds of critical infrastructure in a global city like Singapore to allow it to control and command global flows. Developing more integrated seamless connectivity for cargo and goods to transfer between its maritime and airport hubs perhaps best exemplifies this desire to attract global flows. In other words, the different gateways in and out of a global city previously tasked with separately servicing specific flows (maritime, aviation

18 Thomas Friedman, 'Bumper to bumper'. *The New York Times*, 23 May 2010, <http://www.nytimes.com/2010/05/23/opinion/23friedman.html?_r=0> accessed 24 June 2013.

19 Michael Leifer. *Singapore: Coping with Vulnerability*. Singapore: Routledge (2000), 39.

20 Ibid., 36.

21 Wong Kan Seng, 'Singapore Perspectives 2011 Conference' (speech, Singapore, 17 January 2011) <http://www.nptd.gov.sg/content/NPTD/news/_jcr_content/par_content/download_18/file.res/Keynote%20address%20by%20DPM%20Wong%20Kan%20Seng%20at%20the%20Singapore%20Perspectives%202011%20Conference%20170111.pdf> accessed 18 January 2013.

etc.) can now more efficiently turn around and transform these flows from one domain (maritime) into another (aviation) as they are processed into the global system. Apart from aviation, maritime and financial flows, the city-state has also recently positioned itself as an information and data hub to capture some of the ever-increasing information flows circulating around the world today. However, associated with each of these domains of connectivity, Singapore has also experienced global risks. Even its high level of Internet penetration is a cause of concern: 'our vulnerability has increased because of our inter-connectivity, the cache of classified information that can potentially be stolen through electronic media, and our heavy reliance on IT systems for essential services'.[22]

The continual, never-ending process to ensure its relevance has manifested through assiduously cultivating different avenues of connectivity with global flows. The analyses conducted in previous chapters have attempted to dissemble and unpack what has hitherto been a mostly monolithic notion of 'Singapore the global city'. In doing so, it has shown which particular sectors and actors of the global city help bring about its connectivity and at the same time how these actors are also affected most adversely by global risks. Is it economic indicators (measured by employment, growth and human development indicators), particular industries (travel, financial services, computer networks, shipping), environmental health, or especially vulnerable cross-sections of their populations (such as frontline security staff or medical personnel) that are most affected? Consider Prime Minister Lee's claim that 'shocks will be transmitted more quickly and widely, economic cycles will become shorter and more unpredictable, and the potential for worldwide contagion will be much greater, whether in financial crises or global pandemics'.[23] Lee's use of the word 'contagion' in a broader sense beyond financial crises alone is suggestive here. It suggests an emerging concern with global risks that share a common feature: shocks easily affect Singapore because of the global city's intense sensitivity to circulating global flows and mobilities. For Zygmunt Bauman, an event like September 11th highlighted dramatically how accelerating mobilities and flows had brought a 'symbolic end to an era of space' where security was inherently linked to territorial boundaries.[24] Being so connected, global cities literally have nowhere to hide from Beck's notion of de-spatialised global risks; they have no strategic buffer zone to speak of. This is a point raised

22 Teo Chee Hean, 'Internal Security Department's Heritage Centre 10th Anniversary' (speech. Singapore, 20 March 2012) <http://www.mha.gov.sg/news_details.aspx?nid=MjQxNA%3D%3D-iGqNbuFLKwI%3D> accessed 21 March 2013.

23 Lee Hsien Loong, 'Economic Society of Singapore Annual Dinner' (speech, Singapore, 23 June 2012) <http://www.pmo.gov.sg/content/pmosite/mediacentre/speechesninterviews/primeminister/2012/June/speech_by_prime_ministerleehsienloongateconomicsocietyofsingapor.html#.U4KsV3KSySo> accessed 24 June 2013.

24 Zygmunt Bauman, 'Reconnaissance wars of the planetary frontierland', *Theory, Culture and Society* 19:4 (2002), 81.

in Singapore's National Security Strategy in 2004: vulnerability no longer stems only from the island's traditional proximity to larger neighbours or its need to secure its water supply. Indeed, the Strategy admits that Singapore had previously 'a conventional army geared towards fighting a conventional war' tasked with meeting clear military challenges from state-based threats.[25] The strategy points to a 'new security environment' in the global age.[26] This is why one of Singapore's leading foresight thinkers, Peter Ho, observed that the long-standing dangers of conventional inter-state warfare have been supplemented by non-traditional threats such as pandemics, cyber-threats, piracy, terrorism and nuclear proliferation – which worry security and defence strategists.[27] These dangers may not yet fully manifest themselves but 'they could emerge as game-changers'.[28]

Scholars such as Cha writing about the security implications of globalisation have long warned that 'the definition of security and the fight for it will occur not on battlefields but in unconventional places against non-traditional security adversaries'.[29] This can pose real headaches for security planners because 'what used to protect us (distance, classic defence methods) has been weakened, and now offers little or no protection'.[30] Consider the array of recent security challenges that global cities have faced, such as terrorism, WMD proliferation, or financial contagion. Singapore as a global city has become vulnerable to global risks transmitted through the very same critical infrastructure in global cities that attract, coordinate and circulate global flows of various types. In this sense, the security experiences of hyper-connected global cities like Singapore in recent years vindicates the argument that 'today's primary danger lies not in the nuclear overkill that held much of the world hostage during the cold war, but in the world's increasing complexity and interconnectedness'.[31] Singapore's Deputy Prime Minister Teo Chee Hean agreed that living in an interconnected world means that security challenges in geographically distant regions of the

25 National Security Coordination Centre Singapore, 'The Fight against Terror: Singapore's National Security Strategy'. Singapore: Atlas Associates PTE Singapore (2004), 27.

26 Ibid., 14.

27 Peter Ho, 'Broadening partnerships for an Asian century' (speech, CSIS, Washington D.C., 10 February 2012) <http://csis.org/event/defining-21st-century-strategic-partnership> accessed 12 February 2013.

28 Ibid.

29 Victor Cha, 'Globalisation and the study of international security', *Journal of Peace Research* 37:3 (2000), 400.

30 Javier Solana and Daniel Innerarity, 'The New Grammar of Power', Project Syndicate, 1 August 2011 <http://www.project-syndicate.org/commentary/solana10/English> accessed 1 August 2011.

31 Barry Zellen, 'Singapore aims for enhanced information awareness with RAHS', *Strategic Insights* 6:3 (2007) <http://www.nps.edu/Academics/centers/ccc/publications/OnlineJournal/2007/May/zellenMay07.html> accessed 10 August 2013.

world such as terrorism or piracy can undermine peace and stability.[32] As a result of what Tony Blair once called 'the age of the interconnected',[33] these concerns have also extended to how globalisation might affect racial relations in the global city. Deputy Prime Minister Teo observed that Singapore cannot totally immunise itself from outside influences and therefore had to make sure that religious or ethnic problems in other parts of the world, are not imported into Singapore and cause problems for its multi-cultural and multi-ethic society.[34]

Such concerns about undesirable phenomena that spread easily were vividly demonstrated in the events of September 11th – a dramatic demonstration of a global risk hitting a global city. September 11th can be interpreted in terms of how mobilities also introduce dangers: 'a macabre yet subtle exploitation of the multiple and interconnected mobilities … that sustain global urban capitalism: mobilities of people and machines; mobilities of images and media; mobilities of electronic finance and capital … urban modernity is actually utterly interwoven with fragility and vulnerability'.[35] This very process of urbanisation and the related sets of mobilities underpinning it are now 'saturating the world with the very technologies and techniques that can be harnessed to destroy the urban'.[36] For John Urry, September 11th highlighted how globalisation 'is disordered, full of paradox and the unexpected and of irreversible and juxtaposed complexity'. The world was now characterised by 'complex mobile connection' in such a way that 'wild and safe zones' now became 'highly proximate through the curvatures in space-time' brought about by critical infrastructure such as airports and maritime ports.[37] Audrey Kurth Cronin notes that globalisation and growth of market capitalism has led to less privileged people repelled by the fundamental changes and distortions to traditional ways of life that these forces bring.[38] The intersection point between wild and safe zones often are global cities, being as they are the symbols of globalisation as well as the crossroads of global flows from different parts of the world.

32 Teo Chee Hean. 'Overseas Service Medal Presentation Ceremony' (speech, Singapore, 17 May 2010) <http://www.mindef.gov.sg/imindef/press_room/official_releases/nr/2010/may/19may10_nr2/19may10_speech.html#.U4KxkHKSySo> accessed 18 May 2012.

33 Tony Blair, 'Australian Parliament' (speech, Australia, 27 March 2006) <http://www.theguardian.com/politics/2006/mar/27/uksecurity.terrorism> accessed 27 March 2013.

34 Channel NewsAsia, 'DPM Teo reminds S'poreans of external racial and religious tensions', 10 July 2011 <http://forums.sgclub.com/singapore/dpm_teo_reminds_357145.html> access date 20 April 2014.

35 Stephen Graham, 'In a moment: on glocal mobilities and the terrorized city', *City* 5:3 (2001), 411.

36 Ibid., 411.

37 John Urry, 'The global complexities of September 11th', *Theory, Culture and Society* 19:4 (2002), 57–69.

38 Audrey Kurth Cronin, 'Behind the curve: globalisation and international terrorism', *International Security* 27:3 (2002), 45 .

Singapore's financial core is usually seen as a 'safe zone' given the high-value transactions it processes daily but globalisation and connectivity also means that there is easy access for negative *destructive* flows in the form of global terrorism risks from so-called 'wild zones' that intentionally seek to derail critical global financial systems. In response, anti-terror drills have been held annually with 'Exercise Raffles' simulating explosions in Singapore's financial heart. More than 100 financial institutions take part, including DBS Bank and Citigroup. 'Singapore's financial industry has set the benchmark for the region, and possibly for the world as well', said Rick Cudworth, partner at KPMG LLP.[39] Exercise Raffles III in 2011 simulated both physical and cyber-attacks. Singapore has also supported the policy of pre-emption. As the Press Secretary to the Foreign Minister noted in 2003, 'Should we have waited until the JI exploded bombs in Singapore before acting against it? A small nation in terrorist-infested Southeast Asia does not have this luxury of libertarian posturing'.[40] Free flows of people and openness in a global city meant that the JI plot in Singapore was not entirely home-grown: 'while the surveillance work was conducted by Singaporeans, the planning was done by an Al-Qaeda operative of Arab descent holding a Canadian passport. The bomb maker was an Indonesian living in the Philippines'.[41]

If its financial sector underpinned Singapore's global city claims as well as its exposure to terror threats, the Port Authority of Singapore's tagline on its website – 'The World's Port of Call' – trumpets its ambitions for global maritime connectivity. Some analysts claim that because of its central role coordinating maritime trade flows that are crucial to the world economy, an attack on Singapore's port could generate more devastating ripple-effects and disruptions worldwide than the Lehman Shock of 2008.[42] This comparison of two global risks (financial contagion and global terrorism) reveals the ways in which Singapore's global city infrastructure can be potentially affected by *inadvertent* disruptions or *deliberate* attacks on the various types of global flows that it processes: whether these are financial or maritime. Given terrorists' stated goal to create economic disruption in the world economy, it is likely they will target the various key nodes of maritime and financial activities concentrated in global cities. As the OECD points out, since most seaborne trade arrives in several key port terminals like Singapore, one can easily see the potential for major economic disruption following a terrorist

39 Cited in Bloomberg, 'Singapore stages anti-terror drill for financial industry', 10 May 2006 <http://www.bloomberg.com/apps/news?pid=newsarchive&sid=ap6IhIiSYCuE&refer=asia> accessed 1 April 2010.

40 *The Straits Times*, 'Singapore's support for action on Iraq prompted by wider concerns', 11 June 2003 <http://eresources.nlb.gov.sg/newspapers/Digitised/Article/straitstimes20030611-1.2.26.5.aspx> accessed 16 August 2013.

41 National Security Coordination Centre Singapore, 'The Fight against Terror', 28.

42 Anthony Davis, 'Singapore port attack could be even worse than Lehman's collapse', 25 May 2010 <http://www.defenceiq.com/naval-and-maritime-defence/articles/singapore-port-terror-attack-could-be-worse-than-l/> accessed 18 April 2013.

attack on the maritime transport network'.[43] One can allude to similar dangers in terrorist financing. Here, the concern is not so much destruction but to the contrary, illicit *penetrative* flows of 'dirty money' circulating through Singapore's financial centre depend on the financial system not being unhinged. Just as maritime trade is processed through mega-port hubs like Singapore, likewise, because of the way the global financial system is structured, terrorist financing flows will inevitably encounter a financial hub like Singapore at some point.

Criticisms of Singapore's relentless desire to be a top-tier global city have come from its brightest minds and most capable policy-makers, who argue that the city is always hamstrung by its inherent limitations of size, population, talents and political influence on the world stage. For retired senior civil servant Ngiam Tong Dow, it is delusional to even think that Singapore can join the ranks of top-draw global cities such as New York, London and Tokyo. The best Singapore can hope for is to lead the chasing pack of second-tier global cities.[44] Such doubts certainly linger but based purely on its connectivity and growing amounts of global flows passing through the city, Singapore remains a significant player at least when it comes to circulating financial, maritime and aviation flows.

Global Risk Management: 'Attending' to the Global City Network

In her commentary on the AIDS panic in the late 1980s, the American critic Susan Sontag noted the widespread 'sense of cultural distress or failure' in Western society that seemed to create a need for an 'apocalyptic scenario' and 'fantasies of doom'. This gloomy mood explained the 'striking readiness of so many to envisage the most far-reaching of catastrophes'. It is a case, as Sontag puts it, not of 'Apocalypse Now', but of 'Apocalypse From Now On'.[45] Sontag's sense of despondence corresponds to the sometimes dystopian extreme risk-averse views that permeate Beck's *World Risk Society*. Yet, it has to be said Beck is in truth more optimistic than his detractors claim. Rejecting familiar accusations that he is all about doom and gloom, the 'cosmopolitan' possibilities of reconfiguring relationships at all levels as actors come together to manage shared risks excites him, although he has been silent on what roles global cities play in this brave new world of risk. He stressed the importance of 'the relations of definition' and how certain risks that are successfully 'staged' then gain resonance. The biggest obstacle

43 Organisation for Economic Co-operation and Development (OECD), 'Security in maritime transport, Maritime Transport Committee', July 2003 <http://www.oecd.org/newsroom/4375896.pdf> accessed 28 August 2014, 17.

44 Cited in *The Straits Times*, 'Forget First World Hype', 12 January 2013 <http://newshub.nus.edu.sg/news/1301/PDF/HYPE-st-12jan-pD17.pdf> accessed 17 August 2013, D17.

45 Fitzpatrick, Michael, 'Apocalypse from Now On', Spiked Online, 25 April 2003 <http://www.spiked-online.com/articles/00000006DD71.htm> accessed 8 April 2011.

to more effective trans-national risk management is that 'while the source and scale of most of today's pressing challenges are global, and any effective solution to them must also be global, the policy authority for tackling them remains vested in states'.[46] As Solana and Innerarity claim, what we need is to develop a new mentality and world view centred on ideas of 'the common good – or common bad – rather than of self-interest or national interest'. The notion of 'common bad' can be taken to refer the shared global risks that global cities face. Beck's analysis has so far neglected the reconfiguring of relationships within global cities as multi-level actors work together to manage shared global risks and minimise disruption or exploitation of global flows. Furthermore, the power of such cities is relational, for they shape the framework in which other cities operate in the world economy.[47]

Given their central positions as key nodes orchestrating global flows that sustain the global economy, global cities can potentially play key roles in new transnational risk management initiatives. It has been claimed that cities, not states, can develop templates for governance of the future world order.[48] After all, as this book has argued, the risks and opportunities of globalisation are not only most acutely felt, they are also first and foremost managed in global cities in the frontlines. As such, it is logical that these cities develop the involuntary, enforced 'risk-cosmopolitanism' of a community of shared destiny that Beck speaks of. By shaping perceptions and responses to these exigencies, this book has identified new varieties of multi-level governance based around global cities and the desire to 'attend' to the smooth circulation of global flows in critical infrastructural fields like aviation and finance. As Beaverstock et al. have argued, various actors within and beyond global cities cooperate in order to keep the network functioning and global flows circulating smoothly. Yet, the modus operandi and efficacy of these actors vary across cities, influenced by an assortment of political structures, power relationships and transnational linkages. Existing literature on the role of global cities in IR[49] has thus far focused on identifying the levels of analysis at which cities engage with different layers of governance between cities, local governments, and supra-national levels at the UN. While there has been research published on global cities combating climate change,[50] there has been relatively less in-depth analysis of how regulatory agencies/interest groups/industry and

46 Jorge Heine and Ramesh Thakur, 'Conclusion', in Jorge Heine and Ramesh Thakur (eds), *The Dark Side of Globalisation*. Tokyo: United Nations Press (2011), 278.

47 Arthur S. Alderson and Jason Beckfield, 'Power and position in the world city system' *American Journal of Sociology* 109:4 (2004), 812.

48 Parag Khanna, 'Beyond City Limits', *Foreign Policy* 181, 6 August 2010, 120.

49 See Peter Taylor, 'New Political Geographies: Global civil society and global governance through world city networks', *Political Geography* 24:6 (2005), 703–30. Also Janne Nijman, 'The rising influence of urban actors', *The Broker* 17 (2009), 14–18

50 Harriet Bulkeley and Vanesa Castan Broto, 'Government by experiment? Global cities and the governing of climate change', *Transactions of the Institute of British Geographers* 38:3 (2013), 361–75.

other stakeholders within global cities' critical infrastructural sectors such as financial or maritime industries, perceive or respond to global risks. A global city usually is associated with hard power – in finance, commerce and business – but also needs to project soft power: as a centre of learning and a source of global inspiration to solving global problems. Can cities for instance supplement the state actors who have struggled with financial contagion from the Greek and Italian debt crises? States have developed multilateral groupings such as the G20, with mixed results. The EU has been hobbled by financial contagion; any response is further complicated by its size, complexity, and need for consultation with member states. More nimble and innovative city-based networks are emerging as actors in multi-level governance seeking to manage global risks. The risks of globalisation are mediated by governance responses within and between global cities that have thus far escaped close scrutiny. By examining the interplay between these structural dynamics and networks of global city actors hitherto missing from any detailed or systematic analysis, this project has charted a new path in the analysis of leading urban centres, risk and globalisation. Because these cities and their leaders are by necessity more exposed and vulnerable to global developments, they also have an acute understanding of globalisation's turbulent dynamics. After all, 'cities bear the brunt of the world's financial meltdowns, crime waves and climate crises in ways national governments never will'.[51] Larger countries or even other cities in the same country don't face the same pressures. Cities are said to be humanity's real building blocks because of their economic clout responsible for over two-thirds of the total world economy, population density, political influence, and innovative edge. More frequent interactions and exposure to pressing problems means a 'feedback mechanism' exists that tends to propel innovation and creative solutions in cities.[52]

Three types of city networks currently exist in the literature: 'an inter-state city network with state departments as network-makers, a supra-state city network with UN agencies as network-makers, and a trans-state city network with NGOs as network-makers'.[53] Another form of city level-based transnational governance network might well be emerging, with mayors and provincial governors assuming a central leadership role coordinating with other global cities on global policy issues. A Global Cities Initiative jointly launched by Brookings Institution and JP Morgan seeks to create an international network of leaders from global cities that can trade and grow together. Former New York Mayor Michael Bloomberg's C40 group brings together leading cities to combat climate change by exchanging best-practices in policy initiatives and technologies. At their June 2011 meeting, the C40 announced collaboration with another city-based network, the ICLEI – Local Governments for Sustainability on measuring city greenhouse gas emissions.

---

51 Brad Amburn, 'Global Cities Index', *Foreign Policy* (2008), 68.

52 Luis Bettencourt and Geoffrey West, 'Bigger cities do more with less', *Scientific American*, September 2011.

53 Taylor, 'New political geographies',703.

In 2009, the City of London issued a report arguing that financial sectors and banking actors too have a role to play in combating global climate change.[54] Advocated by former Tokyo Governor Ishihara in 2000, the Asian Network of Major Cities 21 (ANMC 21) undertakes joint projects on crisis management, environmental countermeasures and industrial development. One project develops a permanent network of experts drawn from member cities' administrative, research and medical institutions to enable faster and more efficient action in case of an outbreak of infectious diseases. Collectively, these city-based governance initiatives on specific global risks such as climate change or infectious diseases suggest that Beck's idealised opening up of leadership at a different level from nation-states and 'formal' international relations could be percolating around city-levels of governance.

City governments are clearly operating at an international level, 'responding to the negative forces of globalisation'.[55] This can be seen through the efforts of global cities such as Singapore in managing global risks surveyed in earlier chapters. Yet, Singapore is not alone, as its sister global cities are facing similar risks, and there is ongoing cooperation between these cities. Beginning with global terrorism, 'global cities like New York and London have realised that countering global threats requires a global reach and response'.[56] New York had more resources for counterterrorism than small countries, becoming in the process more active security actors on the international scene.[57] Michael Bloomberg advocated a specific city-focused approach because 'We have no greater responsibility than protecting our City from the threat of terrorism, and we know that New York continues to be at the top of the terrorist target list'.[58] NYPD's slogan is 'Think globally, act locally', an example of how global cities and the experiences of their police forces might well become internationalised and expanded to smaller cities worldwide.[59] NYPD reportedly runs a 500-strong Intelligence Unit led by former CIA operations director David Cohen, which has liaison ties with 11 security agencies in major cities such as Tel Aviv; Amman, Jordan; Toronto; Montreal; Paris and Lyon, France; Madrid; Abu Dhabi; London;

54 City of London, 'Delivering Copenhagen: the role of the City's financial sector in supporting action on climate change', 2009 <http://www.cityoflondon.gov.uk/business/economic-research-and-information/research-publications/Documents/research-2009/Delivering%20Copenhagen.pdf> accessed 19 October 2012.

55 Nijman, 'The rising influence of urban actors', 14.

56 Brian Nussbaum, 'Protecting global cities: New York, London and the Internationalisation of municipal policing for counter-terrorism', *Global Crime* 8:3 (2007), 228.

57 Ibid.

58 New York City Press release, 'Counter-terrorism commissioner appointed', 25 June 2010 <http://www.nyc.gov/html/nypd/html/pr/pr_2010_new_ct_comissioner.shtml> accessed 4 April 2011.

59 Jon Coaffee, *Terrorism, Risk and the Global City: Towards Urban Resilience.* Aldershot: Ashgate (2009).

Singapore; and Santo Domingo. The Singapore Police Force has hosted an NYPD Intelligence Division officer since 2005. This unit conducted lesson-learnt visits to Mumbai after the 2008 terror attacks there, to assess implications for New York. The program is partly funded through a public-private partnership called NYPD Shield that includes business community stakeholders.[60] The origin of NYPD Shield is illustrative of the emulating of best practices across global cities facing the same global risks. New York is not the only global city expanding its reach through cooperation against terrorism. In fact, across the Atlantic, counter-terrorism experiences in London's global business centre 'are increasingly transferred' to New York and other global cities such as Sydney and Mumbai.[61] Project Griffin, launched by the City of London Police in 2004 to help London's financial sector protect against terrorist threats, relies on bringing together various actors from police, fire brigade, private security industry and other government agencies. This project has now been adopted internationally by other cities such as Vancouver. Singapore's 'Project Guardian' program states clearly that it is a 'local adaptation of Project Griffin by the City of London Police' and is 'a public-private partnership to enhance the skills capabilities of private security personnel to augment the Police'.[62] The aforementioned 'NYPD Shield' project in New York also drew inspiration from London. The London approach, which emphasises proportionality of response (maintaining business continuity without creating undue fear or anxiety) is being replicated in central New York, especially Lower Manhattan and its financial core. The London Resilience Partnership, designed to minimise any impact from emergencies such as terrorist attacks, contains more than 170 organisations, including businesses, transport companies, health organisations, central government and local authorities. A similar project called 'Ready New York' is in operation in the Big Apple.

One can identify similar overlapping global city-based linkages emerging with regard to global maritime risks and WMD proliferation. Singapore, together with other leading ports of global cities such as Hong Kong, Tokyo, Dubai and Shanghai are now part of a US-led network of leading ports around the world that have come together to minimise the risks to container security. Singapore was the very first mega-port in Asia to sign up to the Container Security Initiative (CSI), followed quickly by another major node, Yokohama in Japan. U.S. Customs and Border Protection (CBP) Commissioner Robert C. Bonner said, 'This important first step in Asia will provide a significant measure of security for not only Singapore and the United States. It will most importantly provide a significant measure

60 *The Atlantic*, 'Mayor of the world: How Bloomberg flexes New York's diplomatic muscle', 21 September 2011 <http://www.citylab.com/politics/2011/09/mayor-world-how-bloomberg-flexes-new-yorks-diplomatic-muscle/167/> accessed 22 September 2011.

61 Coaffee, *Terrorism, Risk and the Global City*, Preface, xii.

62 Singapore Police Force, 'Project Guardian Scheme' (2014) <http://www.police.gov.sg/cterror/pg_index.htm?_ga=1.111529604.1444508355.1409032448> accessed 2 February 2015.

of security for the global trading system as a whole'.[63] Four years later, when Dubai also signed up, Commissioner Bonner said, 'I applaud the government of Dubai for assuming a leadership role in this region of the world',[64] being the first Middle Eastern port to be part of the network. The CSI works on a reciprocal basis that allows participant ports to send officials to major US ports. For instance, Japanese customs personnel are stationed at the port of Los Angeles targeting sea containers destined for Japan. Mega-ports of global cities also serve as gateways where global maritime flows can enter and exit, so it is only natural that any multi-level initiative to manage global maritime risks (such as WMD proliferation or smuggling) must necessarily involve these port authorities.

Moving on to combating terrorist financing flows, again the various actors in a global city's financial core are coming together. The experience of Singapore with multi-stakeholder and industry involvement is not unique. Similar relationships are emerging in London. The British Bankers' Association organises a one-day 'Managing the Risk of Terrorist Financing Workshop', which teaches delegates how to identify the risks of terrorist financing and ways to reduce exposure and vulnerability. The Wolfsberg Group is an association of 11 global banks based in global cities including giants such as Goldman Sachs (New York), HSBC (Hong Kong), Barclays (London) and Bank of Tokyo-Mitsubishi (Tokyo). It aims to develop financial services industry standards, and related products, for Know Your Customer, Anti-Money Laundering and Counter Terrorist Financing policies. In 2012, the group released its first set of principles and guidelines on anti-money laundering for private banking. The group also works closely with global NGOs such as Transparency International, and academics from the University of Basel.

As for non-intentional penetrative global risks such as pandemics, the Asian Network of Major Cities set up in 2001, has also promoted, amongst others, measures and information sharing on pandemic outbreak. Partners include leading global cities such as Tokyo and Singapore. The networks involve international specialists to swiftly communicate among city administrations, research institutions, and medical institutions. Global cities with their air hubs are usually the first point of entry for pandemics and airborne diseases. This is why for instance, the Tokyo Metropolitan Government in 2009 immediately established a Headquarters of Infectious Disease control and stockpiled vaccines with the H1N1 outbreak. Hospitals and doctors and health agencies in Singapore, Hong Kong, and Toronto are part of the WHO's surveillance and diagnostic networks. Singapore's Changi airport is also engaged in a WHO program cooperating with regional air hubs like Bangkok on pandemic measures.

---

63 Cited in Agence France Press, 'Singapore first Asian port to adopt US security measures', 5 June 2002 <http://www.singapore-window.org/sw02/020605a1.htm> accessed 16 April 2014.

64 United States Customs, 'Port of Dubai to implement the Container Security Initiative', 23 February 2006 <http://www.customs.ustreas.gov/xp/cgov/newsroom/press_releases/archives/2005_press_releases/0032005/03282005.xml> accessed 28 April 2008.

At the same time, global cities have to constantly strike a balance between their need for openness and connectivity as a global node and the requirements for security.[65] One must bear in mind that global cities thrive on permeability and connectivity. Faced with a plethora of global risks, global cities increasingly have to calibrate and adjust that openness while at the same time making sure that they retain the capability to attract, command and command the circulation of global flows. The danger of over-reaction to global risks certainly exists. As the U.S. National Capital Urban Design and Security Plan of 2002 points out, 'potentially extreme security responses undermine its objectives for a vibrant capital city that showcases ideals of openness and accessibility'.[66] Indeed, 'the main threat to cities comes not from terrorism but from the policy responses to terrorism that could undermine the freedom of thought and movement that are the lifeblood of cities'.[67] With many stakeholders and community groups affected by these security measures, the City of London faced numerous complaints from civil liberty groups in its counter-terrorism measures but the City remained steadfastly focused on its overarching desire to ensure resilience and sustained continuity of business in the square mile.[68] Security measures are designed to curtail 'the permeability of spaces by potential perpetrators of attack'. Indeed, there are 'concerns about the impact that such features may have upon the urban fabric and for the permeability and liveability of places'.[69]

Yet, as the World Economic Forum's 'Global Risks Report 2011' notes, there is a real danger of global governance failures and a lack of will in coordination to address the global risks. Indeed, one still has to grapple with divergent interests of the Great Powers, the inequality of the international system and differentials in governance capabilities of many states. Rather than nuclear war, the number-one risk today is 'de-globalization – the failure of the global system to cope with the complex issues we are confronted with'.[70] The range of global risks surveyed in previous chapters taken together constitute a spread of issues across different spheres of governance (economic, health, travel, political, military) whereby a range of different actors have attempted to generate risk management responses. In doing so, they allow us to open up analysis to the role of global cities in multi-level networks seeking to mitigate risks related to globalisation. The importance of these issues for the politics of network formation and governance is likely to compound in the future. The scale of governance built around networks of interlinked cities, their size, flexibility, agility to respond and policy innovation are some attributes that cities possess over

65 Coaffee, *Terrorism, Risk and the Global City*, 217.

66 National Capital Urban design and Security Plan, 'Designing and testing of perimeter security elements'. Washington D.C., 2002, National Capital Planning Commission, A-8.

67 T. Swanstrom, 'Are fear and urbanism at war?', *Urban Affairs Review* 38:1 (2002), 135.

68 Coaffee, *Terrorism, Risk and the Global City*, 223.

69 Ibid., 239–41.

70 World Economic Forum 2011 News Release, 'In East Asia, concerns about the world's response to global risks', 12 June 2011 <http://www.weforum.org/news/east-asia-concerns-about-world%E2%80%99s-response-global-risks> accessed 20 June 2011.

states with their centralised administrations. This is why looking at the role of global cities like Singapore is insightful and important at the same time.

While not replicable across the board, for some global cities, their local government leaders, NGOs and businesses can use their experiences to shape global agendas on shared global risks. For New York Mayor Michael Bloomberg has been extolling the advantages that cities have over states when it comes to tackling global problems: 'We're the level of government closest to the majority of the world's people. While nations talk, but too often drag their heels – cities act'. Indeed, returning to political scientist Benjamin Barber's 2013 book *If Mayors Ruled the World* that was discussed in the Introduction, it does precisely raise the question of alternative forms of global city-led governance, suggesting Singapore and New York were ideal potential leaders in this endeavour. City managers such as mayors, councils, officials and bureaucrats of these global cities are therefore involved in defining and responding to risks and opportunities that potentially propel them into a complex and historically specific set of global relationships. For instance, the C40 Climate Leadership Group is a grouping of iconic cities combining to address climate change. It includes local government leaders and mayors from New York, London, Tokyo and Shanghai. It has also joined hands with the Clinton Climate Initiative's Cities Program.

Having considered the broader roles that other global cities can play in tackling global risks, what insights can be learned from Singapore's experience thus far? Not all global cities respond in the same manner. What is the significance of specific sets of actors, interests and power relationships within different global cities for the different governance responses to globalisation? What is it about the power relationships ascendant within particular global cities that produce more effective policy in one area (for instance environment) than another (such as disease)? For Singapore, it is also unique as a city-state, with sovereign powers and a strong centralised government with long successful history of investing in and developing critical industries, such as aviation and finance. One governance response in particular stands out: a comprehensive inter-agency whole-of-society approach to global risks involving as many stakeholders and vested interests as possible. As its former Senior Minister Jayakumar noted,

> a networked, whole-of-government approach is necessary as our resources are limited and our capabilities distributed. Achieving resilience requires connecting the right agencies, creating the right synergies, and coordinating the right functions. A number of Inter-Ministry Committees have also been set up to coordinate efforts across several domains, including aviation security, maritime security, land transport security, cyber security, critical infrastructure protection, and securing sensitive material.[71]

71 S. Jayakumar, 'General Meeting of the Global Futures Forum: "Building resilience in the face of global shocks"' (speech, Singapore, 13 September 2010) <http://app.nscs.gov.sg/public/download.ashx?id=261> accessed 14 October 2012.

It is significant that the 'domains' Jayakumar refers to also correspond closely to gateways (information, aviation, maritime) through which global flows enter and exit a highly-connected global city. Singapore however goes beyond simply 'whole-of-government' approaches. It is working on 'whole-of-society' approaches 'that engages the academia, business, NGOs, the media and community groups to fortify our social resilience'.[72] Like London's Resilience Partnerships, there are regular meetings with businesses and a Community Engagement Programme to inculcate resilience from the bottom-up. Industry actors such as global container line APL have also worked with port authorities in Singapore, Settle and Yokohama on counter-terrorism drills. As a small tightly-run city-state where the range of conflicting interests that needs to be reconciled is far less complex, the level of resistance and complaints from affected stakeholders has not been as sustained or intense, compared to London. Taken together, these responses to global risks at multiple levels of governance address the question of agency in Beck's 'cosmopolitan vision'. The various stakeholders that enable a global city to function, from regulatory agencies to global organisations and industry associations, are brought together because of a shared concern over global risks. Once again, context matters.

Another governance response that Singapore has pioneered is to better understand and forecast global risks posed by global flows, seared as it has by its experience as an open connected global city over the past decade. The OECD recommends more emphasis on early warning systems and foresight capacities that can help 'produce a probability of the transmission of risks through complex and interdependent systems'.[73] With regard to financial risks, Schinasi also argues that the rate at which private financial practices innovate evolve so quickly, now outpaces the ability of public supervisory and regulatory frameworks when it comes to measuring and managing systemic risk. With increasing global complexity and interconnectivity, Beck warns that the cause-effect relationship cannot be precisely determined because 'global financial risks, like global ecological crises, cannot be confined to the economic subsystem but mutate into social upheavals and thus into political threats'.[74] Economist Joseph Stiglitz highlighted how fall-out from the Euro debt crisis manifested in unpredictable ways,

> Contagion is almost inevitable … globalisation has meant that we have become more interdependent: what happens in one part of the world has repercussions elsewhere … .[75]

---

72 Ibid.

73 Organisation for Economic Co-operation and Development (OECD), 'Future Global Shocks', June 2011 <http://www.oecd.org/governance/48256382.pdf> accessed 9 July 2013, 3.

74 Beck, *World at Risk*, 200.

75 Joseph Stiglitz, 'Europe's travails and our collective fate'. *The New York Times*, 19 July 2011 <http://www.nytimes.com/2011/07/20/opinion/20iht-edstiglitz20.html> accessed 14 July 2013.

To try to systematically address global risks of terrorism for instance, Coaffee has shown how policies reflecting Beck's risk society claims are increasingly pre-emptive and such anticipatory logic is embedded into everyday life in the city through all sorts of preparedness exercises, risk assessment through horizon scanning and foresight programs and national risk registers.[76] One way in which Singapore has tried to build greater resilience is to prepare for future surprises. Prime Minister Lee has also used classic terminology from risk studies: 'there are dark clouds on the horizon … whether it is revolutions in the Middle East … whether it is Europe with its debt problems … All these are known unknowns but there are also many unknown unknowns which we must prepare for and expect'.[77] As Peter Ho, former permanent secretary in the Ministry of Defence recounted, it was Singapore's traumatic and unexpected encounter with SARS in 2003 that led to a horizon scanning initiative being launched.[78] The Horizon Scanning Centre was set up in 2007 as part of the National Security Coordination Secretariat. It has worked with other agencies, such as conducting a case study with the Risk Analysis Branch of the Communicable Diseases Division and the Contingency & Scenario Planning Branch of the Operations Readiness Control Division in Ministry of Health. Former Coordinating Minister for National Security Jayakumar explained the 'RAHS has provided a strategic opportunity to change mindsets at various levels of government and embrace whole-of-government approach to horizon scanning'.[79] In 2009, a new Centre for Strategic Futures was established to coordinate research on futures and foster inter-agency cooperation. In 2010 the government launched a Strategic Futures Network drawing together the Deputy Secretaries from all government ministries and chaired by the Head of Civil Service to discuss emerging risks, and share experiences on foresight projects.[80] In the aviation sector, the CAAS has a 'Futures and Planning Office' based in Changi Airport tasked with organisation-wide and whole-of-government coordination in integrating strategic foresight on risks and opportunities to help shape Singapore's air hub for the future. Amongst the leading global cities, Singapore appears to be taking horizon-scanning most seriously, backed up by support from the national government in terms of staffing and resources. Other global cities such as Hong Kong may not have the same impetus, resources, or political will to develop similar

76 Coaffee, *Terrorism, Risk and the Global City*, 299.

77 Lee Hsien Loong, 'People's Action Party Youth Wing 25th Anniversary Rally' (speech, Singapore, 17 April 2011) <http://maintmp.pap.org.sg/uploads/ap/8170/documents/pmspchyp25thanniversaryrallyeng.pdf> accessed 18 March 2013.

78 Peter Ho, 'The RAHS Story', in Tan Hong Ngoh and Hoo Tiang Boon (eds), *Thinking about the future: strategic anticipation and RAHS*. Singapore: National Security Coordination Secretariat and Rajaratnam School of International Studies (2008), xvi.

79 Cited in S. Ramesh, 'Singapore sets up new centre to enhance risk assessment capability', Channel NewsAsia, 19 March 2007 <http://www.channelnewsasia.com/stories/singaporelocalnews/view/264941/1/.html> accessed 8 April 2010.

80 Jayakumar, 'General Meeting of the Global Futures Forum'.

governance structures. As Peter Ho stated, 'we have probably the world's first and only Risk Assessment and Horizon Scanning system. We see the RAHS system as a tool that will help us to better anticipate strategic shocks that may be lurking just over the horizon'.[81] Above all, Singapore remains determined to proceed on its global city path, despite the pitfalls from global risks. As the Economic Strategies committee reiterated in 2010, 'Singapore's future must rest on being a global city. New York and London are what they are, not because of the specific economic activities they conduct, but because people want to be there. That too, has to be Singapore's key advantage in the future. Being a global city and a meeting point in Asia for enterprise, talent, cultures and ideas, will be a source of competitiveness and growth in its own right'.[82]

Another governance trait in Singapore's response to global risks lies in how its leaders embody a strong competitive streak and desire to maintain its comparative advantages as a global city even in the face of global risks. As former Prime Minister Goh noted in 2007, 'we are on the right track to become a truly global city … it is very much a work in progress and there is no room for complacency'.[83] Former head of civil service Peter Ho argued that Singapore's global city status cannot be taken for granted and 'we must always look for new ways of doing things, and of doing things better, in order to stay ahead of the competition'.[84] This relentless drive for upgrading and improving can be seen in each of the three critical infrastructures that underpin Singapore's global city status, analysed in previous chapters. In the maritime domain, Lee Kuan Yew reminded port administrators that Singapore's raison d'être, its Port was facing severe competition from challenges in the region and Singapore's value proposition had to be continuously enhanced.[85] In 2012, it was announced that the current five container terminals constituting Singapore's port will be moved and consolidated into a new mega-port based in Tuas, western Singapore. This new port, according to Transport Minister Lui, is designed to handle 65 million TEUs annually, and crucially will allow Singapore to plan for the future, 'provide us a clean slate and the opportunity to introduce even more

81 Peter Ho, 'The Interdisciplinary Conference: Adaptation, Order and Emergence – A Tribute to John Holland' (speech, Singapore, 12 February 2009) <http://www3.ntu.edu.sg/CorpComms2/Documents/2009/Feb/GOH%20Speech_090212_JohnHollandConf.pdf> accessed 12 March 2012.

82 Ministry of Finance, 'Economic Strategies Committee Report', February 2010 <http://app.mof.gov.sg/data/cmsresource/ESC%20Report/ESC%20Full%20Report.pdf> accessed 15 April 2011, 9.

83 Goh Chok Tong, 'Making Singapore a Global City' (speech, Singapore Institute of Architects 46th Annual Dinner, 4 May 2007 <http://www.nas.gov.sg/archivesonline/speeches/record-details/7e73fd0e-115d-11e3–83d5–0050568939ad>.

84 Peter Ho, 'Strategic Perspectives Conference' (speech, Singapore, 4 September 2006) <http://www.mfa.gov.sg/content/mfa/overseasmission/washington/newsroom/press_statements/2006/200609/press_200609_01.html> accessed 5 October 2012.

85 Cited in Paul Richardson, 'The Singapore maritime story', *Singapore Nautilis*, (Q1 2008); Port Authority of Singapore (PSA), 'Sage Advice'. Singapore: Portview (Q2 2010), 11.

advanced technology and processes to meet future challenges'.[86] MPA and PSA jointly launched the Port Technology Research and Development Program, which is designed to optimise the use of newly emerging technologies in port operations. Other regional competitor ports are not standing still. A case in point is how in February 2014, Hong Kong announced plans for a new inter-agency maritime body to develop its port further to better keep pace with other mega-ports such as Singapore. As for aviation connectivity, there is a multi-agency Changi 2036 Steering Committee to plan ahead for how Changi Airport's future might look like in 2036, in the face of competing emerging hubs like Seoul, Bangkok and Kuala Lumpur. As an 'infrastructure' approach to the study of global cities might suggest, there is relentless competition to upgrade their infrastructural ability to attract, service, and coordinate the circulation of various types of global flows. In January 2013, Beijing unveiled plans for another new airport to ease congestion in aviation passenger flows. This would place the Chinese capital alongside other competitors such as London, Paris and Tokyo that have multiple airports within the global city. Even a long-established air hub like London is also wrestling with the question of how to enhance its hubbing capacity crucial to the 'maintenance of connectivity by air to key business markets'.[87] Singapore has plans for a fifth terminal as well as a committee called 'Changi 2036' tasked with developing its air hub status well into the future over the next two decades. Likewise in the economic and financial sphere, there is an Economic Strategies Committee that is periodically convened to map out and assess long-term strategies. Singapore's case is thus symptomatic of how global cities are driven by 'relentless competition, struggling to capture ever more command-and-control functions that comprise their very essence … competitive angst is built into world city politics'.[88] The City of London's financial centre was beset by angst when, in 2012, its position as the world's top financial centre was taken by New York, with Asian hubs Hong Kong and Singapore snapping at its heels. In early 1995, former Deputy Prime Minister Lee Hsien Loong told students that 'we are doing well, but like a sports champion, our position is never secure. After winning one tournament, the champion must immediately start training for the next one'.[89] While it is severely exposed to global financial crises such as in 2008, Lee noted that Singapore must also restock and rebuild so as to be ready

86 Cited in 'Singapore to erect a mega Tuas port', *Singapore Business Review*, 2 October 2012 <http://sbr.com.sg/transport-logistics/news/singapore-erect-tuas-mega-port> accessed 9 April 2014.

87 City of London Corporation and York Aviation, 'London's Air connectivity: the importance to London of having world class aviation hubbing capacity' December 2012 <http://www.cityoflondon.gov.uk/business/economic-research-and-information/research-publications/Documents/research-2012/Londons_Air_Connectivity1_PDFOnlineVersion.pdf> accessed 8 January 2013.

88 John Friedmann, 'Where We Stand: A Decade of World City Research', in Paul Knox and Peter J. Taylor (eds), *World Cities in a World-System*. New York: Cambridge University Press (1995), 23.

89 Lee Hsien Loong, 'Singapore's Stake in 21st Century and the Role of Undergraduates' (speech at Nanyang Technological University, Singapore, 10 February

to capitalise on any recovery.[90] Faced with yet another global financial crisis 10 years earlier in 1998, this exact same set of sentiments was expressed by Lee's predecessor Goh Chok Tong, 'we need to ... use this period to gain a head start for the race ahead after the storm has subsided'.[91] Singapore has had to undergo under 'relentless reinvention' just to stay paddling above water.[92]

Yet, Singapore does not just roll over and absorb the shocks thrown at it. To the contrary, its leaders have consistently been mindful that when it is hit by global risks, this also provides impetus for reassessment and reflection for upgrading. Each time Singapore experienced an economic or financial downturn, its leaders have launched major branch-to-root reviews of fundamentals.[93] During the 1997 Asian Financial crisis, a committee was tasked with identifying ways to achieve future growth in the financial sector. This happened again after the 2008 global financial crisis. In his 2010 speech, Prime Minister Lee observed that 'we better learn some lessons from how we managed the downturn because despite all our preparations and precautions, sometime, somewhere, something will happen again and there will be future crises and we should be ready for them'.[94] It has become somewhat of a characteristic trait that Singapore leaders tend to find opportunities to consolidate and prepare for future growth, even in the face of global risks. The trick for global cities such as Singapore is to maintain existing advantages but also seek out new ones. As Kenneth Paul Tan observes, 'the national life cycle of Singapore must be sustained by a perpetual sense of crisis that leads not to despair but to collective hope and self-renewal'.[95] Above all, it has to 'maintain

---

1995) <http://www.nas.gov.sg/archivesonline/speeches/record-details/70b2a54b-115d-11e3-83d5-0050568939ad> accessed 19 July 2014.

90 Lee Hsien Loong, 'National Day Rally' (speech, Singapore, 17 August 2008) <http://www.pmo.gov.sg/content/pmosite/mediacentre/speechesninterviews/primeminister/2008/August/transcript_of_primeministerleehsienloongsnationaldayrally2008spe.html#.U4KqI3KSySo> accessed 18 October 2012.

91 Ibid.

92 Monetary Authority of Singapore (MAS), 'Coping with the Asian Financial Crisis: The Singapore Experience' (speech at Nomura Securities 'Singapore Seminar', Tokyo, Japan, 30 September 1998) <http://www.mas.gov.sg/news_room/statements/1998/Coping_With_the_Asian_Financial_Crisis_The_Singapore_Experience__30_Sep_1998.html> accessed 9 April 2011.

93 Lee Hsien Loong, 'In Parliament' (speech, Singapore, 27 May 2009) <http://www.pmo.gov.sg/content/pmosite/mediacentre/speechesninterviews/primeminister/2009/May/transcript_of_primeministerleehsienloongsspeechinparliamenton27m.html#.U4KqjHKSySo> accessed 28 May 2013.

94 Lee Hsien Loong, 'National Day Rally' (speech, Singapore, 29 August 2010) <http://www.pmo.gov.sg/content/pmosite/mediacentre/speechesninterviews/primeminister/2010/August/national_day_rallyspeechenglishbyprimeministerleehsienloongon29a.html#.U4KrBXKSySo> accessed 30 October 2012.

95 Kenneth Paul Tan, 'Crisis, Self-Reflection, and Rebirth in Singapore's National Life Cycle', in Daljit Singh and Chin Kin Wah (eds), *Southeast Asian Affairs 2003*. Singapore: ISEAS (2003), 256.

singularities: distinctive qualities which protect its position; an ability to stay ahead and to be seen as something like a desirable and intriguing place to go, as well as a useful model for others'.[96] To avoid being marginalised, Singapore has consistently had to be flexible and nimble in its adaption strategies, to continue to make sure that it stays relevant.[97] Speaking about the Economic Development Board, Prime Minister Lee lauded the benefits of 'strategic alignment ... tactical coherence and agility'.[98] Singapore has focused on upgrading and expanding its financial, port and air hub facilities: critical infrastructure that makes itself indispensable to attracting and servicing global flows as a key global city. It has also continually sought out new value-added sectors such as bio-medical and pharmaceutical services and positioning itself as an information data hub.

According to Lee Hsien Loong, 'there is no final vision' for Singapore; it is a city which perpetually remains a 'work in progress'.[99] One needs no reminder that within the global urban hierarchy, cities may rise and fall all too quickly.[100] A small and nimble global city-state therefore needs to be extremely dextrous when riding the waves of globalisation, like a small piece of flotsam bobbing up and down on ocean currents. Lee referred to how Singapore needs to 'compete for global opportunities, and soar high to catch the wind like a kite'.[101] Prime Minister Lee again deployed this nautical imagery to claim success of his Resilience Budget in prompting recovery after the 2008 financial crisis, 'Because of what we did, we recovered fast and caught the wind and last year (2010) our economy grew 14.5 per cent'.[102] Globalisation clearly brought opportunities for Singapore but it also had little choice but to unfurl bigger sails in order to catch whatever favourable winds blow to maximise opportunities.[103] This nautical theme of a boat catching the wind in its sails is one that keeps getting deployed to explain the Singapore government's efforts navigating the global city

96 Karl Hack and Jean-Louis Margolin, 'Singapore: Reinventing the Global City', in Karl Hack and Jean-Louis Margolin (eds), *Singapore from Temasek to the 21st century: reinventing the global city*. Singapore: National University of Singapore Press (2010), 30.

97 Cited in Leifer, *Singapore: Coping with Vulnerability*, 20.

98 *The Business Times*, 'Singapore stays the course on fundamentals: PM', *The Business Times* (Singapore), 2 August 2011 <https://singaporepropertyhighlights.wordpress.com/2011/08/02/spore-stays-fundamentals-pm/> accessed 2 August 2013.

99 Prime Minister Office Singapore, 'Transcript of PM interview on Chicago Tonight', 16 April 2010 <http://www.pmo.gov.sg/content/pmosite/mediacentre/speechesninterviews/primeminister/2010/April/transcript_of_primeministerleehsienloongsinterviewonchicagotonig.html> accessed 8 April 2011.

100 Friedmann, 'Where We Stand', 26.

101 Lee Hsien Loong, 'Meritus Mandarin Hotel' (speech, Singapore, 19 October 2004) <http://www.nas.gov.sg/archivesonline/speeches/record-details/78c8b964-115d-11e3-83d5-0050568939ad> accessed 19 October 2013.

102 Lee, 'People's Action Party Youth Wing 25th Anniversary Rally'

103 S. Rajaratnam School of International Studies and the National Security Coordination Secretariat, Dialogue session at *5th Asia-Pacific Programme for Senior National Security Officers (APPSNO)*, 21 April 2011.

through upsides and downsides of globalisation, but at the same time it is also utilised for nation-building purposes to consolidate a sense of national identity, cohesion, and unity in the face of adversity and global challenges. Successfully navigating the perils of globalisation can also serve to enhance the legitimacy and competence of the ruling party in the eyes of the electorate. Lee described the need for 'our little ship' to be sufficiently robust to survive large waves.[104] Singapore has also been compared to a tiny speed-boat capable of flexible, nimble, rapid changes in direction as required, but a speed boat also is not the safest or most comfortable place to be when the waves get rough.[105] Indeed, as Lee explained the nautical theme again to Fareed Zakaria, 'What worries us in Singapore is not that the world will not prosper, but (whether) in the ups and downs of the world, a small boat like Singapore, with not very much room to maneuvre, can you make sure that every time you catch a wave head-on you are not flipped over?'[106]

How Singapore is Different From the Other Global Cities

The preceding discussion has shown how being a tiny and vulnerable 'small boat' has conditioned the ways in which Singapore's leaders have worked to minimise the downsides of globalisation for a global city. Singapore's long-ruling party 'never misses an opportunity to convey how the small city must cope with and exploit (ride) global and systemic change in an aggressive and strategic fashion'.[107] Yet even within global cities as a 'category', the impact of global risks can and do vary according to factors such as political systems; types of stakeholders; hinterland and geographical size, and degree of integration with the global economy in certain policy domains. This in turn shapes the ability to respond to global risks. As a city-state, its small size means that tightly-run centralised government agencies have both the resources and authority to engage with private sector and industry stakeholders to raise awareness and build consensus for managing global risks. The national government in Singapore also represents the 'global city' at

104 Lee Hsien Loong, 'Ang Mo Kio-Hougang National Day Dinner' (speech, Singapore, 21 August 2011) <http:// https://sg.news.yahoo.com/blogs/singaporescene/poreans-must-play-part-country-progress-160156832.html> accessed 22 August 2013.

105 Burhan Gafoor, 'MEDEF Université Debate at L'Ecole Polytechnique' (speech, Singapore, 28 August 2008) <http://app.mfa.gov.sg/data/paris/statements/REMARKS_FOR_MEDEF_28_Aug_08.html> accessed 28 August 2012.

106 *TODAY*, 'Interview on CNN's Fareed Zakaria GPS', transcript available at 'Of superpowers and the small boat', *TODAYonline*, 7 February 2012 <http://www.todayonline.com/Singapore/EDC120207–0000021/Of-superpowers-and-the-small-boat-Spore> accessed 16 August 2012.

107 Kris Olds and Henry Yeung, 'Pathways to global city formation: a view from the developmental city-state of Singapore', *Review of International Political Economy* 11:3 (2004), 491.

international fora and crucially, it can also swiftly channel resources where they are needed to boost critical infrastructure such as airports or financial centres.

Other global cities such as London or Tokyo, represented by their respective metropolitan mayors, have to, not only contend with far more complex domestic politics; they also have to navigate inter-city relations with other urban centres and lobby national governments within their home countries. This adds several layers of governance that Singapore as a global *city-state* does not have to grapple with to the same extent. Despite Singapore's comparative advantages in size and policy flexibility, on other hand, leaders of large mega global cities such as New York can compensate through having far more considerable resources such as larger populations and hinterland at their disposal, achieving economies of scale that other smaller cities lack.

For Singapore, it has no 'hinterland' comparable to what London or Tokyo have in Britain and Japan respectively. Singapore's hinterland effectively becomes other regions of South-East Asia and distant parts of the world. It is also the only global city that is *also* a full-fledged state. This in turn brings additional responsibilities and duties as well as a 'broader range of policy tools than the other places analysts commonly deem global/world cities'.[108] Clearly, what we are talking about here is a need to appreciate the diversity that exists across global cities, and the different ways through which they have become what they are.[109] One global city is not the same as another, and therefore across-the-board conclusions can be dangerous and misleading. According to Olds and Yeung, there is a need to be sensitive to the diversity of cities and hence they classify global cities according to: 1. hyper-global cities; 2. emerging global cities; 3. global city-states.[110] Hyper-global cities such as New York or London are most comprehensively integrated into the global economy and 'have strong embedded relationships with their immediate hinterland, the so-called 'global city-region'.[111] Other ways of categorising global cities by Jonathon Beaverstock and Peter Taylor rank them as 'Alpha', 'Beta' or 'Gamma' cities.[112]

Just within Asia's global cities, one can identify several different types that exist: global cities that are also states (Singapore) and global cities that are important parts of states (Mumbai, Sydney, Shanghai, Melbourne); global cities that are capitals of states (Tokyo) and global cities that are enclaves (Hong Kong). They encompass different political regimes and political economies, enabling consideration of how differing power relationships, political alliances and ideologies might mediate the way that urbanisation and globalisation play out in any given city. Singaporean leaders consistently recognise how they face different challenges from other leading global cities: 'Other global cities such as

108 Ibid., 490.

109 Ibid., 513.

110 Ibid., 503–4.

111 Ibid., 503.

112 J.V. Beaverstock, et al. 'World city network: a new metageography?', *Annals of the Association of American Geographers* 90:1 (2000), 123–34.

New York, London, Tokyo and Hong Kong, are part of far larger countries. They are connected to wider hinterlands which provide a constant source of skills and labour to sustain their competitiveness. As a small city state, we are not like New York, London or Tokyo. Our city is also our country and our home'.[113]

Clearly, by appreciating the diversity that exists, one is tempted to conclude that 'the replicability of global city models is in serious doubt',[114] whether in terms of city formation or indeed, for the purposes of this book, in terms of global risk management. Indeed, while Tokyo and New York are both top-notch leading global cities, they also have major differences such that there is no such thing as some 'generally applicable model of the 'global city'.[115] Instead, when it comes to analyses of global cities: one should rightly be wary of a 'one city tells all' approach.[116] Singapore and Hong Kong are somewhat unique global cities because 'the state is contained within a fully urbanised and spatially constrained territorial unit'.[117] Indeed, Sassen points out that in Singapore's case, 'In a sense, the whole city is a government-driven project – they have constructed themselves as global cities, and very significant ones'.[118] An interesting comparison of Singapore's policy response to financial crises can be made here with another global city that was also affected severely by the Asian economic contagion in 1998: Hong Kong. Singapore, like Hong Kong also has a colonial past that helped to bring about openness to change and outward-oriented sensibility.[119] However, as Linda Lim points out, despite their similarities, there was a 'dramatic difference'. Hong Kong authorities launched unprecedented market interventions such as massive purchasing of stocks to support the stock market and imposed new measures to restrict speculative activity. Singapore adopted completely opposite measures, with not only the continuation of its open market policies, but also further liberalisation of financial markets and openness to foreign capital. This was 'mainly due to differences in domestic political systems and circumstances of each location'.[120]

---

113 Wong, 'Singapore Perspectives 2011 Conference'.

114 Henry Wai-Chung Yeung, 'Globalisation Singapore: One Global City, Global Production Networks and the Developmental State', in Tarn Tan How (eds), *Singapore Perspectives 2010*. Singapore: World Scientific (2010), 118.

115 M. Harloe and S.S. Fainstein, 'Conclusion: the divided cities', in Susan S. Fainstein, Ian Gordon and Michael Harloe (eds), *Divided Cities: New York and London in the Contemporary World*. Oxford: Blackwell (1992), 246.

116 Olds and Yeung, 'Pathways to global city formation', 497.

117 Yeung, 'Globalisation Singapore': 111.

118 Christina Larson, 'Swoons over Miami', Interview with Saskia Sassen, *Foreign Policy*, 27 August 2010 <http://www.foreignpolicy.com/articles/2010/08/27/miami_swoon?page=0,1> accessed 29 October 2012.

119 Yeung, 'Globalisation Singapore', 112–13.

120 Linda Y.C. Lim, 'Free Market Fancies: Hong Kong, Singapore, and the Asian Financial Crisis', in T.J. Pempel (ed.), *The Politics of the Asian Economic Crisis*. Ithaca: Cornell University Press (1999), 101.

These differences in governance in Singapore and Hong Kong raises questions about the broad applicability of key debates about the growing power and autonomy of such global/world cities that can be divorced from national authority. The global city's autonomy is also bolstered by its involvement in a network of other global cities.[121] Singapore as a global city-state has the political capacity and legitimacy to mobilise strategic resources to achieve national objectives that are otherwise unimaginable in non-city-state global cities. It is represented and governed by the state in all of its roles. This is where the unique nature and capacities of the global city-state becomes all the more evident. Other leading global cities in larger nations, like Tokyo, are governed in relatively more complex, less coherent and less strategic fashion, often confronted with complex inter-city politics that are absent in a city-state. Singapore is also not constrained by tensions in national-versus-urban politics or regional development politics that plague many countries that try to develop their 'global cities' for instance Shanghai versus Beijing. There is much less competition for resources.

Singapore is also a centralised developmental state, No other global city has the capacity to tightly regulate immigration for instance, that Singapore has. 'The net outcome of this control is that the state is able to mobilize social actors and tremendous resources to meet its national objectives' as a global city.[122] It is perhaps in the maritime domain where one can see the crucial role national policies can play in creating Singapore's global city status. For instance, the conscious application of information communication technology to enhance its global container transport hub was a strategic development tool to transform Singapore's maritime competitiveness.[123] Whereas Singapore was ranked a lowly 21st busiest port in 1976, by 1997 it had displaced Hong Kong as the world's busiest. In the 1995 World Competitiveness Report, Singapore ranked first among 48 developed and newly industrialised nations in terms of port infrastructure meeting business requirements.[124] Government investment also went into education and learning-based economy since an educated workforce is better able to take advance of information-based knowledge. Software such as Computer Integrated Terminal Operations System (CITOS) directs container handling operations in real-time to ensure best loading and unloading sequences: reduces cost and turn-around times for vessels. 'Singapore's meteoric rise as a transport logistics platform is directly tied to the policies of the developmental states, one that very early on engaged the global economy to remain regionally competitive'.[125]

121 P.J. Taylor, 'Leading world cities: empirical evaluations of urban nodes in multiple networks', *Urban Studies* 42:9 (2001), 1593–608.

122 Ibid., 115.

123 C.A. Airiess, 'Regional production, information-communication technology, and the developmental state: the rise of Singapore as a global container hub', *Geoforum* 32 (2001), 236.

124 Ibid., 239.

125 Ibid., 251.

While Singapore's global city project has clearly benefited from resources directed at it by the developmental city-state, the danger is that in a fluid uncertain post-2008 financial crisis world characterised by complexity, a centrally directed developmental state model might be ill-equipped to cope. Yet the state with its accumulated experience of transforming Singapore remains central to the continuing remaking of its economy into something more versatile and resilient in the face of global risks.[126] Additionally, being a nation-state as well as global city raises tensions with regard to this inherently dualistic character that can often pull in opposite directions. Indeed, 'a nation-state and a global city require different management ethos. Conventional arguments for cultural and ideological protectionism may sit well with the character of nation-states but are increasingly incongruent with the functions of global cities'.[127] How to reconcile the nation-state's traditional focus on sovereignty, identity, and control with a global city's openness to mobilities and typically fluid sense of borders is most clearly felt in a global city-state like Singapore. As a result, 'in the case of global city-states, the dialectical contest between the nation state and global forces is becoming even more apparent'.[128]An intermestic approach to security must now recognise that the transnational global risks that imperil global cities like Singapore have blurred traditional divisions between internal and external security.[129]

Singapore: Microcosm of the Urban and Global

French writer Jean Baudrillard described the events of September 11th as 'one that questions the very process of globalization', pointing to not only the inequalities and resentment generated by globalisation but also how New York as a global city itself symbolised this process.[130] A global city that became too closely associated with globalisation and its inequalities could certainly be targeted as a result, but it is also their connectivity and critical infrastructure that exposes them to these global risks. As Gideon Rose pointed out, 'the problem lies in an American economy and society that put a premium on openness and the free flow of goods and people, and that this created a situation in which security and homeland defence were low priorities'.[131] The 2008 terror attacks on Mumbai were ample evidence that

126 Yeung, 'Globalisation Singapore', 120.

127 Marystella Amaldas, 'The Management of Globalisation in Singapore: Twentieth Century Lessons for the Early Decades of the New century', *Journal of Alternative Perspectives in the Social Sciences* 1:3 (2009), 987.

128 Olds and Yeung, 'Pathways to global city formation', 511.

129 Cha, 'Globalisation and the study of international security', 397.

130 Jean Baudrillard, 'L'Esprit du terrorisme', *Harper's Magazine*, February 2002 <http://harpers.org/archive/2002/02/lesprit-du-terrorisme/> accessed 2 August 2011.

131 Gideon Rose, 'Why did September 11th happen?', Council on Foreign Relations, 26 November 2001 <http://www.cfr.org/terrorist-attacks/gideon-rose-why-did-september-11-happen/p4211> accessed 8 April 2012.

'terrorists can think strategically'. Mumbai was chosen because it was India's financial centre and had iconic value. The lesson of Mumbai according to Brian Jenkins is that 'nationally and internationally recognized venues that offer ease of access, certainty of tactical success, and the opportunity to kill in quantity will guide target selection'.[132] Global cities fit all these prerequisites.

This book has argued that in Beck's *World Risk Society*, global cities are either providing gateways for global risks to circulate or they are themselves targeted because of their unique set of capabilities to connect flows around the world. This is where the global city-global risk nexus at the heart of this book comes into play. Cities have long been deliberately targeted in warfare. Living on the cusp of the urban age in the twenty-first century, the majority of the human population now lives in urban areas. The potentially widespread disruption and destruction that can arise from an untoward event such as pandemics outbreak or terrorist attack is sufficient cause for alarm. Yet, the traditional 'city-as-target' model must be updated to take account of the various transmission mechanisms through which global cities are at the mercy of global risks. The analytical framework deployed here recognises the significance of the so-called 'mobilities' turn in global cities studies, for it captures exactly what global cities are set up to do: attract, capture and facilitate different types of mobilities and circulate them around the world. Castells' notion of global cities as 'spaces of flows' further suggests that it is within these mobilities and flows that scholars should look for evidence of a global city's connectivity. The 'infrastructure approach' reminds us that the range of critical infrastructure – financial, maritime, aviation – that generates connectivity in turn serves to enhance its exposure to global risks. The key challenge for global cities then is to ensure it balances its core function of facilitating desirable positive flows while at the same time minimising the importation or circulation of undesirable flows such as pandemics or WMD proliferation. Regardless of Singapore's unique features as a global city-state, this challenge is common to all global cities as spaces of flows facing global risks. The case of Singapore has been instructive particularly because of the multi-sectoral connectivity from maritime, aviation, and financial links that drive its global city status. Founding Prime Minister Lee Kuan Yew was asked in 2012 what makes a good city. He replied, 'most important is connectivity ... we became a hub because of the convenience'.[133] At the same time that Singapore has benefited from commanding, coordinating and circulating these global flows through its port hub; airport; and financial centre, it has also had to face up to associated risks: WMD proliferation and maritime terrorism; pandemics and aviation terrorism; financial crises and terrorist financing. A further

132 Brian Michael Jenkins, 'Why terrorists attack airports', CNN, 25 January 2011 <http://articles.cnn.com/2011–01–25/opinion/jenkins.moscow.bombing_1_terrorists-lod-airport-airline-targets?_s=PM:OPINION> accessed 6 April 2012.

133 Cited in *The Straits Times*, 'Lee Kuan Yew's chance of a lifetime', 16 February 2013 <http://www.stasiareport.com/supplements/saturday-special-report/story/lee-kuan-yews-chance-lifetime-20130216> accessed 17 February 2014.

sub-division was made in order to analyse these risks more precisely: whether they were inadvertent penetrative flows that ironically depend on Singapore's ability to circulate global flows worldwide; or deliberate destructive risks that seek to destroy or disrupt that ability to circulate.

The term 'little red dot' was once coined by former Indonesian President Habibie in a desultory way to highlight Singapore's vulnerability and its precarious strategic environment encircled by larger neighbours: 'look at that map. All the green is Indonesia. And that red dot is Singapore'.[134] This traditional understanding of vulnerability long associated with being surrounded potentially hostile neighbours now needs to be supplemented. As a deliberately open and hyper-connected global city on several key measures of connectivity from air, maritime and financial links, the basic hypothesis presented throughout this book is that Singapore also faces an added security challenge from global risks that could potentially course through its critical infrastructure. The vulnerabilities and opportunities of globalisation are most acutely felt in global cities such as Singapore.[135] A case in point is the data and information flows associated with the Internet digital age. As we have seen in previous chapters, Singapore has been relentlessly seeking out all sorts of niche markets to capture as large a percentage of global flows as it can, venturing most recently into information and data flows. The Intelligent Nation 2015 Masterplan seeks to transform Singapore into 'An Intelligent Nation, A Global City, Powered by Infocomm'.[136] Singapore is already one of the most connected cities in Asia with over 67 terabits of submarine cable capacity and hosts over 50 per cent of commercial and area neutral data center space in South East Asia.[137] Yet, in positioning Singapore as a secure and trusted Infocomm hub by global companies, there are also global risks lurking in the form of hacking, virus attacks and cyber terrorism. It is no surprise that these risks are once again related to Singapore's critical infrastructure: this time in its ability to attract, process, coordinate and circulate information and data flows. Hence, the Infocomm Security Masterplan 2 (MP2) was launched in 2008 to protect the information infrastructure from such risks. In 2012, a new Security Response Center in Singapore was inaugurated to increase cybersecurity threat collection and analysis to help it become a hub for data management. The dual nature of globalisation's benefits and downsides seen in Singapore's attempts to

---

134 Dow Jones Wires, 'Singapore Strains/Habibie -2: Complains of Timing of Note', 3 August 1998, accessed 22 September 2012.

135 Yee-Kuang Heng, 'A Global City and in Age of Global Risks: Singapore's evolving discourse on vulnerability', *Contemporary Southeast Asia* 35(3), (2013), 423–46.

136 Infocomm Development Authority of Singapore, 'Strategy and Masterplan' <http://www.ida.gov.sg/About-Us/What-We-Do/Strategy-and-Masterplan.aspx#.UPpTTWd2KL8> accessed 8 April 2011.

137 Richard Pain, 'New security response centre opens in Singapore', Asia Pacific FutureGov, 10 August 2012 <http://www.futuregov.asia/articles/2012/aug/01/new-security-response-center-opens-singapore/> accessed 27 October 2012.

attract global data flows is merely the latest manifestation of the assortment of global risks Singapore has confronted as a global city.

Singapore's developmental experience should remind us that there is no such thing as 'the global city', as if it automatically materialises and discharges its functions by magic on cue. Instead, one can identify a set of actors that actively bring about and enable a global city's connectivity, who in turn have shared interests in protecting that connectivity from global risks. Ranging from city municipal authorities; state-level governments and regulatory agencies, to industry stakeholders such as airport associations and maritime shipping agents and banks, these share one thing in common: their interests are best served by ensuring uninterrupted circulation of desirable global flows, from aviation to maritime and financial. Singapore being a global city-state might have had limited salience to other global cities that have different access to resources as well as policy formulation processes and implementation. Yet, the overarching ways and means through which Singapore has responded to the range of global risks it faces: by extending cooperation outwards at all levels with a range of actors (private industry stakeholders, domestic government agencies, global trade bodies and international organisations), is instructive for other global cities that have common stakes in ensuring their core function of smoothly circulating global flows. Further, the attempt to build a whole-of-society approach to resilience in the face of global risks has resonance with similar other initiatives being undertaken in New York and London. The focus on horizon-scanning and foresight projects in Singapore to better understand global risks such as pandemics can also be extended to cooperation with other like-minded global cities for instance Tokyo and Hong Kong. In a nutshell, these attempts taken together can be seen as risk management initiatives designed to minimise either the possibility of disruption or destruction of smooth circulation of global flows or to reduce the chances these flows could be exploited to circulate undesirable capital/people/materials/viruses around the world. Indeed, we have already seen global cities like New York taking initiatives with counter-terrorism programs as well as on climate change. London's counter-terrorism strategies that involve multi-level stakeholders are being adopted in global cities like New York and Singapore, precisely because these urban nodes share similar perceptions of global risks to their financial cores. Hong Kong, Tokyo and Singapore have shared plans to combat pandemic outbreaks: their air hubs and medical professionals are learning from each other. These same cities, from their port authorities to shipping cargo agents, are also part of maritime container security initiatives to prevent WMD proliferation.

Singapore's experience as a global city perhaps is a microcosm of what the world is experiencing: it is smack in the middle of two intersecting global trends. This is an age of not just intensifying globalisation but also accelerating urbanisation. If cities are increasingly gaining influence in the globalised world today, the leading global cities will shine the brightest because of their abilities to propel and sustain globalisation's key flows. One should however also add another potent global trend to the mix: the rising profile of rapidly spreading global risks that characterise Beck's *World Risk Society* also means global cities are not only especially vulnerable, they also have the greatest incentives to manage them efficiently. The implications for security studies and global politics can be immense, both from a theoretical and policy angle. Going beyond what has already been attempted here, Security Studies scholars have to further broaden their scope of analysis beyond dominant state-centric approaches, and incorporate new emerging multi-level relationships based around global cities as they come to grips with global politics and security in the twenty-first century.

Bibliography

Aaltola, Mika. 'The international airport: the hub-and-spoke pedagogy of the American empire', *Global Networks* 5:3 (2005), 262–78.

Acharya, Amitav. *Singapore's Foreign Policy: The Search for Regional Order*. Singapore: World Scientific (2008).

Acuto, Michele. *Global Cities, Governance and Diplomacy: The Urban Link*, London: Routledge (2013).

Adey, Peter. 'Surveillance at the airport: surveilling mobility/mobilising surveillance', *Environment and Planning* 36:8 (2004), 1365–80.

Agence France Presse. 'Osama bin Laden footprints surround "vulnerable" Singapore', 1 October 2001 <http:// http://www.mindef.gov.sg/imindef/publications/pointer/supplements/IFC/_jcr_content/imindefPars/0006/file.res/MINDEF_Pointer%20IFC%20Supplement%20FINAL.pdf> accessed 16 August 2013.

Agence France Presse. 'Singapore first Asian port to adopt US security measures', 5 June 2002 <http://www.singapore-window.org/sw02/020605a1.htm> accessed 16 April 2014.

Agre, Phil. 'Imagining the next war: infrastructural warfare and the conditions of democracy', *Radical Urban Theory*, 14 September 2001 <http://www.rut.com/911/Phil-agre.html> accessed 19 April 2005.

Airriess, C.A. 'Regional production, information-communication technology, and the developmental state: the rise of Singapore as a global container hub', *Geoforum* 32:2 (2001), 235–54.

Albrow, Martin. *The Global Age: State and Society Beyond Modernity*. Cambridge: Polity Press (1996).

Alderson, Arthur S. and Beckfield, Jason. 'Power and position in the world city system', *American Journal of Sociology* 109:4 (2004), 811–51.

Ali, S. Harris and Keil, Roger. 'Global Cities and the Spread of Infectious Disease: The Spread of Severe Acute Respiratory Syndrome (SARS) in Toronto, Canada', *Urban Studies* 43:3 (2006), 491–509.

Ali, S. Harris and Keil, Roger. 'Introduction: Networked Disease', in S. Harris and Roger Keil, *Networked Disease: Emerging Infections in the Global City*. Malden, MA: Wiley-Blackwell (2008), 10–12.

Ali, S. Harris and Keil, Roger. 'Securitising networked flows: infectious diseases and airports', in Stephen Graham (ed.), *Disrupted Cities: When Infrastructure Fails*. London: Routledge (2010), 97–110.

Alvar, Philip. 'Singapore holds maritime drill to combat terrorism, piracy', Bloomberg, 29 August 2006 <http://www.bloomberg.com/apps/news?pid=newsarchive&sid=ajg9HuWQn9aM> accessed 1 April 2010.

Amaldas, Marystella. 'The Management of Globalisation in Singapore: Twentieth Century Lessons for the Early Decades of the New Century', *Journal of Alternative Perspectives in the Social Sciences* 1:3 (2009), 982–1002.

Amburn, Brad. 'Global Cities Index', *Foreign Policy* (2008), 68.

Amen, Mark, Toly, Noah J., McCarney, Patricia L. and Segbers, Klaus (eds). *Cities and Global Governance: New Sites for International Relations*. Farnham: Ashgate (2011).

Appadurai, Arjun. *Modernity at Large: Cultural Dimensions of Globalization*. Minneapolis: University of Minnesota Press (1996).

Aquino, Kristine. 'Singapore overtakes Japan as Asia's top foreign exchange hub', Bloomberg, 6 September 2013 <http://www.bloomberg.com/news/2013-09-05/singapore-overtakes-japan-as-asia-s-biggest-foreign-exchange-hub.html> accessed 8 September 2013.

Aradau, Claudia and Van Munster, Rens. 'Governing terrorism through risk', *European Journal of International Relations* 13:1 (2007), 89–115.

Arnold, Wayne. 'The nanny state makes a bet', *The New York Times*, 23 May 2006 <http://www.nytimes.com/2006/05/23/business/worldbusiness/23casino.html?pagewanted=all&_r=0> accessed 19 August 2014.

ASEAN Focus Group. 'The strategic intent of a global hub of hubs', Asian Analysis, August 2005 <http://www.law.smu.edu.sg/research/documents/the_strategic_intent_global_hub.pdf> accessed 8 January 2012.

Association of Banks in Singapore, The. 'Principles and Guidelines for Restructuring of Corporate Debt: The Singapore Approach' <http://www.abs.org.sg/pdfs/Publications/spore_approach.pdf> accessed 14 September 2012.

Atlantic, The. 'Mayor of the world: How Bloomberg flexes New York's diplomatic muscle', 21 September 2011 <http://www.citylab.com/politics/2011/09/mayor-world-how-bloomberg-flexes-new-yorks-diplomatic-muscle/167/> accessed 22 September 2011.

Balakrishnan, Angela. 'Singapore slides into recession', *Guardian*, 10 October 2008 <http://www.guardian.co.uk/business/2008/oct/10/creditcrunch-marketturmoil1?INTCMP=SRCH> accessed 9 April 2012.

Barber, Benjamin. *If Mayors Ruled the World*. New Haven: Yale University Press (2013).

Barnes, Paul H. and Oloruntoba, Richard. 'Assurance of security in maritime supply chains: conceptual issues of vulnerability and crisis management', *Journal of International Management* 11:4 (2005), 519–40.

Basu Das, Sanchita. *Road to Recovery: Singapore's Journey Through the Global Crisis*. Singapore: ISEAS (2010).

Baudrillard, Jean. 'L'Esprit du terrorisme', *Harper's Magazine*, February 2002 <http://harpers.org/archive/2002/02/lesprit-du-terrorisme/> accessed 2 August 2011.

Bauman, Zygmunt. *Liquid Fear*. Cambridge: Polity Press (2006).

Bauman, Zygmunt. 'Reconnaissance wars of the planetary frontierland', *Theory, Culture and Society* 19:4 (2002), 81–90.

BBC News. 'SARS deters Singapore visitors', 5 May 2003 <http://news.bbc.co.uk/2/hi/business/3001717.stm> accessed 14 October 2012.

BBC News. 'Singapore Air in worst-ever crisis', 21 May 2003 <http://news.bbc.co.uk/2/hi/business/3047203.stm> accessed 23 November 2012.

BBC News. 'Singapore Airlines staff accept pay cut', 3 July 2003 <http://news.bbc.co.uk/2/hi/business/3042310.stm> accessed 23 November 2012.

Beaverstock, J., Doel, M.A., Hubbard, P.J. and Taylor, P.J. 'Attending to the world: competition, cooperation and connectivity in the world city network', *Global Networks: A Journal of Transnational Affairs* 2:2 (2002), 111–32.

Beaverstock, J., Smith, R.G. and Taylor, P.J. 'A roster of world cities', *Cities* 16:6 (1999), 445–58.

Beaverstock, J.V., Smith, R.G. and Taylor, P.J. 'World city network: a new metageography?', *Annals of the Association of American Geographers* 90:1 (2000), 123–34.

Beck, Ulrich. *Cosmopolitan Vision*. Cambridge: Polity Press (2006).

Beck, Ulrich. 'Global Risk Society', in George Ritzer (ed.), *The Wiley-Blackwell Encyclopedia of Globalization*. London: Wiley-Blackwell (2012), 836–8.

Beck, Ulrich. 'In the new, anxious world, leaders must learn to think beyond borders', *Guardian*, 13 July 2007 <http://www.guardian.co.uk/commentisfree/story/0,2125317,00.html> accessed 12 November 2007.

Beck, Ulrich. 'Living in the world risk society', *Economy and Society* 35:3 (2006), 329–45.

Beck, Ulrich. *The Brave New World of Work*. Cambridge: Polity Press (2000).

Beck, Ulrich. 'The Cosmopolitan State: Towards a Realistic Utopia' <http://www.eurozine.com/articles/2001-12-05-beck-en.html> accessed 14 November 2007.

Beck, Ulrich. 'The silence of words: on terror and war', *Security Dialogue* 34:3 (2009), 255–67.

Beck, Ulrich. 'The terrorist threat: world risk society revisited', *Theory, Culture and Society* 19:4 (1999), 5–26.

Beck, Ulrich. *Twenty Observations on a World in Turmoil*. Cambridge: Polity Press (2012).

Beck, Ulrich. *What is Globalisation?* Cambridge: Polity Press (2000).

Beck, Ulrich. *World at Risk*. Cambridge: Polity Press (2009).

Beck, Ulrich. *World Risk Society*. Cambridge: Polity Press (1999).

Bettencourt, Luis and West, Geoffrey. 'Bigger cities do more with less', *Scientific American*, September 2011.

Bilder, Richard B. 'The role of cities and states in foreign relations', *American Journal of International Law* 83:4 (1989), 821–31.

Bishop, Ryan, Clancey, Gregory and Phillips, John W. *The City as Target*. London: Routledge (2012).

Bisignani, Giovanni. '2011 International Air Traffic Association (IATA) Annual General Meeting' (speech, Singapore, 7 June 2011) <http://www.iata.org/pressroom/Documents/annual-report-2011.pdf> accessed 7 June 2012.

Blair, Tony. 'Australian Parliament' (speech, Australia, 27 March 2006), <http://www.theguardian.com/politics/2006/mar/27/uksecurity.terrorism> accessed 27 March 2013.

Blair, Tony. 'Doctrine of the International Community' (speech, Economic Club of Chicago, 24 April 1999) <http://www.pbs.org/newshour/bb/international-jan-june99-blair_doctrine4-23/> accessed 9 April 2014.

Blair, Tony. 'Joint Session of Congress' (speech, Washington D.C. 17 July 2003), <http://www.cnn.com/2003/US/07/17/blair.transcript/> accessed 19 September 2014.

Blair, Tony. 'The Iraq Crisis: Speech to the House of Commons' (speech, London, 18 March 2003 <http://www.guardian.co.uk/politics/2003/mar/18/foreignpolicy.iraq1> accessed 24 August 2008.

Bloomberg. 'Singapore bonds beat peers in shrinking AAA pool', Bloomberg, 17 August 2012 <http://www.bloomberg.com/news/2012-08-16/singapore-bonds-beat-peers-in-shrinking-aaa-pool-southeast-asia.html> accessed 20 August 2012.

Bloomberg. 'Singapore holds maritime drill to combat terrorism, piracy', Bloomberg, 29 August 2006 <http://www.bloomberg.com/apps/news?pid=newsarchive&sid=ajg9HuWQn9aM> accessed 1 April 2010.

Bloomberg. 'Singapore stages anti-terror drill for financial industry', Bloomberg, 10 May 2006 <http://www.bloomberg.com/apps/news?pid=newsarchive&sid=ap6IhIiSYCuE&refer=asia> accessed 1 April 2010.

Borsuk, Richard and Chua, Reginald. 'Singapore strains relations with Indonesia's President', *The Wall Streeet Journal* <http://www.wsj.com/articles/SB902170180588248000, 04 August 1998> accessed 9 August 2014.

Bowen, John T. and Laroe, Christian. 'Airline networks and the international diffusion of severe acute respiratory syndrome (SARS)', *The Geographical Journal* 172:2 (2006), 130–44.

Brandt, Ben. 'Terrorist threats to commercial aviation: a contemporary assessment', November 2011, Combating Terrorism Centre, West Point Military Academy <http://www.ctc.usma.edu/posts/terrorist-threats-to-commercial-aviation-a-contemporary-assessment> accessed 8 April 2012.

Brenner, Neil and Keil, Roger. 'Editors' Introduction', in Neil Brenner and Roger Keil (eds), *The Global Cities Reader*. London: Routledge (2006), 46–69.

Bulder, Richard B. 'The role of cities and states in foreign relations', *American Journal of International Law* 83:4 (1989), 821–31.

Bulkeley, Harriet and Castan Broto, Vanesa. 'Government by experiment? Global cities and the governing of climate change', *Transactions of the Institute of British Geographers* 38:3 (2013), 361–75.

Bureau of International Narcotics and Law Enforcement Affairs. '2009 INCSR: Country Reports – Moldova through Singapore', 2009 International Narcotics Control Strategy Report (INCSR), 27 February 2009 <http://www.state.gov/j/inl/rls/nrcrpt/2009/vol2/116545.htm> accessed 9 October 2011.

Burgess, J. Peter (ed.). *The Routledge Handbook of New Security Studies*. Abingdon: Routledge (2013).

Business Times, The. 'Singapore stays the course on fundamentals: PM', *The Business Times*, Singapore, 2 August 2011 <https://singaporepropertyhighlights.wordpress.com/2011/08/02/spore-stays-fundamentals-pm/> accessed 2 August 2013.

Callon, Michael and Law, John. 'Guest editorial', *Environment and Planning D: Society and Space* 22 (2004), 3–11.

Campbell, Kurt. 'Globalization's first war', *The Washington Quarterly* 25:1 (2002), 7–14.

Carver, Terrell. 'Materializing the metaphors of global cities: Singapore and Silicon Valley', *Globalizations* 7:3 (2010), 383–93.

Castells, Manuel. *The Rise of the Network Society*. Oxford: Wiley-Blackwell (2000).

Catterall, Bob. 'Cities under siege: September 11th and after', *City* 5:3 (2001), 383.

Cavelty, Myriam Dunn and Victor Mauer. *The Routledge Handbook of Security Studies*. Abingdon: Routledge (2012).

Cha, Victor. 'Globalisation and the study of international security', *Journal of Peace Research* 37:3 (2000), 391–403.

Chan, Francis. 'Twenty years after SQ117, terror threat looms larger', *The Straits Times*, 29 March 2011 <http://soufangroup.com/20-years-after-sq117-terror-threat-looms-larger/> accessed 9 December 2012.

Chan, Margaret. 'Concern over flu pandemic justified' (speech, 62nd World Health Assembly Geneva, Switzerland, 18 May 2009) <http://www.who.int/dg/speeches/2009/62nd_assembly_address_20090518/en/> accessed 19 May 2009.

Changi Airport Singapore. 'Air Cargo: Set Your Sights Further'. Singapore: Changi Airport Group Brochure (2011).

Changi Airport Group. 'Cargo connectivity', 1 December 2011 <http://www.changiairportgroup.com/cag/html/business-partners/air-cargo/cargo-connectivity.html> accessed 15 March 2012.

Changi Airport. 'Facts and Statistics' <http://www.changiairport.com/our-business/about-changi-airport/facts-statistics> accessed on 1 March 2012.

Channel NewsAsia. 'Border security system sees results', Channel NewsAsia, 12 October 2011 <http://www.channelnewsasia.com/stories/singaporelocalnews/view/1158831/1/.html> accessed 8 December 2012.

Channel NewsAsia. 'DPM Teo reminds S'poreans of external racial and religious tensions', Channel NewsAsia, 10 July 2011 <http://forums.sgclub.com/singapore/dpm_teo_reminds_357145.html> access date 20 April 2014.

Channel NewsAsia. 'Hong Kong pips Singapore as most popular city for international business', Channel NewsAsia, 20 July 2011 <http://www.channelnewsasia.com/stories/singaporebusinessnews/view/1141966/1/.html> accessed 20 July 2011.

Chia, Siow Yue. 'The Asian Financial Crisis: Singapore's experience and response', in H.W. Arndt and Hal Hill, *Southeast Asia's Economic Crisis: Origins, Lessons and the Way Forward.* Singapore: ISEAS (1999), 51–66.

Chiu, Stephen Wing-kai and Ho, Kong-Chong. *City-States in the Global Economy: Industrial Restructuring in Hong Kong and Singapore.* Colorado: Westview Press (1998).

Chong, Alan. '"Global City Foreign Policy": The Propaganda of Enlargement and Integration of an IT-Connected Asian City' in Alan Chong and Faizal bin Yahya (eds), *State, Society, and Information Technology in Asia.* Farnham: Ashgate (2014), 135–72.

Chong, Terence. 'Singapore's cultural policy and its consequences', *Critical Asian Studies* 37:4 (2005), 553–68.

Chou, Mark. 'The subject of analysis: global cities and International Relations', *Global Peace, Change, and Security* 24:2 (2012).

Chua, Beng Huat. 'SARS Epidemic and the Disclosure of Singapore Nation', *Cultural Politics* 2:1 (2006), 77–86.

Chua, Beng Huat. 'SARS Epidemic and the Disclosure of Singapore Nation', in John H. Powers and Xiaosui Xiao (eds), *The Social Construction of SARS: Studies of a Health Communication Crisis.* Amsterdam: John Benjamins Publishing Company (2008), 163–77.

Chua, Chin Hon. 'Nuclear terrorism: it's real', *The Straits Times*, 14 April 2010.

Chua, Lee Hoong. 'Strengthen financial safety nets, G20 urged', *The Straits Times*, 28 January 2012.

City of London. 'Delivering Copenhagen: the role of the City's financial sector in supporting action on climate change', 2009 <http://www.cityoflondon.gov.uk/business/economic-research-and-information/research-publications/Documents/research-2009/Delivering%20Copenhagen.pdf> accessed 19 October 2012.

City of London Corporation and York Aviation. 'London's Air connectivity: the importance to London of having world class aviation hubbing capacity' December 2012 <http://www.cityoflondon.gov.uk/business/economic-research-and-information/research-publications/Documents/research-2012/Londons_Air_Connectivity1_PDFOnlineVersion.pdf> accessed 8 January 2013.

Civil Aviation Authority of Singapore (CAAS). 'Asia-Pacific Aviation Security Action Plan jointly presented by Singapore and Japan'. 47th Conference of Directors General of Civil Aviation Asia Pacific Regions, China Macao, 25–9 October, 2010.

Civil Aviation Authority of Singapore (CAAS). 'Air Transport Statistic', May 2002 and May 2003.

Civil Aviation Authority of Singapore (CAAS). 'Bridging Skies: toward sustainable growth', February 2012 <http://www.bridgingskies.com/wp-content/uploads/2012/09/Bridging%20Skies%20Print%20-%20Feb%202012.pdf> accessed 7 July 2012.

Civil Aviation Authority of Singapore (CAAS). 'Empowering Growth in Singapore Aviation', Annual Report 2010/2011.

Civil Aviation Authority of Singapore (CAAS). 'Keeping security threats at bay', *Bridging Skies*, July 2010, 8.

Clark, David. *Urban World/Global City*. London: Routledge (2003).

Cliff, A.D., Haggett, P. and Smallman-Raynor, M.R. *Island Epidemics*. New York: Oxford University Press (1998).

Coaffee, Jon. *Terrorism, Risk and the Global City: Towards Urban Resilience*. Aldershot: Ashgate (2009).

Coaffee, Jon and Wood, Murakami. 'Security is coming home: Rethinking scale and constructing resilience in the global urban response to terrorist risk'. *International Relations* 20:4 (2006), 504.

Coker, Christopher. *War in an Age of Risk*. Cambridge: Polity Press (2009).

Commercial Affairs Department Singapore. 'Annual Report 2011' <http://www.cad.gov.sg/NR/rdonlyres/4B459ADE-5B86-4034-8403-5E8E24A4DC08/28122/CAD_AR2011_web.pdf> accessed 8 July 2012.

Commercial Affairs Department Singapore. 'CAD Anti-Money Laundering and Counter-Terrorism Financing Handbook', 3rd edition. Singapore: Integrated Press Pte Ltd (2010).

Connor, David. 'ABS 35th Annual Dinner' (speech, Singapore, 27 June 2008) <http://www.abs.org.sg/pdfs/Newsroom/Speeches/2008/Speech_270608_MrDavid.pdf> accessed 27 June 2013.

Connor, David. 'Outgoing chairman of ABS', (annual dinner, 26 June 2009) <http://www.abs.org.sg/pdfs/Newsroom/Speeches/2009/Speech_260609_MrDavid.pdf> accessed 8 January 2010.

Cowen, Deborah. 'Containing insecurity: logistic space, U.S. port cities and the "war on terror"', in Stephen Graham (ed.), *Disrupted Cities*. London: Routledge (2010), 69–84.

Crang, Mike. 'Between places: producing hubs, flows, and networks', *Environment and Planning A* 34:4 (2002), 569–71.

Creswell, Tim. *On the Move: Mobility in the Modern Western World*. London: Routledge (2006).

Croft, Stuart. 'What future for security studies', in Paul Williams (ed.), *Security Studies: An Introduction*. Abingdon: Routledge (2008).

Croissant, Aurel and Barlow, Daniel. 'Following the money trail: terrorist financing and government responses in Southeast Asia', *Studies in Conflict & Terrorism* 30:2 (2007), 131–56.

Cronin, Audrey Kurth. 'Behind the curve: globalisation and international terrorism', *International Security* 27:3 (2002), 30–58.

Curley, Melissa and Thomas, Nicholas. 'Human security and public health in Southeast Asia: the SARS outbreak', *Australian Journal of International Affairs* 58:1 (2010), 17–32.

Curphey, M. 'The Chancellor's emergency measures', *Guardian*, 26 February 2003 <http://www.theguardian.com/politics/2003/feb/26/economy.uk> accessed 27 February 2012.

Daipi, Hawazi bin. 'Globalisation and its impact on social cohesion and rootedness' (speech, Singapore, 5 November 2002) <http://www.moe.gov.sg/media/speeches/2002/sp05112002.htm> accessed 5 November 2012.

Davis, Anthony. 'Singapore port attack could be even worse than Lehman's collapse', 25 May 2010 <http://www.defenceiq.com/naval-and-maritime-defence/articles/singapore-port-terror-attack-could-be-worse-than-l/> accessed 18 April 2013.

Davis, Lynn S. *The Security Implications of Globalisation*. Santa Monica, CA: RAND (2003).

Deer, Patrick. 'The ends of war and the limits of war culture', *Social Text* 25:2 (2007), 1–11.

Deleuze, Gilles and Guattari, Félix. 'City/State', *Zone 1/2* (1997).

Derudder, Ben, Timberlake, Michael and Witlox, Frank. 'Pathways of change: shifting connectivities in the world city network 2000–08', *Urban studies* 47:9 (2010), 1861–77.

Derudder, Ben, Witlox, Frank, Faulconbridge, James and Beaverstock, Jon. 'Airline data for global city network research: reviewing and refining existing approaches', *Geojournal* 71 (2008): 5–18.

Desker, Barry and Osman, Mohd Nawab Mohd. 'S. Rajaratnam and the Making of Singapore Foreign Policy', in Kwa Chong Guan (ed.), *S. Rajaratnam on Singapore: From Ideas to Reality*. Singapore: World Scientific (2006).

Devichand, Mukul. 'Where East meets West', *Guardian*, 27 Nov 2008 <http://www.guardian.co.uk/commentisfree/2008/nov/27/mumbai-terror-attacks-india6> accessed 18 April 2009.

Dillon, Michael. 'Global security in the 21st century: Circulation, complexity and contingency', in *The Globalisation of Security*, Chatham House ISP/NSC Briefing Paper 05/02, December 2005.

Douglass, Mike. 'From global intercity competition to cooperation for livable cities and economic resilience', *Environment and Urbanisation* 14:1 (2002), 53–68.

Earth Hour. 'Singapore – home of Earth Hour', 20 February 2012 <http://www.earthhour.org/singapore-home-of-earth-hour> accessed 4 March 2012.

Economic Development Board. 'A Dynamic Global City', 29 April 2009 <http://www.sedb.com/edb/sg/en_uk/index/why_singapore/dynamic_global_city.html> accessed 16 June 2011.

Economic Development Board. 'Why Singapore: unparalleled connectivity and infrastructure', 19 May 2011 <http://www.edb.gov.sg/content/edb/sg/en_uk/index/why_singapore/connected.print.html> accessed 16 October 2014.

Economic Review Committee. 'Positioning Singapore as the pre-eminent financial centre in Asia', September 2002 <http://www.mti.gov.sg/ResearchRoom/Documents/app.mti.gov.sg/data/pages/507/doc/12%20ERC_Services_Financial.pdf> accessed 7 March 2011.

Economic Strategy Committee. 'Making Singapore a Leading Global City', 4 February 2010 <http://www.news.gov.sg/public/sgpc/en/media_releases/agencies/mof/press_release/P-20100204-3/AttachmentPar/0/file/

Subcommittee%20on%20Making%20Singapore%20a%20Leading%20Global%20City.pdf> accessed 7 June 2011.

Edinburgh Evening News. 'Terror attack on finance hub is inevitable', 10 August 2005 <http://www.edinburgnews.scotsman.com/uk.cfm?id=1759222005> accessed 11 September 2013.

Ee, Khor Hoe and Zhang, Kit Wei. 'Ten years from the financial crisis: managing the challenges posed by capital flows', MAS Staff Paper No. 48, November 2007.

Elbe, Stefan. 'Microbes take to the sky: pandemic threats and national security', in Stefan Elbe, *Security and Global Health: Toward the Medicalization of Insecurity*. Cambridge: Polity Press (2000), 30–65.

Elias, Bart. 'Airport Passenger Screening: background and issues for Congress'. Congressional Research Service, Washington D.C., R4053, 2009.

Ernst & Young. 'Globalization Index 2010' <http://www.ey.com/SG/en/Newsroom/News-releases/News-release---Singapore-takes-third-spot-on-Globalization-Index-2010> accessed 1 July 2011.

Faiola, Anthony. 'Globalisation's demise sinking Singapore', *Washington Post*, 9 March 2012 <http://www.theage.com.au/business/globalisations-demise-sinking-singapore-20090308-8sfe.html> accessed 10 April 2012.

Fang, Nicholas. 'Drawn to a wealth magnet', *TODAYonline*, 4 September 2011 <http://sglinks.com/pages/1468043-sunday-st-regis-perspectives-drawn-wealth-magnet> accessed 5 September 2013.

Feldman, Allen. 'Securocratic wars of public safety', *Interventions: International Journal of Postcolonial Studies* 6:3 (2004), 330–50.

Fidler, David. *SARS: Governance and the Globalization of Disease*. New York: Palgrave Macmillan (2004).

Financial Action Task Force. 'Third Mutual Evaluation Report on Anti-Money Laundering and Combating the Financing of Terrorism Singapore'. Paris: FATF/OECD (2008).

Financial Crimes Enforcement Network. 'Suspicious Activity Reporting Guidance for Casinos, U.S. Treasury', 2003 <http://www.fincen.gov/statutes_regs/guidance/pdf/casinosarguidancefinal1203.pdf> accessed 8 December 2011.

Findlay, A.M., Li, F.L.N., Jowett, A.J. and Skeldon R. 'Skilled international migration and the global city: a study of expatriates in Hong Kong', *Transactions of the Institute of British Geographers* 21:1 (1996), 49–61.

Fitzpatrick, Michael. 'Apocalypse from Now On', Spiked Online, 25 April 2003 <http://www.spiked-online.com/articles/00000006DD71.htm> accessed 8 April 2011.

Florida, Richard. 'What if mayors ruled the world', *The Atlantic*, 13 June 2012 <http://www.citylab.com/politics/2012/06/what-if-mayors-ruled-world/1505/> accessed 13 June 2013.

Flynn, Stephen. 'Written testimony on "Neutralizing the nuclear and radiological threat: securing the global supply chain" before a hearing of the Permanent Subcommittee of Investigations', Committee on Homeland Security, U.S. Senate, Washington D.C., 28 March 2006.

Forbes, Kristin J. and Warnock, Francis E. 'Capital Flow Waves', Macroeconomic Review Special Feature B, Monetary Authority of Singapore Economic Policy Group, October 2011 <http://web.mit.edu/kjforbes/www/Papers/MAS%20Article-Macro%20Review-Oct%202011.pdf> accessed 16 April 2012.

Foreign Policy. 'Measuring Globalisation', March/April 2004.

Foreign Policy. 'The Globalisation Index 2007', November/December 2007.

Foreign Policy. 'The Globalisation Index 2008', 15 October 2008.

Fox, Liam. 'Oral evidence before the House of Commons Defence Committee on the SDSR and NSS' (speech, London, 9 March 2011) <https://www.gov.uk/government/news/dr-liam-fox-responds-to-defence-committee-report-on-sdsr> accessed 9 March 2013.

Friedmann, John. 'The World City Hypothesis', *Development and Change* 17:1 (1986), 69–83.

Friedmann, John. 'Where We Stand: A Decade of World City Research', in Paul Knox and Peter J. Taylor (eds), *World Cities in a World-System*. New York: Cambridge University Press (1995), 21–47.

Friedman, Thomas. 'Bumper to bumper'. *The New York Times*, 23 May 2010 <http://www.nytimes.com/2010/05/23/opinion/23friedman.html?_r=0> accessed 24 June 2013.

Fu, Grace. 'Singapore gears up to meet security deadline', 11 February 2004 <http://www.mpa.gov.sg/sites/global_navigation/news_center/mpa_news/mpa_news_detail.page?filename=040211.xml> accessed 27 March 2010.

Gafoor, Burhan. 'MEDEF Université debate at L'Ecole Polytechnique' (Paris, 28 August 2008) <http://app.mfa.gov.sg/data/paris/statements/REMARKS_FOR_MEDEF_28_Aug_08.html> accessed 28 August 2012.

Gallery, Andrew. 'City of Plagues? Toronto, SARS and the anxieties of globalisation', *Explorations in Anthropology* 9:1 (2009), 133–42.

Gan, Kim Yong. 'Remembering SARS: 10 years on' (speech, Singapore, 20 March 2013) <http://www.moh.gov.sg/content/moh_web/home/pressRoom/speeches_d/2013/speech-by-minister-for-health-gan-kim-yong--at-tan-tock-seng-hos.html> accessed 21 March 2014.

Gan, Kim Yong. 'WHO Conference on multi-sectoral collaboration to manage public health risks' (opening remarks, Singapore, 13 October 2011) <http://moh.gov.sg> accessed 13 October 2013.

Garrett, L. *The Coming Plague: Newly Emerging Diseases in a World Out of Balance*. New York: Farrar, Straus and Giroux (1994).

Giddens, Anthony. *Modernity and Self-Identity. Self and Society in the Late Modern Age*. Cambridge: Polity Press (1991).

Giddens, Anthony. *The Consequences of Modernity*. Stanford: Stanford University Press (1990).

Gilbert, Alan. 'World cities and the urban future: the view from Latin America', in Fu-Chen Lo and Yue-man Yeung (eds), *Globalization and the World of Large Cities*. Tokyo: United Nations University Press (1998), 174–203.

Gog, Julia, Ballesteros, Sébastien, Viboud, Cécile, Simonsen, Lone, Bjornstad, Ottar N., Shaman, Jeffrey, Chao, Dennis L., Khan, Farid and Grenfell, Bryan T. 'Spatial transmission of 2009 pandemic influenza in the US', *PLOS Computational Biology* 10:6 (2014).

Goh, Chok Tong. '50th anniversary of the Centre for Development Economics, Williams College, USA' (speech, United States of America, 14 October 2010) <http://www.news.gov.sg/public/sgpc/en/media_releases/agencies/micacsd/speech/S-20101015-1.html> accessed 14 October 2013.

Goh, Chok Tong. 'Making Singapore a Global City' (speech, Singapore Institute of Architects 46th Annual Dinner, 4 May 2007, <http://www.nas.gov.sg/archivesonline/speeches/record-details/7e73fd0e-115d-11e3-83d5-0050568939ad> accessed 16 November 2013.

Goh, Chok Tong. 'Singapore Aviation Centennial Evening Dinner' (speech, Singapore, 16 March 2011) <http://www.pmo.gov.sg/content/pmosite/mediacentre/speechesninterviews/seniorminister/2011/March/Speech_by_Senior_Minister_Goh_Chok_Tong_at_the_Singapore_Aviation_Centennial_Evening_Dinner.html#.U4KneXKSySo> accessed 16 March 2013.

Goh, Chok Tong. 'Singapore Corporate Awards 2010' (speech, Singapore, 10 May 2010) <http://www.mas.gov.sg/news-and-publications/speeches-and-monetary-policy-statements/2010/speech-by-sm-goh-at-the-singapore-corporate-awards-2010.aspx> accessed 10 May 2012.

Goh, Daniel S.P. 'Capital and the transfiguring monumentality of Raffles Hotel', *Mobilities* 5:2 (2010), 175–95.

Goldin, Ian and Mariathasan, Mike. *The Butterfly Defect: How Globalization Creates Systemic Risks*. New Jersey: Princeton University Press (2014).

Goldin, Ian and Vogel, Tiffany. 'Global governance and systemic risk in the 21st century: lessons from the financial crisis', *Global Policy* 1:1 (2010), 4–15.

Gostin, Lawrence O., Bayer, Ronald and Fairchild, Amy L. 'Ethical and legal challenges posed by SARS: implications for the control of severe infectious disease threats', *Journal of the American Medical Association* 290 (2003), 3229–37.

Government of Singapore. 'Background information related to ICAO-WCO-Singapore Joint Conference on Enhancing Air Cargo Security and Facilitation' (Orchard Hotel, Singapore, 5–6 July 2012) <www.news.gov.sg/ … / Background%20info%20on%20ICAO-WCO%20Joint%20Conference%20-%204%20July%202012> accessed 19 October 2012.

Graham, Stephen. *Cities Under Siege*. London: Verso (2010).

Stephen Graham (ed.), *Cities, War, and Terrorism: An Urban Geopolitics*. London: Blackwell (2004).

Graham, Stephen. 'Disruption by Design: Urban Infrastructure and Political Violence', in Stephen Graham (ed.), *Disrupted Cities: When Infrastructure Fails.* London: Routledge (2010).

Graham, Stephen. 'In a moment: on glocal mobilities and the terrorized city', *City* 5:3 (2001), 290–307.

Graham, Stephen. 'Introduction: Cities, Warfare and States of Emergency', in Stephen Graham (ed.), *Cities, War, and Terrorism: An Urban Geopolitics*. London: Blackwell (2004), 31–53.

Graham, Stephen. 'Special collection: reflections on cities, September 11th and the war on terrorism one year on', *International Journal of Urban and Regional Research* 26:3 (2002), 183–8.

Graham, Stephen. 'Urban metabolism as target: Contemporary war as forced demodernisation', in Nik Heynen, Maria Kaika and Erik Swyngedouw (eds), *In the Nature of Cities: Urban Political Ecology and the Politics of Urban Metabolism*. London: Routledge (2006), 234–54.

Graham, Stephen. 'When Infrastructures Fail', in Stephen Graham (ed.), *Disrupted Cities: When Infrastructure Fails*. London: Routledge (2010), 1–26.

Guardian. 'SARS: global death toll tops 630', 19 May 2003 <http://www.guardian.co.uk/world/2003/may/19/china.sars> accessed 8 April 2010.

Guest blog on the US Department of Commerce Website. 'Leading the way for US aerospace companies at the Singapore Air Show', 17 February 2012 <http://www.commerce.gov/blog/2012/02/17/leading-way-us-aerospace-companies-singapore-air-show> accessed 15 January 2013.

Gupta, Piyush. 'Incoming ABS Chairman 38th Annual Dinner' (speech, Singapore, 28 June 2011) <http://www.abs.org.sg/pdfs/Newsroom/Speeches/2011/Speech_280611_MrPiyush.pdf> accessed 29 June 2013.

Hack, Karl and Margolin, Jean-Louis. 'Singapore: Reinventing the Global City', in Karl Hack and Jean-Louis Margolin (eds), *Singapore from Temasek to the 21st Century: Reinventing the Global City*. Singapore: National University of Singapore Press (2010), 3–36.

Hammer, Michael. 'White House National Security Council' (statement, United States of America, 15 November 2009) http:// <http://www.atimes.com/atimes/China/KI26Ad01.html> accessed 15 November 2013.

Hammond, N.G.L. 'International relations of the Greek city-states', *The Classical Review* 64:2 (1950), 65–6.

Hamre, John. 'Foreword', CSIS Commission on Smart Power (2007).

Han, Yingyue. 'Singapore as a global city', *The Diplomat*, 16 March 2012 <http://the-diplomat.com/asean-beat/2012/03/16/singapore-as-a-global-city/> accessed 17 March 2013.

Hannam, Kevin, Sheller, Mimi and Urry, John. 'Editorial: mobilities, immobilities and moorings', *Mobilities* 1:1 (2006), 1–22.

Harloe, Michael and Fainstein, Susan S. 'Conclusion: the divided cities', in Susan S. Fainstein, Ian Gordon and Michael Harloe (eds), *Divided Cities: New York & London in the Contemporary World*. Oxford: Blackwell (1992), 545–66.

Harrald, J.R., Stephens, H.W. and van Dorp, J.R. 'A framework for sustainable port security', *Journal of Homeland security and Emergency Management* 1: 2 (2004), 1–13.

Harrigan, J. and Martin, P. 'Terrorism and the resilience of cities', *FRBNY Economic Policy Review* 8:2, 97–116.

Haveman, Jon D., Jennings, Ethan M., Shatz, Howard J. and Wright, Greg C. 'The Container Security Initiative and Ocean Container Threats', *Journal of Homeland Security and Emergency Management* 4:1 (2007), 1547–7355.

Harvey, David. 'The City as a Body Politic', in Ida Susser and Jane Schneider (eds), *Wounded Cities: Destruction and Reconstruction in a Globalised World.* Oxford: Berg (2003), 25–46.

Haynes, K.E, Hsing, Y.M and Stough R.R. 'Regional port dynamics in a global economy: the case of Kaohsiung', *Maritime Policy and Management* 24:1 (1997), 235–54.

Heine, Jorge and Thakur, Ramesh. 'Conclusion', in Jorge Heine and Ramesh Thakur (eds), *The Dark Side of Globalisation.* Tokyo: United Nations Press (2011).

Heine, Jorg and Thakur, Ramesh. *The Dark Side of Globalization.* United Nations University Press (2011).

Heng, Swee Keat. 'MAS 2008/09 Annual Report Press Conference, (opening remarks, Singapore, 16 July 2009) <http://www.mas.gov.sg/news-and-publications/speeches-and-monetary-policy-statements/2009/opening-remarks-by-managing-director-heng-swee-keat-at-mas-annual-report-2008-09-press-conference.aspx> accessed 17 July 2012.

Heng, Swee Keat. 'The International Institute of Finance Asia Regional Economic Forum' (speech, Singapore, 4 March 2009) <http:// http://blog.finetik.com/2009/03/06/crisis-will-bring-new-opportunities-in-asia-monetary-authority-of-singapore/> accessed 5 March 2009.

Heng, Yee-Kuang, 'A Global City and in Age of Global Risks: Singapore's evolving discourse on vulnerability', *Contemporary Southeast Asia* 35(3), (2013), 423–46.

Heng, Yee-Kuang. *War as Risk Management.* London: Routledge (2006).

Heng, Yee-Kuang and McDonaugh, Kenneth. *Risk, Global Governance and Security: The Other War on Terror*. London: Routledge (2009).

Hicks, Robin. 'Singapore reveals plan behind jobs credit scheme', 24 March 2009 <http://www.futuregov.asia/articles/2009/mar/24/singapore-reveals-plan-behind-jobs-credit-scheme/> accessed 25 March 2012.

Hill, Hal. 'An Overview of the Issues', in H.W. Arndt and Hal Hill (eds), *Southeast Asia's Economic Crisis: Origins, Lessons and the Way Forward.* Singapore: ISEAS (1999), 1–15.

Ho, Joshua. 'The security of sea lanes in Southeast Asia', *Asian Survey* 46:4 (2006), 558–74.

Ho, Peter. 'Broadening partnerships for an Asian century' (speech, CSIS, Washington D.C, 10 February 2012) <http://csis.org/event/defining-21st-century-strategic-partnership> accessed 12 February 2013.

Ho, Peng Kee. 'Counter Terrorism Workshop: Managing Civil Aviation Security In Turbulent Times' (speech, Singapore, 21 July 2003) <http://www.mha.gov.sg/news_details.aspx?nid=OTYx-Rll2t6J02oA%3D> accessed 22 July 2013.

Ho, Peng Kee. 'Launch of the Regulated Air Cargo Agent Regime' (speech, Singapore, 8 September 2008) <http://www.spf.gov.sg/rcar/forms/sms_writeup.pdf> accessed 9 September 2012.

Ho, Peter. 'Strategic Perspectives Conference' (speech, Singapore, 4 September 2006) <http://www.mfa.gov.sg/content/mfa/overseasmission/washington/newsroom/press_statements/2006/200609/press_200609_01.html> accessed 5 October 2012.

Ho, Peter. 'The future of a hub: can Singapore stay on top of the game?', *News Geography* <http://www.newgeography.com/content/001813-the-future-a-hub-can-singapore-stay-on-top-game> accessed 15 October 2010.

Ho, Peter. 'The Interdisciplinary Conference: Adaptation, Order and Emergence – A Tribute to John Holland' (speech, Singapore, 12 February 2009) <http://www3.ntu.edu.sg/CorpComms2/Documents/2009/Feb/GOH%20Speech_090212_JohnHollandConf.pdf> accessed 12 March 2012.

Ho, Peter. 'The RAHS Story', in Tan Hong Ngoh and Hoo Tiang Boon (eds), *Thinking about the Future: Strategic Anticipation and RAHS*. Singapore: National Security Coordination Secretariat and Rajaratnam School of International Studies (2008), xii–xix.

Hong, Mark. 'Singapore's security concerns post-9/11', *RUSI Journal* 148:1 (2003), 52–6.

Hudson, Chris. 'Singapore at war: SARS and its metaphors' in John H. Powers and Xiaosui Xiao (eds), *The Social Construction of SARS: Studies of a health communication crisis*. Amsterdam: John Benjamins Publishing Company (2008), 163–77.

Hughes, Christopher W. and Lai, Yew Meng (eds), *Security Studies: A Reader*. Abingdon: Routledge (2011).

Hulsse, Rainer. 'Creating demand for global governance: the making of a global money-laundering problem', *Global Society* 21:2 (2007), 155–78.

Hung, Hoo-Fung. 'The politics of SARS: containing the perils of globalization by more globalization', *Asian Perspective* 28:1 (2004), 19–44.

IBA Anti-Money Laundering Forum. 'Entry on Singapore', 27 January 2012 <http://www.anti-moneylaundering.org/asiapacific/Singapore.aspx> accessed 13 April 2012.

Iberlings, Hans. *Supermodernism: Architecture in the Age of Globalization*. Rotterdam: NAi (1998).

Idris, Nizam. 'The Future of Singapore as a Global City and its Socio-economic Implications', in Tarn Tan How (ed.), *Singapore Perspectives*. Singapore: World Scientific (2010), 97–106.

Immigration & Checkpoints Authority of Singapore (ICA). 'United States and Singapore governments launch effort to detect terrorist shipments of nuclear material', 10 March 2005 <http://app4.ica.gov.sg/news_details.aspx?nid=3086> accessed 24 April 2011.

Infocomm Development Authority of Singapore. 'Strategy and Masterplan'<http://www.ida.gov.sg/About-Us/What-We-Do/Strategy-and-Masterplan.aspx#.UPpTTWd2KL8> accessed 8 April 2011.

International Air Transport Association (IATA). 'One Stop Security' <http://www.iata.org/whatwedo/safety_security/security/Pages/one-stop.aspx> accessed 9 December 2012.

International Civil Aviation Organization (ICAO). 'Joint Statement of the Regional Conference on Aviation Security' (Kuala Lumpur, 12 January 2012) <http://www.icao.int/Security/Documents/Malaysia%20Regional%20Conference%20Statement%20FINAL.pdf> accessed 6 February 2013.

International Institute for Strategic Studies (IISS) Strategic Dossier. 'Nuclear Black Markets: A. Q Khan and the rise of proliferation networks' (2007).

International Institute for Strategic Studies (IISS) Strategic Dossier. 'Preventing Nuclear Dangers in South-east Asia and Australasia' (2009).

International Monetary Fund (IMF). 'Country Report No.01/177 for Singapore', October 2001 <http://www.imf.org/external/pubs/ft/scr/2001/cr01177.pdf> accessed 10 October 2012.

International Monetary Fund (IMF). 'Country Report No.12/42 for Singapore', February 2012 <http://www.imf.org/external/pubs/ft/scr/2012/cr1242.pdf> accessed 26 August 2012.

International Organisation of Securities Commissions and the World Federation of Exchanges. 'Cyber-crime, securities markets and systemic risks', 16 July 2013 <http://www.csrc.gov.cn/pub/csrc_en/affairs/AffairsIOSCO/201307/W020130719521960468495.pdf> accessed 4 April 2014.

Interview with Charlie Rose on *Chicago Tonight*. 14 April 2010 <http://160.96.2.142/content/pmosite/mediacentre/speechesninterviews/primeminister/2010/April/transcript_of_primeministerleehsienloongsinterviewwithustelevisi.html#.U4KeenKSySo/> accessed 15 March 2012.

Interview with *Le Monde Diplomatique*. 26 March 2009, <http://www.lemonde.fr/livres/article/2009/03/26/saskia-sassen-sociologue-globale_1172727_3260.html#ens_id=1176303> accessed 25 April 2012.

InterVistas-EU Consulting on behalf of IATA. 'Impact of international air service liberalisation on Singapore', July 2009 <http://www.iata.org/SiteCollectionDocuments/Documents/SingaporeReport.pdf> accessed 14 March 2011.

Iyer, Pico. 'Where worlds collide', *Harper's Magazine*, August 1995 <http://harpers.org/archive/1995/08/where-worlds-collide/> accessed 9 January 2012.

Jakarta Globe. 'Terror plot at Singapore's Changi Airport foiled by arrests', 28 July 2009 <http://www.thejakartaglobe.com/home/singapore-airport-terror-plot-foiled-say-solo-police/320409> accessed 27 August 2012.

Javier, Luzi Ann. 'Singapore May Toughen Penalties for Money Laundering, Terrorism Financing', 27 October 2011 <http://www.bloomberg.com/news/2011-10-27/singapore-may-toughen-penalties-for-money-laundering-terrorism-financing.html> accessed 28 October 2011.

Jayakumar, S. 'General Meeting of the Global Futures Forum: "Building resilience in the face of global shocks"' (speech, Singapore, 13 September 2010) <http://app.nscs.gov.sg/public/download.ashx?id=261> accessed 14 October 2012.

Jenkins, Brian Michael. 'Terrorists can think strategically', (testimony presented before the Senate Homeland Security and Governmental Affairs Committee, Washington D.C., 28 January 2009) <http://www.rand.org/pubs/testimonies/CT316.html> accessed 19 August 2012.

Jenkins, Brian Michael. 'Why terrorists attack airports', CNN, 25 January 2011 <http://articles.cnn.com/2011-01-25/opinion/jenkins.moscow.bombing_1_terrorists-lod-airport-airline-targets?_s=PM:OPINION> accessed 6 April 2012.

Joas, Hans. *War and Modernity*. Cambridge: Polity Press (2003), 171–80.

Johnson, Richard. 'Defending ways of life: the (anti) terrorist rhetorics of Bush and Blair', *Theory, Culture and Society* 19:4 (2002), 211–31.

Kahler, Miles. 'Economic security in an era of globalisation: definition and provision', *The Pacific Review* 17:4 (2004), 68–83.

Katz, Bruce. 'Global cities: the drivers of economic growth', Brookings Institution, 20 October 2011 <http://www.brookings.edu/blogs/up-front/posts/2011/10/20-global-cities-katz> accessed 9 January 2013.

Katz, Bruce. 'The enormous challenges of global cities', Spiegel Online, undated <http://www.spiegel.de/international/world/0,1518,589556,00.html> accessed 8 July 2011.

Kaur, Karamjit. '5m fund to help aviation firms expand reach overseas', *The Straits Times*, 29 May 2012.

Kearney, A.T. 'Global cities, present and future', <http://www.atkearney.com/research-studies/global-cities-index/full-report> accessed 9 May 2014.

Keeling, David. 'Transport and the world city paradigm', in Paul Knox and Peter Taylor (eds), *World Cities in a World-System*. Cambridge: Cambridge University Press (1995), 115–31.

Kelly, Rachel. 'Singapore ranked as Asia's leading global city: report', Channel NewsAsia, 15 June 2011 <http://www.channelnewsasia.com/stories/singaporebusinessnews/view/1135350/1/.html> accessed 16 June 2011.

Kennedy, C.A, Cuddihy, J. and Engel Yan, J. 'The changing metabolism of cities', *Journal of Industrial Ecology* (May 2007).

Kessler, Oliver and Daase, Christopher. 'From insecurity to uncertainty: risk and the paradox of security politic', *Alternatives* 33:2 (2008), 211–32.

Khanna, Parag. 'Beyond City Limits', *Foreign Policy* 181, 6 August 2010 <http://foreignpolicy.com/2010/08/06/beyond-city-limits/> accessed 9 April 2014.

Khaw, Boon Wan. 'Opening of Aviation Security Conference' (speech, Singapore, 24 April 2002) <http://www.nas.gov.sg/archivesonline/speeches/record-details/76144877-115d-11e3-83d5-0050568939ad> accessed 25 March 2012.

Khaw, Boon Wan. 'The National Medical Excellence Awards Ceremony' (speech, Singapore, 22 July 2009) <http://www.nuh.com.sg/news/media-articles_442.html> accessed 23 July 2012.

Khoo, Hedy. 'Airport checkpoint of the future?', *The New Paper*, 4 January 2011 <http://www.pvtr.org/pdf/ICPVTRinNews/AirportCheckpointOfTheFuture.pdf> accessed 9 April 2012.

Koh, Annie. 'One Global City', in Tarn How Tan (ed.), *Singapore Perspectives 2010*. Singapore: World Scientific (2010).

Koh, Buck Song. *Brand Singapore: How nation branding built Asia's leading global city*. Singapore: Marshall Cavendish (2011).

Koh, Tommy. 'The new global threat: SARS and its impacts' <http://www.spp.nus.edu.sg/ips/docs/pub/pa_tk_editorial_the%20new%20global%20threat.pdf> accessed 10 April 2012.

Kollewe, Julia. 'Japan drives down yen as volatile trading hits Europe', *Guardian*, 4 August 2011 <http://www.theguardian.com/business/2011/aug/04/japan-yen-crisis-financial> accessed 5 August 2013.

Krahmann, Elke. 'Beck and beyond: selling security in the world risk society', *Review of International Studies* 37:1 (2011), 349–72.

Krause, Linda and Pedro, Patrice (eds). *Global Cities: Cinema, Architecture, and Urbanism in a Digital Age*. London: Rutgers University Press (2003).

Kwa, Chong Guan. 'Relating to the World: Images, Metaphors, and Analogies', in Derek De Cunha (ed.), *Singapore in the New Millennium: Challenges Facing the City-State.* Singapore: ISEAS (2002), 108–32.

Kwok, Jonathan. 'PSA International posts 10.7% rise in profit for 2012', *The Straits Times*, 29 March 2013.

Larson, Christina. 'Swoons over Miami' (interview with Saskia Sassen), *Foreign Policy*, 27 August 2010 <http://www.foreignpolicy.com/articles/2010/08/27/miami_swoon?page=0,1> accessed 29 October 2012.

Latif, Asad. 'Singapore: Surviving the Downside of Globalisation', in Daljit Singh and Chin Kin Wah (eds), *Southeast Asian Affairs 2004*. Singapore: ISEAS, (2004), 253–6.

Latour, Bruno. 'Whose cosmos, which cosmopolitics', *Common Knowledge* 10:3 (2004): 450–62.

Laudicina, Paul. 'The Globalisation Index', *Foreign Policy*, 19 October 2006 <http://foreignpolicy.com/2009/10/12/the-globalization-index-2007/> accessed 20 April 2014.

Lee, Grace and Warner, Malcolm. 'Singapore: a case study', in Grace Lee and Malcolm Warner (eds), *The Political Economy of the SARS Epidemic: The Impact on Human Resources in East Asia*. London: Routledge (2008), 89–103.

Lee, Hsien Loong, '2nd Nuclear Security Summit: Plenary Sessions on "National Measures and International Cooperation to Enhance Nuclear Security, Including Future Commitments"' (speech, Seoul, Republic of Korea, 27 March 2012) <http://160.96.2.142/content/pmosite/mediacentre/speechesninterviews/primeminister/2012/March/interventions_byprimeministerleehsienloongat2ndnuclearsecuritysu.html#.U4KsO3KSySo> accessed 28 March 2013.

Lee, Hsien Loong. '40th Anniversary Dinner of MAS' (speech, Singapore, 28 November 2011) <http://www.mas.gov.sg/news-and-publications/speeches-and-monetary-policy-statements/2011/speech-by-pm-lee-hsien-loong-at-the-mas-40th-anniversary-dinner.aspx> accessed 29 November 2013.

Lee, Hsien Loong. 'Ang Mo Kio-Hougang National Day Dinner' (speech, Singapore, 21 August 2011) <https://sg.news.yahoo.com/blogs/singaporescene/poreans-must-play-part-country-progress-160156832.html> accessed 22 August 2013.

Lee, Hsien Loong. 'APEC CEO Summit' (speech, Singapore, 13 November 2009) <http://www.news.gov.sg/public/sgpc/en/media_releases/agencies/micacsd/speech/S-20091113-2.html> accessed 13 November 2012.

Lee, Hsien Loong. 'Building One Financial World' (keynote address, ACI World Congress, Singapore, 25 May 2001) <http://www.mas.gov.sg/news-and-publications/speeches-and-monetary-policy-statements/2001/building-one-financial-world--25-may-2001.aspx> accessed 25 May 2013.

Lee, Hsien Loong. 'Channel NewsAsia's Question time with the Prime Minister' (speech, Singapore, 12 April 2011) <http://www.youtube.com/watch?v=WlZe8HkUdVY> accessed 13 April 2013.

Lee, Hsien Loong. 'Economic Development Board 50th Anniversary Gala Dinner' (speech, Singapore, 1 August 2011) <http://news.asiaone.com/News/AsiaOne+News/Singapore/Story/A1Story20110802-292220.html> accessed 1 October 2013.

Lee, Hsien Loong. 'Economic Society of Singapore Annual Dinner' (speech, Singapore, 23 June 2012) <http://www.pmo.gov.sg/content/pmosite/mediacentre/speechesninterviews/primeminister/2012/June/speech_by_prime_ministerleehsienloongateconomicsocietyofsingapor.html#.U4KsV3KSySo> accessed 24 June 2013.

Lee, Hsien Loong. 'In Parliament' (speech, Singapore, 27 May 2009) <http://www.pmo.gov.sg/content/pmosite/mediacentre/speechesninterviews/primeminister/2009/May/transcript_of_primeministerleehsienloongsspeechinparliamenton27m.html#.U4KqjHKSySo> accessed 28 May 2013.

Lee, Hsien Loong. 'Keynote Address', in Tarn Tan How (ed.), *Singapore Perspectives 2010*. Singapore: World Scientific (2010), 5–12.

Lee, Hsien Loong. 'Meritus Mandarin Hotel' (speech, Singapore, 19 October 2004) <http://www.nas.gov.sg/archivesonline/speeches/record-details/78c8b964-115d-11e3-83d5-0050568939ad> accessed 19 October 2013.

Lee, Hsien Loong. 'Lloyd's City Dinner' (speech, London, 7 September 2006) <http://www.nas.gov.sg/archivesonline/speeches/record-details/7e6c2509-115d-11e3-83d5-0050568939ad> accessed 8 September 2012.

Lee, Hsien Loong. 'National Day Rally' (speech, Singapore, 17 August 2008) <http://www.pmo.gov.sg/content/pmosite/mediacentre/speechesninterviews/primeminister/2008/August/transcript_of_primeministerleehsienloongsnationaldayrally2008spe.html#.U4KqI3KSySo> accessed 18 October 2012.

Lee, Hsien Loong. 'National Day Rally' (speech, Singapore, 16 August 2009)<http://www.pmo.gov.sg/content/pmosite/mediacentre/speechesninterviews/primeminister/2009/August/national_day_rallyspeech2009part4shapingsingaporetogether> accessed 17 August 2013.

Lee, Hsien Loong. 'National Day Rally' (speech, Singapore, 29 August 2010) <http://www.pmo.gov.sg/content/pmosite/mediacentre/speechesninterviews/primeminister/2010/August/national_day_rallyspeechenglishbyprimeministerleehsienloongon29a.html#.U4KrBXKSySo> accessed 30 October 2012.

Lee, Hsien Loong. 'National Day Rally Speech: Global City, Best Home' (Singapore, 24 August 1997) <http://www.pmo.gov.sg/content/pmosite/mediacentre/speechesninterviews/primeminister/2013/August/prime-minister-lee-hsien-loong-s-national-day-rally-2013--speech.html#.U4KpMnKSySo> accessed 25 August 2012.

Lee, Hsien Loong. 'New Year Message' (statement, Singapore, 2009) <http://www.pmo.gov.sg/content/pmosite/mediacentre/speechesninterviews/primeminister/2008/December/prime_minister_leehsienloongsnewyearmessage2009.html#.U4KqRXKSySo> accessed 19 October 2013.

Lee, Hsien Loong. 'New Year's Day Message' (message, Singapore, 1 January 2005) <http://www.mfa.gov.sg/content/mfa/overseasmission/pretoria/press_statements_speeches/2005/200501/press_200501_02.html> accessed 13 August 2014.

Lee, Hsien Loong. 'Opening address at opening ceremony of UN-Interpol Ministerial meeting and 78th Interpol General Assembly' (speech, Singapore, 12 October 2009) <http://www.pmo.gov.sg/content/pmosite/mediacentre/speechesninterviews/primeminister/2009/October/opening_address_byprimeministerleehsienloongattheopeningceremony.html#.U4VTjnKSySo> accessed 13 October 2010.

Lee, Hsien Loong. 'Opening of Rolls-Royce Seletar Campus' (speech, Singapore, 13 February 2012) <http://www.pmo.gov.sg/content/pmosite/mediacentre/speechesninterviews/primeminister/2012/February/speech_by_prime_ministerleehsienloongattheopeningoftherolls-royc.html#.U4KsAXKSySo> accessed 14 February 2013.

Lee, Hsien Loong. 'People's Action Party Youth Wing 25th Anniversary Rally' (speech, Singapore, 17 April 2011) <http://maintmp.pap.org.sg/uploads/ap/8170/documents/pmspchyp25thanniversaryrallyeng.pdf> accessed 18 March 2013.

Lee, Hsien Loong. 'Singapore International Energy Week' (speech, Singapore, 1 November 2010) <http://www.ema.gov.sg/news/view/232> accessed 2 November 2013.

Lee, Hsien Loong. 'Singapore: long term vision is to become a global city' (*Global: the international briefing*, magazine of the Commonwealth Secretariat, 2011) <http://www.global-briefing.org/2011/01/interview-with-prime-minister-lee-hsien-loong/#auth> accessed 1 January 2013.

Lee, Hsien Loong. 'Singapore Medical Association's 50th Anniversary Dinner on Saturday' (speech, Singapore, 16 May 2009) <http://www.pmo.gov.sg/ … /speechesninterviews/primeminister/ … /speech_by_mr_leehsienloongprimeministeratsingaporemedicalassocia.html> accessed 17 May 2012.

Lee, Hsien Loong. 'Singapore's Stake in 21st Century and the Role of Undergraduates' (speech at Nanyang Technological University, Singapore, 10 February 1995) <http://www.nas.gov.sg/archivesonline/speeches/record-details/70b2a54b-115d-11e3-83d5-0050568939ad> accessed 19 July 2014.

Lee, Hsien Loong. 'Statement to Parliament on the Integrated resorts' (Singapore, Monday 18 April 2005) <https://www.mti.gov.sg/MTIInsights/Documents/PM%20Lee%20Hsien%20Loong-Parliament-18Apr2005.pdf> accessed 18 April 2013.

Lee, Hsien Loong. 'Swearing-in Ceremony of the Seventh President of Singapore' (speech, Singapore, 1 September 2011) <http://news.asiaone.com/News/AsiaOne+News/Singapore/Story/A1Story20110901-297293.html> accessed 2 September 2013.

Lee, Hsien Loong. 'We will do more for middle-income PMETS' (speech, Singapore, 22 February 2009) <http://www.pmo.gov.sg/content/pmosite/mediacentre/speechesninterviews/primeminister/2009/February/we_will_do_more_formiddle-incomepmetspmlee.html> accessed 23 March 2013.

Lee, Kuan Yew. 'The Fundamentals of Singapore's Foreign Policy: Then and Now', (speech, S. Rajaratnam Lecture, Singapore, 9 April 2009) <http://www.news.gov.sg/public/sgpc/en/media_releases/agencies/pmo/speech/S-20090409-1.html> accessed 10 April 2012.

Lee, Taedong. 'Global cities and transnational climate change networks', *Global Environmental Politics* 13:1 (2013), 108–28.

Lee, Vernon J., Chen, Mark I., Chan, Slew Pang, Chia, Siong Wong, Cutter, Jeffrey, Goh, Kee Tai and Tambyah, Paul Anath. 'Influenza pandemics in Singapore, a tropical, globally connected city', *Historical Review* 13:7 (2007), 1052–7.

Lee, Yong Yong. 'The Singaporean economy and macrofinancial linkages', 9 February 2012 <http://www.fairobserver.com/article/singaporean-economy-and-macrofinancial-linkages> accessed 9 February 2013.

Leifer, Michael. *Singapore: Coping with Vulnerability*. Singapore: Routledge (2000).

Leong, Chew Men. 'Foreword', The Information Fusion Centre: Challenges and Perspectives, 30 March 2011, Ministry of Defence Singapore <http://www.mindef.gov.sg/imindef/publications/pointer/supplements/IFC.print.html?Status=1> accessed 9 April 2014.

Libicki, Martin, Chalk, Peter and Sisson, Melanie. *Exploring Terrorist Targeting Preferences*. Santa Monica, CA: RAND Corporation (2007).

Liew, Alvin. 'Singapore bonds beat peers in shrinking AAA pool', Bloomberg, 16 August 2012 <http://www.bloomberg.com/news/2012-08-16/singapore-bonds-beat-peers-in-shrinking-aaa-pool-southeast-asia.html> accessed 20 August 2013.

Lim, Edwin. 'Standing ready in the face of crisis', *Bridging Skies* 15 (2012) <http://www.bridgingskies.com/> accessed 10 January 2013.

Lim, Linda Y.C. 'Free Market Fancies: Hong Kong, Singapore, and the Asian Financial Crisis', in T.J. Pempel (ed.), *The Politics of the Asian Economic Crisis*. Ithaca: Cornell University Press (1999), 101–15.

Lim, Linette. 'Singapore vulnerable in face of looming risks in global economy', *TODAYonline*, 23 May 2011 <https://groups.yahoo.com/neo/groups/RealEdge/conversations/messages/18263> accessed 23 May 2012.

Lim, Meng Kin. 'Global response to pandemic flu: more research needed on a critical front', *Health Research Policy and Systems* 4:8 (2006).

Lim, Nicholas. 'The Information Fusion Centre: A Case for Information Sharing to Enforce Security in the Maritime Domain', *The Information Fusion Centre: Challenges and Perspectives*. Singapore: SAF Pointers Supplement (2011), 3–10.

Lindio-McGovern, Ligaya. *Globalization, Labor Export and Resistance: A Study of Filipino Migrant Domestic Workers in Global Cities*. London: Routledge (2011).

Lloyd's List Daily News Bulletin. 'First Sea Lord warns of al-Qaeda plot to target merchant ships', 5 August 2004 <http://www.lloydslist.com/ll/sector/piracy-and-security/article123388.ece> accessed 29 October 2014.

Lo, Fu-Chen and Yeung, Yue-man. 'Introduction', in Fu-Chen Lo and Yue-man Yeung (eds), *Globalization and the World of Large Cities*. Tokyo: United Nations University Press (1998), 1–13.

Lo, Fu-Chen and Yeung, Yue-man. 'World City Formation in Pacific Asia', in Fu-Chen Lo and Yue-man Yeung (eds), *Globalization and the World of Large Cities*. Tokyo: United Nations University Press (1998), 132–54.

Loh, Dylah. 'Singapore is what it is today because of globalization: Lee Kuan Yew', *TODAYonline*, 21 September 2012 <http://www.channelnewsasia.com/stories/singaporelocalnews/view/1227352/1/.html> accessed 22 September 2013.

Lohmann, Guilherme, Albers, Sascha, Koch, Benjamin and Paylovich, Kathryn. 'From hub to tourist destination – an explorative study of Singapore and Dubai's aviation-based transformation', *Journal of Air Transport Management* 15 (2009), 205–11.

Loy, James M. 'Statement of James M. Loy to the National Commission on Terrorist Attacks Upon The United States' (statement, United States of America, 27 January 2004) <http://www.9-11commission.gov/hearings/hearing7/witness_loy.htm> accessed 15 August 2013.

Lui, Tuck Yew. 'Aviation Community Reception 2013' (speech at Avalon, Marina Bay Sands, 14 May 2013) <http://www.news.gov.sg/public/sgpc/en/media_releases/agencies/mot/speech/S-20130514-1> accessed 15 December 2013.

Lui, Tuck Yew. 'Changi Airline Awards 2011' (speech, Shangri-la Hotel Singapore, 18 July 2011) <http://www.nas.gov.sg/archivesonline/speeches/record-details/813cd11f-115d-11e3-83d5-0050568939ad> accessed 19 July 2013.

Lui, Tuck Yew. 'Official Commissioning of the Port Operations Control' (speech at Changi Naval Base, 25 July 2011) <http://www.mpa.gov.sg/sites/global_navigation/news_center/speeches/speeches_detail.page?filename=sp110725.xml> accessed 10 August 2012.

Lui, Tuck Yew. 'Singapore Maritime Foundation New Year Cocktail Reception 2013' (speech, Singapore, 10 January 2013) <http://www.news.gov.sg/public/sgpc/en/media_releases/agencies/mot/speech/S-20130110-11> accessed 11 January 2014.

Lui, Tuck Yew. 'The Opening of Project 3/12: A Nation Remembers' (speech, City Hall Chambers, Singapore, 3 December 2009) <http://app.mica.gov.sg/default.apsx?tabid=79&ctl=details&mid=540&itemid=1092> accessed 4 December 2012.

Luke, Timothy. 'Everyday Technics as Extraordinary Threats: Urban Technostructures and Non-Places in Terrorist Actions', in S. Graham (ed.), *Cities, War and Terrorism: Towards an Urban Geopolitics*. Malden, MA: Wiley-Blackwell (2004), 120–36

Mabe, Matt. 'The world's most global cities', Bloomberg Businessweek, 29 October 2008 <http://www.businessweek.com/globalbiz/content/oct2008/gb20081029_679467.htm> accessed 08 April 2011.

Maritime and Port Authority of Singapore. 'Conference Program' <http://www.mpa.gov.sg/sites/pdf/030113-b.pdf> accessed 24 March 2011.

Maritime and Port Authority of Singapore. 'Global Port Hub' <http://www.mpa.gov.sg/sites/maritime_singapore/what_maritime_singapore_offer/global_connectivity/global_hub_port.page> accessed 9 January 2013.

Maritime and Port Authority of Singapore. 'Singapore's 2012 maritime performance', 10 January 2013 <http://www.news.gov.sg/public/sgpc/en/media_releases/agencies/mpa/press_release/P-20130110-1> accessed 12 January 2013.

Maritime and Port Authority of Singapore. 'Singapore's 2013 maritime performance', 7 January 2014 <http://www.mpa.gov.sg/sites/global_navigation/news_center/mpa_news/mpa_news_detail.page?filename=nr140107a.xml> accessed 2 January 2015.

Maritime and Port Authority of Singapore, PSA Singapore Terminals and Neptune Orient Lines. 'First Joint Maritime Security Exercise' (MPA Statement, Singapore, 25 May 2004) <http://www.mpa.gov.sg/sites/global_navigation/news_center/mpa_news/mpa_news_detail.page?filename=nr040525.xml> accessed 26 June 2012.

Martell, Luke. 'Beck's cosmopolitan politics', *Contemporary Politics* 14:2 (2008), 129–43.

Matsumoto, Hidenobu. 'International air network structures and air traffic density of world cities', *Transportation Research Part E* 43 (2007), 269–82.

Matsumoto, Hidenobu. 'International urban systems and air passenger and cargo flows: some calculations', *Journal of Air Transport Management* 10 (2004), 241–9.

Mayer, J.D. 'The surveillance and control of emerging infectious diseases', *Applied Geographical Studies* 2:4 (1998), 261–78.

Meier, Barry and Lipton, Eric. 'F.D.A. shift on painkillers was years in the making', *The New York Times*, 27 October 2013 <http://www.nytimes.com/2013/10/28/business/fda-shift-on-painkillers-was-years-in-the-making.html> accessed 28 April 2014.

Meier, Barry and Lipton, Eric. 'In air cargo business, it's speed versus screening, creating weak link in security', *The New York Times*, 1 November 2010 <http://

www.nytimes.com/2010/11/02/business/02cargo.html?pagewanted=all&_r=0> accessed 10 January 2012.

Menon, K.U. and Goh, K.T. 'Transparency and trust: risk communications and the Singapore experience in managing SARS', *Journal of Communication Management* 9:4 (2005), 375–83.

Menon, Ravi. 'A Competent, Trusted and Clean Financial Centre' (speech, Singapore, 28 October 2011) <http://www.mas.gov.sg/news-and-publications/speeches-and-monetary-policy-statements/2011/a-competent-trusted-and-clean-financial-centre-welcome-address-by-mr-ravi-menon-md-mas-at-the-wmi-connection.aspx> accessed 29 October 2013.

Menon, Ravi. 'Asia Anti-money Laundering Conference' (speech, Singapore, 31 July 2003) <http://www.mas.gov.sg/news-and-publications/speeches-and-monetary-policy-statements/2003/combating-money-laundering-and-terrorism-financing.aspx> accessed 30 July 2013.

Menon, Ravi. 'MAS Annual Report 2010/2011 Press Conference' (opening remarks, Singapore, 21 July 2011) <http://www.mas.gov.sg/news_room/statements/2011/Opening_Remarks_at_MAS_AR_2010_11_Press_Conference.html> accessed 22 July 2013.

Menon, Ravi. 'MAS Annual Report 2011/12' (opening remarks, Singapore, 25 July 2012) <http://www.mas.gov.sg/news-and-publications/speeches-and-monetary-policy-statements/2012/mas-annual-report-2011-2012.aspx> accessed 26 July 2013.

Menon, Ravi. 'WMI Connection' (speech, Fullerton Hotel, Singapore, 27 October 2011) <http://www.news.gov.sg/public/sgpc/en/media_releases/agencies/mha%20-%20htuc/speech/S-20100713-1.html> accessed 28 October 2013.

Menon, Vanu Gopala, 'Remarks at Wilton Park Conference on Reforming International Governance, Luxemborg, 15 June 2011' <http://www.mfa.gov.sg/content/mfa/overseasmission/newyork/nyemb_statements/global_governance_group/2011/201102/press_201106_2.html> accessed 12 March 2013.

Meyer, David. 'World cities as financial centres', in Fu-Chen Lo and Yue-man Yeung (eds), *Globalization and the World of Large Cities*. Tokyo: United Nations University Press (1998), 410–32.

Millward, David. 'Spy system for airlines to tackle terrorism', *The Daily Telegraph*, 27 June 2010 <http://www.telegraph.co.uk/finance/newsbysector/transport/7857880/Spy-system-for-airlines-to-tackle-terrorism.html> accessed 20 January 2011.

Ministry of Defence, Singapore. 'Speech at the Overseas Medal Service Presentation Ceremony', 8 October 2010 <http://www.mindef.gov.sg/content/imindef/resources/speeches/2010/08oct10_speech.print.html?Status=1> accessed 9 January 2011.

Ministry of Finance, Singapore. 'Economic Strategies Committee Report', February 2010 <http://app.mof.gov.sg/data/cmsresource/ESC%20Report/ESC%20Full%20Report.pdf> accessed 15 April 2011.

Ministry of Health, Singapore. 'SARS: new measures at airport to curb importation of new cases', 30 March 2003 <http://www.moh.gov.sg/content/moh_web/home/pressRoom/pressRoomItemRelease/2003/SARSnew_measures_at_airport_to_curb_importation_of_new_cases_more_patients_recovering_and_discharged.html> accessed 14 January 2010.

Ministry of Home Affairs, Singapore. 'FATF's Enhanced Measures to Combat Money Laundering, Terrorist Financing And The Financing of Proliferation', 16 February 2012 <http://www.mha.gov.sg/news_details.aspx?nid=MjM2NQ%3D%3D-AL0iTNxUJSI%3D> accessed 17 February 2013.

Ministry of Home Affairs, Singapore. 'Preparing for a Human Influenza Pandemic in Singapore', 2009 <http://app.crisis.gov.sg/Data/Documents/H1N1/NSFP.pdf> accessed 8 January 2010.

Ministry of Manpower, Singapore. 'Labour Market 2008' <http://www.mom.gov.sg/Publications/qtlmr084.pdf> accessed 15 April 2011.

Ministry of Manpower, Singapore. 'Singapore Yearbook of Manpower Statistics, 2012' <http://www.mom.gov.sg/Documents/statistics-publications/yearbook12/mrsd_2012YearBook.pdf> accessed 14 April 2012.

Ministry of Trade and Industry, Singapore. 'Economic Survey of Singapore, 2008' 26 February 2009 <http://www.mti.gov.sg/ResearchRoom/Pages/Economic%20Survey%20of%20Singapore%202008.aspx> accessed 29 October 2014.

Ministry of Trade and Industry, Singapore. 'Report of the Working Group on Logistics, Developing Singapore into a Global Integrated Logistics Hub', September 2002 <http://www.mti.gov.sg/ResearchRoom/Documents/app.mti.gov.sg/data/pages/507/doc/ERC_SVSLOG_MainReport.pdf> accessed 5 October 2012.

Ministry of Transport, Singapore. 'Aviation security' <http://app.mot.gov.sg/page_air.aspx?p=/Air_Transport/Contributions_to_International_Civil_Aviation/Aviation_Security.aspx&AspxAutoDetectCookieSupport=1> accessed 22 December 2012.

Ministry of Transport, Singapore. 'Changi developments to open path to new opportunities', 31 August 2013 <http://app.mot.gov.sg/News_Centre/Latest_News/NewsID/1921B0000710A733/Changi_Developments_To_Open_Path_To_New_Opportunities.aspx> accessed 30 November 2013.

Ministry of Transport, Singapore. 'Liberal air services regime' <http://app.mot.gov.sg/Air_Transport/Aviation_Hub/Liberal_Air_Services_Regime.aspx> accessed 23 December 2012.

Monetary Authority of Singapore (MAS). 'Annual Report 1998/1999' <http://www.mas.gov.sg/~/media/resource/about_us/annual_reports/annual19981999/MASAnnual9899.pdf> accessed 10 April 2014.

Monetary Authority of Singapore (MAS). 'Coping with the Asian Financial Crisis: The Singapore Experience' (speech at Nomura Securities 'Singapore Seminar', Tokyo, Japan, 30 September 1998) <http://www.mas.gov.sg/news_room/statements/1998/Coping_With_the_Asian_Financial_Crisis_The_Singapore_Experience__30_Sep_1998.html> accessed 9 April 2011.

Monetary Authority of Singapore (MAS). 'MAS Annual Report 2011/2012' <http://www.mas.gov.sg/annual_reports/annual20112012/partners01_08.html> accessed 14 September 2012.

Muckstadt, John, Conlin, Sean and Beadling, Walter. 'Securing the air cargo supply chain, expediting the flow of commerce', October 2009 <https://www.securecargo.org/content/securing-the-air-cargo-supply-chain-expediting-the-flow-of-commerce-a-collaborative-approach> accessed 7 March 2011.

Murray, Geoffrey and Perera, Audrey. *Singapore: The Global City-State*. Folkestone: China Library (1996).

Musfirah, Hetty. 'Changi has potential to grow air traffic until at least 2018', Channel NewsAsia <http://www.channelnewsasia.com/stories/singaporelocalnews/view/1243388/1/.html> accessed 18 December 2012.

Mutimer, David. 'Reconstituting security? The practices of proliferation control', *European Journal of International Relations* 4:1 (1998), 99–129.

Mythen, Gabe. *Ulrich Beck: A Critical Introduction to the Risk Society*. Cambridge: Polity Press (2004).

Narayan, K.M. Venkat, Ali, M.K. and Koplan J.P. 'Global non-communicable diseases: where worlds meet', *New England Journal of Medicine* 363 (2010), 1196–8.

Nanto, Dick K. '9/11 terrorism: global economic costs'. Congressional Research Service, 5 October 2004 <http://political-asylum.com/crs_country/CRSReport911TerrorismGlobalEconomicCosts(October5,2004)Updated.pdf> accessed 29 October 2014.

Nathan, S.R. 'Diplomatic Academy's Inaugural S. Rajaratnam Lecture' (speech, Singapore, 10 March 2008) <http://www.mfa.gov.sg/content/mfa/overseasmission/manila/press_statements_speeches/speeches_by_sg_leader/2008/200803/press_200803.html> accessed 11 March 2013.

National Capital Urban design and Security Plan. 'Designing and testing of perimeter security elements'. National Capital Planning Commission, A-8, Washington D.C, 2002, <http://www.ncpc.gov/DocumentDepot/Publications/SecurityPlans/DesignTestPerimSecurity.pdf> accessed 15 July 2013.

National Post, The. 'SARS kills two more in Toronto', 2 April 2003.

National Security Coordination Centre Singapore. 'The Fight against Terror: Singapore's National Security Strategy'. Singapore: Atlas Associates PTE Singapore (2004) <http://www.mindef.gov.sg/dam/publications/eBooks/More_eBooks/FightAgainstTerror.pdf> accessed 15 July 2013.

NATO Parliamentary Assembly Committee Report. 'Policy Implications of the Risk Society', 2005 <http://www.nato-pa.int/Default.asp?SHORTCUT=672> accessed 3 November 2012.

Neptune Orient Lines. 'About Us' <http://www.nol.com.sg/wps/portal/nol/aboutus/corporateresponsibility/security> accessed 9 April 2012.

Neumeister, Larry and Hays, Tom. 'Two NY cooperators give firsthand look at Al Qaida', Associated Press, 7 May 2012 <http://news.yahoo.com/2-ny-cooperators-firsthand-look-al-qaida-211626418.html> accessed 7 May 2012.

New York City press release. 'Counter-terrorism commissioner appointed', 25 June 2010 <http://www.nyc.gov/html/nypd/html/pr/pr_2010_new_ct_comissioner.shtml> accessed 4 April 2011.

Ng, Eng Hen. 'Racial Harmony Day Celebrations' (speech, Singapore, 21 July 2010) <http://www.moe.gov.sg/media/speeches/2010/07/21/speech-by-dr-ng-eng-hen-at-the-38.php> accessed 22 July 2012.

Ng, Sam Sin. 'Society for Trust and Estate Practitioners Asia conference' (speech, Singapore, 1 November 2011) <http://www.mas.gov.sg/News-and-Publications/Speeches-and-Monetary-Policy-Statements/2011/Keynote-Speech-By-Mr-Ng-Nam-Sin-AMD-MAS-STEP-Asia-Conference.aspx> accessed 2 November 2013.

Ngiam, Kee Jin. 'Coping with the Asian Financial Crisis: The Singapore Experience', Speech, Nomura Securities 'Singapore Seminar' (Tokyo, Japan, 30 September 1998) <http://www.mas.gov.sg/news_room/statements/1998/Coping_With_the_Asian_Financial_Crisis__The_Singapore_Experience__30_Sep_1998.html> accessed 31 September 2013.

Nijman, Janne. 'The rising influence of urban actors', *The Broker* 17 (2009), 14–18.

Nussbaum, Brian. 'Protecting global cities: New York, London and the internationalisation of municipal policing for counter-terrorism', *Global Crime* 8:3 (2007), 213–32.

Ooi, Giok Ling and Phua, Kai Hong. 'SARS in Singapore – challenges of a global health threat to local institutions', *Natural Hazards* 48 (2009), 317–27.

Olds, Kris and Yeung, Henry. 'Pathways to global city formation: a view from the developmental city-state of Singapore', *Review of International Political Economy* 11:3 (2004), 489–521.

Organisation for Economic Co-operation and Development (OECD). 'Future Global Shocks', June 2011 <http://www.oecd.org/governance/48256382.pdf> accessed 9 July 2013.

Organisation for Economic Co-operation and Development (OECD). 'Globalisation ups risk of disease', *The Daily Telegraph* (Australia), 28 June 2011, <http://www.dailytelegraph.com.au/news/world/globalisation-ups-risk-of-disease-gfc/story-e6frev00-1226083296018> accessed 29 June 2013.

Organisation for Economic Co-operation and Development (OECD). 'Security in maritime transport', Maritime Transport Committee, July 2003 <http://www.oecd.org/newsroom/4375896.pdf> accessed 28 August 2014.

Osterholm, Michael T. 'Preparing for the next pandemic', *Foreign Affairs*, July/August 2005 <http://www.foreignaffairs.com/articles/60818/michael-t-osterholm/preparing-for-the-next-pandemic> accessed 10 August 2014.

Oswin, Natalie and Yeoh, Brenda. 'Introduction: mobile city Singapore', *Mobilities* 5:2 (2010), 165–75.

Owen, John Wyn and Roberts, Olivia. 'Globalisation, health and foreign policy: emerging linkages and interests', *Globalization and Health* 1:12 (2005), 1–12.

Oxford Economics. ‘Economic Benefits from Air Transport in Singapore’, 2011 <http://www.benefitsofaviation.aero/Documents/Benefits-of-Aviation-Singapore-2011.pdf> accessed 23 April 2012.

Pain, Richard, ‘New security response centre opens in Singapore’, Asia Pacific FutureGov, 10 August 2012 <http://www.futuregov.asia/articles/2012/aug/01/new-security-response-center-opens-singapore/> accessed 27 October 2012.

Pang, Eng Fong. ‘Singapore: positioned to weather the global shock’, East Asia Forum, 2 January 2009 <http://www.eastasiaforum.org/2009/01/02/singapore-positioned-to-weather-the-global-shock> accessed 23 July 2011.

Pang, Kin Keong. ‘Joint Conference on Enhancing Air Cargo Security and Facilitation’ (speech, Orchard Hotel, Singapore 5–6 July 2012) <http://www.customs.gov.sg/NR/rdonlyres/6185D945-DC37-4EA6-B5B7-3EC35CC8C60E/24064/PS_T_OpeningSpeechattheICAOWCOJointConference_Fina.pdf> accessed 7 July 2013.

Pawley, Martin. *Terminal Architecture*. London: Reaktion (1998).

Petrella, Ricardo. ‘World city-states of the future’, *New Perspectives Quarterly* 8:4 (1991), 59–64.

Port of Singapore Authority. ‘About Us’ <http://www.singaporepsa.com/aboutus.php> accessed 8 November 2012.

Port of Singapore Authority. ‘Our Core Business’ <http://www.singaporepsa.com/transhipment.php> accessed 8 November 2012.

Port of Singapore Authority. ‘Sage Advice’. Singapore: Portview (Q2 2010).

Port of Singapore Authority. ‘Security’ <http://www.singaporepsa.com/security.php> accessed 23 January 2013.

Powell, Robert. *Singapore: Architecture of a Global City*. Singapore: Archipelago Press (2000).

Premier Formations (Singapore). ‘AML/CFT policy’ <http://www.premier-formations.com/aboutus/aml.php> accessed 8 April 2012.

Prime Minister Office Singapore. ‘Transcript of PM interview on Chicago Tonight’, 16 April 2010 <http://www.pmo.gov.sg/content/pmosite/mediacentre/speechesninterviews/primeminister/2010/April/transcript_of_primeministerleehsienloongsinterviewonchicagotonig.html> accessed 8 April 2011.

Public Relations Academy. ‘Opening address at the 6th Annual PR Academy Conference: Markets and Brands: Positioning for the 21st century’ (Singapore, 23 May 2007) <http://www.ne.edu.sg/files/Minister%20Speech%206th%20Annual%20Conference%20Media.pdf> accessed 24 May 2013.

Radelet, Steven and Sachs, Jeffrey. ‘Lessons from the Asian financial crisis’ in B.N. Ghosh (ed.), *Global Financial Crises and Reforms: Cases and Caveats*. London: Routledge (2001), 129–56.

Rahil, Siti. ‘More Japanese firms relocating to Singapore’, *The Japan Times*, 14 August 2012 <http://www.japantimes.co.jp/news/2012/08/14/business/more-japanese-firms-relocating-to-singapore/> accessed 15 August 2013.

Rajaratnam, S. 'Singapore: global city' (speech to the Singapore Press Club, 6 February 1972) <http://newshub.nus.edu.sg/news/1202/PDF/GLOBAL-st-6feb-pA17.pdf> accessed 7 February 2012.

Ramesh, S. 'Singapore sets up new centre to enhance risk assessment capability', Channel NewsAsia, 19 March 2007 <http://www.channelnewsasia.com/stories/singaporelocalnews/view/264941/1/.html> accessed 8 April 2010.

Rane, Jordan. '10 of the world's most loved airports', CNNGo, 17 November 2011 <http://www.cnngo.com/explorations/life/10-most-loved-airports-981939?page=0,1> accessed 8 April 2012.

Raymond, Catherine Zara. 'Maritime terrorism in Southeast Asia: a risk assessment', *Terrorism and Political Violence* 18:2 (2006), 239–57.

Raymond, Catherine Zara. 'Maritime terrorism in South-east Asia: potential scenarios', *Terrorism Monitor* 4:7 (2006).

Renn, Ortwin and Walker, Katherine D. (eds), *Global Risk Governance*. Amsterdam: Springer (2008).

Richardson, Michael. *A Time Bomb for Global Trade: Maritime-related Terrorism in an Age of Weapons of Mass Destruction*. Singapore: ISEAS (2004).

Richardson, Paul. 'The Singapore maritime story', *Singapore Nautilus* (Q1 2008).

Rimmer, Peter. 'Transport and Telecommunications Among World Cities', in Fu-Chen Lo and Yue-man Yeung (eds), *Globalization and the World of Large Cities*. Tokyo: United Nations University Press (1998), 433–70.

Robinson, J. 'Global and world cities: a view from off the map', *International Journal of Urban and Regional Research* 26:3 (2002), 531–54.

Rogers, Paul. *Losing Control: Global Security in the Twenty-first Century*. London: Pluto Press (2000).

Rose, Gideon. 'Why did September 11th happen?', Council on Foreign Relations, 26 November 2001 <http://www.cfr.org/terrorist-attacks/gideon-rose-why-did-september-11-happen/p4211> accessed 8 April 2012.

Ross, Robert and Trachte, Kent. 'Global Cities and Global Classes: the peripheralisation of labour in New York city', in Neil Brenner and Roger Keil (eds) *The Global Cities Reader*. New York, NY: Routledge (2006), 104–10.

Roubini, Nouriel. 'The coming financial pandemic', *Foreign Policy*, 2008 <http://www.foreignpolicy.com/articles/2009/02/19/the_coming_financial_pandemic> accessed 10 April 2013.

Roy, Ananya and Ong, Aihwa (eds). *Worlding Cities: Asian Experiments and the Art of Being Global*. Malden, MA: Wiley-Blackwell (2011).

Rubin, Harvey. *Future Global Shocks: Pandemics*. Paris: OECD (2011).

S. Rajaratnam School of International Studies and the National Security Coordination Secretariat. Dialogue session at 5th Asia-Pacific Programme for Senior National Security Officers (APPSNO), 21 April 2011.

Sadasivan, Balaji. 'Opening Ceremony of the Global Outbreak Alert and Response Network Steering Committee Meeting' (speech, Singapore, 7 December 2005) <http://www.moh.gov.sg/content/moh_web/home/pressRoom/

speeches_d/2005/opening_ceremony_of_the_global_outbreak_alert_and_response_network_steering_committee_meeting.html> accessed 8 December 2013.

Salter, Mark B. 'Imagining numbers: risk, quantification, and aviation security', *Security Dialogue* 39:2 (2008), 243–66.

Samers, Michael. 'Immigration and the Global City Hypothesis: Towards an Alternative Research Agenda', in Neil Brenner and Roger Keil (eds), *The Global Cities Reader*. London: Routledge (2006), 384–91.

Sassen, Saskia. 'On concentration and centrality in the global city', in Paul Knox and Peter Taylor (eds), *World cities in a World-System*. Cambridge: Cambridge University Press (1995), 63–78.

Sassen, Saskia, *The Global City: London, New York, Tokyo*. New Jersey: Princeton University Press (2001).

Sassen, Saskia. 'The global city: strategic site/new frontier', Globalization: A symposium on the challenges of closer global integration, July 2001 <http://www.india-seminar.com/2001/503/503%20saskia%20sassen.htm> accessed 8 June 2011.

Saywell, T. and Borsuk, R. 'The fallout of the Bali bombings on regional economies: the neighbourhood takes a hit', *Far Eastern Economic Review*, 24 October 2002.

Schamotta, Karl. 'EU row over Greek aid sparks fears crisis could spread', *The Straits Times*, 12 July 2011.

Scheffer, Jaap de Hoop. 'Meeting the Security Challenges of Globalisation', (speech, Tokyo, Japan, 13 December 2007) <http://www.nato.int/cps/en/natohq/opinions_9636.htm?selectedLocale=en> accessed 15 July 2013.

Schinasi, Garry J., Drees, Burkhard and Lee, William. 'Managing global finance and risk', *Finance and Development: a quarterly magazine of the IMF* 36:4 (1999) <http://www.imf.org/external/pubs/ft/fandd/1999/12/schinasi.htm> accessed 26 May 2014.

Securities Industry Association. 'The Key Building Blocks of World Class Financial Centres' <http://www.ita.doc.gov/td/finance/publications/World_Class_Financial_Center.pdf> accessed 26 March 2010.

Seng, Tan See. 'Faced with the dragon: perils and prospects in Singapore's ambivalent relationship with China', *Chinese Journal of International Politics* 5:3 (2012), 245–65.

Shanmugam, K. '13th Annual Meeting of Asia-Pacific Group on Money Laundering' (speech, Singapore, 13 July 2010) <https://www.mha.gov.sg/news_details.aspx?nid=MTc2MA%3D%3D-g0QQBHqhZ%2FQ%3D> accessed 14 July 2013.

Shanmugam, K. 'Opening Ceremony of 13th Annual Meeting of Asia-Pacific Group on Money Laundering' (speech, Singapore, 13 July 2010) <http://www.news.gov.sg/public/sgpc/en/media_releases/agencies/mha%20-%20htuc/speech/S-20100713-1.html> accessed 14 July 2012.

Shanmugam, K. 'Singapore Corporate Awards' (speech, Singapore, 23 April 2009) <http://www.mlaw.gov.sg/news/speeches/speech-by-law-minister-k-shanmugam-at-the-singapore-corporate-awards-2009.html> accessed 24 April 2012.

Shanmugam, K. 'Statement at the UN General Assembly General Debate' (27 September 2011) <http://gadebate.un.org/66/singapore> accessed 29 August 2014.

Shanmugaratnam, Tharman. '39th Association of Banks in Singapore Annual Dinner' (speech, Singapore, 28 June 2012) <http://app.mof.gov.sg/newsroom_details.aspx?type=speech&cmpar_year=2012&news_sid=20120629148451891878> accessed 29 June 2013.

Shanmugaratnam, Tharman. 'ASEAN Day Reception' (speech, Singapore, 2 August 2012) <http://www.mfa.gov.sg/content/mfa/media_centre/press_room/if/2012/201208/infocus_20120802_03.html> accessed 3 August 2013.

Shanmugaratnam, Tharman. 'Budget Statement' (speech, Singapore, 22 January 2009)<http://www.nas.gov.sg/archivesonline/speeches/record-details/8008b212-115d-11e3-83d5-0050568939ad> accessed 23 January 2013.

Shanmugaratnam, Tharman. 'Chairman of the Monetary Authority of Singapore at the 39th Association of Banks in Singapore (ABS) Annual Dinner' (speech, Singapore, 28 June 2012) <http://app.mof.gov.sg/newsroom_details.aspx?type=speech&cmpar_year=2012&news_sid=20120629148451891878> accessed 29 June 2013.

Shanmugaratnam, Tharman. 'Singapore Human Capital Summit' (speech, Singapore, 19 September 2012) <http://app.mof.gov.sg/newsroom_details.aspx?type=speech&cmpar_year=2012&news_sid=20120919503641796214> accessed 20 September 2013.

Shanmugaratnam, Tharman. 'Singapore Perspectives 2012 conference' (speech, Singapore, 16 January 2012) <http://app.mof.gov.sg/newsroom_details.aspx?type=media&cmpar_year=2012&news_sid=20120121608784777037> accessed 17 January 2013.

Sherbinin, Alex de, Schiller, Andrew and Pulsiper, Alex. 'The vulnerability of global cities to climate hazards', *Environment & Urbanisation* 19:1 (2007), 39–64.

Sheridan, Greg. 'Thoughtful wisdom from Lee Hsien Loong', *The Australian*, 29 September 2012 <http://www.theaustralian.com.au/national-affairs/thoughtful-wisdom-from-lee-hsien-loong-a-leader-with-proven-record/story-fn59niix-1226483762571> accessed 5 October 2012.

Short, John Rennie. *Global Metropolitan*. London: Routledge (2004).

Short, John Rennie and Kim, Yeong Hyun. *Globalisation and the City*. London: Longman (1999).

Singapore Business News. <http://singaporebusiness.asia/don%E2%80%99t-grope-the-passengers-iata-pleads-for-strip-search-free-airline-check-in-in-singapore/#axzz2G38SLx5B> accessed 23 December 2012.

Singapore Customs. 'All exports to be declared in advance come 2013' (media release, 12 January 2012) <http://www.customs.gov.sg/NR/rdonlyres/6185D945-DC37-4EA6-B5B7-3EC35CC8C60E/23735/PressReleaseonAEDImplementation_FinalWeb.pdf> accessed 14 January 2013.

Singapore Customs. 'Forging global partnerships to strengthen air cargo security'. *Insync: Singapore Customs E-Newsletter* 19 (July/August 2012).

Singapore Customs. 'Joint communique on enhancing air cargo security and facilitiation: synergy through cooperation, Singapore', 6 July 2012 <http://www.customs.gov.sg/NR/rdonlyres/806059B3-FEBE-4D85-9717-C4270BE42857/24081/JointCommuniqueMOTSCICAO.pdf> accessed 10 November 2012.

Singapore Customs. 'Secure Trade Partnership' <http://www.customs.gov.sg/leftNav/trad/Supply+Chain+Security.htm> accessed 18 April 2010.

Singapore Customs. 'Singapore Customs rattles sabre against WMD proliferation'. *Insync: Singapore Customs E-Newsletter* 7 (2010).

Singapore Embassy. 'Singapore 2006: Global city, world of opportunities' (an update from the Singapore Embassy, October/November 2005) <http://www.mfa.gov.sg/washington/Oct_Nov_05.pdf> accessed 16 June 2011.

Singapore International Airlines (SIA). 'Annual Report' (2003/2004) <http://www.singaporeair.com/pdf/Investor-Relations/Annual-Report/annualreport0304.pdf> accessed 10 August 2014.

Singapore Tourism Board. *Singapore: Global City for the Arts* (2000). Singapore: STB.

Singh, Bilveer. 'Why Singapore is an iconic target', *TODAYonline*, 22 July 2011 <http://www.themalaysianinsider.com/sideviews/article/why-spore-is-an-iconic-target-for-terrorists-bilveer-singh> accessed 10 April 2012.

Skilling, David. 'How small countries thrive in a big world', *The Straits Times*, 16 June 2011 <http://forums.vr-zone.com/chit-chatting/1445051-how-small-countries-thrive-big-world.html> accessed 20 September 2012.

Smith, David A. and Timberlake, Michael. 'Cities in Global Matrices: Toward Mapping the World-System's City-System', in Paul L. Knox and Peter J. Taylor (eds), *World Cities in a World-System*. New York: Cambridge University Press (1995), 79–97.

Smith, Michael Peter. 'The Global Cities Discourse: A Return to the Master Narrative', in Neil Brenner and Roger Keil (eds), *The Global Cities Reader*. London: Routledge (2006), 377–83.

Smith, Shelley. 'Hong Kong and Singapore vulnerable to global slump, Nomura says', Bloomberg News, 25 May 2009 <http://www.bloomberg.com/apps/news?pid=newsarchive&sid=aUgbgKSCnM6I> accessed 8 April 2011.

Solana, Javier and Innerarity, Daniel. 'The New Grammar of Power', Project Syndicate, 1 August 2011 <http://www.project-syndicate.org/commentary/solana10/English> accessed 1 August 2011.

Stewart, Heather. 'Is this the end of globalisation?', *The Observer*, 5 March 2006 <http://www.theguardian.com/business/2006/mar/05/money.theobserver> accessed 15 July 2013.

Stiglitz, Joseph. 'Europe's travails and our collective fate', *The New York Times*, 19 July 2011 <http://www.nytimes.com/2011/07/20/opinion/20iht-edstiglitz20.html> accessed 14 July 2013.

Stone, Charles A. and Zissu, Anne. 'Registered traveler program: the financial value of registering the good guys', *Review of Policy Research* 24:5 (2007), 433–67.

Straits Times, The. 'Forget First World Hype', 12 January 2013 <http://newshub.nus.edu.sg/news/1301/PDF/HYPE-st-12jan-pD17.pdf> accessed 17 August 2013.

Straits Times, The. 'Lee Kuan Yew's chance of a lifetime', 16 February 2013 <http://www.stasiareport.com/supplements/saturday-special-report/story/lee-kuan-yews-chance-lifetime-20130216> accessed 17 February 2014.

Straits Times, The. 'Singapore's support for action on Iraq prompted by wider concerns', 11 June 2003 <http://eresources.nlb.gov.sg/newspapers/Digitised/Article/straitstimes20030611-1.2.26.5.aspx> accessed 16 August 2013.

Sunday Times, The. 'Connected to the world', *Sunday Times*, special on 'Singapore Airshow 2014', 9 February 2014.

Sunday Times, The. 'Key aviation hub', *Sunday Times*, special on 'Singapore Airshow 2014', 11 February 2014 <http://business.asiaone.com/news/key-aviation-hub> accessed 19 April 2014.

Sunday Times, The. 'Soaring to new heights', *Sunday Times*, special on 'Singapore Airshow 2014', 9 February 2014 <http://business.asiaone.com/news/soaring-new-heights> accessed 18 April 2014.

Susser, Ida and Schneider, Jane. 'Wounded Cities: Destruction and Reconstruction in a Globalized World', in Ida Susser and Jane Schneider (eds), *Wounded Cities: Destruction and Reconstruction in a Globalized World*. Oxford: Berg (2003), 1–20.

Swanstrom T. 'Are fear and urbanism at war?', *Urban Affairs Review* 38:1 (2002), 135–40.

Tan, Andrew. 'Singapore's cooperation with the Trilateral Security Dialogue Partners in the war against global terrorism', *Defence Studies* 7:2 (2007), 193–207.

Tan, Chuan-Jin. 'Opening of the Singapore Summit' (speech, Singapore, 27 September 2012) <http://mom.gov.sg/newsroom/Pages/SpeechesDetail.aspx?listid=409> accessed 28 September 2013.

Tan, Kenneth Paul. 'Crisis, Self-Reflection, and Rebirth in Singapore's National Life Cycle', in Daljit Singh and Chin Kin Wah (eds), *Southeast Asian Affairs 2003*. Singapore: ISEAS (2003), 241–58.

Tan, Tony. 'Maritime security after September 11' (speech at the IISS Conference Plenary Session, Singapore, 1 June 2003) <http://www.mindef.gov.sg/imindef/press_room/official_releases/nr/2003/jun/01jun03_nr2.html#.U4VY7HKSySo> accessed 2 June 2013.

Tay, Victor. 'Acting CEO Singapore Business Federation at Business Continuity Management (BCM) Conference 2011' (speech, Singapore, 10 March 2011) <http://www.sbf.org.sg/public/newsroom/details/20110310sp.jsp> accessed 11 March 2013.

Taylor, P.J. 'Competition and cooperation between cities in globalization', GaWC Research Bulletin 351, Loughborough University, 2011 <http://www.lboro.ac.uk/gawc/rb/rb351.html> accessed 8 January 2012.

Taylor, P.J. 'Leading world cities: empirical evaluations of urban nodes in multiple networks', *Urban Studies* 42:9 (2001), 1593–608.

Taylor, Peter. 'New Political Geographies: Global civil society and global governance through world city networks', *Political Geography* 24:6 (2005), 703–30.

Taylor, Peter J. 'World cities and territorial states: the rise and fall of their mutuality', in Paul Knox and Peter J. Taylor (eds), *World Cities in a World System*. Cambridge: Cambridge University Press (1995), 48–62.

Teo, Chee Hean. 'Asia Pacific Security Conference' (opening address, Singapore, 22 February 2004) <http://www.mindef.gov.sg/imindef/press_room/official_releases/sp/2004/22feb04_speech.html#.U4KxLHKSySo> accessed 23 February 2012.

Teo, Chee Hean. 'Emerging Security Trends: Challenges for Singapore and South-east Asia' (speech, Institute of Defence and Strategic Analysis, New Delhi, India, 2004) <http://www.mfa.gov.sg/content/mfa/overseasmission/new_delhi/press_statements_speeches/2004/200401/press_200401_01.html> accessed 10 April 2013.

Teo, Chee Hean. 'Exercise Deep Sabre II' (opening address, Singapore, 27 October 2009) <http://www.mindef.gov.sg/imindef/press_room/official_releases/nr/2009/oct/27oct09_nr/27oct09_speech.html#.U4KxWXKSySo> accessed 28 October 2013.

Teo, Chee Hean. 'Internal Security Department's Heritage Centre 10th Anniversary' (speech, Singapore, 20 March 2012) <http://www.mha.gov.sg/news_details.aspx?nid=MjQxNA%3D%3D-iGqNbuFLKwI%3D> accessed 21 March 2013.

Teo, Chee Hean. 'Opening ceremony of Singapore International Water Week 2010' (speech, Singapore, 28 June 2010) <http://www.nas.gov.sg/archivesonline/speeches/record-details/80c63ef8-115d-11e3-83d5-0050568939ad> accessed 29 June 2012.

Teo, Chee Hean. 'Overseas Medal Service Presentation Ceremony' (speech, 8 October 2010 <http://www.mindef.gov.sg/content/imindef/resources/speeches/2010/08oct10_speech.print.html?Status=1> accessed 9 October 2012.

Teo, Chee Hean. 'Overseas Service Medal Presentation Ceremony' (speech, Singapore, 17 May 2010) <http://www.mindef.gov.sg/imindef/press_room/official_releases/nr/2010/may/19may10_nr2/19may10_speech.html#.U4KxkHKSySo> accessed 18 May 2012.

Teo, Chee Hean. 'Speech by Teo Chee Hean' (Singapore Global Dialogue, 21 September 2011) <http://www.mha.gov.sg/news_details.aspx?nid=MjY0Mg%3D%3D-tXzor6yjYbs%3D> accessed 22 September 2013.

Teo, Eng Cheong. 'Global Trade Controls – Asia Conference' (speech, Singapore, 25 May 2006) <http://www.customs.gov.sg/NR/rdonlyres/29789BF9-39F4-4E7C-BADD-5E0DC1561422/22486/GTCAddress.pdf> accessed 26 May 2012.

Teo, Josephine. 'Ministry of Finance Committee of Supply' (speech, Singapore, 7 March 2014) <http://app.mof.gov.sg/newsroom_details.aspx?type=speech&cmpar_year=2014&news_sid=20140307334420702206> accessed 7 April 2014.

Teo, Josephine. 'World Maritime Day Hamper Presentation Ceremony' (speech, Singapore, 29 September 2011) <http://www.mpa.gov.sg/sites/global_navigation/news_center/speeches/speeches_detail.page?filename=sp110929.xml> accessed 30 September 2013.

TODAY. 'Interview on CNN's Fareed Zakaria GPS', transcript available at 'Of superpowers and the small boat', *TODAYonline* <http://www.todayonline.com/Singapore/EDC120207-0000021/Of-superpowers-and-the-small-boat-Spore> accessed 16 August 2012.

TODAY. 'New Changi Airport can handle 135m passengers', *TODAYonline*, 31 August 2013 <http://www.todayonline.com/singapore/new-changi-airport-can-handle-135m-passengers> accessed 7 September 2013.

Toh, Elgin. 'Regulating tightly not always feasible', *The Straits Times*, 8 October 2012 <http://www.straitstimes.com/breaking-news/singapore/story/regulating-banks-tightly-not-always-feasible-pm-lee-20121008> accessed 10 October 2013.

Transport Ministers, 'Transport Ministers' Statement on Terrorism' (Tokyo, Japan, 15 January 2002) <http://www.internationaltransportforum.org/IntOrg/ecmt/crime/pdf/Tokyo2002.pdf> accessed 16 January 2014.

Tsing, Anna. *Friction: An Ethnography of Global Connection*. New Jersey: Princeton University Press (2005).

Tyler, Tony. 'Singapore Air Show' (speech, Singapore, 16 February 2012) <http://www.iata.org/pressroom/speeches/pages/2012-02-13-01.aspx> accessed 17 February 2013.

Tyler, Tony. 'We can make airport security faster and more secure', *The Business Times*, Singapore, 22 October 2012 <http://www.iata.org/pressroom/Documents/OpEd-Airport-Security-Faster-moreSecure-October2012.pdf> accessed 23 October 2013.

UNCTAD, Review of Maritime Transport. Geneva: United Nations Conference on Trade and Development (2013).

UNCTAD, Review of Maritime Transport. Geneva: United Nations Conference on Trade and Development (2014), Chapter 4.

United Nations Habitat Program. 'State of the World's Cities'. Nairobi, Kenya: UNHP (2007).

United States Customs. 'Port of Dubai to implement the Container Security Initiative', 23 February 2006 <http://www.customs.ustreas.gov/xp/cgov/newsroom/press_releases/archives/2005_press_releases/0032005/03282005.xml> accessed 28 April 2008.

United States Department of State Bureau for International Narcotics and Law Enforcement Affairs. 'International Narcotics Control Strategy Report. Volume II: Money Laundering and Financial Crimes', March 2012 <http://www.state.gov/j/inl/rls/nrcrpt/2012/index.htm> accessed 30 March 2013.

United States Senate. 'US vulnerabilities to money laundering, drugs, and terrorist financing: HSBC Case History', 17 July, 2012 <http://www.hsgac.senate.gov/subcommittees/investigations/hearings/us-vulnerabilities-to-money-laundering-drugs-and-terrorist-financing-hsbc-case-history> access date 27 August 2014.

Urry, John. *Mobilities*. Cambridge: Polity Press (2007).

Urry, John. *Sociology Beyond Societies*. London: Routledge (2000).

Urry, John. 'The global complexities of September 11th', *Theory, Culture and Society* 19:4 (2002), 57–69.

U.S. Department of State. 'Country Reports on Terrorism'. Washington D.C., 2010 <http://www.state.gov/j/ct/rls/crt/> accessed 27 August 2014.

Vigneswaran, Darshan. 'The territorial strategy of the Italian city-state', *International Relations* 21:4 (2007), 427–44.

Wagner, E. Van. 'Toward a Dialectical Understanding of Networked Disease in the Global City: Vulnerability, Connectivity, Topologies', in S. Harris Ali and Roger Keil (eds), *Networked Disease: Emerging Infections in the Global City*. London: Wiley-Blackwell (2008), 13–26.

Wallis, Rodney. *How Safe Are Our Skies?* Santa Barbara: Greenwood Publishing, 69.

Warren, Adam, Bell, Morag and Budd, Lucy. 'Airports, localities and disease: representations of global travel during the H1N1 pandemic', *Health & Place* 16 (2010), 727–35.

Wechsler, Willam F. 'Follow the money', *Foreign Affairs* 80:4 (2001) <http://www.foreignaffairs.com/articles/57052/william-f-wechsler/follow-the-money> accessed 12 May 2013.

Whimster, Sam and Budd, Leslie. 'Introduction', in Sam Whimster and Leslie Budd (eds), *Global Finance and Urban Living: A Study of Metropolitan Change*. London: Routledge (1992), 1–29.

White House, The. 'A National Security Strategy for a New Century'. Washington D.C.: The White House (December 1999), Chapter I.

Williams, Michael J. *NATO, Security, and Risk Management*. London: Routledge (2009).

Wilson, Ara, 'Bangkok, the Bubble City', in Ida Susser and Jane Schneider (eds), *Wounded Cities: Destruction and Reconstruction in a Globalized World*. Oxford: Berg (2003).

Wilson, Ara. *The Intimate Economies of Bangkok: Tomboys, Tycoons and Avon Ladies in the Global City*. Los Angeles: University of California Press (2004).

Wijaya, Megawati. 'A dent in Singapore's financial hub dream', *Asia Times*, 6 November 2008 <http://www.atimes.com/atimes/Southeast_Asia/JK06Ae01.html> accessed 8 January 2009.

Wojcik, Daruisz. 'The dark side of NY-LON: financial centres and the global financial crisis'. Oxford Working Papers in Employment, Work and Finance 11–12, Oxford (2011).

World Economic Forum. 'Global Risks Report 2011: Executive Summary', January 2011 <http://www.weforum.org/reports/global-risks-executive-summary-2011> accessed 15 July 2013.

World Economic Forum. 'Global Risks Report 2012' <http://www.weforum.org/reports/global-risks-2012-seventh-edition> accessed 10 August 2014.

World Economic Forum, 'Global Risks Report 2013' <http://www.weforum.org/reports/global-risks-2013-eighth-edition> accessed 4 June 2015.

World Economic Forum 2011 News Release. 'In East Asia, concerns about the world's response to global risks', 12 June 2011 <http://www.weforum.org/news/east-asia-concerns-about-world%E2%80%99s-response-global-risks> accessed 20 June 2011.

World Health Organization, 'Situation updates', SARS update #53, 12 May 2003 <http://www.who.int/csr/sars/archive/en/> accessed 13 June 2013.

World Port Source. 'Port of Singapore' <http://www.worldportsource.com/ports/commerce/SGP_Port_of_Singapore_244.php> accessed 9 November 2012.

World Trade Organization (WTO). 'Trade Policy Review, Report by Singapore'. Trade Policy Review Body, WT/TPR/G/202. Geneva: World Trade Organization (2008).

World Trade Organization (WTO). 'Trade profile: Singapore', October 2011 <http://stat.wto.org/CountryProfile/WSDBCountryPFView.aspx?Language=F&Country=SG> accessed 8 April 2012.

Wong, Kan Seng. '8th National Security Seminar' (speech, Singapore, 9 November 2010) <http://www.singaporeunited.sg/cep/index.php/Our-News/DPM-Coordinating-Minister-for-National-Security-Mr-Wong-Kan-Seng-8th-National-Security-Seminar> accessed 10 November 2012.

Wong, Kan Seng. 'Administrative Service Singapore' (speech, Singapore, 28 March 2011) <http://app.psd.gov.sg/data/Admin%20Service%20Dinner%202011%20on%2028%20March%202011%20-%20Speech%20by%20DPM%20Wong%20Kan%20Seng.pdf> accessed 29 March 2013.

Wong, Kan Seng. 'Singapore Perspectives 2011 Conference' (speech, Singapore, 17 January 2011) <http://www.nptd.gov.sg/content/NPTD/news/_jcr_content/par_content/download_18/file.res/Keynote%20address%20by%20DPM%20Wong%20Kan%20Seng%20at%20the%20Singapore%20Perspectives%202011%20Conference%20170111.pdf> accessed 18 January 2013.

Wong, Kan Seng. 'The Second Reading of the Terrorism (Suppression of Financing) Bill' (speech, Singapore, 8 July 2002) <http://www.mha.gov.sg/news_details.aspx?nid=ODQ3-D78tel4qsXU%3D> accessed 9 July 2013.

Yeo, Cheow Tong. 'Maritime Security Should Be Beefed Up at the Multilateral, National and Individual Levels' (speech, International Maritime and Port Security Conference, 21 January 2003) <http://www.mpa.gov.sg/sites/global_navigation/news_center/mpa_news/mpa_news_detail.page?filename=030121.xml> accessed 10 December 2013.

Yeoh, Brenda. 'Global/globalizing cities', *Progress in Human Geography* 23:4 (1999), 607–16.

Yeoh, Brenda. 'The global cultural city? Spatial imagineering and politics in the (multi-) cultural marketplaces of South-east Asia', *Urban Studies* 42:5/6 (2005), 945–58.

Yeoh, Brenda and Chang, T.C. 'Globalising Singapore: debating transnational flows in the city', *Urban Studies* 38:7 (2001), 1025–44.

Yeung, Bernard. 'Foreword', in Sanchita Basu Das, *Road to Recovery: Singapore's Journey Through the Global Crisis*. Singapore: ISEAS (2010).

Yeung, Henry Wai-Chung, 'Global cities and developmental states: understanding Singapore's global reach', GaWC Annual Lecture 2000, 3 March 2000, <http://www.lboro.ac.uk/gawc/rb/al2.html> accessed 8 August 2014.

Yeung, Henry Wai-Chung. 'Globalisation Singapore: One Global City, Global Production Networks and the Developmental State', in Tarn Tan How (eds), *Singapore Perspectives 2010*. Singapore: World Scientific (2010), 109–21.

Yong, Ying-I. 'Developing a Regional Infectious Disease Hub' (speech by Ministry of Health Permanent Secretary, Singapore, 21 March 2009) <https://www.moh.gov.sg/content/moh_web/home/pressRoom/speeches_d/2009/developing_a_regional_infectious_disease_hub.html> accessed 10 August 2014.

Young, Adam J. and Valencia, Mark J. 'Conflation of piracy and terrorism in Southeast Asia: rectitude and utility', *Contemporary Southeast Asia* 25:2 (2003), 269–83.

Yudhoyono, Susilo Bambang (speech at the IISS Asian Security Conference, Singapore, 6 June 2012) <http://www.thejakartapost.com/news/2012/06/01/keynote-speech-11th-iiss-asia-security-summit-shangri-la-dialogue.html> accessed 7 June 2013.

Zellen, Barry. 'Singapore aims for enhanced information awareness with RAHS', *Strategic Insights* 6:3 (2007) <http://www.nps.edu/Academics/centers/ccc/publications/OnlineJournal/2007/May/zellenMay07.html> accessed 10 August 2013.

Zielonka, Jan. 'Europe as a global actor: empire by example?' *International Affairs* 84:3 (2008), 471–84.

Zukin, Sharon. 'The City as a Landscape of Power: London and New York as Global Financial Capitals', in Sam Whimster and Leslie Budd (eds), *Global Finance and Urban Living: A Study of Metropolitan Change*. London: Routledge (1992), 198–226.

9/11 Commission, January 27 2004 <http://www.9–11commission.gov/hearings/hearing7/witness_loy.html> accessed 13 January 2012.

Index